Lecture Notes in Computer Science 1428

Edited by G. Goos, J. Hartmanis and J. van Leeuwen

Springer-Verlag Berlin Heidelberg GmbH

Jens Knoop

Optimal Interprocedural Program Optimization

A New Framework and Its Application

 Springer

Series Editors

Gerhard Goos, Karlsruhe University, Germany
Juris Hartmanis, Cornell University, NY, USA
Jan van Leeuwen, Utrecht University, The Netherlands

Author

Jens Knoop
Universität Passau, Fakultät für Mathematik und Informatik
Innstrasse 33, D-94032 Passau, Germany
E-mail: knoop@fmi.uni-passau.de

Cataloging-in-Publication data applied for

Die Deutsche Bibliothek - CIP-Einheitsaufnahme

Knoop, Jens:
Optimal interprocedural program optimization : a new framework and
its application / Jens Knoop. - Berlin ; Heidelberg ; New York ;
Barcelona ; Budapest ; Hong Kong ; London ; Milan ; Paris ;
Singapore ; Tokyo : Springer, 1998
  (Lecture notes in computer science ; Vol. 1428)
  ISBN 978-3-540-65123-9

CR Subject Classification (1991): F.3, D.3, D.2.4

ISSN 0302-9743
ISBN 978-3-540-65123-9   ISBN 978-3-540-49639-7 (eBook)
DOI 10.1007/978-3-540-49639-7

Typesetting: Camera-ready by author
SPIN 10637566   06/3142 – 5 4 3 2 1 0   Printed on acid-free paper

Foreword

The typical development of a successful theory in computer science traverses three sometimes overlapping phases: an *experimental phase*, where phenomena are studied almost in a trial and error fashion, a busy *phase of realization*, where people use the results of the experimental phase in an "uncoordinated" fashion, and a *contemplative phase*, where people look for the essence of what has been previously achieved. In *compiler optimization* these three phases currently coexist. New heuristics are still being proposed and purely evaluated on some benchmarks, and known techniques are still being implemented specifically for a new operating system or variants of programming languages, but increasingly many attempts now try to understand the full picture of compiler optimization in order to develop general frameworks and generators.

This monograph is a typical contribution to third phase activities in that it presents a uniform framework capturing a large class of imperative programming languages and their corresponding transformations, together with directions for cookbook style implementation. Thus besides clarifying appropriateness and limitations of the considered methods it also tries to open these methods even to non-experts.

More technically, the monograph adresses the issue of extension: which principles are stable, i.e., remain valid when extending intraprocedurally successful methods to the interprocedural case, and what needs to be done in order to overcome the problems and anomalies arising from this extension. This investigation characterizes the power and flexibility of procedure mechanisms from the data flow analysis point of view.

Even though all the algorithms considered evolve quite naturally from basic principles, which directly leads to accessible correctness and optimality considerations, they often outperform their "tricky" handwritten counterpart. Thus they constitute a convincing example for the superiority of *concept-driven* software development.

The monograph presents a full formal development for so-called *syntactic* program analysis and transformation methods including complete proofs, which may be quite hard to digest in full detail. This rigorous development, on purpose structurally repetitive, is tailored to stress similarities and differences between the intraprocedural and interprocedural setting, down to the very last detail. However, the reader is not forced to follow the technical level. Rather, details can be consulted on demand, providing students with a deep yet intuitive and accessible introduction to central principles of intraprocedural and interprocedural optimization, compiler experts with precise information about the obstacles when moving from the intraprocedural to the interprocedural case, and developers with concise specifications of easy to implement yet high-performance interprocedural analyses.

Summarizing, this thesis can be regarded as a comprehensive account of what, from the practical point of view, are the most important program analysis and transformation methods for imperative languages. I therefore recommend it to everybody interested in a conceptual, yet far reaching entry into the world of optimizing compilers.

Bernhard Steffen

Prologue

The present monograph is based on the doctoral dissertation of the author [Kn1]. It presents a new framework for optimal *interprocedural program optimization*, which covers the full range of language features of imperative programming languages. It captures programs with (mutually) recursive procedures, global, local, and external variables, value, reference, and procedure parameters. In spite of this unique generality, it is tailored for practical use. It supports the design and implementation of provably optimal program optimizations in a cookbook style. In essence, this is achieved by decomposing the design process of a program optimization and the proof of its optimality with respect to a specific optimality criterion into a small number of elementary steps, which can independently be proved using only knowledge about the specification of the optimization. This contrasts with heuristically based approaches to program optimization, which are still dominant in practice, and often ad hoc. The application of the framework is demonstrated by means of the *computationally* and *lifetime optimal* elimination of *partially redundant computations* in a program, a practically relevant optimization, whose intraprocedural variant is part of many advanced compiler environments. The purpose of considering its interprocedural counterpart is twofold. On the one hand, it demonstrates the analogies between designing intraprocedural and interprocedural optimizations. On the other hand, it reveals essential differences which must usually be faced when extending intraprocedural optimizations interprocedurally. Optimality criteria satisfiable in the intraprocedural setting can impossible to be met in the interprocedural one. Optimization strategies being successful in the intraprocedural setting can fail interprocedurally. The elimination of partially redundant computations is well-suited for demonstration. In contrast to the intraprocedural setting, computational and lifetime optimal results are in general impossible in the interprocedural setting. The placement strategies leading to computationally and lifetime optimal results in the intraprocedural setting, can even fail to guarantee profitability in the interprocedural setting. We propose a natural constraint applying to a large class of programs, which is sufficient for the successful transfer of the intraprocedural elimination techniques to the interprocedural setting. Under this constraint, the resulting algorithm generates interprocedurally computationally and lifetime optimal results, making it unique. It is not only more powerful than its heuristic predecessors but also more efficient, and reduces in the absence of procedures to its intraprocedural counterpart.

The remainder of this prologue summarizes the background of this monograph, and provides a brief introduction to program optimization intended to make its presentation more easily amenable to novice readers in the field.

Optimizing Compilers. In essence, a *compiler* is a program translating programs of some source language $\mathcal{L}_1$ into semantically equivalent programs of some target language $\mathcal{L}_2$. One of the most typical applications of a compiler is the translation of a source program written in a high-level programming language into a machine program (often simply called "machine code" or just "code"), which can be executed on the computer the compiler is implemented on. Of course, compilers are expected to produce highly efficient code, which has led to the construction of *optimizing compilers* [ASU, WG, Mor].

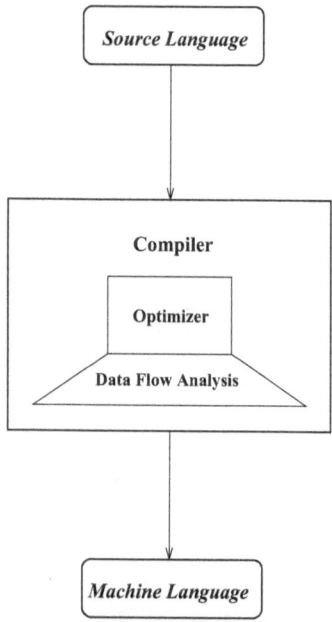

Fig. 1.1. Structure of an optimizing compiler

Figure 1.1 illustrates the general structure of an optimizing compiler. The central component is called an *optimizer*. Basically, this is a program designed for detecting and removing inefficiencies in a program by means of appropriate performance improving transformations. Traditionally, these transformations are called *program optimizations*. This general term, however, is slightly misleading because program optimization cannot usually be expected to transform a program of "bad" performance into a program of "good" or even "optimal" performance. There are two quite obvious reasons for this limitation. First, "bad," "good," and "optimal" are qualitative properties lacking a (precise) quantitative meaning. Second, interpreting the term optimization naively, does not impose any restrictions on the kind of transformations considered possible; restrictions, for example, which are usually imposed by automation requirements. Following the naive interpretation, optimization would require replacing a sorting algorithm of quadratic time complexity by a completely different sorting algorithm where the second factor is replaced by a logarithmic one. Optimizations of this kind would require a profound understanding of the semantics of the program under consideration, which is usually far beyond the capabilities of an automatic analysis.

The original domain of program optimization is different. Usually, it leaves the inherent structure of the algorithms invariant, and improves their performance by *avoiding* or *reducing* the computational effort at run-time, or by *shifting* it from the run-time into the compile-time. Typical examples are *loop invariant code motion*, *strength reduction*, and *constant folding*. Loop invariant code motion moves computations yielding always the same value inside a loop to a program point outside of it, which avoids unnecessary recomputations of the value at run-time. Strength reduction replaces operations that are "expensive" by "cheaper" operations, which reduces the computational effort at run-time. Constant folding evaluates and replaces complex computations, whose operands are known at compile-time, by their values, which shifts the computational effort from the run-time to the compile-time of the program.

In practice, the power of an optimization is often validated by means of benchmark tests, i.e., by measuring the performance gain on a sample of programs in order to provide empirical evidence of its effectivity. The limitations of this approach are obvious. It cannot reveal how "good" an optimization really is concerning the relevant optimization potential. In addition, it is questionable to which extent a performance improvement observed can be considered a reliable prediction in general. This would require that the sample programs are "statistically representative" because the performance gain of a specific optimization depends highly on the program under consideration.

In this monograph, we contrast this empirical approach by a mathematical approach, which focuses on *proving* the effectivity of an optimization. Central is the introduction of *formal optimality criteria*, and proof of the effectivity or even optimality of an optimization with respect to the criteria considered. Usually, these criteria exclude the existence of a certain kind of inefficiencies. Following this approach optimality gets a formal meaning. An optimization satisfying a specific optimality criterion guarantees that a program subjected to it cannot be improved any further with respect to this criterion, or hence with respect to the source of inefficiencies it addresses. Thus, rather than aiming at assuring of a specific percentage of performance improvement, our approach guarantees that a specific kind of inefficiency is proved to be absent after optimization.

Data Flow Analysis. Optimization must preserve semantics. It is thus usually preceded by a static analysis of the argument program, usually called *data flow analysis (DFA)*, which checks the side-conditions under which an optimization is applicable. For imperative programming languages like Algol, Pascal, or Modula, an important classification of DFA techniques is derived from the treatment of programs with procedures. *Intraprocedural* DFA is characterized by a separate and independent investigation of the procedures of a program making explicit worst-case assumptions for procedure calls. *Interprocedural* DFA takes the semantics of procedure calls into account, and is thus theoretically and practically much more ambitious than intraprocedural DFA. In contrast, *local* DFA considering (maximal sequences of) straight-line code only, so-called *basic blocks*, which are investigated separately and independently, is considerably simpler, but also less powerful than intraprocedural and interprocedural DFA. In distinction to local DFA, intraprocedural and interprocedural DFA are also called *global* DFA. Figure 1.2 illustrates this classification of DFA techniques, which carries over to program optimization, i.e., local, intraprocedural, and interprocedural optimization are based on local, intraprocedural, and interprocedural DFA, respectively.

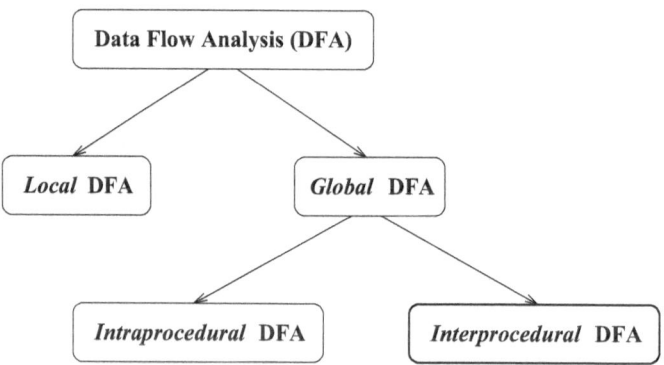

Fig. 1.2. Taxonomy of data flow analysis

DFA is usually performed on an intermediate program representation. A flexible and widely used representation is the *control flow graph (CFG)* of a program. This is a directed graph, whose nodes and edges represent the statements and the branching structure of the underlying program. Figure 1.3 shows an illustrative example. In order to avoid undecidability of DFA the branching structure of a CFG is usually nondeterministically interpreted. This means, whenever the control reaches a branch node, it is assumed that the program execution can be continued with any successor of the branch node within the CFG. Programs containing several procedures can naturally be represented by systems of CFGs. The control flow caused by procedure calls can be made explicit by combining them to a single graph, the *inter-*

procedural flow graph; intuitively, by connecting the call sites with the flow graphs representing the called procedures.

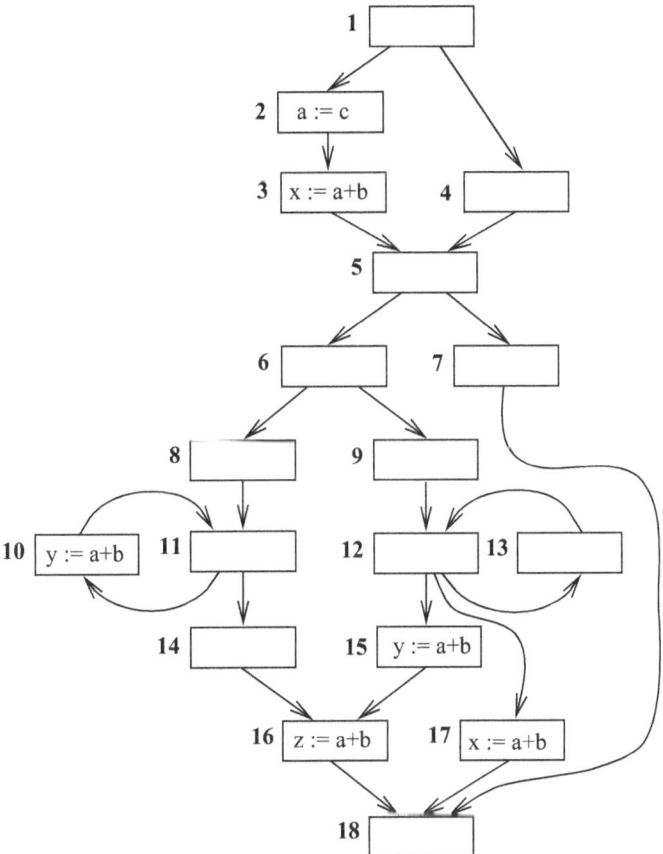

Fig. 1.3. Control flow graph

Code Motion: A Practically Relevant Optimization. Code motion is one of the most widely used program optimizations in practice, for which there are two quite natural optimization goals concerning the number of computations performed at run-time, and the lifetimes of temporaries, which are unavoidably introduced as a side-effect of the transformation. Code motion is thus well suited for demonstrating the practicality of our optimization framework because it is designed for supporting the construction of provably optimal optimizations. The code motion transformation we develop (interprocedurally with respect to a natural side-condition) satisfies both optimality criteria informally sketched above: it generates programs which are *computationally* and *lifetime optimal*. The corresponding transformation to meet these criteria is not only unique, it is even more efficient than its heuristic predecessors. In the following we illustrate the central idea underlying this transformation in the intraprocedural context.

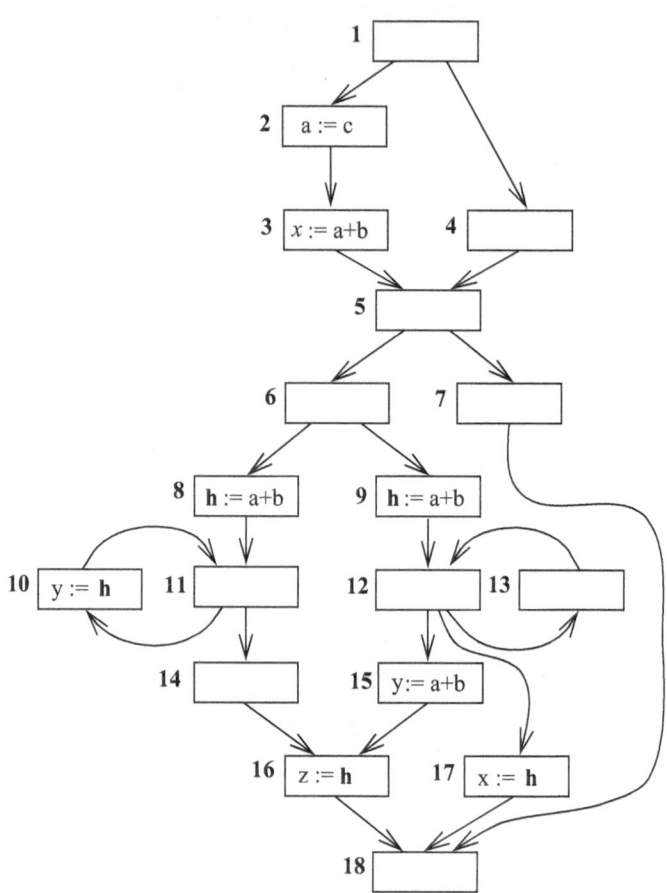

Fig. 1.4. A first code motion optimization

In essence, code motion improves the efficiency of a program by avoiding unnecessary recomputations of values at run-time. For example, in the program of Figure 1.3 the computation of $a + b$ at node **10** always yields the same value. Thus, it is unnecessarily recomputed if the loop is executed more than once at run-time. Code motion eliminates unnecessary recomputations by replacing the original computations of a program by temporaries (or registers), which are correctly initialized at appropriate program points. For example, in the program of Figure 1.3 the original computations of $a + b$ occurring at the nodes **10**, **16**, and **17** can be replaced by a temporary **h**, which is initialized by $a + b$ at the nodes **8** and **9** as illustrated in Figure 1.4.

Admissible Code Motion

Code motion must preserve the semantics of the argument program. This leads to the notion of *admissible* code motion. Intuitively, admissibility requires that the temporaries introduced for replacing the original computations of a program are correctly initialized at certain program points as illustrated above. In addition, it requires that the initializations of the temporaries do not introduce computations of new values on paths because this could introduce new run-time errors. Illustrating this by means of the program of Figure 1.3, the second requirement would be violated by initializing the temporary **h** at node **5** as shown in Figure 1.5. This introduces a computation of $a + b$ on the path $(1, 4, 5, 7, 18)$, which is free of a computation of $a + b$ in the original program. Under the admissibility requirement, we can obtain *computationally* and *lifetime optimal* results as indicated below.

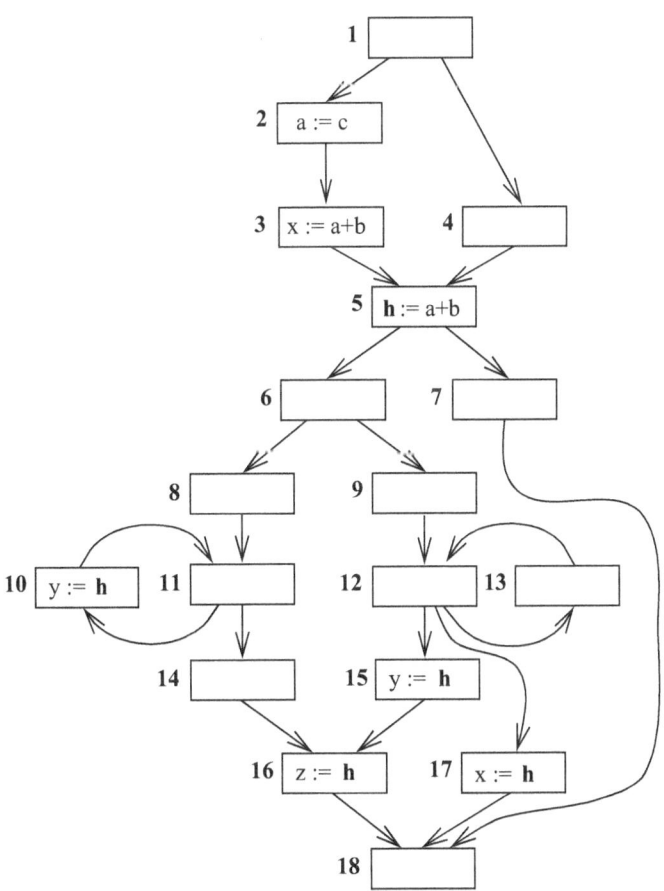

Fig. 1.5. No admissible code motion optimization

Computationally Optimal Code Motion

Intuitively, an admissible code motion is *computationally optimal*, if the number of computations on every program path cannot be reduced any further by means of admissible code motion. Achieving computationally optimal results is the primary goal of code motion. The central idea to meet this goal is to place computations

– *as early as possible*, while maintaining admissibility.

This is illustrated in Figure 1.6 showing the program, which results from the program of Figure 1.3 by means of the "as-early-as-possible" placing strategy. All unnecessary recomputations of $a + b$ are avoided by storing the value of $a+b$ in the temporary **h** and replacing all original computations of $a+b$ by **h**. Note that this program cannot be improved any further. It is computationally optimal.

Lifetime Optimal Code Motion

The "as-early-as-possible" placing strategy moves computations even if there is no run-time gain. In the running example this is particularly obvious when considering the computation of $a + b$ at node **3**, which is moved without any run-time gain. Though unnecessary code motion does not increase the number of computations on a path, it can be the source of superfluous *register pressure*, which is a major problem in practice. The secondary goal of code motion therefore is to avoid any unnecessary motions of computations while maintaining computational optimality. This is illustrated in Figure 1.7 for the running example of Figure 1.3.

Like the program of Figure 1.6, it is computationally optimal. However, computations are only moved, if it is profitable: the computations of $a + b$ at nodes **3** and **17**, which cannot be moved with run-time gain, are not touched at all. The problem of unnecessary code motions is addressed by the criterion of lifetime optimality. Intuitively, a computationally optimal code motion transformation is *lifetime optimal*, if the lifetimes of temporaries cannot be reduced any further by means of computationally optimal code motion. Intuitively, this means that in any other program resulting from a computationally optimal code motion transformation, the lifetimes of temporaries are at least as long as in the lifetime optimal one. The central idea to achieve lifetime optimality is to place computations

– *as late as possible*, while maintaining computational optimality.

The "as-late-as-possible" placing strategy transforms computationally optimal programs into a unique lifetime optimal program. This is an important difference to computational optimality. Whereas computationally optimal results can usually be achieved by several transformations, lifetime optimality is achieved by a single transformation only.

Figures 1.8 and 1.9 illustrate the lifetime ranges of the temporary **h** for the programs of Figures 1.6 and 1.7, respectively.

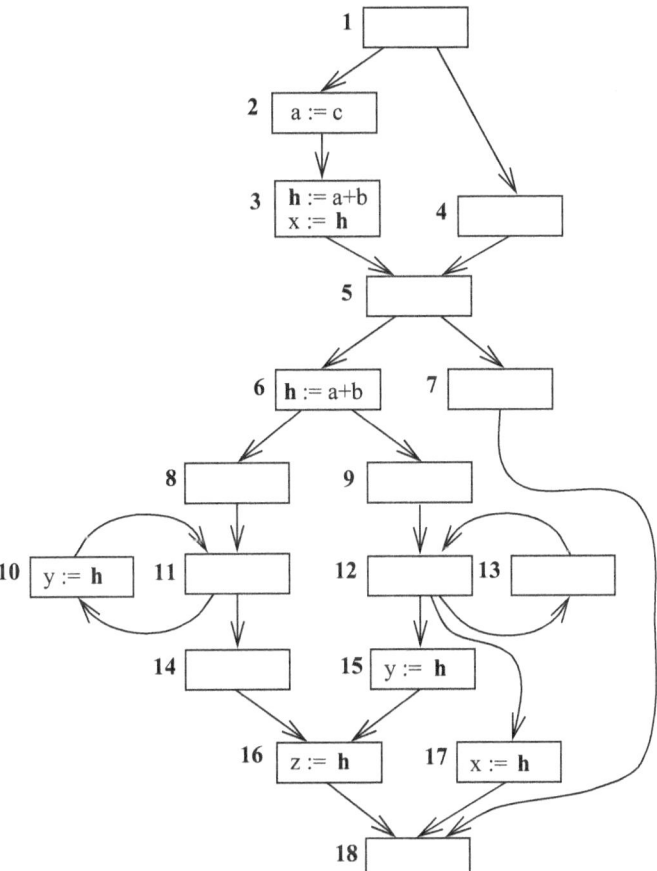

Fig. 1.6. A computationally optimal program

Summarizing, the "as-early-as-possible" code motion transformation of Figure 1.6 moves computations as far as *possible* in order to achieve computationally optimal results; the "as-late-as-possible" code motion transformation of Figure 1.7 moves computations only as far as *necessary*. Therefore, we call the first transformation the *busy* code motion transformation and the second one the *lazy* code motion transformation, or for short the *BCM*- and *LCM*-transformation.

In this monograph, we will show how to construct intraprocedural and interprocedural program optimizations like the *BCM*- and *LCM*-transformation systematically. However, we also demonstrate that usually essential differences have to be taken into account when extending intraprocedural optimizations interprocedurally. We illustrate this by developing the interprocedural counterparts of the *BCM*- and *LCM*-transformation for programs with recursive procedures, global, local, and external variables, value, reference and procedure parameters. We show that interprocedurally computationally and

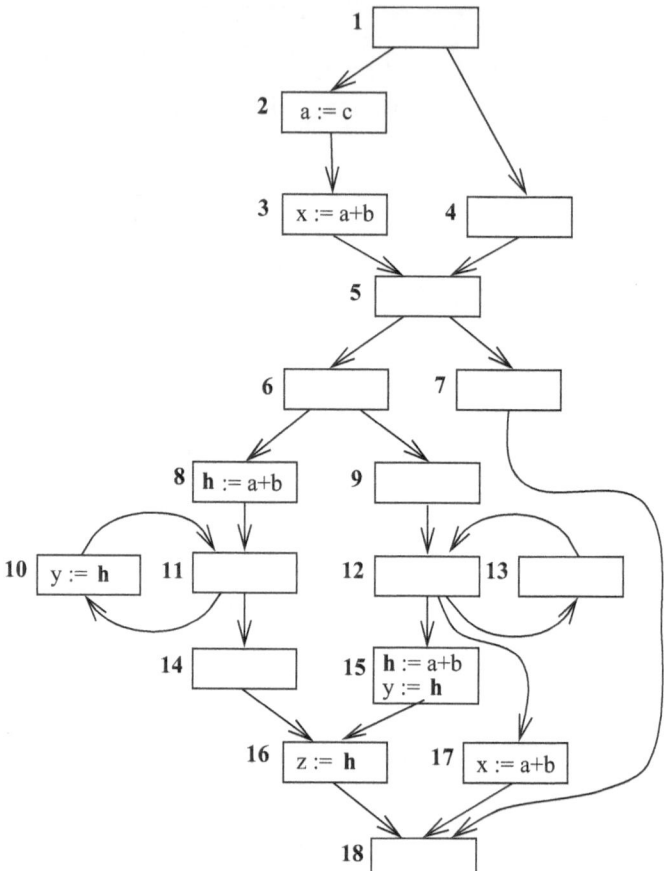

Fig. 1.7. The computationally and lifetime optimal program

lifetime optimal results are in general impossible. Therefore, we propose a natural constraint which is sufficient to meet both criteria for a large class of programs. The resulting algorithms are unique in achieving interprocedurally computationally and lifetime optimal results for this program class. Their power is illustrated by a complex example in Section 10.6. Additionally, a detailed account of the example considered in the prologue for illustrating the intraprocedural versions of busy and lazy code motion can be found in Section 3.5.

Acknowledgements

I am greatly indebted to many people, in particular, my academic teachers, colleagues, friends, and parents, who contributed in various, quite different

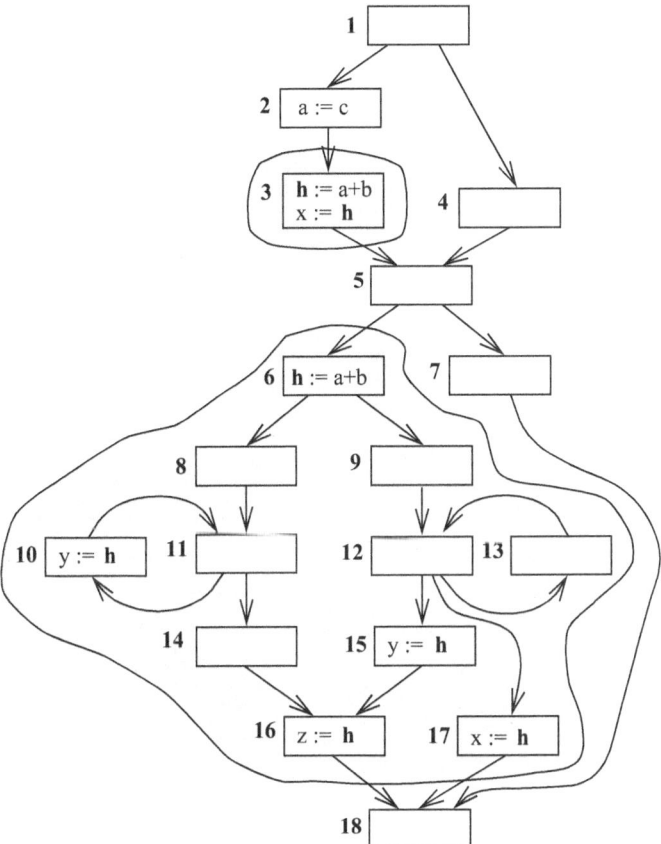

Fig. 1.8. Lifetime ranges after the *BCM*-transformation

ways to the origin of this monograph, and I wish to express my deepest gratitude to all of them.

Both I and my research, and as a consequence the present monograph, owe a lot to my academic teachers and my colleagues at Kiel and Passau University, above all to Hans Langmaack and to Bernhard Steffen. Professor Langmaack introduced me to the foundations of computer science and the specifics of compiler construction from the very beginnings of my studies, and later on I conducted my research for the doctoral dissertation underlying this monograph as a member of his research group. I am very grateful for the valuable and inspiring advice he gave, for his constant motivation and support. These thanks belong to the same extent to Professor Steffen. It was Bernhard who aroused my interest for the theory of abstract interpretation and its application to program optimization, the topic of this monograph, and also the general theme of in the meantime more than 10 years of most intensive, enjoyable, and fruitful collaboration going far beyond the joint publications we accomplished over the years. In particular, I would like to

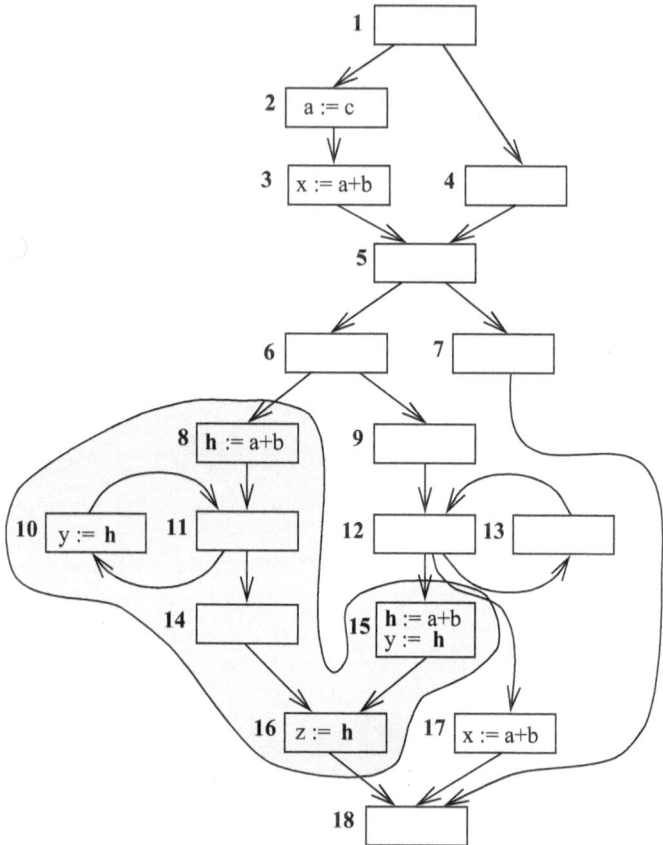

Fig. 1.9. Lifetime ranges after the LCM-transformation

thank Bernhard for writing the foreword to this monograph. Moreover, I am also very grateful to Oliver Rüthing, my close colleague at Kiel University, and collaborator on several joint publications in the field of program analysis and optimization. Not just because we shared an office, Oliver accompanied the development of my doctoral dissertation at very close range, and I would like to thank him cordially for many discussions on technical and nontechnical topics, and invaluable comments, which helped improving it.

I would also like to thank Dhananjay M. Dhamdhere, Rajiv Gupta, Flemming Nielson, Robert Paige, Thomas Reps, Barry K. Rosen, and F. Kenneth Zadeck for many stimulating discussions, mostly during conferences and Professor Nielson's guest professorship at Kiel University. I am also grateful to Hardi Hungar for his hints on recent references to decidability and complexity results concerning formal reachability, and to Thomas Noll and Gerald Lüttgen for their careful proof-reading of a preliminary version of this monograph. My special thanks belong to Reinhard Wilhelm for taking over the third report on the underlying thesis.

Moreover, I greatly acknowledge the financial support of the Deutsche Forschungsgemeinschaft for providing me a research fellowship at Kiel University for several years, and also its generous support for joining several conferences, in particular, the ACM SIGPLAN'92 Conference on Programming Languages Design and Implementation in San Francisco, where the intraprocedural version of the lazy code motion transformation considered as a running example in this monograph was originally presented. Without this support, conducting my research would have been much more difficult.

I am also especially grateful to Gerhard Goos, editor-in-chief of the series of Lecture Notes in Computer Science, and an anonymous referee for reviewing my doctoral dissertation for publication in this series. I greatly acknowledge their helpful comments and suggestions for improving the current presentation. Last but not least, I would cordially like to thank Alfred Hofmann at Springer-Verlag for the smooth and competent cooperation, his assistance and thoroughness in publishing this monograph, and particularly for his patience in awaiting the final version of the manuscript.

My deepest gratitude, finally, belongs to my parents for their continuous encouragement, support, and love.

Passau, May 1998   Jens Knoop

Table of Contents

Part II. = The Framework

Part III. = The Application

1. Preface

1.1 Summary

A new framework for interprocedural program optimization is presented, which is tailored for supporting the construction of interprocedural program optimizations satisfying formal optimality criteria in a cookbook style. The framework is unique in capturing programs with statically nested (mutually) recursive procedures, global and local variables, value, reference, and procedure parameters. In addition, it supports separate compilation and the construction of software libraries by dealing with external procedures and external variables. An important feature of the framework is that it strictly separates the specification of an optimizing transformation and the proof of its optimality from the specification of the data flow analysis algorithms computing the program properties involved in the definition of the transformation and the proofs of their precision. This structures and simplifies the development of optimal program transformations, and allows us to hide all details of the framework which are irrelevant for application. In particular, this holds for the higher order data flow analysis concerning formal procedure calls, which is organized as an independent preprocess. The power and flexibility of the framework is demonstrated by a practically relevant optimization: the computationally and lifetime optimal elimination of interprocedurally partially redundant computations in a program. As a side-effect this application reveals essential differences, which usually must be taken into account when extending intraprocedural optimizations interprocedurally. Concerning the application considered here, this means that computationally and lifetime optimal results are interprocedurally in general impossible. However, we propose a natural constraint which is sufficient to meet these optimality criteria for a large class of programs. Under this constraint the algorithm developed is not only unique in satisfying both optimality criteria, it is also more efficient than its heuristic predecessors.

1.2 Motivation

Program optimization is traditionally the general term of program transformations, which are intended to improve the run-time or the storage efficiency

J. Knoop: Optimal Interprocedural Program Optimization, LNCS 1428, pp. 1-12, 1998.
© Springer-Verlag Berlin Heidelberg 1998

of a program.[1] In the imperative programming paradigm an important classification of program optimization is derived from the treatment of programs with procedures. *Intraprocedural* program optimization is characterized by a separate and independent investigation of the procedures of a program where explicit worst-case assumptions are made for procedure calls. *Interprocedural* program optimization takes the semantics of procedure calls into account, and is thus theoretically and practically more ambitious than intraprocedural optimization.

Ideally, optimizing program transformations preserve the semantics of the argument program, improve their run-time efficiency, and satisfy *formal optimality criteria*. This is worth to be noted because in practice heuristically based transformations are still dominant. Even transformations which sometimes impair the run-time efficiency are considered program optimizations. In [CLZ] they are called *non-strict* in contrast to *strict* optimizations, which are required to be always run-time improving. In contrast to this pragmatic approach, we are interested in *optimal* program optimization, i.e., in program transformations which are strict in the sense of [CLZ], and provably optimal with respect to *formal optimality criteria*.

The construction of provably optimal program transformations has been studied in detail in the intraprocedural case. Conceptually, it is important to separate the specification of a program transformation and the proof of its optimality from the specification of the *data flow analysis (DFA)* algorithms computing the program properties involved in the definition of the transformation, and the proof that they compute these properties precisely. This leads to the following two-step structure:

1. Specify a program transformation and prove its optimality with respect to a specific formal optimality criterion of interest.
2. Specify the DFA-algorithms and prove that they precisely compute the program properties involved in the definition of the transformation of the first step.

The first step can be directed by general guide-lines fixing the elementary steps which are necessary for proving the optimality of a transformation. The details, of course, depend on the concrete transformation and the optimality criterion under consideration. The second step can be organized in greater detail. In essence, its specification part reduces to specifying the DFA-information of interest for a given program property, and the way in which it is computed by the elementary statements of a procedure. The concrete DFA-algorithm results then automatically from instantiating a generic DFA-algorithm by the specification. Proving its precision for the program property under consideration can be split into three elementary substeps, which only

---

[1] In general there is a trade-off between run-time and storage improving transformations (e.g., procedure inlining, loop unrolling). In this monograph we focus on the run-time, which is the major concern in practice.

concern the domain of the specification, and can independently be proved. The theory of abstract interpretation (cf. [CC1, CC3, CC4, Ma, Nie1, Nie2]), and the well-known Coincidence Theorem 2.2.2 of Kildall [Ki1] and Kam and Ullman [KU2] giving a sufficient condition for the coincidence of the *specifying* meet over all paths solution and the *algorithmic* maximal fixed point solution of a DFA-problem are central for the simplicity and elegance of this approach.

1.2.1 The Framework

We present a framework for *interprocedural program optimization*, which evolves as an extension and generalization of the stack-based framework for *interprocedural data flow analysis (IDFA)* of [KS1]. The new framework applies to Algol-like programming languages, and supports the optimization of complete programs as well as of program modules, which is required for separate compilation and the construction of software libraries. It is unique in capturing programs with

– statically nested mutually recursive procedures,
– global and local variables,
– value, reference, and procedure parameters, and
– external variables and procedures.

The new framework maintains the two-step structure of intraprocedural program optimization: the specification and the optimality proof of an interprocedural program transformation is separated from the specification and the precision proofs of the IDFA-algorithms computing the program properties involved in the definition of the transformation under consideration. Moreover, both steps are organized like their intraprocedural counterparts. This means, the first step is directed by general guide-lines fixing the obligations for specifying and proving the optimality of an interprocedural program transformation. The second step, considering the specification part first, reduces as in the intraprocedural case essentially to specifying the DFA-information of interest for a given program property, and the way in which it is computed by the elementary statements of a program. The only difference to the intraprocedural setting is the necessity of specifying the effect of return nodes in order to deal with local variables and value parameters of recursive procedures. The concrete IDFA-algorithm results as intraprocedurally automatically from instantiating the generic IDFA-algorithms of the interprocedural framework by the specification. Proving its precision for the property under consideration requires only a single step in addition to the intraprocedural case. This step is concerned with the effect of return nodes. The precision proof of the generated IDFA-algorithm consists of four elementary substeps, whose proofs are usually straightforward as in the intraprocedural case and concern the domain of the specification only. Central for achieving this is the Interprocedural Coincidence Theorem of [KS1], which is an interprocedural generalization of the Coincidence Theorem of [Ki1, KU2]. It gives a sufficient condition for the coincidence of the *specifying* interprocedural meet over all paths (*IMOP*) solution and the *algorithmic* interprocedural maximal fixed point (*IMFP*) solution of an IDFA-problem. In comparison to the presentation of [KS1], the framework and the coincidence theorem are extended in order to deal with static procedure nesting, external variables and procedures, and reference and procedure parameters. Whereas the extension to static procedure nesting and to external variables and procedures is straightforward, the extension to procedure parameters is more intricate, and requires a *higher order data flow analysis* (*HO-DFA*). As a side-effect, it turns out that the HO-DFA covers uniformly also reference and name parameters offering a conceptually new approach to the computation of alias information.

Higher Order Data Flow Analysis. The central idea to handle formal procedure calls in our framework is to consider formal procedure calls as "higher order" branch statements and to interpret them nondeterministically during IDFA. This can be considered the natural analogue to the nondeterministic treatment of ordinary branch statements in intraprocedural DFA. Moreover, it allows us to organize the HO-DFA as a preprocess of the "usual" IDFA, and to hide all details of the HO-DFA from the subsequent IDFA. Its intent is to determine for every formal procedure call in a program the set of procedures it can call at run-time *as precisely as possible*. This is closely related to approaches for constructing the procedure call graph of a program (cf. [CCHK, HK, Lak, Ry, Wal]).[2] These approaches, however, are mostly heuristically based,[3] and concentrate on the correctness (safety) of their approximation. They do not systematically deal with precision or decidability in general. This contrasts with our approach, where investigating correctness and precision, and addressing the theoretical and practical limitations of computing the set of procedures, which can be invoked by a formal procedure call, and integrating the results obtained into IDFA, is central. We show that the problem of determining the set of procedures which can be invoked by a formal procedure call is a refinement of the well-known *formal reachability* problem (cf. [La1]). We therefore call the refined problem the *formal callability* problem. Formal callability yields as a by-product the solution of the formal reachability problem. This is important because of the well-known undecidability of formal reachability in general (cf. [La1]) as it directly implies that also formal callability is in general not decidable. It is true that formal reachability is decidable for finite mode languages (e.g., ISO-Pascal [ISO]) [La1],[4] but the mode depth dramatically affects the computational complexity: whereas for programming languages of mode depth 2

---

[2] In [Lak] a different set-up is considered with procedure valued variables instead of procedure parameters.

[3] For example, the algorithm of [Ry] is restricted to programs without recursion.

[4] Intuitively, in a program with finite mode depth procedure parameters can completely be specified without using mode equations as it is necessary for certain procedure parameters of programs with infinite mode depth (Consider e.g. self-

(e.g., Wirth's Pascal [Wth, HW]) and a limit on the length of parameter lists, formal reachability is decidable in quadratic time [Ar3], it is P-space hard in the general case of unbounded finite mode depth languages [Ar3, Wi2].

Motivated by the theoretical limitations of deciding formal callability, and the practical limitations imposed by the efficiency requirements of compilers, we introduce a correct (safe) approximation of formal callability, called *potential passability*, which can efficiently be computed. Moreover, for programs of mode depth 2 without global formal procedure parameters, our approximation is precise for formal callability, i.e., potential passability and formal callability coincide.

Reference and Name Parameters. Reference and name parameters can be regarded as parameterless procedure parameters. This observation is the key to uniformly deal with procedure parameters, reference and name parameters.[5] Using this identification the HO-DFA can directly be used for computing (safe approximations of) the set of may-aliases of a reference parameter. Moreover, it can easily be modified for computing also (safe approximations of) the set of must-aliases of a reference parameter.

Interprocedural Data Flow Analysis. In IDFA we focus on programs, which satisfy the *strong formal most recent* (*sfmr*) property (cf. [Ka]); a property, which holds trivially for programs without formal procedure calls.[6] The point of concentrating on programs with this property is that in sfmr-programs[7] formal procedure calls can be handled in a most recent fashion like ordinary procedure calls, and thus, as efficiently as ordinary procedure calls.[8] The validity of the sfmr-property guarantees that the simplified and more efficient treatment of formal procedure calls is correct: so-called most recent errors in accessing non-local variables, which are known from early implementations of run-time systems, do not occur (cf. [McG]).

We recall that the sfmr-property is decidable at compile-time [Ka]. However, similar to formal reachability the mode depth is crucial for the computational complexity: for programming languages of mode depth 2 and a limit on the length of parameter lists, the sfmr-property is decidable in polynomial time [Ar2], but it is P-space complete in the general case of Algol-like

---

application of a procedure π as in the call statement *"call $\pi(\pi)$"*. Self-application is illegal in a language with finite mode depth!).

[5] Note that call-by-reference and call-by-name coincide as long as there are no complex data structures.

[6] Intuitively, this means that in the run-time stack maintaining the activation records of the procedures, which have been called but not yet terminated, the static pointer of each activation record created by a call of a procedure π always refers to the most recent activation record created by a call of the static predecessor of π (cf. [Ar2]). We remark that our HO-DFA does not rely on this property.

[7] I.e., programs satisfying the sfmr-property.

[8] In our approach to IDFA programs are treated in the sense of the mr-copy rule ("most recent"-copy rule), which for sfmr-programs coincides with the static scope copy rule in the sense of Algol60 (cf. [Ol2]).

languages, even if at most 4 local (procedure) parameters per procedure are allowed [Wi1, Wi2]. Thus, for most practical applications additional criteria, which are sufficient for the sfmr-property and can efficiently be checked, will be necessary (cf. [McG]). A simple syntactic criterion is that a program does not contain statically nested procedures [Wi2]. Of course, this looks arbitrary and quite restrictive. It is thus worth noting that C is an example of a widely used programming language, which does not allow statically nested procedures. In addition, the nesting criterion is also important because programs with statically nested procedures can often effectively be transformed into formally equivalent programs without statically nested procedures.[9] This is known as the *modularity* property of a program (cf. [La2]).[10] A program satisfies the modularity property if and only if it has a regular formal call tree [Ol1]. Based on the technique of *accompanying parameters* of [La2], there is an effective procedure that transforms an Algol-like program with a regular formal call tree into a formally equivalent Algol-like program without statically nested procedures [Ol1]. Unfortunately, the modularity property is not decidable in general [Ol1].[11] Thus, the following result of [La2] is here particularly important: there is an effective procedure transforming every Algol-like program without global formal procedure parameters into a formally equivalent Algol-like program without statically nested procedures.[12]

Summarizing, the advantages of focusing IDFA on sfmr-programs are as follows:

1. HO-DFA can be organized as a preprocess which can be hidden from IDFA:
   ↝Formal procedure calls do not affect the construction and the efficiency of IDFA-applications.
2. Formal procedure calls can be interpreted as nondeterministic higher order branch statements which can be treated in a most recent fashion like ordinary procedure calls:
   ↝Formal procedure calls fit uniformly into the standard techniques of static program analysis, and can be treated as efficiently as ordinary procedure calls.
3. sfmr-programs can effectively be transformed into formally equivalent programs without statically nested procedures:

---

[9] Formal equivalence of programs induce their functional equivalence [La4].

[10] This directly implies that sfmr-programs are *universal* in the sense that for every program satisfying the modularity property there is a formally equivalent program satisfying the sfmr-property.

[11] The set of programs satisfying the sfmr-property is a proper (decidable) subset of the set of programs satisfying the modularity property [Ol1].

[12] In [La2] the transformation is developed for Algol60-P, which stands for *pure* Algol60. Details on Algol60-P can be found in [La1].

⤳IFDA-applications on programs without statically nested procedures are often more efficient.[13]

We remark that the HO-DFA of our framework is primarily designed as an efficient preprocess for the interprocedural analysis of sfmr-programs with formal procedure calls. However, the problem underlying it, formal callability, and the correctness, precision, and complexity results concerning potential passability are closely related to classical problems of compiler optimization like formal reachability and formal recursivity. In contrast to the latter two problems, which have thoroughly been studied in the literature concerning both their decidability and their inherent complexity (cf. [Ar1, Ar2, Ar3, La1, Wi1, Wi2]), formal callability has not yet been investigated systematically to the knowledge of the author (except for the pragmatic approaches of call graph analysis (cf. [CCHK, HK, Lak, Ry, Wal]).[14] Our main result concerning formal callability that it can be computed in quadratic time for programs of mode depth 2 without global formal procedure parameters, if there is a limit on the length of parameter lists, is a direct analogue to the central result of [Ar3] that the coarser problem of formal reachability is decidable in quadratic time for programs of mode depth 2 and a limit on the length of parameter lists. In addition, our HO-DFA yields a new approach for computing alias information for reference parameters, which is conceptually significantly different from traditional approaches to the alias problem (cf. [Ban, Co, CpK2, LH, We]).

1.2.2 The Application

After developing the new framework for interprocedural program optimization, we demonstrate its power and flexibility by means of a practically relevant application, the *computationally* and *lifetime optimal* elimination of *interprocedurally partially redundant computations* in a program. The data flow analyses involved can rather straigthforward be deduced from their intraprocedural counterparts. However, we demonstrate that in the interprocedural setting computationally and lifetime optimal results are in general impossible. Therefore, we propose a natural sufficient constraint together with an algorithm, which meets both optimality criteria for a large class of programs. The algorithm evolves as the interprocedural counterpart of the algorithm for *lazy code motion* of [KRS1, KRS2]. Under the constraint proposed the new algorithm is not only more powerful than its heuristic predecessors (cf. [Mo, MR2, SW]), but also more efficient.

---

[13] This also holds for the application developed in Chapter 10 and Chapter 11. However, the trade-off between the costs of eliminating static procedure nesting, which usually increases the program size, and the efficiency gain of IDFA must be taken into account.

[14] In [Ar2] a similar notion was introduced defining when a procedure π formally calls a procedure π'. This, however, is still a coarser notion than formal callability, which defines when a specific call site in π formally calls procedure π'.

1.2.3 Related Work

There is a large variety of approaches to interprocedural DFA and optimization. In essence, they can be classified into three major groups. Approaches, which

1. reduce interprocedural DFA to intraprocedural DFA (e.g., by means of procedure inlining), or which use interprocedural information (e.g., which variables are *used* or *modified* by a procedure call) for intraprocedural program optimization [AGS, HC, Ri, RG].
2. deal with specific problems of interprocedural program optimization, e.g., *constant propagation* [CCpKT, GT], *loop invariant code motion* [SW], *partial redundancy elimination* [Mo, MR2], *register allocation* [SH], *branch elimination* [BGS], *slicing* [HRB], *alias information* [Bu, Co, CpK2, CpK3, De, ERH, LH, LR, My, We], or information whether a specific variable is *used*, *modified* or *preserved* by a procedure call [All2, Ban, Bth, Bu, CpK1, HS, Ro].
3. aim at a unifying framework for interprocedural DFA and interprocedural program optimization [Ba1, Ba2, Bou, CC2, SRH2, KS1, JM, RHS, SP, SRH1].

Approaches of the first group are not truly interprocedural. They aim at performing traditional intraprocedural techniques "more accurately" by weakening the worst-case assumptions of specific procedure calls. The results of Richardson and Ganapathi [Ri, RG] show that the effect of such approaches on the efficiency of a program is limited in practice.

Approaches of the second group are tailored for specific applications. Usually, it is not clear how to modify these specialized approaches in order to arrive at a uniform framework for interprocedural DFA or interprocedural program optimization.

Approaches of the third group have been pioneered by Cousot and Cousot [CC2], Barth [Ba1, Ba2], Sharir and Pnueli [SP], Jones and Muchnick [JM], and more recently by Bourdoncle [Bou]. These approaches address mainly correctness of an interprocedural DFA, and their applicability is limited as they do not properly deal with local variables of recursive procedures, which would require a mechanism to store information about local variables when treating a recursive call. The proper treatment of local variables and parameters of recursive procedures was a major achievement of the stack-based framework of Knoop and Steffen [KS1]. Fundamental was the introduction of so-called *DFA-stacks* and *return functions*, which allow an analysis to distinguish between effects on global and local variables after returning from a procedure call. This turned out to be the key for constructing a generic algorithm, which computes the "intuitively desired" solution of an interprocedural DFA-problem, and handles local variables properly.

The framework presented here is based on the approach of [KS1], but in addition to the specification, correctness and precision of interprocedural

DFA-algorithms, the framework here addresses also the specification, correctness and optimality of interprocedural program optimizations based thereof. Moreover, it is enhanced in order to capture reference and procedure parameters, external variables, and external procedures making the framework unique. In addition, the following features are central. (1) The framework is general: it is not restricted to certain problem classes. (2) It is optimal: DFA-algorithms and optimizations based thereon are precise even in the presence of recursive procedures. (3) It is tailored for practical use: all details, which are irrelevant for a specific application are hidden. This point is particularly important in practice because the framework allows the construction of optimal interprocedural program optimizations in a cookbook style. This contrasts to previous approaches, which often have a foundational character. The use of their techniques requires usually a detailed understanding of the underlying frameworks.

Recently, two efficiency oriented approaches for interprocedural DFA have been introduced by Reps, Horwitz, and Sagiv, and Duesterwald, Gupta, and Soffa, respectively, which also address the treatment of local variables. The framework presented here can be regarded as the theoretical backbone for proving the correctness of these approaches, which we therefore discuss in more detail here.

Reps, Horwitz, and Sagiv proposed in [RHS] an algorithm for solving interprocedural DFA-problems over finite lattices in a way, which captures global and local variables, and value and reference parameters. They achieve the proper treatment of local variables by means of two separate functions, which mimic the return functions originally introduced in [KS1]:[15] one function for extracting the globally relevant part from the data flow information, which is valid at the termination time of the called procedure. And another function for extracting the data flow information about local variables, which must be re-established after finishing the call, from the data flow information, which is valid immediately before the call. This *implicit* treatment of return functions allows them to reduce an interesting class of DFA-problems to graph reachability problems that can efficiently be solved, and to compute the effect of procedure calls in a by-need fashion. Moreover, it enables the treatment of some potentially infinite abstract domains [SRH1]. However, the introduction of the two "artifical" functions introduces additional paths in the graph used to represent the program, which do not correspond to a standard program execution path. As a consequence, when one encodes a problem in their framework(s), the proof of correctness for the encoding in the sense of the meet over all paths approach must account for these paths. This proof can be simplified by means of the theorems applying to the framework here. It is sufficient to prove the equivalence to the *IMFP*-solution. The Interprocedural Coincidence Theorem 8.4.2 then yields that it coincides as

---

[15] This was made explicit in a private communication with Thomas Reps (November 1994).

desired with the *IMOP*-solution, and thus, with the intuitively desired solution of the IDFA-problem under consideration. Moreover, following the lines of [KRS4] proving the equivalence to the *IMFP*-solution does not require the consideration of DFA-stacks at all, which must be part of any sound *IMOP*-solution capturing local variables and value parameters.

Duesterwald, Gupta, and Soffa proposed in [DGS1, DGS2] an algorithm for demand-driven interprocedural DFA, which works for programs with global and local variables, value and reference parameters. The point of their algorithm is to compute data flow information for a given program point without performing an exhaustive analysis of the argument program. In practice, this may be used e.g. for the debugging of a program during its development. The effect of the return functions of [KS1] to handle local variables can problem specifically be encoded in the *binding functions*, which realize the mapping between the address space of the calling procedure and the called procedure. Like in [RHS] a formal correctness proof for this approach depends on the correspondence between the computed solution and the operational understanding of a procedural program, and can be established by means of the results applying to the framework presented here. We remark that another and conceptually quite different algorithm for demand-driven DFA, which is based on magic-set transformations, has recently been proposed by Reps [Re1, Re2].

1.2.4 Organization of the Monograph

The monograph consists of four parts. In the first part we revisit the standard framework for intraprocedural program optimization in a cookbook view. Subsequently, we illustrate the framework by means of the practically relevant algorithm for lazy code motion (*LCM*) of [KRS1, KRS2]. This algorithm was the first one to eliminate partially redundant computations in a procedure in a computationally and lifetime optimal fashion. In contrast to the presentation of [KRS1, KRS2], the essential step of proving the precision of the DFA-algorithms involved in the *LCM*-transformation is here based on the Coincidence Theorem 2.2.2. Whereas intraprocedurally the impact of this different proceeding is mostly of technical nature, it turns out that it is quite advantageous interprocedurally because it significantly simplifies and shortens the precision proofs.

After the introductory first part, the second and the third part are central for the monograph. In the second part we introduce the new framework for interprocedural program optimization. Besides the treatment of formal procedure calls, and external variables and procedures, the cookbook view of the interprocedural framework is particularly important as it stresses the analogies and differences to the intraprocedural setting. Subsequently, we illustrate in the third part the interprocedural framework by means of the interprocedural extensions of the algorithms for busy and lazy code motion. We show that interprocedurally computational and lifetime optimality are in general impossible, but that both criteria can be met under a natural sufficient side-condition for a large class of programs.

In the fourth part, finally, we discuss a variety of pragmatic aspects related to interprocedural code motion and the new framework, and give directions to future work.

Note that highlighting the analogies and differences of the intraprocedural and interprocedural setting as mentioned above, as well as underlining the similarity of the proceeding for different data flow problems, when applying the framework, is a central concern of our presentation. To this end proofs for (most) theorems applying to the intraprocedural setting are given in full detail, even though they are corollaries of their interprocedural counterparts. In particular, this concerns theorems on properties of DFA-algorithms considered for illustrating the intra- and interprocedural framework. However, this presentation principle, sometimes even re-picking up a paragraph almost verbatim, is not restricted to proofs. It also recurs in the presentation of the underlying specifications of the DFA-algorithms as well as in the presentation of the intra- and interprocedural frameworks, and culminates in their cookbook summaries.

We conclude this section with a more detailed sketch of the contents of the following chapters.

- Part I: Introduction
  - Chapter 2 revisits the standard framework for intraprocedural program optimization in a cookbook view.
  - Chapter 3 and Chapter 4 illustrate the intraprocedural framework by recalling the transformations for busy (*BCM*-) and lazy code motion (*LCM*-transformation), and specifying the DFA-algorithms for computing the program properties involved in the *BCM*- and *LCM*-transformation, respectively. The precision proofs of the DFA-algorithms differ from the original proofs of [KRS1, KRS2], and are thus explicitly given.
- Part II: The Framework
  - Chapter 5 introduces the programming language representing the common of Algol-like languages, which we consider during the development and application of the interprocedural framework.
  - Chapter 6 presents the HO-DFA dealing with formal procedure calls. Central is to introduce the notion of formal callability, which we show to yield a refinement of the formal reachability problem. Like formal reachability it turns out that formal callability is not decidable in general. Thus, we introduce a correct (safe) approximation of formal callability, called potential passability, which can efficiently be computed. Moreover, for programs of mode depth 2 without global formal procedure parameters we prove that formal callability and potential passability coincide.
  - Chapter 7 completes the setting of IDFA. In particular, we fix the interface between HO-DFA and IDFA. Additionally, we introduce flow graph

systems and interprocedural flow graphs as representations of programs
with procedures.
- Chapter 8 presents the stack-based framework of IDFA. Central is the
  introduction of DFA-stacks and return functions, which are the prerequisite for defining the interprocedural versions of the meet over all paths
  approach and the maximal fixed point approach. The solutions of these
  approaches define the "specifying" and the "algorithmic" solution of an
  IDFA-problem, respectively. The main results of this chapter are the
  Interprocedural Correctness Theorem 8.4.1 and the Interprocedural Coincidence Theorem 8.4.2, which give sufficient conditions for the correctness and the precision of the algorithmic solution with respect to the
  specifying solution of an IDFA-problem. Finally, the specification of an
  IDFA-problem is formalized, and the generic fixed point algorithms for
  computing the algorithmic solution of a given IDFA-problem are presented.
- Chapter 9 summarizes the presentation of the second part. In this chapter we take the view of a designer of an interprocedural program optimization, and arrive at a cookbook for optimal interprocedural program
  optimization.
- Part III: The Application
  - Chapter 10 illustrates the framework for interprocedural program op-
    timization by means of the interprocedural extensions of the BCM-
    transformation and the LCM-transformation. It demonstrates that in
    contrast to the data flow analyses, which can rather straightforward
    be transferred from the intraprocedural setting, transformations based
    thereon usually require additional care. In particular, it shows that com-
    putationally and lifetime optimal results are interprocedurally in general
    impossible. Under a natural side-condition, however, the interprocedural
    extensions of the BCM- and LCM-transformation are proved to satisfy
    for a large class of programs both optimality criteria.
  - Chapter 11 presents the IDFA-algorithms for computing the program
    properties involved in the $IBCM$- and the $ILCM$-transformation to-
    gether with the proofs of their precision.
- Part IV: Conclusion
  - Chapter 12 discusses a variety of pragmatic aspects related to interpro-
    cedural code motion and the framework presented, and gives directions
    to future work.

The monograph closes with the bibliography and an index for simplifying
the access to definitions and technical terms. In particular, the index entry
"notations" can be used as a quick-reference to symbols and abbreviations.

2. The Intraprocedural Framework

In this chapter we revisit the standard framework for intraprocedural program optimization. Beyond recalling the framework for the convenience of the reader, the point of this revision is to structure and summarize it in a fashion, which allows the construction of provably optimal program optimizations in a cookbook style. This is important as in Part II we will show how to lift this cookbook oriented presentation of the intraprocedural framework to the interprocedural setting. As a by-product, this reveals and highlights the essential analogies and differences of the intraprocedural and interprocedural setting.

2.1 Intraprocedural Program Optimization

Program optimization is traditionally used as general term for program transformations, which are intended to *improve* the run-time or storage efficiency of a program. Thus, speaking of program optimization does usually not imply the generation of truly "optimal" programs as suggested by the term. In practice, one is often satisfied by heuristically based optimizations. Even transformations which sometimes impair the efficiency of a program are often considered program optimizations. Cytron, Lowry, and Zadeck distinguish *strict* transformations, which are required to always improve the efficiency, and *non-strict* transformations, which sometimes may fail to do this (cf. [CLZ]).

In contrast to these pragmatic approaches, we are interested in *optimal* program optimization, i.e., in program transformations which are provably optimal with respect to *formal optimality criteria*.[1] Toward this end we decompose program optimization into two steps. In the first step, we fix a class of program transformations $\mathcal{T}$ together with a formal optimality criterion $\mathcal{O}$. In the second step, we fix a transformation $Tr_{opt} \in \mathcal{T}$, and prove that it is optimal with respect to $\mathcal{O}$, or more briefly, that it is $\mathcal{O}$-optimal. In general, the ingredients of this two-step approach must be defined by the designer of

---

[1] In the following we will focus on run-time improving transformations, which are the major concern in practice. The framework, however, applies to storage improving transformations as well.

J. Knoop: Optimal Interprocedural Program Optimization, LNCS 1428, pp. 15-29, 1998.
© Springer-Verlag Berlin Heidelberg 1998

the optimization. Usually, the optimality criterion $\mathcal{O}$ is based on a pre-order, which fixes the standard of comparison between different programs. The program transformations of $\mathcal{T}$ are typically defined in terms of a set of program properties ϕ, which fix the side conditions under which a transformation is applicable. The validity of these properties must be verified before the transformation can be performed. This is the task of *data flow analysis* (DFA), which usually precedes every optimizing program transformation. Of course, in order to guarantee that the transformation induced by the results of the DFA is correct or even $\mathcal{O}$-optimal, the program properties involved must be computed precisely by the DFA (or at least conservatively, i.e., safely approximated). This leads to the notions of φ-*precise* and φ-*correct* DFA-algorithms, which we will consider in more detail in the following sections presenting our two-step approach for optimal program optimization.

After recalling flow graphs as an appropriate representation of procedures in Section 2.1.1, we introduce our two-step scheme of optimal program optimization in Section 2.1.2, and informally present the notion of provably precise (correct) DFA-algorithms in Section 2.1.3. Subsequently, we recall in Section 2.2 the theory of abstract interpretation, which provides the theoretical foundation of precise (correct) DFA-algorithms, and give a formal definition of a DFA-specification. Finally, we summarize in Section 2.3 our revision of the intraprocedural framework for optimal program optimization in a concise and structured form, which allows us to construct and prove the optimality and precision of program transformations and DFA-algorithms, respectively, in a cookbook style.

2.1.1 Procedures and Flow Graphs

Intraprocedural program optimization is characterized by a separate and independent investigation of the procedures of a program. As usual, we represent the procedures of a program as *directed flow graphs* $G = (N, E, \mathbf{s}, \mathbf{e})$ with node set N and edge set E.[2] Nodes $n \in N$ represent the statements, and edges $(n, m) \in E$ the nondeterministic branching structure of the underlying procedure; $\mathbf{s}$ and $\mathbf{e}$ denote the unique *start node* and *end node* of G, which are assumed to have no incoming and outgoing edges, respectively.[3]

For every flow graph G, we denote the set of immediate predecessors and successors of a node n by $pred_G(n) =_{df} \{ m \mid (m, n) \in E \}$ and $succ_G(n) =_{df} \{ m \mid (n, m) \in E \}$. A *finite path* in G is a sequence $(n_1, \ldots, n_q)$ of nodes such that $(n_j, n_{j+1}) \in E$ for $j \in \{1, \ldots, q-1\}$. Moreover, $\mathbf{P}_G[m, n]$ denotes the set of all finite paths from m to n, $\mathbf{P}_G[m, n[$ the set of all finite paths from m to a predecessor of n, and $\mathbf{P}_G]m, n]$ the set of all finite paths from a successor of m to n. Program paths reaching the end node

---

[2] The construction of flow graphs is described in [All1].

[3] This does not impose any restrictions as it is always possible to introduce a new start node and stop node enjoying these properties by need.

of G are called *terminating*. We assume that every node of a flow graph G lies on a terminating path starting in $\mathbf{s}$. The operator ";" denotes the concatenation of two paths. The *length* of a path p is given by the number of its node occurrences and denoted by λ_p. In particular, we denote the unique path of length 0 by ε. For a path p and an index $1 \le i \le \lambda_p$, the i-th component of p is denoted by p_i. A path q is a *subpath* of p, in signs $q \sqsubseteq p$, if there is an index $i \in \{1, \dots, \lambda_p\}$ such that $i + \lambda_q - 1 \le \lambda_p$ and $q_j = p_{i+j-1}$ for all $j \in \{1, \dots, \lambda_q\}$. Moreover, for i, $j \le \lambda_p$, $p[i,j]$, $p[i,j[$, and $p]i,j]$ denote the subpaths $(n_i, \dots, n_j)$, $(n_i, \dots, n_{j-1})$, and $(n_{i+1}, \dots, n_j)$ of p, respectively. If $i > j$, $p[i,j]$ means ε. The subpath relation $\sqsubseteq$ defined on paths can naturally be extended to sets of paths P and Q: $P \sqsubseteq Q \Longleftrightarrow_{df} \forall p \in P \; \exists q \in Q.\; p \sqsubseteq q$. Finally, for every path $p = (n_1, \dots, n_{\lambda_p})$ in G, we introduce the *reversed path* $\tilde{p}$ of p defined by $(n_{\lambda_p}, \dots, n_1)$.

2.1.2 Provably Optimal Program Transformations

Let G be a flow graph, $\mathcal{T}$ be a class of program transformations, and Tr be a transformation of $\mathcal{T}$. Additionally, let G_{Tr} denote the flow graph resulting from the application of Tr to G, and let $G_{\mathcal{T}} =_{df} \{G\} \cup \{G_{Tr} \mid Tr \in \mathcal{T}\}$ denote the set of all programs resulting from a transformation of $\mathcal{T}$ extended by G itself. By means of these definitions, we can present our two-step approach of optimal program optimization.

> *Step 1:* Fix a class of program transformations $\mathcal{T}$ and a relation $\le_{\mathcal{T}} \subseteq G_{\mathcal{T}} \times G_{\mathcal{T}}$.

Intuitively, the relation $\le_{\mathcal{T}}$ compares the "quality" of transformations $Tr, Tr' \in \mathcal{T}$. Usually, $\le_{\mathcal{T}}$ is a pre-order, and $G_{Tr} <_{\mathcal{T}} G_{Tr'}$ can informally be read as "Tr is *better* than Tr'". This directly induces a formal optimality criterion, which we call $\mathcal{O}_{\le_{\mathcal{T}}}$-optimality.

Definition 2.1.1 ($\mathcal{O}_{\le_{\mathcal{T}}}$-Optimality).
A transformation $Tr \in \mathcal{T}$ is $\mathcal{O}_{\le_{\mathcal{T}}}$-optimal, if for all $Tr' \in \mathcal{T}$ holds: $G_{Tr} \le_{\mathcal{T}} G_{Tr'}$.

> *Step 2:* Fix a transformation $Tr_{opt} \in \mathcal{T}$ and prove that it is $\mathcal{O}_{\le_{\mathcal{T}}}$-optimal.

As mentioned before, the transformations $Tr \in \mathcal{T}$ are typically defined in terms of a set of program properties Φ. Every $\varphi \in \Phi$ is a pair of functions $(N\text{-}\varphi, X\text{-}\varphi)$, whose domain and range are the sets of nodes of G and the Boolean truth values *true* and *false* of $\mathcal{B}$, respectively, i.e.,

$$N\text{-}\varphi, X\text{-}\varphi : N \to \mathcal{B}$$

Intuitively, the truth values $N\text{-}\varphi\ (n)$ and $X\text{-}\varphi\ (n)$, $n \in N$, indicate whether φ holds at the entry and at the exit of the argument node n, respectively.

It is worth noting that proving the $\mathcal{O}_{\leq_T}$-optimality of a given program transformation $Tr_{opt} \in \mathcal{T}$ does not rely on the particular choice of an algorithm $\mathcal{A}$ computing the program properties involved in the definition of Tr_{opt}. In fact, proving that an algorithm $\mathcal{A}$ computes a certain property of interest can be done separately. This is important because it structures and simplifies the overall proof by decomposing it into two independent steps.

2.1.3 Provably Precise Data Flow Analyses

In the context of our two-step scheme for optimal program optimization the task of DFA is to compute the program properties φ, which are involved in the transformation Tr_{opt}. Technically, this requires a static program analysis of G, which is performed by an appropriate DFA-algorithm computing the set of program points enjoying a program property φ of interest. This rises the questions of correctness and precision of DFA-algorithms. Intuitively, a DFA-algorithm is φ-*precise*, if it computes the set of nodes of G enjoying φ precisely, and it is φ-*correct*, if it approximates this set of nodes conservatively, i.e., if it computes a subset of the nodes of G enjoying φ.[4] Once the DFA-algorithms have been proved precise for the program properties involved in Tr_{opt}, it is usually easy to perform the transformation itself, and the program resulting from the transformation is guaranteed to be $\mathcal{O}_{\leq_T}$-optimal.[5] Theoretically well-founded are DFA-algorithms that are based on *abstract interpretation*, which has proved to be powerful and uniform framework for static program analyses (cf. [CC1, CC3, CC4, Ma, Nie1, Nie2]).

2.2 Abstract Interpretation

The central idea of abstract interpretation is to replace the "full" semantics of a procedure by a simpler more abstract version, which is tailored for a specific problem.[6] Usually, an abstract interpretation consists of two components: a domain of relevant data flow information, and a local semantic functional which specifies the effect of elementary statements on the domain under consideration. Together both components induce two variants of a corresponding global abstract semantics of a flow graph, an *operational* one specifying the intuitively desired solution of a DFA-problem, and a *denotational* one inducing a computation procedure.

---

[4] φ-precision and φ-correctness are formally defined in Section 2.2.6.

[5] ϕ-correctness is usually not sufficient to draw this conclusion (cf. Section 2.3).

[6] Here, to compute a program property φ.

2.2.1 Data Flow Information

The domain of data flow information is typically given by a complete semi-lattice[7]

$$(\mathcal{C}, \sqcap, \sqsubseteq, \bot, \top)$$

with least element $\bot$ and greatest element $\top$. The elements of $\mathcal{C}$ are assumed to express the data flow information of interest. For practical applications lattices satisfying the descending chain condition are particularly important.

Definition 2.2.1 (Descending Chain Condition).
The lattice $(\mathcal{C}, \sqcap, \sqsubseteq, \bot, \top)$ *satisfies the* descending chain condition *if and only if for every subset* $C' \subseteq \mathcal{C}$ *and every sequence of elements of* C' *with*

$$c_1 \sqsupseteq c_2 \sqsupseteq c_3 \sqsupseteq c_4 \sqsupseteq \cdots$$

there is an index k_0 *such that* $c_j = c_{k_0}$ *for every* $j \geq k_0$.

In the following $\mathcal{C}$ will always denote a complete semi-lattice.

2.2.2 Local Abstract Semantics

The *local* abstract semantics of a flow graph G is given by a semantic functional

$$[\![\ ]\!] : N \rightarrow (\mathcal{C} \rightarrow \mathcal{C})$$

which gives meaning to every node $n \in N$ in terms of a transformation on $\mathcal{C}$. Without loss of generality, we assume that **s** and **e** are associated with the identity on $\mathcal{C}$ denoted by $Id_{\mathcal{C}}$. Note that a local abstract semantics $[\![\ ]\!]$ can easily be extended to cover finite paths. For every path $p \in \mathbf{P}_G[m, n]$, we define:

$$[\![\, p \,]\!] =_{df} \begin{cases} Id_{\mathcal{C}} & \text{if } p = \varepsilon \\ [\![\, p[2, \lambda_p] \,]\!] \circ [\![\, p_1 \,]\!] & \text{otherwise} \end{cases}$$

2.2.3 Global Abstract Semantics

As mentioned before, the global abstract semantics of G results from one of the following two globalization approaches of a local abstract semantics: the "operational" *meet over all paths* (*MOP*) approach, and the "denotational" *maximal fixed point* (*MFP*) approach in the sense of Kam and Ullman [KU2]. The solutions of these approaches define the *specifying* and the *algorithmic* solution of a DFA-problem, respectively. The *MOP*-approach directly mimics possible program executions: it "meets" (intersects) all informations, which belong to a program path reaching the program point under consideration.

---

[7] A complete semi-lattice is a complete lattice as well. DFA-algorithms, however, usually consider only the join operation or the meet operation of $\mathcal{C}$. We emphasize this by considering $\mathcal{C}$ a semi-lattice.

Definition 2.2.2 (The *MOP*-Solution).
Given a flow graph $G = (N, E, \mathbf{s}, \mathbf{e})$, a complete semi-lattice $\mathcal{C}$, and a local abstract semantics $[\![\ ]\!]$, the MOP-solution is defined by:[8]

$$\forall c_s \in \mathcal{C} \ \forall n \in N. \ MOP_{([\![\ ]\!],c_s)}(n) =_{df} (\, N\text{-}MOP_{([\![\ ]\!],c_s)}(n), \ X\text{-}MOP_{([\![\ ]\!],c_s)}(n)\,)$$

where

$$N\text{-}MOP_{([\![\ ]\!],c_s)}(n) =_{df} \sqcap \{\, [\![p]\!](c_s) \mid p \in \mathbf{P}_G[\mathbf{s}, n[\,\}$$
$$X\text{-}MOP_{([\![\ ]\!],c_s)}(n) =_{df} \sqcap \{\, [\![p]\!](c_s) \mid p \in \mathbf{P}_G[\mathbf{s}, n]\,\}$$

This definition directly reflects our desires. However, it does not specify an effective computation procedure in general.[9] In contrast, the *MFP*-approach iteratively approximates the greatest solution of a system of equations which express consistency between pre-conditions and post-conditions expressed in terms of $\mathcal{C}$ with respect to a start information $c_s \in \mathcal{C}$:

Equation System 2.2.3.

$$\mathbf{pre}(n) \quad = \quad \begin{cases} c_s & \text{if } n = \mathbf{s} \\ \sqcap \{\, \mathbf{post}(m) \mid m \in pred_G(n) \,\} & \text{otherwise} \end{cases}$$

$$\mathbf{post}(n) \quad = \quad [\![n]\!](\mathbf{pre}(n))$$

Denoting the greatest solution of Equation System 2.2.3 with respect to a given start information c_s by $\mathbf{pre}_{c_s}$ and $\mathbf{post}_{c_s}$, respectively, the solution of the *MFP*-approach is defined by:

Definition 2.2.4 (The *MFP*-Solution).
Given a flow graph $G = (N, E, \mathbf{s}, \mathbf{e})$, a complete semi-lattice $\mathcal{C}$ and a local abstract semantics $[\![\ ]\!]$, the MFP-solution is defined by:

$$\forall c_s \in \mathcal{C} \ \forall n \in N. \ MFP_{([\![\ ]\!],c_s)}(n) =_{df} (\, N\text{-}MFP_{([\![\ ]\!],c_s)}(n), \ X\text{-}MFP_{([\![\ ]\!],c_s)}(n)\,)$$

where

$$N\text{-}MFP_{([\![\ ]\!],c_s)}(n) =_{df} \mathbf{pre}_{c_s}(n) \qquad and \qquad X\text{-}MFP_{([\![\ ]\!],c_s)}(n) =_{df} \mathbf{post}_{c_s}(n)$$

In general, this definition leads to a suboptimal but algorithmic description. Thus, there are two global notions of semantics here: an operational one, which precisely mimics our intuition, and a denotational one, which has an algorithmic character and induces a computation procedure. In fact, we thus consider the *MOP*-approach as a mean for the direct specification of a DFA, and the *MFP*-approach as its algorithmic realization.[10] This rises the questions of *MOP-correctness* and *MOP-precision* of such algorithms, which have elegantly be answered by Kildall, and Kam and Ullman.

---

[8] Remember, "N" and "X" stand for entry and exit of a node, respectively.
[9] Think e.g. of loops in a program.
[10] An explicit generic algorithm is given in Section 2.2.5.

2.2.4 *MOP*-Correctness and *MOP*-Precision

The key for answering the questions of *MOP*-correctness and *MOP*-precision are the following two notions on functions on a complete semi-lattice $(\mathcal{C}, \sqcap, \sqsubseteq, \bot, \top)$. A function $f : \mathcal{C} \to \mathcal{C}$ on $\mathcal{C}$ is called

- *monotonic* if and only if $\forall c, c' \in \mathcal{C}.\ c \sqsubseteq c'$ implies $f(c) \sqsubseteq f(c')$
- *distributive* if and only if $\forall \emptyset \neq C' \subseteq \mathcal{C}.\ f(\sqcap C') = \sqcap \{f(c) \,|\, c \in C'\}$

We recall that distributivity is a stronger requirement than monotonicity in the following sense:

Lemma 2.2.1.
A function $f : \mathcal{C} \to \mathcal{C}$ is monotonic iff $\forall C' \subseteq \mathcal{C}.\ f(\sqcap C') \sqsubseteq \sqcap \{f(c) \,|\, c \in C'\}$.

As demonstrated by Kam and Ullman, monotonicity of the semantic functions is sufficient to guarantee correctness of the *MFP*-solution with respect to the *MOP*-solution. We have (cf. [KU2]):

Theorem 2.2.1 (Correctness Theorem).
Given a flow graph $G = (N, E, \mathbf{s}, \mathbf{e})$, the MFP-solution is a correct approximation of the MOP-solution, i.e.,

$$\forall c_s \in \mathcal{C}\ \forall n \in N.\ \mathit{MFP}_{([\![\ ]\!], c_s)}(n) \sqsubseteq \mathit{MOP}_{([\![\ ]\!], c_s)}(n)$$

if all the semantic functions $[\![\, n \,]\!]$, $n \in N$, are monotonic.

Distributivity of the semantic functions yields precision. This follows from the well-known intraprocedural Coincidence Theorem 2.2.2 of Kildall [Ki1], and Kam and Ullman [KU2]:

Theorem 2.2.2 (Coincidence Theorem).
Given a flow graph $G = (N, E, \mathbf{s}, \mathbf{e})$, the MFP-solution is precise for the MOP-solution, i.e.,

$$\forall c_s \in \mathcal{C}\ \forall n \in N.\ \mathit{MFP}_{([\![\ ]\!], c_s)}(n) = \mathit{MOP}_{([\![\ ]\!], c_s)}(n)$$

if all the semantic functions $[\![\, n \,]\!]$, $n \in N$, are distributive.

2.2.5 The Generic Fixed Point Algorithm

In contrast to the *MOP*-approach, the *MFP*-approach is practically relevant because it directly specifies an iterative procedure for computing the *MFP*-solution. In this section we present a generic computation procedure, which is parameterized in the argument flow graph, the lattice of data flow information, the local semantic functional, and a start information.

Algorithm 2.2.5 (Computing the *MFP*-Solution).

Input: A flow graph $G = (N, E, \mathbf{s}, \mathbf{e})$, a complete semi-lattice $\mathcal{C}$, a local semantic functional $[\![\ ]\!] : N \to (\mathcal{C} \to \mathcal{C})$, and a start information $c_s \in \mathcal{C}$.

Output: An annotation of G with data flow informations, i.e., an annotation with pre-informations (stored in *pre*) and post-informations (stored in *post*) of elements of $\mathcal{C}$, which represent valid data flow information at the entry and exit of every node of G, respectively.

Remark: The variable *workset* controls the iterative process. Its elements are pairs, whose first components are nodes of G, and whose second components are elements of $\mathcal{C}$, which specify a new approximation for the pre-information of the node of the first component.

(Initialization of the annotation arrays *pre* and *post*, and the variable *workset*)
FORALL $n \in N$ **DO**
     $pre[n] := \top;$
     $post[n] := [\![n]\!](\top)$
OD;
$workset := \{ (\mathbf{s}, c_s) \} \cup \{ (n, post[m]) \mid n \in succ_G(m) \wedge post[m] \sqsubset \top \};$

(Iterative fixed point computation)
WHILE $workset \neq \emptyset$ **DO**
      LET $(m, c) \in workset$
          BEGIN
                $workset := workset \backslash \{ (m, c) \};$
                $meet := pre[m] \sqcap c;$
                IF $pre[m] \sqsupset meet$
                    THEN
                          $pre[m] := meet;$
                          $post[m] := [\![m]\!](pre[m]);$
                          $workset := workset \cup \{ (n, post[m]) \mid n \in succ_G(m) \}$
          FI
          END
OD.

Denoting the values of *workset*, *pre*[n], and *post*[n] after the k-th execution of the while-loop by $workset^k$, $pre^k[n]$, and $post^k[n]$, respectively, one can easily prove the following monotonicity property of Algorithm 2.2.5:

Lemma 2.2.2. *If the semantic functions $[\![n]\!]$, $n \in N$, are monotonic, we have:*

$$\forall n \in N \ \forall k \in I\!\!N. \ (pre^{k+1}[n], post^{k+1}[n]) \sqsubseteq (pre^k[n], post^k[n])$$

Moreover, by means of Lemma 2.2.2 we can prove:

Theorem 2.2.3 (Algorithm 2.2.5).
If the semantic functions $[\![\, n \,]\!]$, $n \in N$, are monotonic, we have:

1. *If $\mathcal{C}$ satisfies the descending chain condition, there is a $k_0 \in I\!N$ with*

$$\forall\, k \geq k_0.\; (pre^k[n], post^k[n]) = (pre^{k_0}[n], post^{k_0}[n])$$

2. *$\forall\, n \in N.\; MFP_{([\![\,]\!], c_s)}(n) = (\bigsqcap\{pre^k[n] \mid k \geq 0\}, \bigsqcap\{post^k[n] \mid k \geq 0\})$*

As an immediate corollary of Theorem 2.2.3 we obtain:

Corollary 2.2.1 (Algorithm 2.2.5).
If the semantic functions $[\![\, n \,]\!]$, $n \in N$, are monotonic, we have:

1. *Algorithm 2.2.5 terminates, if $\mathcal{C}$ satisfies the descending chain condition.*

2. *After the termination of Algorithm 2.2.5 holds:*
   $\forall\, n \in N.\; MFP_{([\![\,]\!], c_s)}(n) = (pre[n], post[n])$

2.2.6 Formal Specification of DFA-Algorithms

Following the presentation of the previous sections, a DFA $\mathcal{A}$ is specified by a triple $(\mathcal{C}, [\![\,]\!], c_s)$, which consists of a lattice $\mathcal{C}$, a local semantic functional $[\![\,]\!]$, and a start information c_s. The specification of a DFA $\mathcal{A}$ can directly be fed into the generic Algorithm 2.2.5, which yields the DFA-algorithm induced by $\mathcal{A}$.

Definition 2.2.6 (Specification of a DFA-Algorithm).
The specification of a DFA $\mathcal{A}$ is a triple $(\mathcal{C}, [\![\,]\!], c_s)$, where

1. *$\mathcal{C} = (\mathcal{C}, \sqcap, \sqsubseteq, \bot, \top)$ is a complete semi-lattice,*
2. *$[\![\,]\!] : N \rightarrow (\mathcal{C} \rightarrow \mathcal{C})$ a local semantic functional, and*
3. *$c_s \in \mathcal{C}$ a start information.*

The DFA-algorithm $Alg(\mathcal{A})$ induced by $\mathcal{A}$ results from instantiating the generic Algorithm 2.2.5 with $(\mathcal{C}, [\![\,]\!], c_s)$. The MOP-solution of $\mathcal{A}$ and the MFP-solution of $Alg(\mathcal{A})$ are the specifying *and the* algorithmic *solutions of $\mathcal{A}$, respectively.*

A DFA $\mathcal{A}$ expresses the information of interest in terms of lattice elements. In general, there is thus a gap between a DFA $\mathcal{A}$ and a program property φ, which is a Boolean predicate. This gap is closed by means of an *interpretation* function *Int*, which interprets the data flow information computed by $\mathcal{A}$ in Boolean truth values leading to the central notions of φ-correctness and φ-precision of a DFA.

Definition 2.2.7 (φ-Correctness and φ-Precision of a DFA).
Let φ be a program property, $\mathcal{A} = (\mathcal{C}, [\![\ ]\!], c_s)$ a DFA, and $Int : \mathcal{C} \to \mathcal{B}$ an interpretation of $\mathcal{C}$ in $\mathcal{B}$. Then $\mathcal{A}$ is

1. *φ-correct if and only if*   *(i)* $Int \circ N\text{-}MOP_{([\![\ ]\!],c_s)} \Rightarrow N\text{-}\varphi$
                                   (ii) $Int \circ X\text{-}MOP_{([\![\ ]\!],c_s)} \Rightarrow X\text{-}\varphi$
2. *φ-precise if and only if*   *(i)* $Int \circ N\text{-}MOP_{([\![\ ]\!],c_s)} \iff N\text{-}\varphi$
                                   (ii) $Int \circ X\text{-}MOP_{([\![\ ]\!],c_s)} \iff X\text{-}\varphi$

The notions of φ-correctness and φ-precision relate the specifying solution of a DFA $\mathcal{A}$ to a property φ. In order to close the gap between the algorithmic solution of $\mathcal{A}$ and φ, we introduce next the notions of *MOP*-correctness and *MOP*-precision, which relate the algorithmic solution to the specifying solution of $\mathcal{A}$. Additionally, we introduce the notion of a terminating DFA. The separation of concerns resulting from these definitions simplifies the proofs of φ-correctness and φ-precision of a DFA significantly because proving the algorithmic solution of a DFA to be terminating, and correct or precise for φ reduces to checking the preconditions of the Correctness Theorem 2.2.1 or the Coincidence Theorem 2.2.2, respectively. This is particularly beneficial in the interprocedural case.

Definition 2.2.8 (*MOP*-Correctness, *MOP*-Precision, Termination).

A DFA $\mathcal{A} = (\mathcal{C}, [\![\ ]\!], c_s)$ is

1. *MOP-correct if and only if $MFP_{([\![\ ]\!],c_s)} \sqsubseteq MOP_{([\![\ ]\!],c_s)}$*
2. *MOP-precise if and only if $MFP_{([\![\ ]\!],c_s)} = MOP_{([\![\ ]\!],c_s)}$*
3. *terminating, if its induced DFA-algorithm $Alg(\mathcal{A})$ terminates.*

MOP-correctness, *MOP*-precision, and the termination of a DFA can usually be proved straightforward by a few substeps. This is a consequence of Theorem 2.2.4, which results from combining the Correctness Theorem 2.2.1, the Coincidence Theorem 2.2.2, and Corollary 2.2.1, and gives sufficient conditions guaranteeing these properties of a DFA.

Theorem 2.2.4 (*MOP*-Correctness, *MOP*-Precision, Termination).
A DFA $\mathcal{A} = (\mathcal{C}, [\![\ ]\!], c_s)$ is

1. *MOP-correct, if all semantic functions $[\![\, n \,]\!]$, $n \in N$, are monotonic.*
2. *MOP-precise, if all semantic functions $[\![\, n \,]\!]$, $n \in N$, are distributive.*
3. *terminating, if (i)* $\mathcal{C}$ *satisfies the descending chain condition, and*
                        (ii)   *all semantic functions $[\![\, n \,]\!]$, $n \in N$, are monotonic.*

For convenience, we finally introduce an abbreviation, which both expresses the termination of a DFA $\mathcal{A}$ with respect to a given program property φ and its φ-correctness (φ-precision).

Definition 2.2.9 (Correctness and Precision of a DFA).
Let φ be a program property and $\mathcal{A}$ be a DFA. Then $\mathcal{A}$ is called correct
(precise) for φ if and only if $\mathcal{A}$ is (i) terminating and (ii) φ-correct (φ-precise).

2.2.7 Forward, Backward, and Bidirectional DFA-Algorithms

An important classification of DFA-algorithms, which we did not consider yet, is induced by the direction of information flow. Typically, DFA-algorithms are grouped into *forward*, *backward*, and *bidirectional* algorithms depending on the direction of information flow (cf. [He]). A DFA-algorithm is called *forward*, if information is propagated in the same direction as control flow, it is called *backward*, if information is propagated in the opposite direction of control flow, and it is called *bidirectional*, if information is mutually dependently propagated in both directions. As usual, we formulated our framework for forward analyses. However, backward analyses can be dealt with by forward analyses in our framework simply after inverting the flow of control. In contrast, bidirectional analyses cause more problems because they lack a natural operational (or *MOP-*) interpretation. *Information flow paths*, which have been introduced by Dhamdhere and Khedker in order to characterize the information flow of bidirectional analyses do usually not correspond to possible program executions (cf. [DK1, DK2]). Bidirectional problems are in fact conceptually and computationally more complex than unidirectional ones in general: in contrast to the unidirectional case, where reducible programs can be dealt with in $O(n \, log(n))$ time (cf. [AU, GW, HU1, HU2, Ke2, KU1, Ta1, Ta2, Ta3, Ull]), the best known estimation for bidirectional analyses is $O(n^2)$ (cf. [Dh3, DK1, DRZ, DP]), where n characterizes the size of the argument program (e.g., number of statements).[11] An elegant way to overcome this problem is to decompose bidirectional DFA-algorithms into sequences of unidirectional ones. Chapter 3 shows the result of such a decomposition: the originally bidirectional flow of DFA-information for code motion (cf. [Ch, Dh1, Dh2, Dh3, DS1, MR1, So]) is structured into a sequence of a backward analysis followed by a forward analysis [KRS1, KRS2], a decomposition, which was first proposed by Steffen (cf. [St1]). Besides yielding clarity, this decomposition was also the key to open the algorithm for modifications. By enhancing it by two further unidirectional analyses we arrived at a code motion algorithm which was the first

---

[11] In [DK1] the complexity of bidirectional problems has been estimated by $O(n*w)$, where w denotes the *width* of a flow graph. In contrast to the well-known notion of *depth* (cf. [He]) traditional estimations are based on, width is not a structural property of a flow graph, but varies with the problem under consideration. In particular, it is larger for bidirectional problems than for unidirectional ones, and in the worst case it is linear in the size of the flow graph.

one to achieve (intraprocedurally) *computationally* and *lifetime optimal* programs [KRS1, KRS2]. Intuitively, computational optimality means that the number of computations on each program path cannot be reduced any further by means of semantics preserving code motion; lifetime optimality means that no computation has been moved unnecessarily far, i.e., without run-time gain. The flexibility resulting from the decomposition was also demonstrated by Drechsler and Stadel, who proposed a variant of the computationally and lifetime optimal algorithm, which inserts computations on edges rather than in nodes (cf. [DS2]).

2.3 A Cookbook for Optimal Intraprocedural Program Optimization

In this section we summarize the revision of the intraprocedural framework for optimal program optimization for constructing a program optimization from the designer's point of view. The point is to arrive at a presentation, which supports the designer of a program optimization by structuring the construction process, and hiding all details of the framework that are irrelevant for its application. In fact, following the lines of this section the construction and the proof of optimality of a program transformation as well as the proofs of precision of the corresponding DFA-algorithms can be done in a cookbook style.

2.3.1 Optimal Program Optimization

Fixing the Program Transformations and the Optimality Criterion.
According to the two-step scheme of our approach to optimal program optimization, we first have to fix the class of program transformations and the optimality criterion of interest. Following Section 2.1.2, this requires:

Define ...

1. a set of appropriate program properties Φ
2. the class of program transformations $\mathcal{T}$ of interest in terms of a subset $\Phi_C \subseteq \Phi$
3. a relation $\leq_{\mathcal{T}} \subseteq G_{\mathcal{T}} \times G_{\mathcal{T}}$,[12] which induces the optimality criterion of interest

---

The optimality criterion induced by $\leq_{\mathcal{T}}$ is the criterion of $\mathcal{O}_{\leq_{\mathcal{T}}}$-optimality in the sense of Definition 2.1.1, i.e.:

A transformation $Tr \in \mathcal{T}$ is $\mathcal{O}_{\leq_{\mathcal{T}}}$-optimal, if for all $Tr' \in \mathcal{T}$ holds:
$$G_{Tr} \leq_{\mathcal{T}} G_{Tr'}$$

---

[12] In general, $\leq_{\mathcal{T}}$ will be a pre-order.

Fixing the Optimal Program Transformation. Next, the (optimal) program transformation must be defined. Similar to the class of program transformations $\mathcal{T}$, it is defined in terms of a subset of the properties of Φ, i.e.:

Define ...

    4. the program transformation Tr_{opt} of interest in terms of a subset $\Phi_T \subseteq \Phi$

Subsequently, we have to prove that Tr_{opt} is a member of the transformation class under consideration and satisfies the optimality criterion of interest. Thus:

Prove ...

    5. $Tr_{opt} \in \mathcal{T}$

    6. Tr_{opt} is $\mathcal{O}_{\leq_{\iota}}$-optimal

2.3.2 Precise Data Flow Analysis

After proving the optimality of Tr_{opt}, we have to define for each property $\varphi \in \Phi_T$ involved in the definition of Tr_{opt} a DFA $\mathcal{A}_\varphi$ computing the set of program points enjoying φ. Without loss of generality, we thus consider an arbitrary, but fixed property φ of Φ_T in the following.

Specifying the DFA $\mathcal{A}_\varphi$. According to Section 2.2.6 the specification of the DFA $\mathcal{A}_\varphi$, and the proof that it is precise for φ requires the following components:

Specify ...

    7. a complete semi-lattice $(\mathcal{C}, \sqcap, \sqsubseteq, \bot, \top)$

    8. a local semantic functional $[\![\ ]\!] : N \to (\mathcal{C} \to \mathcal{C})$

    9. a start information $c_s \in \mathcal{C}$

   10. an interpretation $Int : \mathcal{C} \to \mathcal{B}$

The lattice $\mathcal{C}$ represents the data flow information of interest, the local semantic functional gives meaning to the elementary statements of the argument program, and the start information c_s represents the data flow information which is assumed to be valid immediately before the execution of the argument program starts. The function Int, finally, interprets the elements of $\mathcal{C}$ as Boolean truth values, which closes the gap between the data flow information computed and the program property φ of interest.

Handling Backward Analyses: We recall that backward analyses can be handled by forward analyses simply after inverting the flow of control.

Proving Precision of $\mathcal{A}_\varphi$. At this stage, we have to verify that $\mathcal{A}_\varphi$ is precise for φ in the sense of Definition 2.2.9, i.e., that $\mathcal{A}_\varphi$ is terminating and φ-precise. Applying Definition 2.2.7 and Theorem 2.2.4 the following proof steps are sufficient:

Prove ...

11. the lattice $\mathcal{C}$ satisfies the descending chain condition
12. the local semantic functions $[\![\,n\,]\!]$, $n \in N$, are distributive
13. the specifying solution of $\mathcal{A}_\varphi$ is φ-precise, i.e.:
    (i) $\mathit{Int} \circ N\text{-}\mathit{MOP}_{([\![\,]\!],c_s)} \iff N\text{-}\varphi$
    (ii) $\mathit{Int} \circ X\text{-}\mathit{MOP}_{([\![\,]\!],c_s)} \iff X\text{-}\varphi$

Combining Definition 2.2.7, Theorem 2.2.4, and the propositions of the steps 11, 12, and 13 we directly obtain the desired precision result.

Theorem 2.3.1 ($\mathcal{A}_\varphi$-Precision).
$\mathcal{A}_\varphi$ is precise for φ, i.e., $\mathcal{A}_\varphi$ is terminating and φ-precise.

After proving Theorem 2.3.1 for each DFA $\mathcal{A}_\varphi$, $\varphi \in \Phi_T$, we obtain that the transformation Tr_{opt} and the transformation $\mathit{Tr}_{\{\mathcal{A}_\varphi \mid \varphi \in \Phi_T\}}$ induced by the algorithmic solutions of the DFA-algorithms $\mathcal{A}_\varphi$, $\varphi \in \Phi_T$, coincide. Thus, we have the desired optimality result:

Theorem 2.3.2 ($\mathcal{O}$-Optimality).
The transformation $\mathit{Tr}_{\{\mathcal{A}_\varphi \mid \varphi \in \Phi_T\}}$ is $\mathcal{O}_{\leq_T}$-optimal.

Monotonic DFA-Problems: Additional Proof Obligations. In contrast to *distributive* DFA-problems, which are characterized by the fact that the local semantic functions are distributive, *monotonic* DFA-problems, i.e., problems, where the local semantic functions are monotonic (but not distributive), impose additional proof obligations. A prominent representative of this class of DFA-problems is the problem of computing the set of *simple constants* of a program (cf. [Ki1, Ki2, RL1, RL2]). Intuitively, a program term t is a simple constant, if it is a program constant, or if all its subterms are simple constants. The value c of a simple constant t can be computed at compile-time. The original and possibly complex program term t can then be replaced by its value c in order to improve the run-time efficiency of the argument program.

For a monotonic DFA-problem, i.e., if step 12 holds for monotonicity instead of distributivity only, the Correctness Theorem 2.2.1 still yields the *MOP*-correctness of $\mathcal{A}_\varphi$. Together with step 13, this even implies φ-correctness of $\mathcal{A}_\varphi$. In general, however, this is not sufficient in order to guarantee that the program $G_{\mathit{Tr}_{\{\mathcal{A}_\varphi \mid \varphi \in \Phi_T\}}}$ resulting from the transformation

$Tr_{\{A_\varphi \mid \varphi \in \Phi_T\}}$ is correct or even $\mathcal{O}_{\leq_T}$-optimal. Analogously, this also holds if step 13 holds for φ-correctness instead of φ-precision only. In both cases the following two proof obligations must additionally be verified in order to guarantee correctness and profitability of the induced transformation:

Prove ...

14. $Tr_{\{A_\varphi \mid \varphi \in \Phi_T\}} \in \mathcal{T}$

15. $G_{Tr_{\{A_\varphi \mid \varphi \in \Phi_T\}}} \leq_T G$

Application: Intraprocedural Code Motion. We conclude this section with an outlook to the code motion application, which we consider in Chapter 3 for illustrating the usage of the cookbook. For this application the set of program properties Φ is basically given by the set of predicates *safe, correct, down-safe, earliest, latest,* and *isolated.* The class of program transformations $\mathcal{T}$ is given by the set of *admissible code motion transformations* which are defined in terms of the predicates *safe* and *correct.* The predicates *down-safe* and *earliest* are used for defining the computationally optimal transformation of *busy* code motion, and the predicates *latest* and *isolated* for defining the computationally and lifetime optimal transformation of *lazy* code motion.

3. Optimal Intraprocedural Code Motion: The Transformations

In this chapter we consider a practically relevant optimization, the *elimination of partially redundant computations* in a procedure, in order to illustrate the two-step approach of our framework for optimal intraprocedural program optimization. In particular, we demonstrate how to apply the cookbook of Section 2.3. To this end we recall the *busy* and the *lazy code motion* transformation of [KRS1, KRS2] for partial redundancy elimination. They result in *computationally* and *lifetime optimal* programs, respectively. We remark that lifetime optimality implies computational optimality. The optimality theorems applying to the busy and the lazy code motion transformation were originally proved in [KRS1, KRS2]. Here, they are corollaries of their interprocedural counterparts proved in Chapter 10. We thus omit proofs in this chapter, which allows us to focus on illustrating the two-step approach. In the following we denote the transformations of busy and lazy code motion more briefly as BCM-transformation and LCM-transformation. The variants of the original transformations of [KRS1, KRS2] presented in the following are slightly enhanced in order to work on parallel assignments.

After introducing the basic definitions, which are necessary for defining the BCM-transformation and the LCM-transformation in Section 3.1, we present the BCM-transformation and the theorems showing its computational optimality in Section 3.3. Subsequently, we present the LCM-transformation together with the theorems demonstrating its lifetime optimality in Section 3.4. In Section 3.5, finally, we demonstrate the power of both transformations by means of an illustrating example, which highlights their essential features.

3.1 Preliminaries

We develop the BCM-transformation and the LCM-transformation with respect to an arbitrary but fixed flow graph $G = (N, E, \mathbf{s}, \mathbf{e})$, and an arbitrary but fixed program term $t \in \mathbf{T}$. This allows us a simple and unparameterized notation. As usual, we assume that terms are inductively composed of variables, operators, and constants.

Parallel Assignments, Modifications, and Computations. We assume that the nodes of G represent *parallel assignments* of the form

J. Knoop: Optimal Interprocedural Program Optimization, LNCS 1428, pp. 31-48, 1998.
© Springer-Verlag Berlin Heidelberg 1998

$(x_1, \ldots, x_k) := (t_1, \ldots, t_k)$, where $i \neq j$ implies $x_i \neq x_j$. A parallel assignment is called a *modification* of t, if it assigns to an operand of t. It is called a *computation* of t, if t is a subexpression of one of its right-hand side terms. Moreover, the occurrences of t occurring in computations of G are called *original computations*.

Local Predicates *Comp* **and** *Transp*. Central for defining the *BCM*-transformation and the *LCM*-transformation are two local predicates *Transp* and *Comp*, which are defined for every node $n \in N$. Intuitively, these predicates indicate whether t is modified or computed by the assignment of node n.[1]

- *Transp* (n): n is *transparent* for t, i.e., n is not a modification of t.
- *Comp* (n): n is a *computation* of t, i.e., n contains an original computation of t.

Convention: As in [KRS2], we extend a predicate *Predicate*, which is defined on nodes n, to paths p by means of the following convention:

- $Predicate^{\forall}(p) \iff \forall 1 \leq i \leq \lambda_p. \ Predicate(p_i)$
- $Predicate^{\exists}(p) \iff \exists 1 \leq i \leq \lambda_p. \ Predicate(p_i)$

Note that the formulas $\neg Predicate^{\forall}(p)$ and $\neg Predicate^{\exists}(p)$ are abbreviations of the formulas $\exists 1 \leq i \leq \lambda_p. \ \neg Predicate(p_i)$ and $\forall 1 \leq i \leq \lambda_p. \ \neg Predicate(p_i)$ according to this convention.

Critical Edges. In this section we recall the well-known fact that in completely arbitrary graph structures code motion may be blocked by *critical edges*, i.e., by edges leading from nodes with more than one successor to nodes with more than one predecessor (cf. [Dh1, Dh3, DRZ, DS1, KRS1, KRS2, KRS3, RWZ, SKR1, SKR2]). In order to exploit the full power of code motion, critical edges must be removed in the argument flow graph as it is illustrated below.

In Figure 3.1(a) the computation of "$a+b$" at node **3** is partially redundant with respect to the computation of "$a + b$" at node **1**. However, this partial redundancy cannot safely be eliminated by moving the computation of "$a + b$" to its preceding nodes because this may introduce a new computation on a path leaving node **2** on the right branch. On the other hand, it can safely be eliminated after inserting a synthetic node **4** in the critical edge $(\mathbf{2}, \mathbf{3})$, as illustrated in Figure 3.1(b).

In the following we assume that all edges in G leading to a node with more than one predecessor have been split by inserting a synthetic node. Besides guaranteeing that all critical edges have been split, this simple transformation simplifies the process of code motion because computationally and lifetime optimal programs can now be obtained by moving all computations to node

---

[1] In [MR1] the predicate *Comp* is called *Antloc*, which stands for "local anticipability".

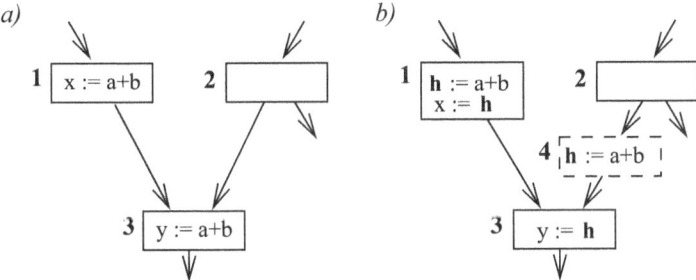

Fig. 3.1. Critical edges

entries (cf. [KRS1]). In essence, this is a consequence of the Control Flow
Lemma 3.1.1, which characterizes the branching structure of G after the
insertion of synthetic nodes (cf. [KRS2]).

Lemma 3.1.1 (Control Flow Lemma).

1. $\forall n \in N. \ | \, pred_G(n) \, | \ \geq 2 \Rightarrow succ_G(pred_G(n)) = \{n\}$
2. $\forall n \in N. \ | \, succ_G(n) \, | \ \geq 2 \Rightarrow pred_G(succ_G(n)) = \{n\}$

3.2 Intraprocedural Code Motion Transformations

In accordance to the first step of our two-step approach for program optimization, we fix in this section the set of program transformations of interest,
the set of *admissible code motion transformations*. In essence, code motion
transformations are characterized by the following three-step procedure: (1)
Declare a new temporary **h** in the argument flow graph for storing the value
of the computation under consideration, (2) insert assignments of the form
h := t at some nodes of G, and (3) replace some of the original computations
of t in G by **h**.

The first step of declaring the temporary is shared by all code motion
transformations. Thus, the specification of a code motion transformation *CM*
reduces to defining two predicates *Insert*$_{CM}$ and *Replace*$_{CM}$, which denote
the set of program points where an initialization must be inserted and an
original computation must be replaced. Without loss of generality we assume
that *Replace*$_{CM}$ implies *Comp*, and that the conjunction of *Insert*$_{CM}$ and
Comp implies *Replace*$_{CM}$. Note that this does not impose any restrictions to
our approach. It only avoids transformations which keep an original computation even after an insertion into the corresponding node making the original
computation locally redundant.

> - *Declare a new temporary* **h** *for storing the value of t in the argument flow graph.*
> - *Insert at the entry of every node satisfying Insert$_{CM}$ the assignment* **h** $:= t$.
> - *Replace every original computation of t in nodes satisfying Replace$_{CM}$ by* **h**.

Table 3.1: Scheme of intraprocedural code motion transformations

In the following we denote the set of all code motion transformations with respect to t, i.e., the set of all transformations matching the scheme of Table 3.1, by $\mathcal{CM}$. In the following section, we will restrict $\mathcal{CM}$ to the set of admissible transformations, which are guaranteed to preserve the semantics of their argument programs. We consider this a necessary constraint of optimizing program transformations.

3.2.1 Admissible Transformations

A code motion transformation *CM* is *admissible*, if it preserves the semantics of its argument programs. Intuitively, this requires that *CM* is *safe* and *correct*. "Safe" means that there is no program path on which the computation of a new value is introduced by inserting a computation of t; "correct" means that **h** always represents the same value as t when it is replaced by **h**. Formally, two computations of t represent the *same value* on a path if and only if no operand is modified between them. This is reflected in the following definition, which defines when inserting and replacing a computation of t is *safe* and *correct* in a node $n \in N$.

Definition 3.2.1 (Safety and Correctness).
For all nodes $n \in N$ we define:

1. Safety: $Safe(n) \Longleftrightarrow_{df} \forall p \in \mathbf{P}_G[\mathbf{s},\mathbf{e}] \; \forall j. \; (p_j = n) \Rightarrow$
    a) $\exists i < j. \; Comp(p_i) \wedge Transp^{\forall}(p[i,j[) \; \vee$
    b) $\exists i \geq j. \; Comp(p_i) \wedge Transp^{\forall}(p[j,i[)$
2. Strong Safety: $S\text{-}Safe(n) \Longleftrightarrow_{df} N\text{-}USafe(n) \vee N\text{-}DSafe(n),$ *where*
   a) $N\text{-}USafe(n) \Longleftrightarrow_{df}$
   $ \forall p \in \mathbf{P}_G[\mathbf{s},n] \; \exists i < \lambda_p. \; Comp(p_i) \wedge Transp^{\forall}(p[i,\lambda_p[)$
   b) $N\text{-}DSafe(n) \Longleftrightarrow_{df}$
   $ \forall p \in \mathbf{P}_G[n,\mathbf{e}] \; \exists i \leq \lambda_p. \; Comp(p_i) \wedge Transp^{\forall}(p[1,i[)$
3. Correctness: Let $CM \in \mathcal{CM}$. *Then:*
   $Correct_{CM}(n) \Longleftrightarrow_{df}$
   $ \forall p \in \mathbf{P}_G[\mathbf{s},n] \; \exists i \leq \lambda_p. \; Insert_{CM}(p_i) \wedge Transp^{\forall}(p[i,\lambda_p[)$

In the intraprocedural setting, there is no difference between safety and strong safety. The backward implication is quite obvious from the definitions of safety and strong safety. The converse implication is essentially a consequence of the fact that we are only considering nondeterministic branching, which makes the set of all paths in G a *regular* set. Each path in $\mathbf{P}_G[\mathbf{s}, n]$ leading to a node n can be completed by every program continuation starting in n, i.e., by every path in $\mathbf{P}_G[n, \mathbf{e}]$. In particular, each path violating the up-safety condition at a node n, can be linked to every path violating the down-safety condition at this node. This yields a path violating the safety condition at n, and proves the contrapositive of the forward implication. As we will see in Chapter 10, this is an important difference to the interprocedural setting. Though we consider in the interprocedural setting nondeterministic branching as well this equivalence gets lost. Essentially, this is a consequence of the fact that the set of interprocedurally valid program paths is given by a *context-free* set (cf. Chapter 7).

Lemma 3.2.1 (Safety Lemma).

$$\forall\, n \in N.\ Safe(n) \ \Longleftrightarrow\ S\text{-}Safe(n)$$

The predicates for safety and correctness allow us to define the class of *admissible* code motion transformations.

Definition 3.2.2 (Admissible Code Motion).
A code motion transformation $CM \in \mathcal{CM}$ *is* admissible *if and only if every node* $n \in N$ *satisfies the following two conditions:*

1. $Insert_{CM}(n) \Rightarrow Safe(n)$
2. $Replace_{CM}(n) \Rightarrow Correct_{CM}(n)$

The set of all admissible code motion transformations is denoted by $\mathcal{CM}_{Adm}$.

We have (cf. [KRS2]):

Lemma 3.2.2 (Correctness Lemma).

$$\forall\, CM \in \mathcal{CM}_{Adm}\ \forall\, n \in N.\ Correct_{CM}(n) \Rightarrow Safe(n)$$

Note that admissibility of a code motion transformation does not require that insertions are really used. Condition (2) of Definition 3.2.2 holds trivially if the predicate *Replace* is false for every node. Thus, we additionally introduce the subset of *canonic* transformations. Intuitively, an admissible code motion transformation is canonic, if insertions are used on every program continuation. Canonic transformations are particularly important in the interprocedural setting.

Definition 3.2.3 (Canonic Code Motion).
An admissible code motion transformation $CM \in CM_{Adm}$ *is* canonic *if and only if for every node* $n \in N$ *the following condition holds:*

$Insert_{CM}(n) \Rightarrow$

$$\forall p \in \mathbf{P}_G[n, \mathbf{e}] \; \exists 1 \leq i \leq \lambda_p. \; Replace_{CM}(p_i) \wedge \neg Insert_{CM}^{\exists}(p[2, i])$$

We denote the set of all canonic code motion transformations by CM_{Can}. *Programs resulting from a transformation of* CM_{Can} *are called canonic, too.*

Having now fixed the set of program transformations of interest, we proceed further along the lines of our two-step approach for optimal program optimization, and introduce next the optimality criteria of interest: *computational* and *lifetime optimality*.

3.2.2 Computationally Optimal Transformations

The primary goal of code motion is to minimize the number of computations on every program path. This intent is reflected by the relation "computationally better". It requires the local predicate $Comp_{CM}$, which is true for nodes containing a computation of t after applying the code motion transformation it is annotated with, i.e.:

$$Comp_{CM}(n) =_{df} Insert_{CM}(n) \vee (Comp(n) \wedge \neg Replace_{CM}(n))$$

Using this notation, a code motion transformation $CM \in CM_{Adm}$ is *computationally better* than a code motion transformation $CM' \in CM_{Adm}$ if and only if

$$\forall p \in \mathbf{P}_G[\mathbf{s}, \mathbf{e}]. \; | \; \{i \mid Comp_{CM}(p_i)\} \; | \; \leq \; | \; \{i \mid Comp_{CM'}(p_i)\} \; |$$

Note that the relation "computationally better" is reflexive. Thus, *computationally at least as good* would be the more precise but uglier term. Nonetheless, by means of this relation, we can now define:

Definition 3.2.4 (Computationally Optimal Code Motion).
An admissible code motion transformation $CM \in CM_{Adm}$ *is* computationally optimal *if and only if it is computationally better than any other admissible code motion transformation. The set of all computationally optimal code motion transformations is denoted by* CM_{CmpOpt}.

Intraprocedurally, computationally optimal code motion transformations are canonic. In fact, we have:

Theorem 3.2.1 (Computational Optimality and Canonicity).

$$CM_{CmpOpt} \subseteq CM_{Can}$$

As we will demonstrate in Chapter 10 this theorem does not carry over to the interprocedural setting, which reveals an important and essential difference between intraprocedural and interprocedural code motion. Moreover, canonicity will be shown of being the key for successfully enhancing the intraprocedural code motion techniques interprocedurally.

3.2.3 Lifetime Optimal Transformations

Besides the primary goal of code motion of avoiding unnecessary recomputations of values, its secondary goal is to avoid unnecessarily far motions of computations because they can cause superfluous register pressure. This requires to minimize the lifetimes of temporaries, which are introduced by a computationally optimal code motion transformation. Intuitively, a computationally optimal code motion transformation is lifetime optimal, if the lifetime ranges of temporaries are minimal. In essence, a lifetime range is a path from an initialization site to a use site of **h** which is free of redefinitions of **h**.

Definition 3.2.5 (Lifetime Ranges).
Let $CM \in \mathcal{CM}_{Adm}$. The set of lifetime ranges *of CM is defined by*

$$LtRg(CM) =_{df} \{ p \mid Insert_{CM}(p_1) \wedge Replace_{CM}(p_{\lambda_p}) \wedge \neg Insert^{\exists}_{CM}(p]1, \lambda_p]) \}$$

This leads us to the following definition: a code motion transformation $CM \in \mathcal{CM}_{Adm}$ is *lifetime better* than a code motion transformation $CM' \in \mathcal{CM}_{Adm}$ if and only if

$$\forall p \in LtRg(CM) \ \exists q \in LtRg(CM'). \ p \sqsubseteq q$$

Analogously to the notion of computationally optimal transformations, we can now define the notion of lifetime optimal transformations.

Definition 3.2.6 (Lifetime Optimal Code Motion).
A computationally optimal code motion transformation $CM \in \mathcal{CM}_{CmpOpt}$ is lifetime optimal *if and only if it is lifetime better than any other computationally optimal code motion transformation. The set of all lifetime optimal code motion transformations is denoted by $\mathcal{CM}_{LtOpt}$.*

Intuitively, lifetime optimality guarantees that no computation has been moved without run-time gain. Thus, there is no superfluous register pressure due to unnecessary code motion. In contrast to computational optimality, however, which can be achieved by several admissible code motion transformations, lifetime optimality is achieved at most by one transformation as shown by Theorem 3.2.2 (cf. [KRS2]).

Theorem 3.2.2 (Uniqueness of Lifetime Optimal Code Motion).

$$|\mathcal{CM}_{LtOpt}| \leq 1$$

We conclude this section recalling the notion of *first-use-lifetime ranges*. They are important for the optimality proofs of the *BCM*-transformation and the *LCM*-transformation.

Definition 3.2.7 (First-Use-Lifetime Ranges).
Let $CM \in \mathcal{CM}_{Adm}$. *We define*

$$FU\text{-}LtRg(CM) =_{df} \{\, p \in LtRg(CM) \mid \forall q \in LtRg(CM).\ q \sqsubseteq p \Rightarrow q = p \,\}$$

We have (cf. [KRS2]):

Lemma 3.2.3 (First-Use-Lifetime Range Lemma).
Let $CM \in \mathcal{CM}_{Adm}$, $p \in \mathbf{P}_G[\mathbf{s}, \mathbf{e}]$, *and* $q_1, q_2 \in FU\text{-}LtRg(CM)$ *with* $q_1 \sqsubseteq p$ *and* $q_2 \sqsubseteq p$. *Then either*

- $q_1 = q_2$ *or*
- q_1 *and* q_2 *are disjoint, i.e., they do not have any node occurrence in common.*

We now continue to follow the lines of Section 2.3. We define two program transformations, the *busy* and the *lazy code motion* transformation, which will be shown to satisfy the optimality criteria introduced above. They are computationally and lifetime optimal, respectively.

3.3 The *BCM*-Transformation

In this section we recall the definition of the *BCM*-transformation. It is based on the predicates for down-safety and earliestness.

3.3.1 Specification

Intuitively, a node n is *down-safe* at its entry, if on every terminating program path starting in n there is a computation of t which is not preceded by a modification of t. Analogously, it is *down-safe* at its exit, if on every terminating path starting in a successor of n there is a computation of t which is not preceded by a modification of t.

Definition 3.3.1 (Down-Safety).
Let $n \in N$. n *is*

1. entry-down-safe [*in signs:* $N\text{-}DSafe(n)$] $\iff_{df}$
   $\forall p \in \mathbf{P}_G[n, \mathbf{e}]\ \exists i \leq \lambda_p.\ Comp(p_i) \wedge Transp^{\forall}(p[1, i[)$

2. exit-down-safe [*in signs: X-DSafe*(n)] $\Longleftrightarrow_{df}$
   $\forall\, p \in \mathbf{P}_G]n,\mathbf{e}] \; \exists\, i \leq \lambda_p. \; Comp\,(p_i) \wedge Transp^{\forall}(\,p[1,i[\,)$

Intuitively, a computation is *earliest* at a node n, if an "earlier" computation would not deliver the same value due to a subsequent modification or would not be down-safe. In other words, a computation is earliest if there is a path from $\mathbf{s}$ to n, where no node prior to n is down-safe and delivers the same value as n when computing t.

Definition 3.3.2 (Earliestness).
Let $n \in N$. n is

1. entry-earliest [*in signs: N-Earliest*(n)] $\Longleftrightarrow_{df}$
   $\exists\, p \in \mathbf{P}_G[\mathbf{s},n[\; \forall\, i \leq \lambda_p. \; N\text{-}DSafe\,(p_i) \Rightarrow \neg\, Transp^{\forall}(\,p[i,\lambda_p]\,)$
2. exit-earliest [*in signs: X-Earliest*(n)] $\Longleftrightarrow_{df}$
   $\exists\, p \in \mathbf{P}_G[\mathbf{s},n] \; \forall\, i \leq \lambda_p. \; N\text{-}DSafe\,(p_i) \Rightarrow \neg\, Transp^{\forall}(\,p[i,\lambda_p]\,)$

Abbreviating *N-DSafe* and *N-Earliest* by *DSafe* and *Earliest*, respectively, Table 3.2 shows the definition of the predicates $Insert_{BCM}$ and $Replace_{BCM}$, which specify the *BCM*-transformation.

- $\forall\, n \in N. \; Insert_{BCM}(n) =_{df} DSafe\,(n) \wedge Earliest\,(n)$
- $\forall\, n \in N. \; Replace_{BCM}(n) =_{df} Comp\,(n)$

Table 3.2: The *BCM*-transformation

Intuitively, the *BCM*-transformation places the computations *as early as possible* in a program while maintaining safety.

3.3.2 Proving Computational Optimality

The *BCM*-transformation yields computationally optimal programs. Central for proving this result is the following lemma (cf. [KRS2]).

Lemma 3.3.1 (*BCM*-Lemma).

1. $\forall\, n \in N. \; Insert_{BCM}(n) \Longleftrightarrow$
   $$Safe(n) \wedge \prod_{m \in pred_G(n)} \neg(\,Transp\,(m) \wedge Safe(m))$$
2. $\forall\, n \in N. \; Correct_{BCM}(n) \Longleftrightarrow Safe(n)$
3. $\forall\, p \in \mathbf{P}_G[\mathbf{s},\mathbf{e}] \; \forall\, i \leq \lambda_p. \; Insert_{BCM}(p_i) \Rightarrow \exists\, j \geq i. \, p[i,j] \in FU\text{-}LtRg\,(BCM)$
4. $\forall\, CM \in \mathcal{CM}_{Adm} \; \forall\, p \in LtRg\,(BCM). \; \neg Replace_{CM}(\lambda_p) \vee Insert^{\exists}_{CM}(p)$

By means of the *BCM*-Lemma 3.3.1, we obtain as desired (cf. [KRS2]):

Theorem 3.3.1 (*BCM*-Optimality).
The BCM -transformation is computationally optimal, i.e., $BCM \in \mathcal{CM}_{CmpOpt}$.

3.4 The *LCM*-Transformation

In this section we recall the definition of the *LCM*-transformation. It is based on the predicates for latestness and isolation.

3.4.1 Specification

In order to avoid any code motion without run-time gain, and therefore any superfluous register pressure, computations must be placed *as late as possible* in a program while maintaining computational optimality. Intuitively, this requires to move the insertions of the *BCM*-transformation in the direction of the control flow to "later" program points. This leads us to the notion of delayability.

Definition 3.4.1 (Delayability).
Let $n \in N$. n is

1. entry-delayable [*in signs: N-Delayable (n)*] $\Longleftrightarrow_{df}$
   $\forall p \in \mathbf{P}_G[\mathbf{s}, n] \; \exists i \leq \lambda_p. \; Insert_{BCM}(p_i) \wedge \neg Comp^{\exists}(p[i, \lambda_p[).$
2. exit-delayable [*in signs: X-Delayable (n)*] $\Longleftrightarrow_{df}$
   $\forall p \in \mathbf{P}_G[\mathbf{s}, n] \; \exists i \leq \lambda_p. \; Insert_{BCM}(p_i) \wedge \neg Comp^{\exists}(p[i, \lambda_p]).$

The following definition characterizes the set of program points, where an insertion of the *BCM*-transformation is "maximally delayed".

Definition 3.4.2 (Latestness).
A node $n \in N$ is latest, *if it satisfies the predicate* Latest *defined by*

$$Latest(n) =_{df} N\text{-}Delayable(n) \wedge (\; Comp(n) \vee \neg \bigwedge_{m \in succ_G(n)} N\text{-}Delayable(m)\;)$$

Intuitively, a node n is latest, if an insertion of t can be delayed to its entry (i.e., *N-Delayable (n)*), and if its further delay is blocked by an original computation of t (i.e., *Comp (n)*) as it does not make sense to initialize after a use site, or if the process of moving the insertions of the *BCM*-transformation to later program points fails for some of the successors of n (i.e., $\neg \bigwedge_{m \in succ_G(n)} N\text{-}Delayable(m)$).

In order to avoid insertions, whose value can only be used in the insertion node itself, we define a predicate identifying "unusable" insertion points, i.e., program points which are lacking a terminating program continuation with a computation of t which is not preceded by a redefinition of **h**.

Definition 3.4.3 (Unusability).
Let $n \in N$. n is

1. entry-unusable [*in signs: N-Unusable (n)*] $\Longleftrightarrow_{df}$
   $\forall p \in \mathbf{P}_G[n, \mathbf{e}] \ \forall i \le \lambda_p. \ Comp(p_i) \Rightarrow Latest^{\exists}(p[1, i])$.
2. exit-unusable [*in signs: X-Unusable (n)*] $\Longleftrightarrow_{df}$
   $\forall p \in \mathbf{P}_G]n, \mathbf{e}] \ \forall i \le \lambda_p. \ Comp(p_i) \Rightarrow Latest^{\exists}(p[1, i])$.

Computations, which are exit-unusable, can only be used in the node itself. We call them thus "isolated".

Definition 3.4.4 (Isolation).
A node $n \in N$ is isolated, *if it satisfies the predicate Isolated defined by*

$$Isolated(n) =_{df} X\text{-}Unusable(n)$$

Table 3.3 shows the definition of the predicates $Insert_{LCM}$ and $Replace_{LCM}$, which specify the *LCM*-transformation.

- $\forall n \in N. \ Insert_{LCM}(n) =_{df} Latest(n) \land \neg Isolated(n)$
- $\forall n \in N. \ Replace_{LCM}(n) =_{df} Comp(n) \land \neg(\, Latest(n) \land Isolated(n)\,)$

Table 3.3: The *LCM*-transformation

As mentioned earlier, the point of the *LCM*-transformation is to place computations *as late as possible* in a program while maintaining computational optimality. This is the main result of the following section.

3.4.2 Proving Lifetime Optimality

The *LCM*-transformation yields lifetime optimal programs. The following lemma is the key for proving this result (cf. [KRS2]).

Lemma 3.4.1 (*LCM*-Lemma).

1. $\forall n \in N. \ N\text{-}Delayable(n) \Rightarrow N\text{-}DSafe(n)$
2. $\forall p \in \mathbf{P}_G[\mathbf{s}, \mathbf{e}] \ \forall l \le \lambda_p. \ N\text{-}Delayable(n_l) \Rightarrow$
   $\exists i \le l \le j. \ p[i, j] \in FU\text{-}LtRg(BCM)$
3. $\forall p \in FU\text{-}LtRg(BCM)). \ Latest^{\exists}(p)$
4. $\forall p \in LtRg(BCM)) \ \forall i \le \lambda_p. \ Latest(p_i) \Rightarrow \neg N\text{-}Delayable^{\exists}(p[i, \lambda_p])$
5. $\forall \ CM \in \mathcal{CM}_{CmpOpt} \ \forall n \in N. \ Comp_{CM}(n) \Rightarrow N\text{-}Delayable(n)$
6. $\forall p \in \mathbf{P}_G[\mathbf{s}, \mathbf{e}] \ (\forall i \le \lambda_p. \ (p_i) \in LtRg(LCM))$
   $\exists p' \in \mathbf{P}_G[\mathbf{s}, \mathbf{e}]. \ p[1, i] = p'[1, i] \land \exists j > i. \ p'[i, j] \in LtRg(LCM)$

By means of the LCM-Lemma 3.4.1 we can prove (cf. [KRS2]):

Theorem 3.4.1 (The LCM-Optimality).
The LCM-transformation is computationally and lifetime optimal, i.e., LCM
$\in \mathcal{CM}_{LtOpt}$.

As a corollary of Theorem 3.2.2 and Theorem 3.4.1 we immediately obtain:

Corollary 3.4.1. $\mathcal{CM}_{LtOpt} = \{ LCM \}$

3.5 An Illustrating Example

In this section we demonstrate the power of the BCM-transformation and the LCM-transformation by discussing the motivating example of [KRS1] displayed in Figure 3.2. The program fragment of this example is complex enough in order to illustrate the essential features of the two transformations. In order to keep the presentation as simple as possible, synthetic nodes that do not occur as insertion points of the BCM-transformation and the LCM-transformation are omitted.

Figure 3.3 shows the result of computing the set of down-safe and of earliest program points. They induce the insertion points of the BCM-transformation. The result of this transformation is displayed in Figure 3.4. Note that the flow graph of this figure is indeed computationally optimal.

Subsequently, Figure 3.5 and Figure 3.6 show the results of computing the sets of delayable and latest, and of latest and isolated program points, respectively. They induce the insertion and replacement points of the LCM-transformation. The result of this transformation is shown in Figure 3.7. It is exceptional, because it eliminates the partially redundant computations of "$a + b$" at node **10** and node **16** by moving them to node **8** and node **15**, but it does not touch the computations of "$a + b$" in node **3** and node **17** which cannot be moved with run-time gain. For the example under consideration, this confirms that computations are only moved by the LCM-transformation, when it is profitable. Note that the flow graph of Figure 3.7 is in fact computationally and lifetime optimal.

We recall that the algorithm for lazy code motion of [KRS1, KRS2] was the first algorithm satisfying these optimality criteria.

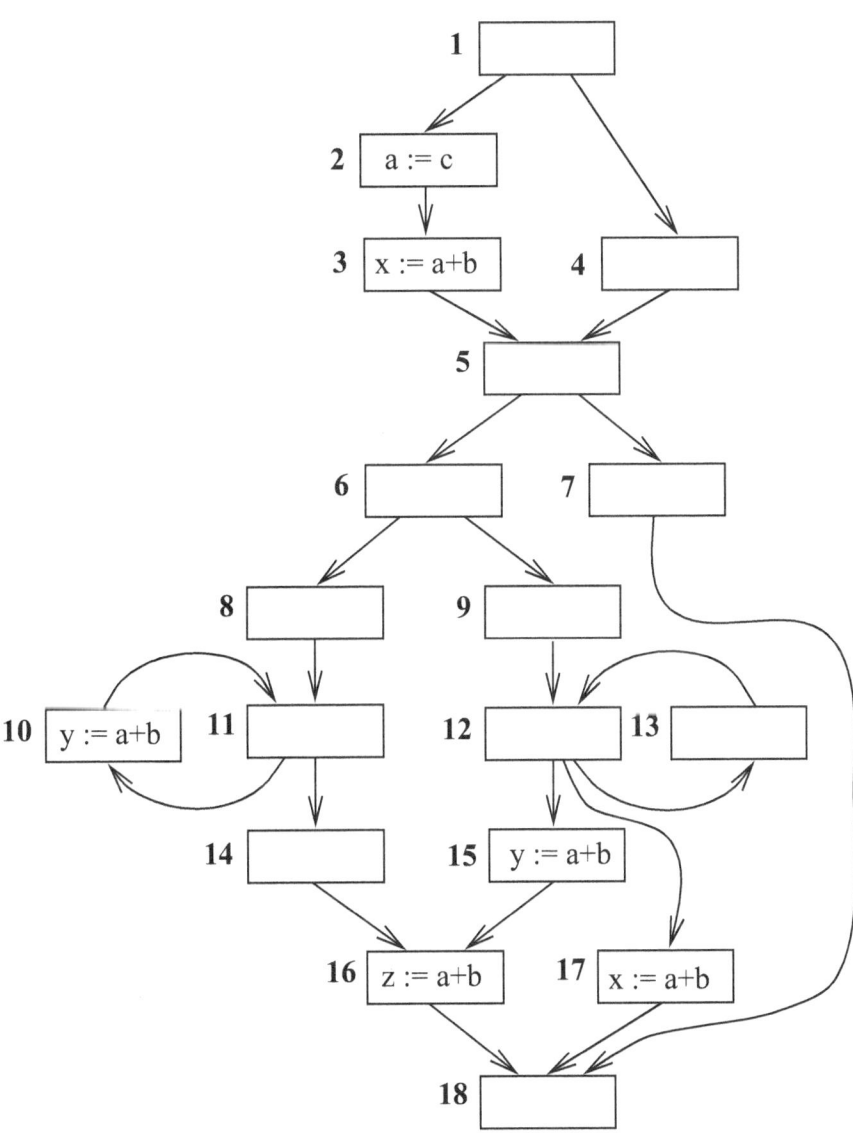

Fig. 3.2. The original program

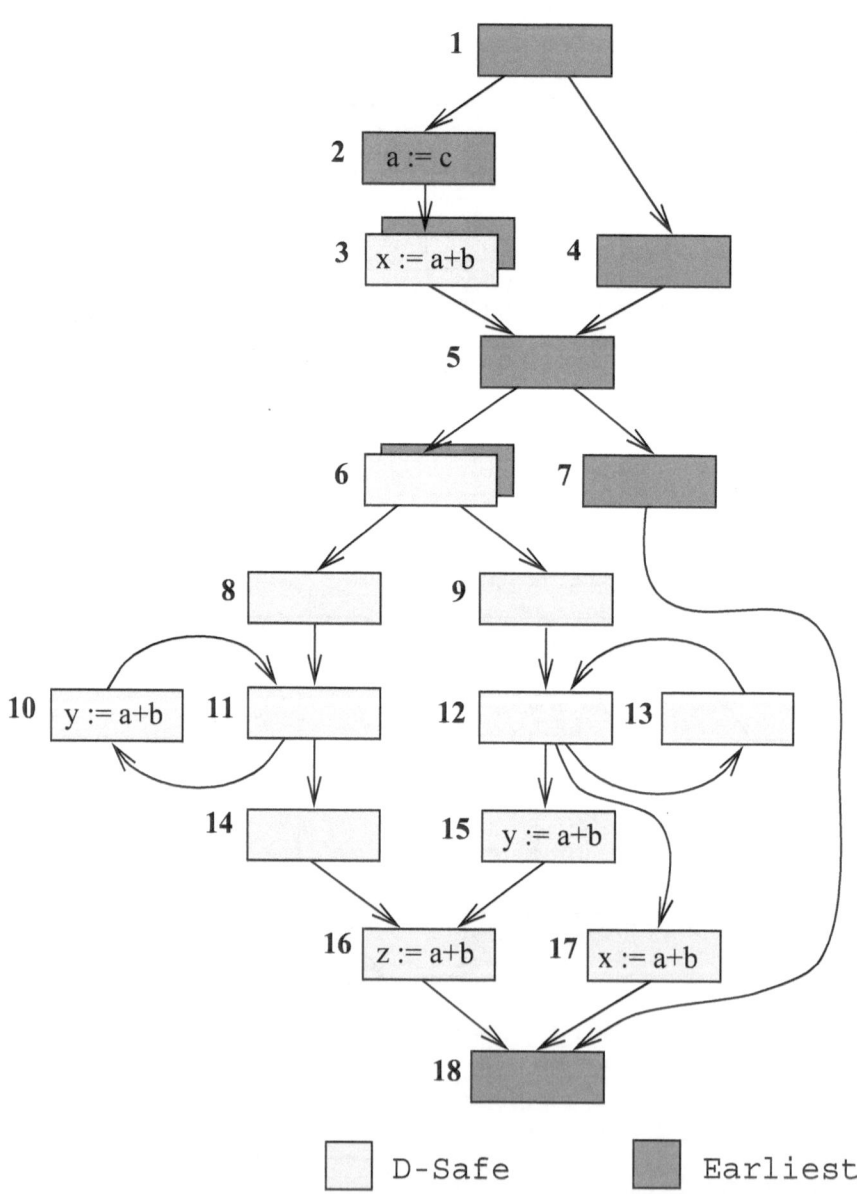

Fig. 3.3. *Down-safe* and *earliest* program points

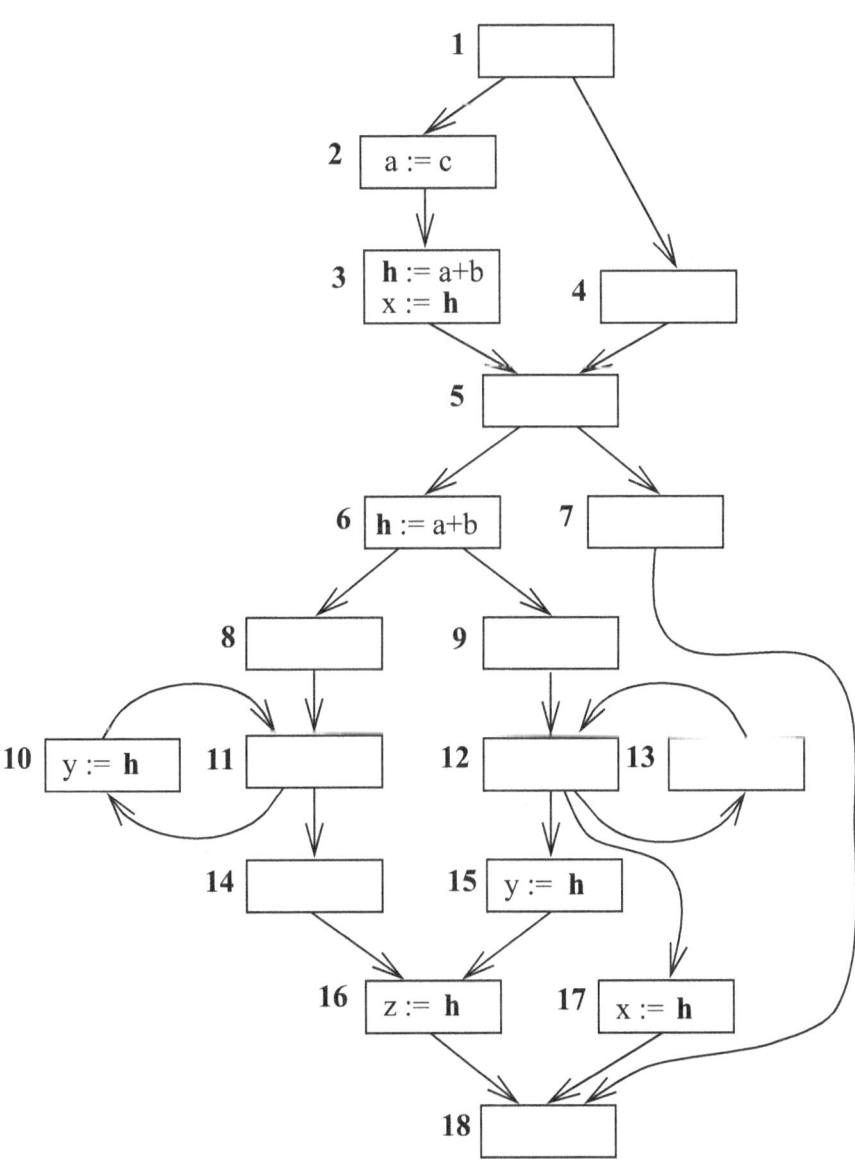

Fig. 3.4. The result of the *BCM*-transformation

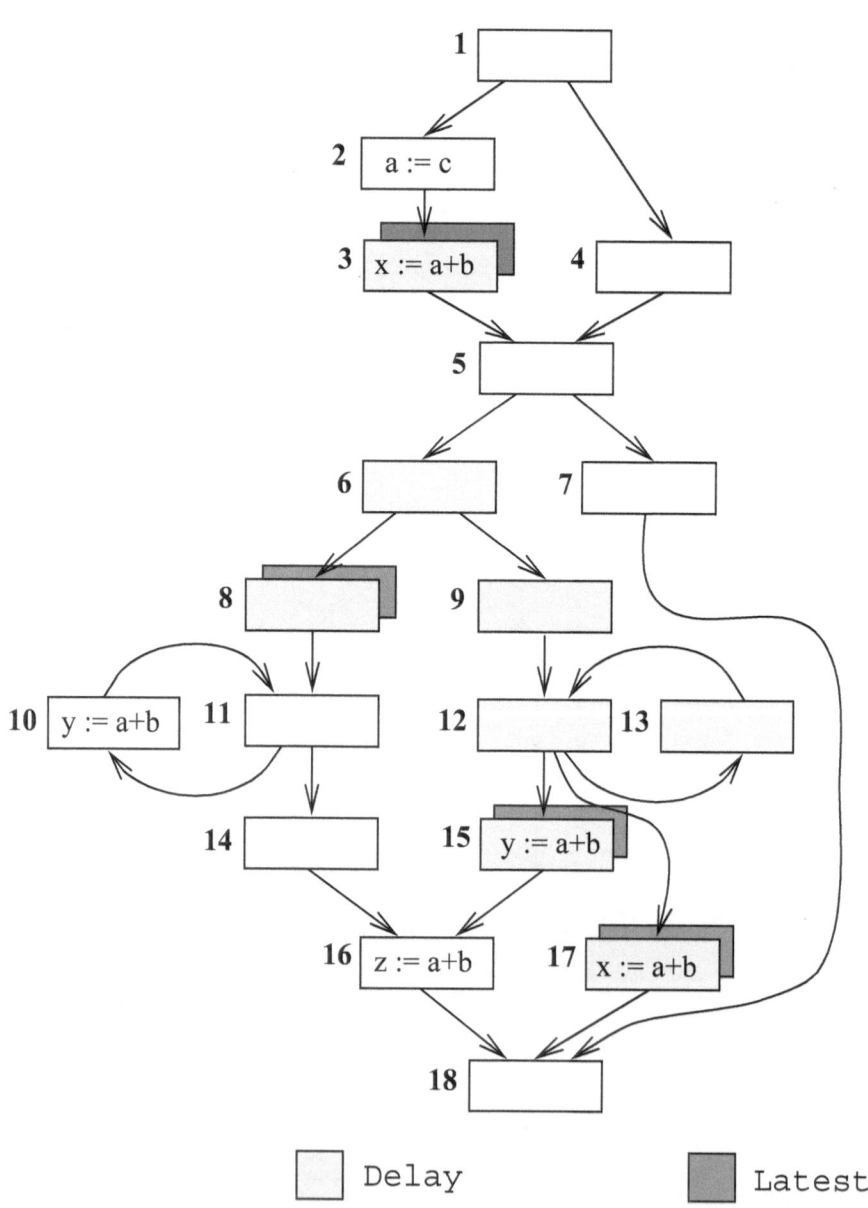

Fig. 3.5. *Delayable* and *latest* program points

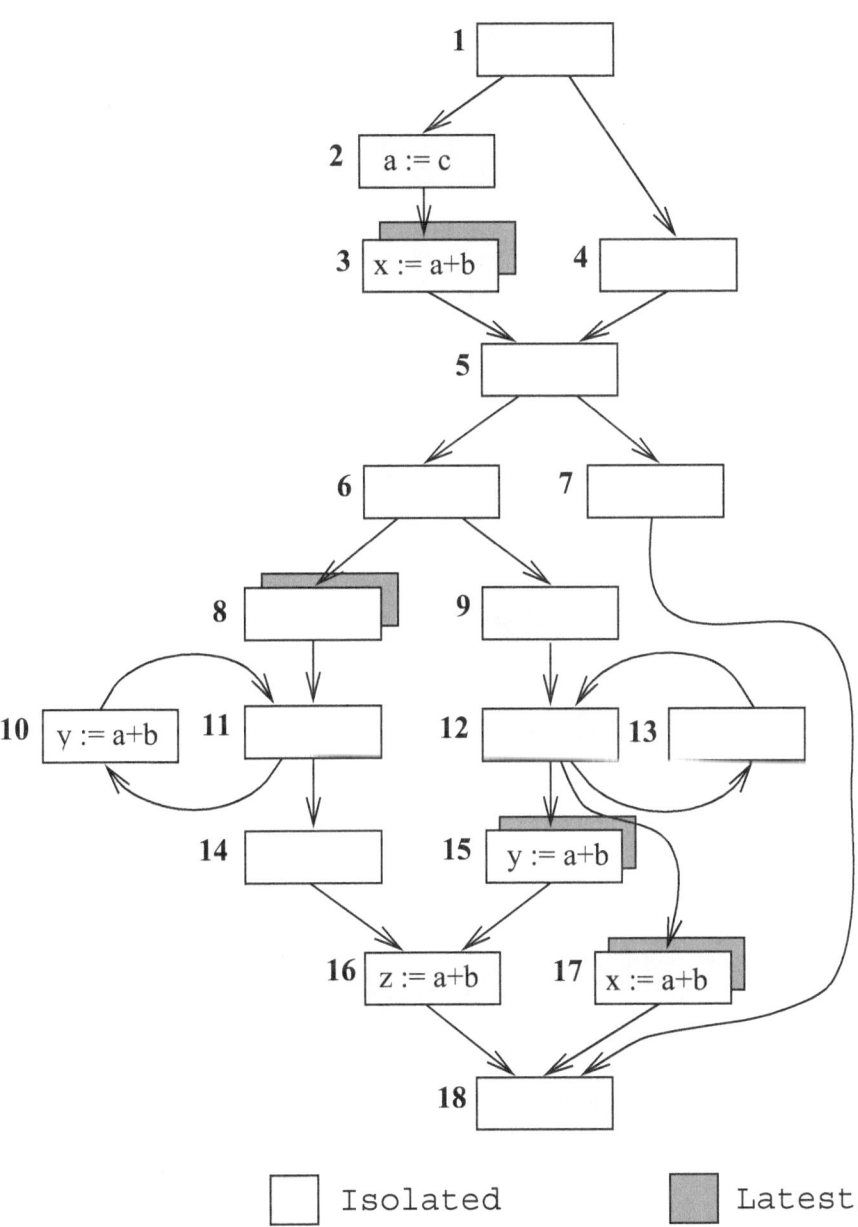

Fig. 3.6. *Latest* and *isolated* program points

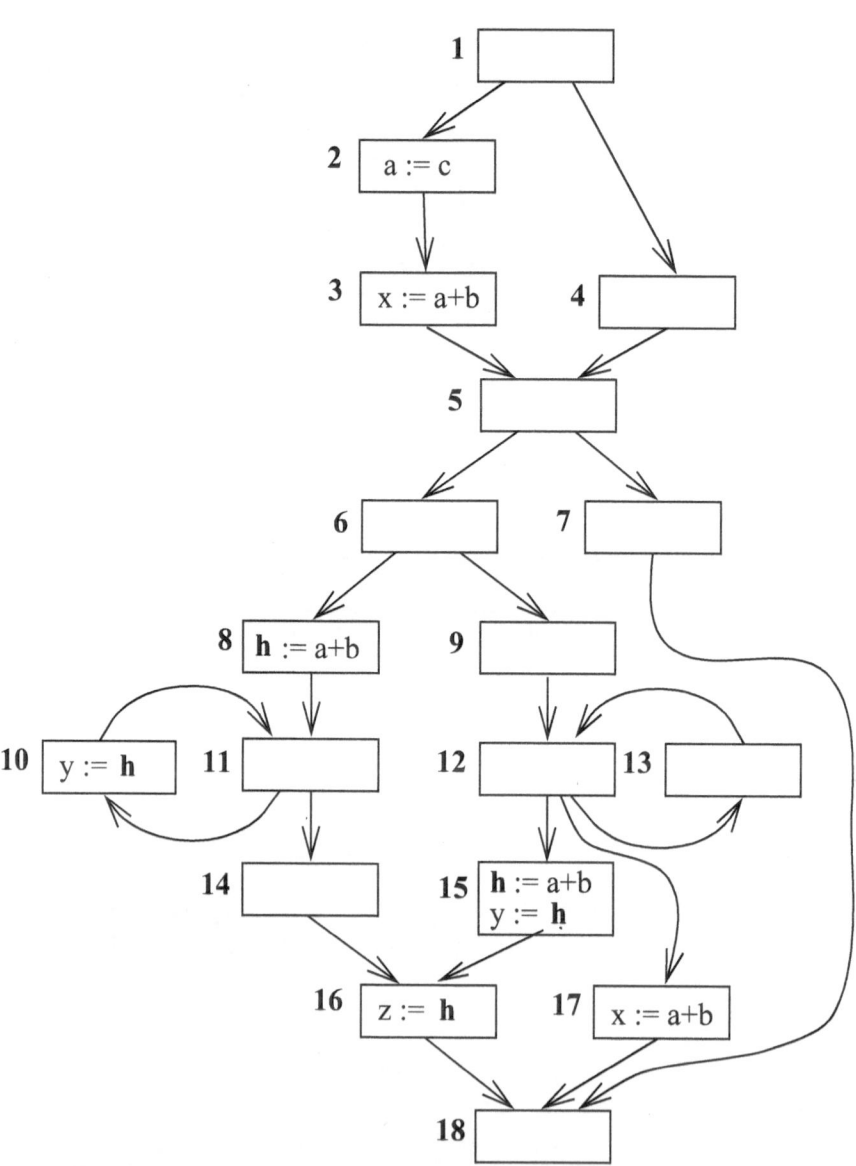

Fig. 3.7. The result of the *LCM*-transformation

4. Optimal Intraprocedural Code Motion: The DFA-Algorithms

In this chapter we specify for every program property involved in the *BCM*-transformation and the *LCM*-transformation a corresponding DFA-algorithm. The specifications follow the cookbook style of Section 2.3. Thus, every DFA-algorithm is defined by a lattice of data flow information, a local semantic functional, a start information, and an interpretation of the lattice elements in the set of Boolean truth values. All DFA-algorithms are precise for the program property they are designed for. The corresponding precision theorems are corollaries of their interprocedural counterparts proved in Chapter 11. In spite of this fact, we still present the proofs of the intraprocedural theorems in full detail. First, in order to demonstrate the analogies and differences to the interprocedural setting, and second, in order to also demonstrate the similarity of precision proofs for different properties. According to the recipe of Section 2.3 this reduces for every DFA-algorithm to proving that the lattice satisfies the descending chain condition, that the local semantic functions are distributive, and that the meet over all paths solution is precise for the program property under consideration. In contrast to [KRS1, KRS2] the central step of the precision proofs is based on the Coincidence Theorem 2.2.2. For convenience, we identify throughout this chapter the specification of a DFA and the DFA-algorithm it induces (cf. Definition 2.2.6).

4.1 DFA-Algorithm $\mathcal{A}_{ds}$: Down-Safety

In this section we present the DFA-algorithm $\mathcal{A}_{ds}$ for computing the set of down-safe program points.[1] The main result applying to this algorithm is the $\mathcal{A}_{ds}$-Precision Theorem 4.1.2. It guarantees that the algorithm is precise for this program property: it terminates with the set of all program points being down-safe in the sense of Definition 3.3.1.

We recall that down-safety requires a backward analysis of the program under consideration. This is reflected in the definition of the local semantic functional (cf. Section 4.1.1), and in the fact that the start information is attached to the end node (cf. Section 4.1.1).

---

[1] The index *ds* stands for down-safety.

J. Knoop: Optimal Interprocedural Program Optimization, LNCS 1428, pp. 49-67, 1998.
© Springer-Verlag Berlin Heidelberg 1998

4.1.1 Specification

Data Flow Information. The domain of data flow information of $\mathcal{A}_{ds}$ is given by the lattice of Boolean truth values

$$(\mathcal{C}, \sqcap, \sqsubseteq, \bot, \top) =_{df} (\mathcal{B}, \wedge, \leq, \mathit{false}, \mathit{true})$$

with $\mathit{false} \leq \mathit{true}$. Intuitively, the data flow information attached to a program point expresses, whether a placement of t is down-safe at this point.

Local Semantic Functional. The local semantic functional $[\![\ ]\!]_{ds} : N \to (\mathcal{B} \to \mathcal{B})$ of $\mathcal{A}_{ds}$ is defined by

$$\forall n \in N \ \forall b \in \mathcal{B}. \ [\![n]\!]_{ds}(b) =_{df} \mathit{Comp}(n) \vee (b \wedge \mathit{Transp}(n))$$

Intuitively, a placement of t is down-safe at the entry of a node n, if it is computed in n (i.e., $\mathit{Comp}(n)$), or if it is down-safe at its exit (i.e., $b = \mathit{true}$) and none of its operands is modified by n (i.e., $\mathit{Transp}(n)$).

Start Information. The start information of $\mathcal{A}_{ds}$ is given by the element

$$\mathit{false} \in \mathcal{B}$$

Intuitively, this choice of the start information expresses that t cannot be used after the termination of the argument program.

Interpretation. The interpretation of lattice elements in $\mathcal{B}$ is given by the identity on $\mathcal{B}$. Thus, the function $\mathit{Int}_{ds} : \mathcal{B} \to \mathcal{B}$ is defined by

$$\mathit{Int}_{ds} =_{df} \mathit{Id}_{\mathcal{B}}$$

4.1.2 Proving Precision

Important for proving the precision of $\mathcal{A}_{ds}$ is the fact that each of the local semantic functions $[\![n]\!]_{ds}$, $n \in N$, is either the constant function Const_{true} or Const_{false}, or the identity $\mathit{Id}_{\mathcal{B}}$ on $\mathcal{B}$. This follows immediately from the definition of the local semantic functions.

Lemma 4.1.1.

$$\forall n \in N. \ [\![n]\!]_{ds} = \begin{cases} \mathit{Const}_{true} & \text{if } \mathit{Comp}(n) \\ \mathit{Id}_{\mathcal{B}} & \text{if } \neg \mathit{Comp}(n) \wedge \mathit{Transp}(n) \\ \mathit{Const}_{false} & \text{if } \neg(\mathit{Comp}(n) \vee \mathit{Transp}(n)) \end{cases}$$

Note that constant functions and the identity on a lattice are distributive. This directly implies that the local semantic functions of the down-safety analysis are distributive, too.

Lemma 4.1.2. *The functions Const_{true}, Const_{false}, and $\mathit{Id}_{\mathcal{B}}$ are distributive.*

The following variant of Lemma 4.1.1 will be convenient for proving the *ds*-Precision Theorem 4.1.1.

Lemma 4.1.3.

1. $\forall n \in N \ \forall b \in \mathcal{B}. \ Comp(n) \Rightarrow [\![n]\!]_{ds}(b) = true$
2. $\forall n \in N \ \forall b \in \mathcal{B}. \ \neg Comp(n) \Rightarrow$
$$([\![n]\!]_{ds}(b) = true \iff b = true \ \wedge \ Transp(n))$$

Descending Chain Condition. The lattice of Boolean truth values is finite. Consequently, every descending chain is finite as well. Thus, we have:

Lemma 4.1.4 (Descending Chain Condition).
The lattice $(\mathcal{B}, \wedge, \leq, false, true)$ *satisfies the descending chain condition.*

Distributivity. The distributivity of the local semantic functions $[\![n]\!]$, $n \in N$, follows immediately from Lemma 4.1.1 and Lemma 4.1.2.

Lemma 4.1.5 ($[\![\ ]\!]_{ds}$-Distributivity).
The local semantic functions $[\![n]\!]_{ds}$, $n \in N$, *are distributive.*

ds-Precision. The last step required for verifying the precision of A_{ds} is to prove that A_{ds} is ds-precise. This means that down-safety in the sense of Definition 3.3.1 coincides with the meet over all paths solution of A_{ds} as expressed by Theorem 4.1.1. Without loss of generality, we will only prove the first part of this theorem. It is the relevant one for defining the *BCM*-transformation, and the second part can be proved in the same fashion.

Theorem 4.1.1 (ds-Precision).
For all nodes $n \in N$ *we have:*

1. $N\text{-}DSafe(n)$ *if and only if* $Int_{ds}(X\text{-}MOP_{([\![\ ]\!]_{ds}, false)}(n))$
2. $X\text{-}DSafe(n)$ *if and only if* $Int_{ds}(N\text{-}MOP_{([\![\ ]\!]_{ds}, false)}(n))$

Proof.
As mentioned above, we concentrate on the first part of Theorem 4.1.1. In order to simplify the notation, we abbreviate $Int_{ds} \circ X\text{-}MOP_{([\![\ ]\!]_{ds}, false)}$ by $X\text{-}MOP$ throughout the proof.

The first implication, "$\Rightarrow$",

$$\forall n \in N. \ N\text{-}DSafe(n) \Rightarrow X\text{-}MOP(n)$$

is proved by showing the even stronger implication

$$\forall p \in \mathbf{P}_G[n, \mathbf{e}]. \ (\exists 1 \leq i \leq \lambda_p. \ Comp(p_i) \wedge Transp^{\forall}(p[1, i[)$$
$$\Rightarrow [\![\tilde{p}]\!]_{ds}(false) = true) \tag{4.1}$$

Implication (4.1) will simultaneously be proved for all nodes $n \in N$ by induction on the length k of all paths $p \in \mathbf{P}_G[n, \mathbf{e}]$ satisfying

$$\exists 1 \leq i \leq \lambda_p = k. \ Comp\,(p_i) \wedge Transp^{\vee}(p[1, i[) \qquad (4.2)$$

Obviously, the case $k = 0$ does not occur. Thus, let p be a path of length $k = 1$. In this case (4.2) yields

$$Comp\,(p_1)$$

Applying Lemma 4.1.3(1) we therefore obtain as desired

$$[\![\,\tilde{p}\,]\!]_{ds}(false) = [\![\,p_1\,]\!]_{ds}(false) = true$$

In order to prove the induction step, let $k > 1$, and assume that (4.1) holds for all paths q with $\lambda_q < k$, i.e.,

(IH) $(\forall q \in \mathbf{P}_G[n, e].\ 1 \leq \lambda_q < k).$

   $(\exists 1 \leq i \leq \lambda_q.\ Comp\,(q_i) \wedge Transp^{\vee}(q[1, i[) \Rightarrow [\![\,\tilde{q}\,]\!]_{ds}(false) = true)$

Now, it is sufficient to show that for every path $p \in \mathbf{P}_G[n, e]$ with $\lambda_p = k$ satisfying (4.2) holds

$$[\![\,\tilde{p}\,]\!]_{ds}(false) = true$$

Without loss of generality, we can assume that there is such a path p, which then can obviously be rewritten as $p = (n);p'$ for some $p' \in \mathbf{P}_G[m, e]$ with $m \in succ_G(n)$. Two cases must be investigated next.

Case 1. $Comp\,(n)$
In this case, Lemma 4.1.3(1) yields as desired

$$[\![\,\tilde{p}\,]\!]_{ds}(false) = [\![\,n\,]\!]_{ds}([\![\,\tilde{p'}\,]\!]_{ds}(false)) = true$$

Case 2. $\neg Comp\,(n)$
In this case, (4.2) guarantees the existence of an index i with $2 \leq i \leq k$ and

$$Comp\,(p_i) \wedge Transp^{\vee}(p[1, i[)$$

Thus, the induction hypothesis (IH) can be applied yielding

$$[\![\,\tilde{p'}\,]\!]_{ds}(false) = true$$

Applying Lemma 4.1.3(2) we now obtain the following sequence of equalities

$$[\![\,\tilde{p}\,]\!]_{ds}(false) = [\![\,n\,]\!]_{ds}([\![\,\tilde{p'}\,]\!]_{ds}(false)) = [\![\,n\,]\!]_{ds}(true) = true$$

which completes the proof of the first implication.

The second implication, "$\Leftarrow$",

$$\forall n \in N.\ X\text{-}MOP(n) \Rightarrow N\text{-}DSafe\,(n)$$

is proved by showing the even stronger implication

$$\forall p \in \mathbf{P}_G[n, \mathbf{e}].$$
$$(\,[\![\, \tilde{p}\,]\!]_{ds}(false) = true \Rightarrow \exists 1 \leq i \leq \lambda_p. \; Comp\,(p_i) \wedge Transp^{\forall}(p[1, i[\,)\,) \tag{4.3}$$

Also this implication is simultaneously proved for all nodes $n \in N$ by induction on the length k of all paths $p \in \mathbf{P}_G[n, \mathbf{e}]$ satisfying

$$[\![\, \tilde{p}\,]\!]_{ds}(false) = true \tag{4.4}$$

As in the proof of the first implication, the case $k = 0$ does not occur, since we are dealing with entry-down-safety. Thus, we can start with considering a path p of length $k = 1$. In this case, equation (4.4) yields

$$[\![\, \tilde{p}\,]\!]_{ds}(false) = [\![\, p_1\,]\!]_{ds}(false) = true$$

By means of Lemma 4.1.3 we therefore obtain

$$Comp\,(p_1)$$

Hence, the induction basis follows for $i = 1$.

For the proof of the induction step, let $k > 1$, and assume that (4.3) holds for all paths q with $\lambda_q < k$, i.e.,

(IH) $(\forall q \in \mathbf{P}_G[n, \mathbf{e}]. \; 1 \leq \lambda_q < k).$
$$(\,[\![\, \tilde{q}\,]\!]_{ds}(false) = true \Rightarrow \exists 1 \leq i \leq \lambda_q. \; Comp\,(q_i) \wedge Transp^{\forall}(q[1, i[\,)\,)$$

It is sufficient to show that for each path $p \in \mathbf{P}_G[n, \mathbf{e}]$ with $\lambda_p = k$ satisfying equation (4.4) holds

$$\exists 1 \leq i \leq \lambda_p = k. \; Comp\,(p_i) \wedge Transp^{\forall}(p[1, i[\,)$$

Without loss of generality, we can assume that there is such a path p. Obviously, this path can be rewritten as $p = (n); p'$ for some $p' \in \mathbf{P}_G[m, \mathbf{e}]$ with $m \in succ_G(n)$. Similarly to the proof of the first implication two cases must be investigated next in order to complete the proof.

Case 1. $Comp\,(n)$
In this case the induction step follows trivially for $i = 1$.

Case 2. $\neg Comp\,(n)$
Applying Lemma 4.1.3(2), we here obtain

$$Transp\,(n) \tag{4.5}$$

and

$$[\![\, \tilde{p}'\,]\!]_{ds}(false) = true \tag{4.6}$$

Applying now the induction hypothesis (IH) to p' we obtain the existence of an index $i_{p'}$ with $1 \leq i_{p'} < k$ and

$$Comp\,(p'_{\,i_{p'}}) \wedge Transp^{\forall}(p'[1, i_{p'}[\,) \tag{4.7}$$

Combining (4.5) and (4.7), the induction step follows for $i = i_{p'}$. This completes the proof of the second implication and finishes the proof of the relevant part of Theorem 4.1.1.   □

Combining Lemma 4.3.4, Lemma 4.1.5, and Theorem 4.1.1, we obtain as desired that $\mathcal{A}_{ds}$ is precise for the predicate down-safe. In particular, this guarantees that the *MFP*-solution computed by $\mathcal{A}_{ds}$ coincides with the set of all program points being down-safe in the sense of Definition 3.3.1.

Theorem 4.1.2 ($\mathcal{A}_{ds}$-Precision).
$\mathcal{A}_{ds}$ is precise for down-safety, i.e., $\mathcal{A}_{ds}$ is terminating and ds-precise.

4.2 DFA-Algorithm $\mathcal{A}_{ea}$: Earliestness

In this section we present the DFA-algorithm $\mathcal{A}_{ea}$ for computing the set of earliest program points.[2] The main result of this section, the $\mathcal{A}_{ea}$-Precison Theorem 4.2.2, yields that it is indeed precise for this property: it terminates with the set of all program points being earliest in the sense of Definition 3.3.2.

4.2.1 Specification

Data Flow Information. The domain of data flow information of $\mathcal{A}_{ea}$ is given by the lattice of Boolean truth values

$$(\mathcal{C}, \sqcap, \sqsubseteq, \bot, \top) =_{df} (\mathcal{B}, \vee, \geq, \textit{true}, \textit{false})$$

Intuitively, the data flow information attached to a program point indicates, whether a placement of t is earliest at this point. In distinction to the down-safety analysis, however, the earliestness analysis uses the corresponding dual lattice. This is necessary because the generic algorithm of Section 2.2.5 is tailored for computing the greatest solution of an equation system, whereas the straightforward specification of the earliestness analysis requires the computation of the least solution.

Local Semantic Functional. The local semantic functional $[\![\ ]\!]_{ea} : N \to (\mathcal{B} \to \mathcal{B})$ of $\mathcal{A}_{ea}$ is defined by[3]

$$\forall n \in N \ \forall b \in \mathcal{B}.\ [\![n]\!]_{ea}(b) =_{df} \neg\, \textit{Transp}\,(n) \vee (b \wedge \neg \textit{DSafe}\,(n))$$

Intuitively, a placement of t is earliest at the exit of a node n, if t is modified by the assignment of node n (i.e., $\neg\,\textit{Transp}\,(n)$), or if it is earliest at its entry (i.e., $b = \textit{true}$), and a placement of t is not down-safe there (i.e., $\neg\textit{DSafe}\,(n)$).

---

[2] The index *ea* stands for earliestness.
[3] Recall that $\textit{DSafe} =_{df} N\text{-}DSafe$ (cf. Section 3.3.1).

Start Information. The start information of $\mathcal{A}_{ea}$ is given by the element

$$true \in \mathcal{B}$$

Intuitively, a computation cannot be placed earlier than at the entry of the start node of a program.

Interpretation. As for down-safety, also for earliestness the interpretation of the lattice elements of $\mathcal{B}$ is given by the identity on $\mathcal{B}$, i.e., the function $Int_{ea} : \mathcal{B} \to \mathcal{B}$ is defined by

$$Int_{ea} =_{df} Id_{\mathcal{B}}$$

4.2.2 Proving Precision

Like the local semantic functions for down-safety, also the local semantic functions for earliestness $[\![\, n \,]\!]_{ea}$, $n \in N$, can be characterized in terms of the identity and the constant functions on $\mathcal{B}$:

Lemma 4.2.1.

$$\forall n \in N. \ [\![\, n \,]\!]_{ea} = \begin{cases} Const_{true} & if \ \neg Transp\,(n) \\ Id_{\mathcal{B}} & if \ Transp\,(n) \wedge \neg DSafe\,(n) \\ Const_{false} & if \ Transp\,(n) \wedge DSafe\,(n) \end{cases}$$

Similar to Lemma 4.1.1 this lemma can be rewritten as shown in Lemma 4.2.2. This variant will be used in the proof of the $\mathcal{A}_{ea}$-Precision Theorem 4.2.2.

Lemma 4.2.2.

1. $\forall n \in N \ \forall b \in \mathcal{B}. \ \neg Transp\,(n) \Rightarrow [\![\, n \,]\!]_{ea}(b) = true$
2. $\forall n \in N \ \forall b \in \mathcal{B}. \ Transp\,(n) \Rightarrow$
$$([\![\, n \,]\!]_{ea}(b) = true \iff \neg DSafe\,(n) \wedge b = true)$$

Descending Chain Condition. The finiteness of $\mathcal{B}$ guarantees:

Lemma 4.2.3 (Descending Chain Condition).
The lattice $(\mathcal{B}, \vee, \geq, true, false)$ *satisfies the descending chain condition.*

Distributivity. Combining Lemma 4.2.1 and Lemma 4.1.2 we obtain as desired the distributivity of the local semantic functions $[\![\, n \,]\!]_{ea}$, $n \in N$.

Lemma 4.2.4 ($[\![\ ]\!]_{ea}$-Distributivity).
The local semantic functions $[\![\, n \,]\!]_{ea}$, $n \in N$, *are distributive.*

ea-**Precision.** Theorem 4.2.1 provides the final step of proving the precision of $\mathcal{A}_{ea}$. It yields the coincidence of earliestness in the sense of Definition 3.3.2 and the meet over all paths solution of $\mathcal{A}_{ea}$. Like for Theorem 4.1.1 we only prove the first part of this theorem. It is the relevant one for defining the *BCM*-transformation. The second part can be proved analogously.

Theorem 4.2.1 (*ea*-Precision).
For all nodes $n \in N$ we have:

1. $N\text{-}Earliest(n)$ *if and only if* $Int_{ea}(N\text{-}MOP_{(\llbracket\ \rrbracket_{ea},true)}(n))$
2. $X\text{-}Earliest(n)$ *if and only if* $Int_{ea}(X\text{-}MOP_{(\llbracket\ \rrbracket_{ea},true)}(n))$

Proof.
As mentioned before, we concentrate on the first part of Theorem 4.2.1, and in order to shorten the notation, we abbreviate $Int_{ea} \circ N\text{-}MOP_{(\llbracket\ \rrbracket_{ea},true)}$ by $N\text{-}MOP$ throughout the proof.

The first implication, "$\Rightarrow$",

$$\forall n \in N.\ \ N\text{-}Earliest(n) \Rightarrow N\text{-}MOP(n)$$

is proved by showing the equivalent formula:

$$\forall p \in \mathbf{P}_G[\mathbf{s}, n[.\ (\forall 1 \le i \le \lambda_p.\ DSafe(p_i) \Rightarrow \neg Transp^\forall(p[i, \lambda_p]))$$
$$\Rightarrow \llbracket p \rrbracket_{ea}(true) = true \tag{4.8}$$

It is simultaneously proved for all nodes $n \in N$ by induction on the length k of all paths $p \in \mathbf{P}_G[\mathbf{s}, n[$ satisfying

$$\forall 1 \le i \le \lambda_p = k.\ DSafe(p_i) \Rightarrow \neg Transp^\forall(p[i, \lambda_p]) \tag{4.9}$$

For $k = 0$, we obtain $n = \mathbf{s}$ and $p = \varepsilon$. In this case the desired equality

$$\llbracket p \rrbracket_{ea}(true) = \llbracket \varepsilon \rrbracket_{ea}(true) = true$$

holds trivially.

In order to prove the induction step, let $k > 0$, and assume that (4.8) holds for all paths q with $\lambda_q < k$, i.e.,

(IH) $(\forall q \in \mathbf{P}_G[\mathbf{s}, n[.\ 0 \le \lambda_q < k).$

$(\forall 1 \le i \le \lambda_q.\ DSafe(q_i) \Rightarrow \neg Transp^\forall(q[i, \lambda_q])) \Rightarrow \llbracket q \rrbracket_{ea}(true) = true$

It is sufficient to show that for every path $p \in \mathbf{P}_G[\mathbf{s}, n[$ with $\lambda_p = k$ satisfying (4.9) holds

$$\llbracket p \rrbracket_{ea}(true) = true$$

Without loss of generality we can assume that there is such a path p, which can then be rewritten as $p = p';(m)$ for some $p' \in \mathbf{P}_G[\mathbf{s}, m[$ with $m \in pred_G(n)$. This leaves us with the investigation of the following two cases.

Case 1. $\neg Transp\,(m)$

In this case, the desired sequence of equalities

$$[\![\,p\,]\!]_{ea}(true) = [\![\,m\,]\!]_{ea}([\![\,p'\,]\!]_{ea}(true)) = true$$

is a direct consequence of Lemma 4.2.2(1).

Case 2. $Transp\,(m)$

According to the choice of p we obtain $\neg DSafe\,(m)$, and therefore

$$\forall\,1 \le i < \lambda_p = k.\ DSafe\,(p_i) \Rightarrow \neg Transp^{\forall}(p[i,k[)$$

Thus, the induction hypothesis (IH) yields

$$[\![\,p'\,]\!]_{ea}(true) = true$$

Combining this with Lemma 4.2.2(2) we obtain as desired

$$[\![\,p\,]\!]_{ea}(true) = [\![\,m\,]\!]_{ea}([\![\,p'\,]\!]_{ea}(true)) = [\![\,m\,]\!]_{ea}(true) = true$$

which completes the proof of the first implication.

The second implication, "$\Leftarrow$",

$$\forall\,n \in N.\ N\text{-}MOP(n) \Rightarrow N\text{-}Earliest\,(n)$$

is equivalent to

$$\forall\,p \in \mathbf{P}_G[\mathbf{s},n[.\ ([\![\,p\,]\!]_{ea}(true) = true) \Rightarrow$$
$$(\forall\,1 \le i \le \lambda_p.\ DSafe\,(p_i) \Rightarrow \neg Transp^{\forall}(p[i,\lambda_p]))\qquad(4.10)$$

This implication is now simultaneously proved for all nodes $n \in N$ by induction on the length k of all paths $p \in \mathbf{P}_G[\mathbf{s},n[$ satisfying

$$[\![\,p\,]\!]_{ea}(true) = true\qquad(4.11)$$

For $k=0$, we obtain $p=\varepsilon$ and the implication

$$\forall\,1 \le i \le 0.\ DSafe\,(p_i) \Rightarrow \neg Transp^{\forall}(p[i,0])$$

holds trivially.

In order to prove the induction step, let $k > 0$, and assume that (4.10) holds for all paths q with $\lambda_q < k$, i.e.,

(IH) $(\forall\,q \in \mathbf{P}_G[\mathbf{s},n[.\ 0 \le \lambda_q < k).$

$([\![\,q\,]\!]_{ea}(true) = true) \Rightarrow (\forall\,1 \le i \le \lambda_q.\ DSafe\,(q_i) \Rightarrow \neg Transp^{\forall}(q[i,\lambda_q]))$

It is sufficient to show that for every path $p \in \mathbf{P}_G[\mathbf{s},n[$ with $\lambda_p = k$ satisfying (4.11) holds

$$\forall\,1 \le i \le \lambda_p = k.\ DSafe\,(p_i) \Rightarrow \neg Transp^{\forall}(p[i,\lambda_p])$$

Hence, we can assume the existence of such a path p, which can obviously be rewritten as $p = p';(m)$ for some $p' \in \mathbf{P}_G[\mathbf{s}, m[$ with $m \in pred_G(n)$. Similarly to the proof of the first implication two cases must be investigated next.

Case 1. $\neg Transp(m)$
In this case the induction step holds trivially because $Transp(p_{\lambda_p})$ does not hold.

Case 2. $Transp(m)$
In this case we obtain by means of (4.11) and Lemma 4.2.2(2)

$$\neg DSafe(m) \,\wedge\, [\![\, p'\,]\!]_{ea}(true) = true$$

Applying now the induction hypothesis (IH) to p' yields as desired the induction step. This completes the proof of the second implication, and finishes the proof of the relevant part of Theorem 4.2.1.   □

Combining Lemma 4.2.3, Lemma 4.2.4, and Theorem 4.1.1 we obtain the desired precision of $\mathcal{A}_{ea}$. In particular, this guarantees that the *MFP*-solution computed by $\mathcal{A}_{ea}$ coincides with the set of all program points being earliest in the sense of Definition 3.3.2.

Theorem 4.2.2 ($\mathcal{A}_{ea}$-Precision).
$\mathcal{A}_{ea}$ *is precise for earliestness, i.e.,* $\mathcal{A}_{ea}$ *is terminating and ea-precise.*

4.3 DFA-Algorithm $\mathcal{A}_{dl}$: Delayability

In this section we present the specification of the DFA-algorithm $\mathcal{A}_{dl}$ for computing the set of delayable program points and prove it to be precise.[4] In fact, this will be guaranteed by the main result of this section, the $\mathcal{A}_{dl}$-Precision Theorem 4.3.2. It yields that $\mathcal{A}_{dl}$ terminates with the set of all program points being delayable in the sense of Definition 3.4.1.

4.3.1 Specification

Data Flow Information. The domain of data flow information of $\mathcal{A}_{dl}$ is given by the lattice of Boolean truth values

$$(\mathcal{C}, \sqcap, \sqsubseteq, \bot, \top) =_{df} (\mathcal{B}, \wedge, \leq, false, true)$$

In the context of this analysis, a data flow information attached to a program point indicates, whether an insertion of the *BCM*-transformation can be delayed to the program point under consideration.

---

[4] The index dl stands for delayability.

Local Semantic Functional. The local semantic functional $[\![\ ]\!]_{dl} : N \rightarrow (\mathcal{B} \rightarrow \mathcal{B})$ of A_{dl} is defined by

$$\forall n \in N \ \forall b \in \mathcal{B}. \ [\![\, n\,]\!]_{dl}(b) =_{df} (\, b \ \vee \ Insert_{BCM}(n)\,) \ \wedge \ \neg Comp\,(n)$$

Intuitively, an insertion of the BCM-transformation can be delayed to the exit of a node n, if the term t under consideration is not blocked by n (i.e., $\neg Comp\,(n)$), and if the insertion can be delayed to the entry of n. This holds trivially, if n is an insertion point of the BCM-transformation (i.e., $Insert_{BCM}(n)$), or, alternatively, if the argument of $[\![\, n\,]\!]_{dl}$ is true (i.e., $b = true$).

Start Information. The start information is given by the element

$$Insert_{BCM}(\mathbf{s}) \in \mathcal{B}$$

Intuitively, this choice of the start information reflects that the process of moving the insertions of the BCM-transformation in the direction of the control flow to "later" program points starts in the insertion points of the BCM-transformation.

Interpretation. The interpretation of lattice elements in $\mathcal{B}$ is given by the identity on $\mathcal{B}$. This means the function $Int_{dl} : \mathcal{B} \rightarrow \mathcal{B}$ is defined by

$$Int_{dl} =_{df} Id_{\mathcal{B}}$$

4.3.2 Proving Precision

Like for down-safety and earliestness, we first introduce a lemma characterizing the local semantic functions of the delayability analysis in terms of the constant functions and the identity on $\mathcal{B}$. This lemma follows immediately from the definition of the local semantic functions. Moreover, we present two further lemmas, which are helpful for proving the A_{dl}-Precision Theorem 4.3.2. The first one is a simple consequence of the definition of intraprocedural delayability (cf. Definition 3.4.1), and the second one is a reformulation of Lemma 4.3.1.

Lemma 4.3.1.

$$\forall n \in N. \ [\![\, n\,]\!]_{dl} = \begin{cases} Const_{true} & \text{if } \neg Comp\,(n) \wedge Insert_{BCM}(n) \\ Id_{\mathcal{B}} & \text{if } \neg(\,Comp\,(n) \vee Insert_{BCM}(n)) \\ Const_{false} & \text{if } Comp\,(n) \end{cases}$$

Lemma 4.3.2. $\forall n \in N. \ N\text{-}Delayable\,(n) \ \Longleftrightarrow \ Insert_{BCM}(n) \ \vee$
$$(\forall p \in \mathbf{P}_G[\mathbf{s}, n[\, \exists\, 1 \leq i \leq \lambda_p. \ Insert_{BCM}(p_i) \wedge \neg Comp^{\exists}(p[i, \lambda_p])$$

Lemma 4.3.3.

1. $\forall n \in N \ \forall b \in \mathcal{B}. \ Comp\,(n) \Rightarrow [\![\, n\,]\!]_{dl}(b) = false$
2. $\forall n \in N \ \forall b \in \mathcal{B}. \ \neg Comp\,(n) \Rightarrow$
$$([\![\, n\,]\!]_{dl}(b) = true \ \Longleftrightarrow \ Insert_{BCM}(n) \vee b = true\,)$$

Descending Chain Condition. The finiteness of $\mathcal{B}$ guarantees that every descending chain in $\mathcal{B}$ is finite. Thus, we have:

Lemma 4.3.4 (Descending Chain Condition).
The lattice $(\mathcal{B}, \wedge, \leq, false, true)$ satisfies the descending chain condition.

Distributivity. Combining Lemma 4.3.1 and Lemma 4.1.2, we get as desired the distributivity of the local semantic functions of the delayability analysis.

Lemma 4.3.5 ($[\![\ ]\!]_{dl}$-Distributivity).
The local semantic functions $[\![n]\!]_{dl}$, $n \in N$, are distributive.

***dl*-Precision.** The last step in proving the precision of $\mathcal{A}_{dl}$ is to prove the coincidence of delayability in the sense of Definition 3.4.1 and the meet over all paths solution of $\mathcal{A}_{dl}$. This coincidence yields the desired *dl*-precision of $\mathcal{A}_{dl}$, which is granted by Theorem 4.3.1. For the same reasons as in the previous sections, we will only prove the first part of this theorem.

Theorem 4.3.1 (*dl*-Precision).
For all nodes $n \in N$ we have:

1. *N-Delayable(n) if and only if $Insert_{BCM}(n) \vee$*
$$Int_{dl}(N\text{-}MOP_{([\![ ]\!]_{dl}, Insert_{BCM}(\mathbf{s}))}(n))$$
2. *X-Delayable(n) if and only if $Int_{dl}(X\text{-}MOP_{([\![ ]\!]_{dl}, Insert_{BCM}(\mathbf{s}))}(n))$*

Proof. As mentioned above we concentrate on the first part of Theorem 4.3.1. In order to simplify the notation, $Int_{dl} \circ N\text{-}MOP_{([\![ ]\!]_{dl}, Insert_{BCM}(\mathbf{s}))}$ is abbreviated by $N\text{-}MOP$ throughout the proof.

According to Lemma 4.3.2 the first implication, "$\Rightarrow$",

$$\forall n \in N. \ N\text{-}Delayable(n) \Rightarrow Insert_{BCM}(n) \vee N\text{-}MOP(n)$$

is equivalent to

$$\forall n \in N. \ (\ Insert_{BCM}(n) \vee$$
$$\forall p \in \mathbf{P}_G[\mathbf{s}, n[. \ (\exists 1 \leq i \leq \lambda_p. \ Insert_{BCM}(p_i) \wedge \neg Comp^{\exists}(p[i, \lambda_p]))(4.12)$$
$$\Rightarrow Insert_{BCM}(n) \vee [\![p]\!]_{dl}(Insert_{BCM}(\mathbf{s})) = true)$$

Obviously, (4.12) is trivial, if n satisfies the predicate $Insert_{BCM}$. In order to complete the proof of (4.12), it is therefore sufficient to show

$$\forall p \in \mathbf{P}_G[\mathbf{s}, n[. \ (\exists 1 \leq i \leq \lambda_p. \ Insert_{BCM}(p_i) \wedge \neg Comp^{\exists}(p[i, \lambda_p]))$$
$$\Rightarrow [\![p]\!]_{dl}(Insert_{BCM}(\mathbf{s})) = true \qquad (4.13)$$

This implication is simultaneously proved for all nodes $n \in N$ by induction on the length k of all paths $p \in \mathbf{P}_G[\mathbf{s}, n[$ satisfying

$$\exists 1 \leq i \leq \lambda_p = k. \ Insert_{BCM}(p_i) \wedge \neg Comp^{\exists}(p[i, \lambda_p]) \qquad (4.14)$$

Obviously, the case $k=0$ does not occur, and therefore, we can start with considering a path p of length $k=1$. In this case (4.14) delivers

$$Insert_{BCM}(p_1) \wedge \neg Comp(p_1)$$

Hence, applying Lemma 4.3.3(2) we obtain as desired

$$[\![\, p \,]\!]_{dl}(Insert_{BCM}(\mathbf{s})) = [\![\, p_1 \,]\!]_{dl}(Insert_{BCM}(\mathbf{s})) = true$$

In order to prove the induction step, let $k > 1$, and assume that (4.13) holds for all paths q with $\lambda_q < k$, i.e.,

(IH) $(\forall q \in \mathbf{P}_G[\mathbf{s}, n[.\ 1 \le \lambda_q < k).$
$$(\exists 1 \le i \le \lambda_q.\ Insert_{BCM}(q_i) \wedge \neg Comp^{\exists}(q[i, \lambda_q]))$$
$$\Rightarrow [\![\, q \,]\!]_{dl}(Insert_{BCM}(\mathbf{s})) = true$$

It is sufficient to show that for every path $p \in \mathbf{P}_G[\mathbf{s}, n[$ with $\lambda_p = k$ satisfying (4.14) holds

$$[\![\, p \,]\!]_{dl}(Insert_{BCM}(\mathbf{s})) = true$$

Thus, without loss of generality we can assume that there is such a path p. This path can then be rewritten as $p = p';(m)$ for some $m \in pred_G(n)$ and $p' \in \mathbf{P}_G[\mathbf{s}, m[$. Next, two cases must be investigated.

Case 1. $Insert_{BCM}(m)$
According to (4.14), $Insert_{BCM}(m)$ directly implies $\neg Comp(m)$. Hence, Lemma 4.3.3(2) yields as desired

$$[\![\, p \,]\!]_{dl}(Insert_{BCM}(\mathbf{s})) = true$$

Case 2. $\neg Insert_{BCM}(m)$
In this case, (4.14) guarantees the existence of an index $1 \le i < k$ satisfying $Insert_{BCM}(p_i)$ and $\neg Comp^{\exists}(p[i, k])$. Thus, by induction hypothesis (IH) we get

$$[\![\, p' \,]\!]_{dl}(Insert_{BCM}(\mathbf{s})) = true$$

Applying now Lemma 4.3.3(2) we get the following sequence of equations

$$[\![\, p \,]\!]_{dl}(Insert_{BCM}(\mathbf{s})) = [\![\, m \,]\!]_{dl}([\![\, p' \,]\!]_{dl}(Insert_{BCM}(\mathbf{s}))) = [\![\, m \,]\!]_{dl}(true) = true$$

which completes the proof of the first implication.

The second implication, "$\Leftarrow$",

$$\forall n \in N.\ Insert_{BCM}(n) \vee N\text{-}MOP(n) \Rightarrow N\text{-}Delayable(n)$$

holds trivially by means of Lemma 4.3.2, if n satisfies the predicate $Insert_{BCM}$. Thus, in order to complete the proof of the second implication it is sufficient to show

$$\forall p \in \mathbf{P}_G[\mathbf{s}, n[. \ ([\![\, p \,]\!]_{dl}(\mathit{Insert}_{BCM}(\mathbf{s})) = \mathit{true}) \Rightarrow$$
$$\exists 1 \leq i \leq \lambda_p. \ \mathit{Insert}_{BCM}(p_i) \wedge \neg \mathit{Comp}^{\exists}(p[i, \lambda_p]) \qquad (4.15)$$

This implication can simultaneously be proved for all nodes $n \in N$ by induction on the length k of all paths $p \in \mathbf{P}_G[\mathbf{s}, n[$ satisfying

$$[\![\, p \,]\!]_{dl}(\mathit{Insert}_{BCM}(\mathbf{s})) = \mathit{true} \qquad (4.16)$$

As in the proof of the first implication, the case $k = 0$ does not occur. Therefore, we can start with considering a path p of length $k = 1$. In this case, (4.16) yields immediately

$$[\![\, p \,]\!]_{dl}(\mathit{Insert}_{BCM}(\mathbf{s})) = [\![\, p_1 \,]\!]_{dl}(\mathit{Insert}_{BCM}(\mathbf{s})) = \mathit{true}$$

By means of Lemma 4.3.3(2) we thus obtain

$$\mathit{Insert}_{BCM}(p_1) \wedge \neg \mathit{Comp}(p_1)$$

which proves the induction basis.

Let now $k > 1$, and assume that (4.15) holds for all paths q with $\lambda_q < k$, i.e.,

(IH) $(\forall q \in \mathbf{P}_G[\mathbf{s}, n[. \ 1 \leq \lambda_q < k).$
$([\![\, q \,]\!]_{dl}(\mathit{Insert}_{BCM}(\mathbf{s})) = \mathit{true}) \Rightarrow$
$\exists 1 \leq i \leq \lambda_q. \ \mathit{Insert}_{BCM}(q_i) \wedge \neg \mathit{Comp}^{\exists}(q[i, \lambda_q])$

It is sufficient to show that for every path $p \in \mathbf{P}_G[\mathbf{s}, n[$ with $\lambda_p = k$ satisfying (4.16) holds

$$\exists 1 \leq i \leq \lambda_p = k. \ \mathit{Insert}_{BCM}(p_i) \wedge \neg \mathit{Comp}^{\exists}(p[i, k])$$

Without loss of generality, we can assume that there is such a path p, which can be rewritten as $p = p'; (m)$ for some $m \in \mathit{pred}_G(n)$ and $p' \in \mathbf{P}_G[\mathbf{s}, m[$. Moreover, Lemma 4.3.3(2) yields directly $\neg \mathit{Comp}(m)$. Similar to the proof of the first implication we are now left with investigating two cases.

Case 1. $\mathit{Insert}_{BCM}(m)$
In this case the induction step follows for $i = k$.

Case 2. $\neg \mathit{Insert}_{BCM}(m)$
In this case we obtain by means of Lemma 4.3.3(2) and the choice of p

$$[\![\, p' \,]\!]_{dl}(\mathit{Insert}_{BCM}(\mathbf{s})) = \mathit{true}$$

Applying the induction hypothesis (IH) to p', we get the existence of an index $i_{p'}$ with $1 \leq i_{p'} < k$ and

$$\mathit{Insert}_{BCM}(p_{i_{p'}}) \wedge \neg \mathit{Comp}^{\exists}(p[i_{p'}, k[) \qquad (4.17)$$

Combining (4.17) and the fact that m does not satisfy *Comp*, the induction step follows for $i = i_{p'}$ in this case. This completes the proof of the second implication and finishes the proof of the relevant part of Theorem 4.3.1. $\square$

Applying Lemma 4.3.4, Lemma 4.3.5, and Theorem 4.3.1 we obtain the desired precision of $\mathcal{A}_{dl}$. In particular, we obtain that the *MFP*-solution computed by $\mathcal{A}_{dl}$ coincides with the set of all program points being delayable in the sense of Definition 3.4.1.

Theorem 4.3.2 ($\mathcal{A}_{dl}$-Precision).
$\mathcal{A}_{dl}$ is precise for delayability, i.e., $\mathcal{A}_{dl}$ is terminating and dl-precise.

4.4 DFA-Algorithm $\mathcal{A}_{un}$: Unusability

In this section we specify the DFA-algorithm $\mathcal{A}_{un}$ for computing the set of unusable insertion points and prove it to be precise.[5] In fact, this is a consequence of the $\mathcal{A}_{un}$-Precision Theorem 4.4.2, which is the main result of this section. It yields that $\mathcal{A}_{un}$ terminates with the set of program points being unusable in the sense of Definition 3.4.3.

4.4.1 Specification

Data Flow Information. The domain of data flow information of $\mathcal{A}_{un}$ is given by the lattice of Boolean truth values

$$(\mathcal{C}, \sqcap, \sqsubseteq, \bot, \top) =_{df} (\mathcal{B}, \wedge, <, \mathit{false}, \mathit{true})$$

where a data flow information attached to a program point indicates, whether a placement of t is unusable at this point.

Local Semantic Functional. The local semantic functional $[\![\ ]\!]_{un} : N \to (\mathcal{B} \to \mathcal{B})$ of $\mathcal{A}_{un}$ is defined by

$$\forall n \in N \ \forall b \in \mathcal{B}.\ [\![n]\!]_{un}(b) =_{df} \mathit{Latest}(n) \vee (\neg\mathit{Comp}(n) \wedge b)$$

Intuitively, a placement of t is unusable at the entry of a node n, if it is latest at the entry of n (i.e., $\mathit{Latest}(n)$), or if it is not computed in n (i.e., $\neg\mathit{Comp}(n)$) and unusable at its exit (i.e., $b = \mathit{true}$). Note that unusability requires like down-safety a backward analysis of the argument program, a fact, which is reflected in the definition of the local semantic functions. For the same reason, the start information of the unusability analysis is associated with the end node.

---

[5] The index un stands for unusability.

Start Information. The start information is given by the element

$$true \in \mathcal{B}$$

Intuitively, a computation cannot be used after the termination of the program under consideration. This is reflected in choosing *true* as start information.

Interpretation. The interpretation of the lattice elements of $\mathcal{B}$ is given by the identity on $\mathcal{B}$, i.e., the function $Int_{un} : \mathcal{B} \to \mathcal{B}$ is defined by

$$Int_{un} =_{df} Id_{\mathcal{B}}$$

4.4.2 Proving Precision

Before proving the precision of $\mathcal{A}_{un}$, we present a lemma, which characterizes the local semantic functions in terms of the constant functions and the identity on $\mathcal{B}$. This lemma, which follows from the definition of the local semantic functional $[\![\ ]\!]_{un}$ of $\mathcal{A}_{un}$, is the key for proving the $[\![\ ]\!]_{un}$-Distributivity Lemma 4.4.4.

Lemma 4.4.1.

$$\forall n \in N. \ [\![n]\!]_{un} = \begin{cases} Const_{true} & \text{if } Latest(n) \\ Id_{\mathcal{B}} & \text{if } \neg(Latest(n) \vee Comp(n)) \\ Const_{false} & \text{if } \neg Latest(n) \wedge Comp(n) \end{cases}$$

Moreover, we present an alternative version of Lemma 4.4.1, which is more convenient for proving the *un*-Precision Theorem 4.4.1.

Lemma 4.4.2.

1. $\forall n \in N \ \forall b \in \mathcal{B}. \ Latest(n) \Rightarrow [\![n]\!]_{un}(b) = true$
2. $\forall n \in N \ \forall b \in \mathcal{B}. \ \neg Latest(n) \Rightarrow$
$$([\![n]\!]_{un}(b) = true \iff \neg Comp(n) \wedge b = true)$$

Descending Chain Condition. Obviously, the finiteness of $\mathcal{B}$ implies:

Lemma 4.4.3 (Descending Chain Condition).
The lattice $(\mathcal{B}, \wedge, \leq, false, true)$ *satisfies the descending chain condition.*

Distributivity. By means of Lemma 4.4.1 and Lemma 4.1.2 we obtain as desired:

Lemma 4.4.4 ($[\![\ ]\!]_{un}$-Distributivity).
The local semantic functions $[\![n]\!]_{un}$, $n \in N$, *are distributive.*

un-Precision. The last step in proving the precision of A_{un} is to prove that unusability in the sense of Definition 3.4.3 and the meet over all paths solution of A_{un} coincide. We obtain this coincidence in the same fashion as in the previous sections. It guarantees that A_{un} is un-precise as it is expressed by Theorem 4.4.1. For the same reasons as in the previous sections, we will prove this time the second part of this theorem only.

Theorem 4.4.1 (un-Precision).
For all nodes $n \in N$ we have:

1. *N-Unusable (n) if and only if $Int_{un}(X\text{-}MOP_{([\![\;]\!]_{un}, true)}(n))$*
2. *X-Unusable (n) if and only if $Int_{un}(N\text{-}MOP_{([\![\;]\!]_{un}, true)}(n))$*

Proof.
As mentioned before we will only prove the second part of Theorem 4.4.1. In order to simplify the notation, we abbreviate $Int_{un} \circ N\text{-}MOP_{([\![\;]\!]_{un}, true)}$ by $N\text{-}MOP$ throughout the proof.

The first implication, "$\Rightarrow$",

$$\forall n \in N. \ X\text{-}Unusable(n) \Rightarrow N\text{-}MOP(n)$$

is proved by showing the even stronger implication

$$\forall p \in \mathbf{P}_G]n, \mathbf{e}]. \ (\forall 1 \le i \le \lambda_p. \\ Comp(p_i) \Rightarrow Latest^{\exists}(p[1,i])) \ \Rightarrow \ [\![\,\tilde{p}\,]\!]_{un}(true) = true \tag{4.18}$$

This implication is now simultaneously proved for all nodes $n \in N$ by induction on the length k of all paths $p \in \mathbf{P}_G]n, \mathbf{e}]$ satisfying

$$\forall 1 \le i \le \lambda_p = k. \ Comp(p_i) \Rightarrow Latest^{\exists}(p[1,i]) \tag{4.19}$$

For $k = 0$, we obtain $p = \varepsilon$ and

$$[\![\,\tilde{p}\,]\!]_{un}(true) = [\![\,\varepsilon\,]\!]_{un}(true) = true$$

holds trivially.

In order to prove the induction step, let $k > 0$, and assume that (4.18) holds for all paths q with $\lambda_q < k$, i.e.,

(IH) $(\forall q \in \mathbf{P}_G]n, \mathbf{e}]. \ 0 \le \lambda_q < k).$
   $(\forall 1 \le i \le \lambda_q. \ Comp(q_i) \Rightarrow Latest^{\exists}(q[1,i])) \ \Rightarrow \ [\![\,\tilde{q}\,]\!]_{un}(true) = true$

It is sufficient to show that for each path $p \in \mathbf{P}_G]n, \mathbf{e}]$ with $\lambda_p = k$ satisfying (4.19) holds

$$[\![\,\tilde{p}\,]\!]_{un}(true) = true$$

Hence, we can assume that there is such a path p, which can then be rewritten as $p = (m);p'$ for some $p' \in \mathbf{P}_G]m, \mathbf{e}]$ with $m \in succ_G(n)$. Now the following two cases must be investigated.

Case 1. *Latest* (m)

In this case, Lemma 4.4.2(1) yields as desired

$$[\![\, \tilde{p}\,]\!]_{un}(true) = [\![\, m\,]\!]_{un}([\![\, \tilde{p}'\,]\!]_{un}(true)) = true$$

Case 2. $\neg Latest\,(m)$

In this case, (4.19) delivers $\neg Comp\,(m)$. Moreover, it guarantees

$$\forall i \geq 2.\ Comp\,(p_i) \Rightarrow Latest^{\exists}(p[2,i])$$

Thus, applying the induction hypothesis (IH) to p' yields

$$[\![\, \tilde{p}'\,]\!]_{un}(true) = true$$

Due to $\neg Latest\,(m)$ and $\neg Comp\,(m)$, we now obtain by means of Lemma 4.4.2(2)

$$[\![\, \tilde{p}\,]\!]_{un}(true) = [\![\, m\,]\!]_{un}([\![\, \tilde{p}'\,]\!]_{un}(true)) = [\![\, m\,]\!]_{un}(true) = true$$

This completes the proof of the first implication.

The second implication, "$\Leftarrow$",

$$\forall n \in N.\ N\text{-}MOP(n) \Rightarrow X\text{-}Unusable\,(n)$$

is proved by showing the even stronger implication

$$\forall p \in \mathbf{P}_G]n, \mathbf{e}].\ ([\![\, \tilde{p}\,]\!]_{un}(true) = true) \Rightarrow \atop (\forall 1 \leq i \leq \lambda_p.\ Comp\,(p_i) \Rightarrow Latest^{\exists}(p[1,i]))\ \ \ (4.20)$$

It will simultaneously be proved for all nodes $n \in N$ by induction on the length k of all paths $p \in \mathbf{P}_G]n, \mathbf{e}]$ satisfying

$$[\![\, \tilde{p}\,]\!]_{un}(true) = true \qquad\qquad (4.21)$$

As in the proof of the first implication, the case $k = 0$ holds trivially.

Thus, let $k > 0$, and assume that (4.20) holds for all paths q with $\lambda_q < k$, i.e.,

(IH) $(\forall q \in \mathbf{P}_G]n, \mathbf{e}].\ 0 \leq \lambda_q < k).$

$([\![\, \tilde{q}\,]\!]_{un}(true) = true) \Rightarrow (\forall 1 \leq i \leq \lambda_q.\ Comp\,(q_i) \Rightarrow Latest^{\exists}(q[1,i]))$

It is sufficient to show that for every path $p \in \mathbf{P}_G]n, \mathbf{e}]$ with $\lambda_p = k$ satisfying (4.21) holds

$$\forall 1 \leq i \leq \lambda_p = k.\ Comp\,(p_i) \Rightarrow Latest^{\exists}(p[1,i])$$

We can therefore assume that there is such a path p, which then can be rewritten as $p = (m);p'$ for some $p' \in \mathbf{P}_G]m, \mathbf{e}]$ with $m \in succ_G(n)$. Similar to the proof of the first implication we are left with investigating two cases.

Case 1. *Latest* (m)

In this case the induction step follows trivially because we have *Latest* (p_1).

Case 2. $\neg Latest$ (m)

Here we obtain by means of (4.21) and Lemma 4.4.2(2)

$$\neg Comp\,(m) \,\wedge\, [\![\,\tilde{p}'\,]\!]_{un}(true) = true \qquad (4.22)$$

Applying the induction hypothesis (IH) to p' then yields the induction step as desired. This completes the proof of the second implication, and finishes the proof of the relevant part of Theorem 4.4.1. $\qquad\qquad\square$

By means of Lemma 4.4.3, Lemma 4.4.4, and Theorem 4.4.1, we get the desired precision of A_{un}. In particular, this implies that the *MFP*-solution computed by A_{un} coincides with the set of all program points, where a computation of t would be unusable in the sense of Definition 3.4.3.

Theorem 4.4.2 (A_{un}-Precision).
A_{un} *is precise for unusability, i.e., A_{un} is terminating and un-precise.*

5. The Programming Language

In this chapter we introduce the programming language, which we consider during the development and application of our framework for optimal interprocedural program optimization. The syntactic features of this language, called *Prog*, represent the common of Algol-like programming languages (e.g., Algol, Pascal, Modula, etc.), for which our framework is primarily designed.

5.1 Programs

The programming language *Prog* is an Algol-like imperative programming language. *Prog*-programs Π have statically nested procedures, global and local variables, formal value, reference, and procedure parameters. They are represented as *structured systems* $\Pi = \langle \pi_1, \ldots, \pi_k \rangle$ of (mutually recursive) procedure definitions, where every procedure $\pi \in \Pi$ has a list of formal value parameters $f_1, \ldots, f_q$, $q \geq 0$, a list of formal reference parameters $z_1, \ldots, z_r$, $r \geq 0$, a list of formal procedure parameters $\phi_1, \ldots, \phi_s$, $s \geq 0$, and a list of local variables $v_1, \ldots, v_u$, $u \geq 0$. Additionally, there may be occurrences of external variables and external procedures in a *Prog* program.

5.1.1 Syntax

The syntax of *Prog*-programs is basically given by the contextfree-like production rules given below. Angle brackets are used for expressing the static nesting of procedures. The non-terminal **stmt-part** stands for the *statement part* of a procedure. Its elementary components are *parallel assignments* and *procedure calls* as indicated by the last three rules.

The procedure generated by the rule for **main-proc** is considered the *main procedure* (*main program*) of the corresponding *Prog*-program. It does not have formal parameters, and cannot be called by other procedures. For clarity, we will sometimes add mode information to formal procedure parameters using the key words *val*, *ref*, and *proc* indicating a value, reference, and procedure parameter, respectively. For example, in the declaration of the procedure π below

$$\pi \, (\, : \, : \, \phi \, (val, val : ref : proc(\, : ref : proc)))$$

J. Knoop: Optimal Interprocedural Program Optimization, LNCS 1428, pp. 71-77, 1998.
© Springer-Verlag Berlin Heidelberg 1998

the mode information attached to the parameter ϕ identifies it as a formal procedure having two value, one reference, and one procedure parameter, which itself has a reference and a parameterless procedure parameter.

---

program ::= ⟨main-proc : block⟩

main-proc ::= π

block ::= var-part stmt-part | var-part ⟨proc-part⟩ stmt-part

var-part ::= empty | $v_1, \ldots, v_u$:

proc-part ::= procedure : block | procedure : block, proc-part

stmt-part ::= "statement part"

procedure ::= $\pi(f_1, \ldots, f_q : z_1, \ldots, z_r : \phi_1, \ldots, \phi_s)$

empty ::=

. . .

elem-stmt ::= ass-stm | call-stm

ass-stm ::= $(x_1, \ldots, x_n) := (t_1, \ldots, t_n)$

call-stm ::= call $\pi(t_1, \ldots, t_q : x_1, \ldots, x_r : \iota_1, \ldots, \iota_s)$

Internal and External Identifiers. We split the set of identifiers occurring in a *Prog*-program Π into the sets of internal and external identifiers. An identifier is called *internal*, if it has a defining occurrence inside Π, and *external* otherwise. Similarly, a procedure call in Π is called *internal*, if the identifier denoting the called procedure is an internal identifier. Otherwise, it is called *external*. Additionally, we distinguish ordinary and formal procedure calls. A procedure call in Π is called *formal*, if the defining occurrence of the identifier denoting the called procedure occurs in the formal parameter list of a procedure of Π, and it is called *ordinary*, otherwise. Finally, $Ext(\Pi)$ denotes the set of all external identifiers of Π. It is composed of the sets of external variable and procedure identifiers denoted by $Ext_{\mathbf{V}}(\Pi)$ and $Ext_{\mathbf{P}}(\Pi)$, respectively.

Identifier Bindings. We assume that *Prog* obeys the block structuring and identifier binding and visibility rules of Algol-like programming languages with *static scoping*. Accordingly, every procedure of a program Π, including its main procedure, encloses the set of its *static successors*. The local variables of a procedure are therefore global variables of all its static successors and can be accessed by them. In particular, external identifiers are considered global identifiers of all procedures of Π. Thus, external variables and external procedures can be accessed and called by every procedure like a global variable and an ordinary procedure, respectively. Internal procedures except for the main procedure can be called by (other) internal procedures according to the visibility rules of procedure identifiers. In particular, procedures of the same static level, which have the same static predecessor, can call each other *mutually recursively*.

Distinguished Programs and Correct Procedure Calls. We call a *Prog*-program Π *distinguished*, if the sets of internal and external identifiers are disjoint and if defining occurrences in Π use different identifiers. An ordinary internal procedure call of Π is *correct*, if the numbers of value, reference, and procedure parameters of the call statement coincide with the corresponding numbers of the formal parameters of the procedure called. We remark that this definition can naturally be extended to formal procedure calls, if mode information is given.

5.1.2 Notations

In order to simplify the argumentation about programs and procedures, we introduce a number of further notations.

Identifiers, Operators, and Terms. We denote the set of *identifiers* of *Prog* by **Idf**. It is composed of the disjoint sets of *variable identifiers* **V** and *procedure identifiers* **P**, which itself consists of the disjoint sets of *ordinary procedure identifiers* **OP** and *formal procedure identifiers* **FP**. Usually, we omit the term "identifier", and simply speak of variables and procedures. Identifiers range preferably over lower case Greek letters as e.g., ι or κ. More specifically, we usually denote variables by lower case Latin letters (preferably $x, y, z, ...$), and procedures by lower case Greek letters (preferably $\pi, \pi', ...$ for ordinary procedures, and $\phi, \phi', ...$ for formal procedures). Additionally, we assume a set of operators **O**, and a set of terms $t \in \mathbf{T}$, which are inductively built from variables and operators.

$\mathcal{I}$, *Stmt*, *CalledProc*, *ParLst*, **and Other Functions.** The function $\mathcal{I}$ denotes a polymorphic function, which maps its arguments (e.g., programs, flow graphs, statements, etc.) to the set of identifiers having an occurrence in it. Superposing it by "d", the resulting function $\mathcal{I}^d$ maps its arguments to the set of identifiers having a defining occurrence in them. Subscribing $\mathcal{I}$ and $\mathcal{I}^d$ by a set of identifiers means to restrict the result of $\mathcal{I}$ and $\mathcal{I}^d$ for a given argument to the set of identifiers belonging to the specified subset of identifiers. For example, $\mathcal{I}^d_{\mathbf{FP}}(\pi)$ denotes the set of formal procedure identifiers having a defining occurrence in procedure π.

Additionally, we introduce the polymorphic function *Stmt* defined on programs and procedures of *Prog*, which maps its arguments to the multiset of elementary statements occurring in them. Subscribing *Stmt* with a certain statement type means to project the result of *Stmt* to those statements matching the specified statement type. For example, $Stmt_{call}(\pi)$ denotes the set of procedure call statements occurring in procedure π. Moreover, for every call statement $st \in Stmt_{call}(\Pi)$, *CalledProc*(st) denotes the identifier of the procedure called by *st*. Similarly, the polymorphic function *ParLst* yields the parameter list of its argument, i.e., the *formal parameter list* of a procedure declaration, and the *actual parameter list* of a procedure call. Additionally, $\downarrow_i$ is a polymorphic projection function defined on lists, wich maps an argument list to its ith component. The function *LhsVar* maps every assignment statement $m = (x_1, \ldots, x_n) := (t_1, \ldots, t_n)$ to the set of variables occurring on the left-hand side of m, i.e., $LhsVar(m) =_{df} \{x_1, \ldots, x_n\}$.

Furthermore, we introduce for every program $\Pi = \langle \pi_1, \ldots, \pi_k \rangle \in Prog$ the functions *decl*, *pos*, *c-occ*, *p-occ*, and *occ*. Intuitively, *decl* maps every internal identifier of a program to the procedure of its declaration, *pos* every formal procedure identifier to the position of its defining occurrence in the relevant formal parameter list, *c-occ* every procedure identifier to the set of call statements invoking it, *p-occ* every procedure identifier to the set of call statements, where it is passed as argument, and *occ* every procedure identifier to the set of call statements in which it occurs. As usual IN denotes the set of *natural numbers* starting with 0, and $\mathcal{P}$ the *powerset* operator.

1. $decl : \mathcal{I}(\Pi) \to \Pi$ with $decl(\iota) =_{df} \begin{cases} \pi & \text{if } \iota \in \mathcal{I}^d(\pi) \\ undef & \text{otherwise} \end{cases}$

2. $pos : \mathcal{I}_{\mathbf{FP}}(\Pi) \to \mathrm{IN}$ with $pos(\iota) =_{df} j$ iff $\iota = ParLst(decl(\iota)) \downarrow_j$

3. $c\text{-}occ : \mathcal{I}_{\mathbf{P}}(\Pi) \to \mathcal{P}(Stmt_{call}(\Pi))$ with
$$c\text{-}occ(\iota) =_{df} \{ st \mid st \in Stmt_{call}(\Pi) \land CalledProc(st) = \iota \}$$

4. $p\text{-}occ : \mathcal{I}_{\mathbf{P}}(\Pi) \to \mathcal{P}(Stmt_{call}(\Pi))$ with
$$p\text{-}occ(\iota) =_{df} \{ st \mid st \in Stmt_{call}(\Pi) \land \iota \in ParLst(st) \}$$

5. $occ : \mathcal{I}_{\mathbf{P}}(\Pi) \to \mathcal{P}(Stmt_{call}(\Pi))$ with $occ(\iota) =_{df} c\text{-}occ(\iota) \cup p\text{-}occ(\iota)$.

For every procedure π of Π, we denote its static predecessor by $StatPred(\pi)$. As usual, $StatPred^+$ and $StatPred^*$ denote the transitive and the reflexive-transitive closure of $StatPred$, respectively.[1] Finally, IN^* denotes the set of *lists* (i.e., sequences) of natural numbers, which we usually denote by barred lower Greek letters, preferably by $\bar{\omega}$. In particular, the empty sequence is denoted by $\bar{\varepsilon}$.

5.1.3 Conventions

In order to simplify the notation, we denote the procedures of a program $\Pi \in Prog$ by identifiers of the form $\pi_{\bar{\omega}}$, where the index $\bar{\omega} \in \mathrm{IN}^*$, a finite sequence of natural numbers, is uniquely determined. The length of $\bar{\omega}$ encodes the *static level* the corresponding procedure is declared on; the longest proper prefix of $\bar{\omega}$ gives the index of its unique static predecessor. Thus, given the index of an procedure π the set of all its proper prefixes yields the set of all static predecessors of π. Similarly, the set of indexes of a given length l determines the set of procedures of the static level l. In particular, the main procedure is assumed to have static level 1. Thus, it is denoted by π_1.

---

[1] Note that $StatPred$ induces a relation on Π.

The following example illustrates our naming convention.

$$\Pi = \langle \pi_1 \langle \pi_{11}, \pi_{12} \langle \pi_{121}, \pi_{122} \langle \pi_{1221} \rangle \rangle, \pi_{13} \langle \pi_{131} \rangle \rangle \rangle$$

Π is a program with the following nesting structure of procedures.

$$
\begin{aligned}
\Pi = \langle \pi_1 : \\
\langle \pi_{11} (\ldots : \ldots : \ldots) : \ldots, \\
\pi_{12} (\ldots : \ldots : \ldots) : \\
\langle \pi_{121} (\ldots : \ldots : \ldots) : \ldots, \\
\pi_{122} (\ldots : \ldots : \ldots) : \\
\langle \pi_{1221} (\ldots : \ldots : \ldots) : \ldots \rangle \ldots \rangle \ldots, \\
\pi_{13} (\ldots : \ldots : \ldots) : \\
\langle \pi_{131} (\ldots : \ldots : \ldots) : \ldots \rangle \ldots \rangle \\
\ldots \rangle
\end{aligned}
$$

Note that according to our naming convention, the nesting structure of the procedures of a program is uniquely encoded in the procedure names. Therefore, we will usually omit the angle brackets. For example, for the program Π we will simply write:

$$\Pi = \langle \pi_1, \pi_{11}, \pi_{12}, \pi_{121}, \pi_{122}, \pi_{1221}, \pi_{13}, \pi_{131} \rangle$$

In the following we restrict our attention to *Prog*-programs, which are distinguished and where all procedure calls are correct.

5.2 Sublanguages

An important classification of Algol-like programming languages is induced by the notion of *mode depth* (cf. [Ar3, La5, LLW]). Following [Ar3], the mode depth $\mathcal{MD}$ of an ordinary or a formal procedure identifier f without any procedural arguments or parameters occurring in a call statement or declaration, respectively, is defined to be 1. The mode depth of a procedure identifier g occurring in a context of the form $g(: : h_1, \ldots, h_k)$ is then inductively defined by

$$\mathcal{MD}(g) =_{df} Max(\{\mathcal{MD}(h_i) \mid i \in \{1, \ldots, k\}\}) + 1$$

This notion can easily be enhanced to capture programs. The mode depth of a *Prog*-program Π is given by the maximal mode depths of its procedure identifiers:

$$\mathcal{MD}(\Pi) =_{df} Max(\{\mathcal{MD}(\pi) \mid \pi \in \mathcal{I}_{\mathbf{P}}(\Pi)\})$$

The notion of mode depth divides the family of Algol-like programming languages into two major groups: languages allowing programs with *infinite modes* like Algol68 [vWMPK, vWMPKSLMF] and languages allowing programs with *finite modes* only like ISO-Pascal [ISO]. The importance of this classification stems from the fact that a variety of problems, which are relevant for the construction of a compiler, like *formal reachability* or *formal recursivity* of a procedure are decidable for finite, but undecidable for infinite mode languages [Ar1, La1].[2] Concerning interprocedural program optimization, the problem of formal reachability and its inherent complexity is particularly important as we have to consider a refined version of formal reachability, called *formal callability*, in order to avoid worst-case assumptions for formal procedure calls during optimization (cf. Chapter 6). In the general case of arbitrary finite mode languages formal reachability is P-space hard [Ar3, Wi2]; for languages of mode depth 2, however, formal reachability is decidable in polynomial time, if there is a limit on the length of parameter lists [Ar3]. Intuitively, mode depth 2 means that formal procedure parameters do not have procedures as parameters. Note that the original version of Wirth's Pascal [Wth, HW] is a prominent example of an Algol-like programming language of mode depth 2. In addition to these results on finite mode languages, also the following result of [La1] is important for us: formal reachability is decidable for subsets of Algol-like languages, which do not allow procedures with global formal procedure parameters. This gives rise to the definition of the following sublanguages of *Prog*, which we consider in more detail in the following chapter dealing with *higher order data flow analysis*:

1. $Prog_{fm(k)}$: the set of *Prog*-programs with mode depth $m \leq k$, $k \in \mathbb{N}$,
2. $Prog_{ugfpp}$: the set of *Prog*-programs without global formal procedure parameters,
3. $Prog_{fm(k),ugfpp}$: the set of *Prog*-programs with mode depth k without global formal procedure parameters.

5.3 Separate Compilation and Separate Optimization

Large software systems are typically constructed and organized as a hierarchy of subsystems (*modules*) in order to support a structured and reliable programming. "State-of the-art" languages support this approach of "programming-in-the-large" by allowing the composition of programs out of modules, which import and export procedures from and to other modules, respectively. This has led to the development of compilers offering *separate compilation*, i.e., the ability of compiling single modules as well as complete programs. Besides simplifying the software development process, separate compilation also supports the reuse of software components (modules). However, in order to exploit the full power of separate compilation, it must be enhanced with methods for *separate optimization* in order to support the generation of efficient object code also for separately compiled program modules (cf. [Bu, BC2, SW]). Technically, separate optimization can be organized by

---

[2] The practical impact of these results for the design and the construction of compilers is discussed in [La1].

means of an *optimizer library system*, which stores, manages, and maintains information on previously analysed programs and modules, and intelligently supports the retrieval of this information to enhance the optimization of other modules (cf. [CKT1, CKT2]). In fact, this approach allows a proper treatment of external procedures, which are imported from other modules, and whose implementation is invisible to the module currently under optimization. The two extremes are here as follows: first, the library fully specifies the semantics of an external procedure with respect to the application under consideration; second, the library leaves the semantics of an external procedure completely unspecified, i.e., concerning the application it provides no (positive) information on its behaviour. In this case the external procedure is treated by means of a worst-case assumption. Clearly, the correctness and the optimality of a concrete optimization holds relatively to the correctness of the information stored in the library system. It is worth noting that besides separate optimization also *incremental optimization* is supported by this approach, i.e., after changing a program module it is sufficient to reoptimize the modified module, and those that hierarchically depend on it.

Our framework for interprocedural program optimization takes separate optimization into account by offering an interface to an optimizer library system. However, it can also be used in the absence of a library system because information on external procedures can also manually be fed in. The extreme case that nothing is assumed about (some of) the external procedures is taken care of by extending the program (module) Π under consideration with a fictitious procedure π_0, representing the unspecified external procedures occurring in the environment of Π. In particular, all unspecified external variables of Π are considered local variables of π_0, and all procedure calls of Π to unspecified external procedures are considered ordinary procedure calls of π_0. The procedure π_0 is then treated by means of a *worst case assumption* in order to guarantee the safety of the DFA-results. This leads to a uniform treatment of internal and external procedure calls in our framework, even if their semantics is unspecified. For simplicity, the attribute "unspecified" is omitted in the following, and the term external procedure denotes always an external procedure without a specified semantics.

6. Higher Order Data Flow Analysis

In this chapter we present the *higher order data flow analysis* (*HO-DFA*) of our framework. It allows us a proper treatment of formal procedure calls in interprocedural program optimization by avoiding worst-case assumptions for them. The intent of the HO-DFA is to compute for every formal procedure call in a program the set of procedures, which may actually be called by it. In IDFA, this information can be used by interpreting formal procedure calls as nondeterministic higher-order branch statements. Intuitively, this is closely related to approaches for constructing the procedure call graph of a program (cf. [CCHK, HK, Wal, Lak, Ry]).[1] These approaches, however, are mostly heuristically based, and concentrate on correctness (safety) of the analysis results. They do not systematically deal with precision. In contrast, investigating both correctness and precision, and demonstrating the theoretical and practical limitations of computing the set of procedures which may be called by a formal procedure call is an important point of our approach. Technically, we proceed by showing that computing the set of procedures which may be called by a formal procedure call is a refinement of the well-known *formal reachability* problem (cf. [La1]). We therefore call the refined problem the *formal callability* problem. The undecidability of formal reachability in general (cf. [La1]) directly implies that also formal callability is in general undecidable. Thus, in order to make our approach practical, we introduce an approximation of formal callability, which we call *potential passability*. We prove that it is a correct approximation of formal callability, which can efficiently be computed. Moreover, for programs of mode depth 2 without global formal procedure parameters potential passability and formal callability coincide.

Conceptually as well as technically, the HO-DFA computing potential passability is embedded as a preprocess in our framework for interprocedural program optimization. This is important because all details of this preprocess can be hidden from the designer of an optimization. The construction of an interprocedural optimization proceeds as for programs without formal procedure calls. The results of the HO-DFA are automatically taken care of

---

[1] In [Lak] a different setup is considered with procedure valued variables instead of formal procedure parameters. The algorithm of [Ry] is restricted to programs without recursion.

J. Knoop: Optimal Interprocedural Program Optimization, LNCS 1428, pp. 79-97, 1998.
© Springer-Verlag Berlin Heidelberg 1998

by interpreting formal procedure calls according to these results as higher-order branch statements of ordinary procedure calls during IDFA. Formal procedure calls are thereby handled in a most recent fashion. In Chapter 10 we will thus require that the argument program satisfies the *strong formal most recent* property for guaranteeing the correctness of the IDFA-results (cf. [Ka]). It is worth noting, however, that the HO-DFA does not rely on this premise. It applies to all programs of *Prog*.

6.1 Formal Callability: Formal Reachability Revisited and Refined

Intuitively, *callability* is concerned with the question which procedures can be called by a procedure call statement at run-time. While this is not at all a problem for ordinary procedure calls as the called procedure is unique and statically known, it is in general undecidable for formal procedure calls (cf. Theorem 6.1.2). The distinctive difference is that the procedure actually called by a formal procedure call is given by the argument which is bound to the formal procedure, when reaching the call site. This, however, depends on the particular program execution reaching the call site as illustrated in Example 6.1.1.

Example 6.1.1. Let $\Pi \in Prog_{fm(2)}$ be the program given below, where we assume that the three call statements in the body of π_{13} can sequentially be executed.[2] Note that all formal parameters occurring in Π are procedure parameters, and that the formal procedure parameter ϕ_2 is a global formal procedure parameter of the procedures π_{133} and π_{134}.

$$
\begin{aligned}
&\langle \pi_1 : \\
&\quad \langle \pi_{11} : \dots , \\
&\quad\ \pi_{12} : \dots , \\
&\quad\ \pi_{13} (:: \phi_1, \phi_2) : \\
&\quad\quad \langle \pi_{131} : \dots , \\
&\quad\quad\ \pi_{132} : \dots , \\
&\quad\quad\ \pi_{133} : \dots ; \phi_2; \dots , \\
&\quad\quad\ \pi_{134} : \dots ; \phi_2; \dots \rangle \\
&\quad\quad \dots ; \pi_{13}(:: \pi_{133}, \pi_{131}); \dots ; \pi_{13}(:: \pi_{134}, \pi_{132}); \dots ; \phi_1; \dots \rangle \\
&\quad \pi_{13}(:: \pi_{11}, \pi_{12}) \rangle
\end{aligned}
$$

Considering the program Π of Example 6.1.1 it is easy to check that the formal procedure call of ϕ_1 in π_{13} calls π_{11}, π_{133} and π_{134}, and that the formal procedure calls of ϕ_2 in π_{133} and in π_{134} call the procedures π_{131} and π_{132}, respectively. In general, however, it is not decidable which procedures

---

[2] This can be achieved by adding appropriate branch instructions.

are *actually* called by a formal call statement at run-time. This holds even for programs without any input operations as they are expressive enough to simulate any Turing machine. Thus, *actual callability* must be approximated by a corresponding static property of a program, which we call *formal callability*. It is defined in terms of the *formal execution tree* T_{Π}^{stat} of a program Π. In essence, T_{Π}^{stat} results from successive unfolding the argument program Π by applying the *static scope copy rule* to the procedure calls currently reachable (cf. [La1, Ol2]). In particular, $T_{\Pi}^{stat}(k)$, $k \in \mathbb{N}$, denotes the subtree of T_{Π}^{stat}, in which the distance between the root and its leaves is less or equal than k. This is illustrated in Example 6.1.2, which shows the program resulting from an application of the copy rule to the program of Example 6.1.1:

Example 6.1.2.

$$\langle \pi_1 :$$
$$\langle \pi_{11} : \ldots ,$$
$$\pi_{12} : \ldots ,$$
$$\pi_{13} (::\phi_1, \phi_2) :$$
$$\langle \pi_{131} : \ldots ,$$
$$\pi_{132} : \ldots ,$$
$$\pi_{133} : \ldots; \phi_2; \ldots ,$$
$$\pi_{134} : \ldots; \phi_2; \ldots \rangle$$
$$\ldots; \pi_{13}(::\pi_{133}, \pi_{131}); \ldots; \pi_{13}(::\pi_{134}, \pi_{132}); \ldots; \phi_1; \ldots \rangle$$
$$\{ IGB \} \rangle$$

where IGB is an abbreviation of

$$\langle \pi'_{131} : \ldots ,$$
$$\pi'_{132} : \ldots ,$$
$$\pi'_{133} : \ldots; \pi_{12}; \ldots ,$$
$$\pi'_{134} : \ldots; \pi_{12}; \ldots \rangle$$
$$\ldots; \pi_{13}(::\pi_{133}, \pi_{131}); \ldots; \pi_{13}(::\pi_{134}, \pi_{132}); \ldots; \pi_{11}; \ldots \rangle$$

The acronym IGB used in Example 6.1.2 stands for *innermost generated block*. For clarity the IGB is usually enclosed in curly brackets as shown in the example above (cf. [La1]). The notion of an innermost generated block will be important in the following definitions. Intuitively, the innermost generated block is the modified copy of the procedure body of the procedure invoked by the call statement the copy rule has most recently been applied to. We remark that in programs of T_{Π}^{stat} the copy rule is always applied to procedure calls occurring in the currently innermost generated block.

Definition 6.1.1 (Formal Callability).
Let $\Pi \in Prog$, $\hat{\pi} \in \Pi$, and $\iota \in \mathcal{I}_{\mathbf{P}}(\Pi)$.

1. *A procedure π is k-callable by ι in $\hat{\pi}$ iff there is a call statement st'
   with $CalledProc(st') = \pi$ in the main part of the innermost generated
   block of a program $\Pi' \in T_{\Pi}^{stat}(k)$, which is the copy of a call statement
   $st \in Stmt_{call}(\hat{\pi})$ with $CalledProc(st) = \iota$.*
   *Let $\mathcal{FC}_{\hat{\pi},k}(\iota)$ denote the set of all procedures which are k-callable by ι
   in $\hat{\pi}$.*
2. *A procedure π is formally callable by ι in $\hat{\pi}$ iff $\pi \in \bigcup \{ \mathcal{FC}_{\hat{\pi},k}(\iota) \mid k \in IN \}$.*
   *Let $\mathcal{FC}_{\hat{\pi}}(\iota)$ denote the set of all procedures which are formally callable
   by ι in $\hat{\pi}$.*
3. *A procedure π is formally callable by ι iff $\pi \in \bigcup \{ \mathcal{FC}_{\hat{\pi}}(\iota) \mid \hat{\pi} \in \Pi \}$.*
   *Let $\mathcal{FC}(\iota)$ denote the set of all procedures which are formally callable by
   ι.*

Considering Example 6.1.1, the procedures π_{11}, π_{133} and π_{134} are formally
callable by ϕ_1 in π_{13}, and the procedures π_{131} and π_{132} are formally callable
by ϕ_2 in π_{133} and π_{134}, respectively. As we are going to show next, formal
callability is a direct refinement of *formal reachability* (cf. [La1]), which, intuitively, is concerned with the question, which procedures of a program may
be called at run-time.

Definition 6.1.2 (Formal Reachability).
*Let $\Pi \in Prog$, and $\pi \in \Pi$. The procedure π is formally reachable (in signs:
FormReach(π)) iff there is a program $\Pi' \in T_{\Pi}^{stat}$, whose innermost generated
block is a copy of π.*

*Let $\mathcal{FR}(\Pi) =_{df} \{ \pi \in \Pi \mid FormReach(\pi) \}$ denote the set of all procedures of
Π which are formally reachable.*

Intuitively, formal reachability of a procedure indicates whether it can (actually) be called at run-time. Formal reachability is necessary for actual callability, i.e., a procedure, which is not formally reachable, is guaranteed of being
never called at run-time. The converse implication is in general invalid. In
addition to formal reachability, formal callability even pinpoints those call
statements in a program which are responsible for the reachability. Formal
callability is thus a natural refinement of formal reachability: a procedure π
is formally reachable if and only if it is formally callable by some $\iota \in \mathcal{I}_{\mathbf{P}}(\Pi)$.

Theorem 6.1.1 (Refinement Theorem).

$$\forall \Pi \in Prog \; \forall \pi \in \Pi. \; FormReach(\pi) \iff \pi \in \bigcup \{ \mathcal{FC}(\iota) \mid \iota \in \mathcal{I}_{\mathbf{P}}(\Pi) \}$$

As a consequence of the Refinement Theorem 6.1.1 we directly obtain that every decision procedure for formal callability is a decision procedure for formal reachability as well. As it is known that formal reachability is not decidable in general (cf. [La1]), we have the following negative result:

Theorem 6.1.2 (Undecidability of Formal Callability).
It is undecidable, whether a procedure π of a Prog-program Π is formally callable by a procedure identifier ι.

Note that Theorem 6.1.2 does not exclude the decidability of formal callability for sublanguages of *Prog*. However, the Refinement Theorem 6.1.1 yields that a decision procedure for formal callability is computationally at least as complex as a decision procedure for formal reachability. This is important because the results concerning the computational complexity of formal reachability for sublanguages of *Prog* carry over to the computational complexity of formal callability. At first sight these results are discouraging. In the general case of unbounded finite mode languages (e.g., ISO-Pascal [ISO]), the formal reachability problem is *P-space hard* [Ar3, Wi2]. More encouraging, for programming languages of mode depth 2 (e.g., Wirth's Pascal [Wth, HW]) and a limit on the length of parameter lists formal reachability is decidable in polynomial time [Ar3]. However, formal reachability is too coarse in order to avoid worst-case assumptions for formal procedure calls because it only yields the existence of a procedure call statement calling a particular procedure, but it does not explicitly pinpoint the set of statements that are responsible for its reachability as it is done by formal callability (cf. Refinement Theorem 6.1.1). Even more, as demonstrated in Example 6.1.1, formal callability distinguishes even occurrences of formal procedure calls of the same formal procedure identifier which are located in different procedures. In fact, the set of procedures which is callable by a formal procedure identifier ι depends on the procedure containing the formal call statement of ι.

The theoretical limitations of deciding formal callability, and the efficiency requirements imposed by program optimization give rise to consider approximations of formal callability which satisfy the following requirements:

1. formal callability is *correctly (safely)* approximated,
2. for every program $\Pi \in Prog$, the approximation is *efficiently* computable, and
3. for certain sublanguages of *Prog*, the approximation is *precise* for formal callability.

In Section 6.2 and Section 6.3 we stepwise develop an approximation satisfying these requirements. Central are the notions of *formal passability* and *potential passability*. The results on potential passability presented in Section 6.4 show that potential passability meets the requirements introduced above.

6.2 Formal Passability

Intuitively, *formal passability* deals with the question, which procedures can be passed as an argument to a procedure parameter. Formal passability of a procedure π to a procedure parameter ι is thus a necessary condition for the formal callability of π by ι (cf. Theorem 6.2.1). As we will show, for programs of $Prog_{ugfpp}$ it is even sufficient. This means, for programs without global formal procedure parameters formal callability and formal passability coincide (cf. Theorem 6.2.3).

Definition 6.2.1 (Formal Passability).
Let $\Pi \in Prog$, and $\iota \in \mathcal{I}_{\mathbf{FP}}(\Pi)$.

1. *A procedure π is k-passable to ι iff there is a call statement st' with $CalledProc(st') = decl(\iota)$ in the main part of the innermost generated block of a program $\Pi' \in T_{\Pi}^{stat}(k)$ such that $ParLst(st')\downarrow_{pos(\iota)} = \pi$.*
   Let $\mathcal{FP}_k(\iota)$ denote the set of all procedures which are k-passable to ι.
2. *A procedure π is formally passable to ι iff $\pi \in \bigcup \{\mathcal{FP}_k(\iota) \mid k \in \mathbb{N}\}$.*
   Let $\mathcal{FP}(\iota)$ denote the set of all procedures which are formally passable to ι.

It can easily be proved that formal callability implies formal passability.

Theorem 6.2.1 (Passability).

$$\forall \Pi \in Prog \; \forall \iota \in \mathcal{I}_{\mathbf{FP}}(\Pi). \; \mathcal{FC}(\iota) \subseteq \mathcal{FP}(\iota)$$

In general, the inclusion in the Passability Theorem 6.2.1 is proper as illustrated by the program of Example 6.1.1. For this example it can easily be checked that $\mathcal{FC}_{\pi_{133}}(\phi_2) = \{\pi_{131}\}$, and $\mathcal{FC}_{\pi_{134}}(\phi_2) = \{\pi_{132}\}$, whereas $\mathcal{FP}(\phi_2) = \{\pi_{12}, \pi_{131}, \pi_{132}\}$, and that both procedures π_{133} and π_{134} are formally reachable. As a consequence of this example we thus directly obtain:

Theorem 6.2.2.

1. $\exists \Pi \in Prog_{fm(2)} \; \exists \iota \in \mathcal{I}_{\mathbf{FP}}(\Pi) \; (\exists \pi \in \mathcal{FR}(\Pi).$
   $c\text{-}occ_\pi(\iota) \neq \emptyset). \; \mathcal{FC}_\pi(\iota) \subset \mathcal{FP}(\iota)$
2. $\exists \Pi \in Prog_{fm(2)} \; \exists \iota \in \mathcal{I}_{\mathbf{FP}}(\Pi)$
   $(\exists \pi, \pi' \in \mathcal{FR}(\Pi). \; c\text{-}occ_\pi(\iota) \neq \emptyset \wedge c\text{-}occ_{\pi'}(\iota) \neq \emptyset). \; \mathcal{FC}_\pi(\iota) \neq \mathcal{FC}_{\pi'}(\iota)$

Theorem 6.2.2 shows that even for programs of mode depth 2 formal callability and formal passability are in general not equivalent. The point here is that $Prog_{fm(2)}$-programs may have global formal procedure parameters. In fact, for programs without global formal procedure parameters, i.e., for $Prog_{ugfpp}$-programs, we have:

Theorem 6.2.3 ($Prog_{ugfpp}$)**.**

$\forall \Pi \in Prog_{ugfpp}$ $(\forall \iota \in \mathcal{I}_{\mathbf{FP}}(\Pi).\ c\text{-}occ(\iota) \neq \emptyset).\ \mathcal{FC}(\iota) = \mathcal{FC}_{decl(\iota)}(\iota) = \mathcal{FP}(\iota)$

Theorem 6.2.3 does not depend on the mode depth of the program under consideration. However, computing formal passability for $Prog_{fm(k),ugfpp}$-programs with $k \geq 3$ causes similar problems as for programs of mode depth 2 and global formal procedure parameters. This is illustrated by the two program fragments of Example 6.2.1.

Example 6.2.1.

Let $\Pi_1 \in Prog_{fm(2)}$ and $\Pi_2 \in Prog_{fm(3),ugfpp}$ be the programs shown below. Note that all parameters occurring in Π_1 and Π_2 are procedure parameters.

$$\Pi_1 = \langle \pi_1 :$$
$$\langle \pi_{11} : \ldots,$$
$$\pi_{12} : \ldots,$$
$$\pi_{13} (::\phi_1,\phi_2) :$$
$$\langle \pi_{131} (::\phi_3) : \ldots; \phi_3; \ldots,$$
$$\pi_{132} : \ldots,$$
$$\pi_{133} : \ldots,$$
$$\pi_{134} : \ldots; \phi_2; \ldots; \pi_{131}(::\phi_2); \ldots,$$
$$\pi_{135} : \ldots; \phi_2; \ldots \rangle$$
$$\ldots; \pi_{13}(::\pi_{134},\pi_{132}); \ldots; \pi_{13}(::\pi_{135},\pi_{133}); \ldots; \phi_1; \ldots \rangle$$
$$\pi_{13}(::\pi_{11},\pi_{12}) \rangle$$

$$\Pi_2 = \langle \pi_1 :$$
$$\langle \pi_{11} (::\phi_1(::proc),\phi_2) :$$
$$\langle \pi_{111} (::\phi_3) : \ldots,$$
$$\pi_{112} : \ldots \rangle$$
$$\ldots; \phi_1(::\phi_2); \ldots; \pi_{11}(::\pi_{111},\pi_{112}); \ldots,$$
$$\pi_{12} (::\phi_4) : \ldots; \phi_4; \ldots,$$
$$\pi_{13} : \ldots \rangle$$
$$\pi_{11}(::\pi_{12},\pi_{13}) \rangle$$

Considering first program Π_1, we obtain that the procedures π_{131}, π_{134}, and π_{135} of Π_1 are formally reachable. Moreover, we can easily check the inclusion

$$\mathcal{FP}(\phi_3) = \{\pi_{132}\} \subset \{\pi_{12},\pi_{132},\pi_{133}\} = \mathcal{FP}(\phi_2)$$

Hence, $\mathcal{FP}(\phi_3)$ is a proper subset of $\mathcal{FP}(\phi_2)$. Considering now the program Π_2, we similarly get the inclusion

$$\mathcal{FP}(\phi_4) = \{\pi_{13}\} \subset \{\pi_{13},\pi_{112}\} = \mathcal{FP}(\phi_2)$$

which is proper as well.

Note that in the program Π_1 of Example 6.2.1, the set $\mathcal{FP}(\phi_3)$ depends directly on the actual values of ϕ_2 only, but indirectly also on the actual values of ϕ_1. Intuitively, this is because the procedure π_{134} is only reachable for particular pairs of elements of $\mathcal{FP}(\phi_1)$ and $\mathcal{FP}(\phi_2)$. Therefore, detecting the equality $\mathcal{FP}(\phi_3) = \{\pi_{132}\}$ requires a bookkeeping over all combinations of arguments occurring in a call of procedure π_{13} in T_Π^{stat}. Clearly, this is much more complex than a bookkeeping which for every procedure parameter separately keeps track of the set of arguments. In fact, in the first case we have up to

$$|\mathcal{I}_{\mathbf{FP}}(\pi)|^{|\Pi|}$$

different parameter combinations for a procedure π, whereas in the second case this number can be estimated by

$$|\mathcal{I}_{\mathbf{FP}}(\pi)| * |\Pi|$$

Similar effects occur in programs with finite mode depth greater than 2, even if they are free of global formal procedure parameters. This is illustrated by the program Π_2 of Example 6.2.1, which originally was given in [Ar3] in order to illustrate the intractability of the formal reachability problem for programs with finite mode depths greater than 2. Similarly to the parameter ϕ_2 in program Π_1, the actual values of ϕ_4 in Π_2 depend directly only on the actual values of ϕ_2, but indirectly also on the values of ϕ_1. Detecting this requires a bookkeeping over all combinations of arguments occurring in procedure calls. Thus, deciding formal passability for programs of mode depth greater than 2 even without global formal procedure identifiers is in general expensive.

In contrast, for programs of mode depth 2 without global formal procedure parameters effects as illustrated above do not occur. In essence, this is a consequence of Property (6.1) of $Prog_{fm(2)}$-programs. Intuitively, it means that in programs with mode depth 2 formal procedure calls do not have procedures as arguments.

$$\forall\, st \in Stmt_{call}(\Pi).CalledProc(st) \in \mathcal{I}_{\mathbf{FP}}(\Pi) \tag{6.1}$$
$$\Rightarrow ParLst(st) \cap \mathcal{I}_{\mathbf{P}}(\Pi) = \emptyset$$

This property is the key for constructing an algorithm, which computes formal callability for $Prog_{fm(2),ugfpp}$-programs efficiently. It relies on the notion of *potential passability*.

6.3 Potential Passability

Like formal passability, *potential passability* deals with the question, which procedures are passable as an argument to a procedure parameter. Parameterized with a correct (safe) approximation of the set of formally reachable procedures of the argument program, it yields a correct (safe) approximation of formal passability. However, in contrast to formal passability, potential passability can efficiently be computed for all *Prog*-programs. Moreover, for *Prog*$_{fm(2),ugfpp}$-programs potential passability (parameterized with the set of formally reachable procedures of the argument program), formal passability and formal callability coincide.

The computation of potential passability proceeds in two steps. First, computing a correct (safe) approximation of formal reachability, and second, computing potential passability with respect to the reachability information of the first step.

Note that formal reachability is correctly (safely) approximated by the elements of the set

$$\mathcal{FR}_{App}(\Pi)=_{df}\{\,A\,|\,\mathcal{FR}(\Pi)\subseteq A\,\}$$

Obviously, we have $\mathcal{FR}_{App}(\Pi)\neq\emptyset$ because of $\Pi\in\mathcal{FR}_{App}(\Pi)$. This implies that there is always a safe, though trivial, approximation of formal reachability, even for programming languages, for which formal reachability is undecidable. Note, however, that the accuracy of potential passability with respect to formal passability depends on the accuracy of the reachability information. Thus, it is important to recall that for programs with mode depth 2 and a limit on the length of parameter lists formal reachability is computable in polynomial time (cf. [Ar3]).

The second step of computing potential passability is characterized by Equation System 6.3.1, where $A\in\mathcal{FR}_{App}(\Pi)$.

Equation System 6.3.1 (Potential Passability).

$$\mathbf{pp}(\iota)\;=\;\begin{cases}\{\iota\} & \text{if } \iota\in\mathcal{I}_{\mathbf{OP}}(\Pi)\\[2mm]\bigcup\{\,\mathbf{pp}(ParLst(st)\!\downarrow_{pos(\iota)})\,|\\\quad st\in c\text{-}occ_{Stmt(A)}(\{\,\kappa\,|\,decl(\iota)\in\mathbf{pp}(\kappa)\,\})\,\} & \text{otherwise}\end{cases}$$

Denoting the least solution of Equation System 6.3.3 with respect to A by $\mathcal{PP}_A$ potential passability is defined as follows:

Definition 6.3.2 (Potential Passability).
Let $\Pi\in Prog$, $A\in\mathcal{FR}_{App}(\Pi)$, and $\iota\in\mathcal{I}_{\mathbf{FP}}(\Pi)$. A procedure π is potentially passable *to* ι if and only if $\pi\in\mathcal{PP}_A(\iota)$.

Obviously, we have:

$$\forall\,\pi\in\mathcal{I}_{\mathbf{OP}}(\Pi).\ \mathcal{PP}_A(\pi)=\{\pi\}$$

Theorem 6.3.1 yields that potential passability is a correct (safe) approximation of formal passability, and thus, by means of the Passability Theorem 6.2.1 also a correct (safe) approximation of formal callability.

Theorem 6.3.1 (Correctness (Safety)).

$$\forall \Pi \in Prog \ \forall A \in \mathcal{FR}_{App}(\Pi) \ \forall \iota \in \mathcal{I}_{\mathbf{FP}}(\Pi). \ \mathcal{FP}(\iota) \subseteq \mathcal{PP}_A(\iota)$$

Proof. Let $\iota \in \mathcal{I}_{\mathbf{P}}(\Pi)$ and $\pi \in \mathcal{FP}(\iota)$. According to Definition 6.2.1 there is a $k \in \mathbb{N}$, a program $\Pi' \in T_{\Pi}^{stat}(k)$, and a call statement st' with $CalledProc(st') = decl(\iota)$ in the main part of the innermost generated block of Π' with $ParLst(st')\!\downarrow_{pos(\iota)} = \pi$. Under this assumption we have to show:

$$\pi \in \mathcal{PP}_A(\iota) \tag{6.2}$$

This is proved by induction on the number k of applications of the copy rule, which are necessary to obtain program Π'.

For $k = 0$, we have $\Pi' = \Pi$. Moreover, there is a call statement st in Π with $CalledProc(st) = decl(\iota) \in \mathcal{I}_{\mathbf{OP}}(\Pi)$ and $ParLst(st)\!\downarrow_{pos(\iota)} = \pi$. Obviously, we have $st \in Stmt_{call}(\pi_1)$, and therefore, $st \in c\text{-}occ_{Stmt(A)}(decl(\iota))$. Moreover, we have $\pi \in \mathcal{I}_{\mathbf{OP}}(\Pi)$. The induction base follows now from the following sequence of inclusions:

$$
\begin{aligned}
\mathcal{PP}_A(\iota) \ &= \ \bigcup \{ \mathcal{PP}_A(ParLst(\hat{st})\!\downarrow_{pos(\iota)}) \mid \hat{st} \in \\
& \qquad c\text{-}occ_{Stmt(A)}(\{ \kappa \mid decl(\iota) \in \mathcal{PP}_A(\kappa) \}) \} \\
(\ decl(\iota) \in \mathcal{I}_{\mathbf{OP}}(\Pi)\ ) \ &\supseteq \ \bigcup \{ \mathcal{PP}_A(ParLst(\hat{st})\!\downarrow_{pos(\iota)}) \mid \\
& \qquad \hat{st} \in c\text{-}occ_{Stmt(A)}(\ decl(\iota)\ ) \} \\
(\ st \in c\text{-}occ_{Stmt(A)}(decl(\iota))\ ) \ &\supseteq \ \mathcal{PP}_A(ParLst(st)\!\downarrow_{pos(\iota)}) \\
(\ ParLst(st)\!\downarrow_{pos(\iota)} = \pi\ ) \ &= \ \mathcal{PP}_A(\pi) \\
(\ \pi \in \mathcal{I}_{\mathbf{OP}}(\Pi)\ ) \ &= \ \{ \pi \}
\end{aligned}
$$

The induction step for $k > 0$ can now be proved under the induction hypothesis

$$\forall \iota \in \mathcal{I}_{\mathbf{FP}}(\Pi) \ \forall 0 \leq l < k. \ \pi \in \mathcal{FP}_l(\iota) \Rightarrow \pi \in \mathcal{PP}_A(\iota) \tag{IH}$$

It is sufficient to show that for every $\iota \in \mathcal{I}_{\mathbf{P}}(\Pi)$ and every $\pi \in \mathcal{FP}_k(\iota) \backslash \mathcal{FP}_{k-1}(\iota)$ holds:

$$\pi \in \mathcal{PP}_A(\iota)$$

Without loss of generality, we can assume that there is a $\pi \in \mathcal{FP}_k(\iota) \backslash \mathcal{FP}_{k-1}(\iota)$ for some $\iota \in \mathcal{I}_{\mathbf{P}}(\Pi)$, since otherwise the induction hypothesis would suffice. Then there is a call statement st' in Π' with $CalledProc(st') = decl(\iota) \in \mathcal{I}_{\mathbf{OP}}(\Pi)$ and $ParLst(st')\!\downarrow_{pos(\iota)} = \pi \in \mathcal{I}_{\mathbf{OP}}(\Pi)$, which is the copy of a call statement st of Π with $CalledProc(st) = \kappa$, and $ParLst(st)\!\downarrow_{pos(\iota)} = \phi$. Moreover, we have $st \in c\text{-}occ_A(\kappa)$. Thus, we are left with investigating the following four cases.

Case 1. $\kappa,\ \phi \in \mathcal{I}_{\mathbf{OP}}(\Pi)$.

In this case we obtain $\kappa = decl(\iota)$ and $\phi = \pi$. Then the following sequence of inclusions

$$
\begin{aligned}
\mathcal{PP}_A(\iota) &= \bigcup\{\,\mathcal{PP}_A(ParLst(\hat{st})\!\downarrow_{pos(\iota)})\,| \\
&\qquad \hat{st} \in c\text{-}occ_{Stmt(A)}(\{\,\hat{\kappa}\,|\,decl(\iota) \in \mathcal{PP}_A(\hat{\kappa})\,\})\,\} \\
(\,decl(\iota) \in \mathcal{PP}_A(\kappa)\,) &\supseteq \bigcup\{\,\mathcal{PP}_A(ParLst(\hat{st})\!\downarrow_{pos(\iota)})\,| \\
&\qquad \hat{st} \in c\text{-}occ_{Stmt(A)}(\kappa)\,\} \\
(\,st \in c\text{-}occ_{Stmt(A)}(\kappa)\,) &\supseteq \mathcal{PP}_A(ParLst(st)\!\downarrow_{pos(\iota)}) \\
(\,ParLst(st)\!\downarrow_{pos(\iota)} = \phi\,) &= \mathcal{PP}_A(\phi) \\
(\,\pi = \phi\,) &= \{\pi\}
\end{aligned}
$$

completes the proof of Case 1.

Case 2. $\kappa \in \mathcal{I}_{\mathbf{OP}}(\Pi),\ \phi \in \mathcal{I}_{\mathbf{FP}}(\Pi)$.

In this case we have $\kappa = decl(\iota)$. Moreover, there is a call statement st'' in a predecessor Π'' of Π' in $T_{\Pi}^{stat}(k)$ with $CalledProc(st'') = decl(\phi)$, and $ParLst(st'')\!\downarrow_{pos(\phi)} = \pi$. Thus, we have $\pi \in \mathcal{FP}_{k-1}(\phi)$, and therefore by means of the induction hypothesis (IH) $\pi \in \mathcal{PP}_A(\phi)$. Similarly as in Case 1 we obtain

$$
\begin{aligned}
\mathcal{PP}_A(\iota) &= \bigcup\{\,\mathcal{PP}_A(ParLst(\hat{st})\!\downarrow_{pos(\iota)})\,| \\
&\qquad \hat{st} \in c\text{-}occ_{Stmt(A)}(\{\,\hat{\kappa}\,|\,decl(\iota) \in \mathcal{PP}_A(\hat{\kappa})\,\})\,\} \\
(\,decl(\iota) \in \mathcal{PP}_A(\kappa)\,) &\supseteq \bigcup\{\,\mathcal{PP}_A(ParLst(\hat{st})\!\downarrow_{pos(\iota)})\,| \\
&\qquad \hat{st} \in c\text{-}occ_{Stmt(A)}(\kappa)\,\} \\
(\,st \in c\text{-}occ_{Stmt(A)}(\kappa)\,) &\supseteq \mathcal{PP}_A(ParLst(st)\!\downarrow_{pos(\iota)}) \\
(\,ParLst(st)\!\downarrow_{pos(\iota)} = \phi\,) &= \mathcal{PP}_A(\phi) \\
(\,\pi \in \mathcal{PP}_A(\phi)\,) &\supseteq \{\pi\}
\end{aligned}
$$

which completes the proof of Case 2.

Case 3. $\kappa \in \mathcal{I}_{\mathbf{FP}}(\Pi),\ \phi \in \mathcal{I}_{\mathbf{OP}}(\Pi)$.

Here, we have $\phi = \pi$. Additionally, there is a call statement st'' in a predecessor Π'' of Π' in $T_{\Pi}^{stat}(k)$ with $CalledProc(st'') = decl(\kappa)$, and $ParLst(st'')\!\downarrow_{pos(\kappa)} = decl(\iota)$. Thus, we obtain $decl(\iota) \in \mathcal{FP}_{k-1}(\kappa)$, and therefore by means of the induction hypothesis (IH) $decl(\iota) \in \mathcal{PP}_A(\kappa)$. Hence, we have:

$$
\begin{aligned}
\mathcal{PP}_A(\iota) &= \bigcup\{\,\mathcal{PP}_A(ParLst(\hat{st})\!\downarrow_{pos(\iota)})\,| \\
&\qquad \hat{st} \in c\text{-}occ_{Stmt(A)}(\{\,\hat{\kappa}\,|\,decl(\iota) \in \mathcal{PP}_A(\hat{\kappa})\,\})\,\} \\
(\,decl(\iota) \in \mathcal{PP}_A(\kappa)\,) &\supseteq \bigcup\{\,\mathcal{PP}_A(ParLst(\hat{st})\!\downarrow_{pos(\iota)})\,| \\
&\qquad \hat{st} \in c\text{-}occ_{Stmt(A)}(\kappa)\,\}
\end{aligned}
$$

$$(st \in c\text{-}occ_{Stmt(A)}(\kappa)) \quad \supseteq \quad \mathcal{PP}_A(ParLst(st)\!\downarrow_{pos(\iota)})$$
$$(ParLst(st)\!\downarrow_{pos(\iota)} = \phi) \quad = \quad \mathcal{PP}_A(\phi)$$
$$(\pi = \phi) \quad = \quad \{\pi\}$$

which completes the proof of Case 3.

Case 4. $\kappa,\ \phi \in \mathcal{I}_{\mathbf{FP}}(\Pi)$.
First, there is a call statement st'' in a predecessor Π'' of Π' in $T_\Pi^{stat}(k)$ with $CalledProc(st'') = decl(\kappa)$, and $ParLst(st'')\!\downarrow_{pos(\kappa)} = decl(\iota)$. Hence, we obtain $decl(\iota) \in \mathcal{FP}_{k-1}(\kappa)$, and therefore by means of the induction hypothesis (IH) $decl(\iota) \in \mathcal{PP}_A(\kappa)$. Second, there is a call statement $\bar{st}$ in a predecessor $\bar{\Pi}$ of Π' in $T_\Pi^{stat}(k)$ with $CalledProc(\bar{st}) = decl(\phi)$, and $ParLst(\bar{st})\!\downarrow_{pos(\phi)} = \pi$. Thus, we have $\pi \in \mathcal{FP}_{k-1}(\phi)$, and therefore again by means of the induction hypothesis (IH) $\pi \in \mathcal{PP}_A(\phi)$. Summarizing, we obtain

$$\mathcal{PP}_A(\iota) \quad = \quad \bigcup\{\mathcal{PP}_A(ParLst(\hat{st})\!\downarrow_{pos(\iota)})\,|$$
$$\hat{st} \in c\text{-}occ_{Stmt(A)}(\{\,\hat{\kappa}\,|\,decl(\iota) \in \mathcal{PP}_A(\hat{\kappa})\,\}\,))\}$$
$$(decl(\iota) \in \mathcal{PP}_A(\kappa)) \quad \supseteq \quad \bigcup\{\mathcal{PP}_A(ParLst(\hat{st})\!\downarrow_{pos(\iota)})\,|$$
$$\hat{st} \in c\text{-}occ_{Stmt(A)}(\kappa)\,\}$$
$$(st \in c\text{-}occ_{Stmt(A)}(\kappa)) \quad \supseteq \quad \mathcal{PP}_A(ParLst(st)\!\downarrow_{pos(\iota)})$$
$$(ParLst(st)\!\downarrow_{pos(\iota)} = \phi) \quad = \quad \mathcal{PP}_A(\phi)$$
$$(\pi \in \mathcal{PP}_A(\phi)) \quad \supseteq \quad \{\pi\}$$

This completes the proof of Case 4, and finishes the proof of Theorem 6.3.1.
$\square$

In general, the converse inclusion of Theorem 6.3.1 does not hold. This can be demonstrated for example by the programs Π_1 and Π_2 of Example 6.2.1. It is easy to check the validity of the inclusions

$$\mathcal{FP}(\phi_3) = \{\pi_{132}\} \subset \{\pi_{12}, \pi_{132}, \pi_{133}\} = \mathcal{PP}_{\mathcal{FR}(\Pi)}(\phi_3)$$

and

$$\mathcal{FP}(\phi_4) = \{\pi_{13}\} \subset \{\pi_{13}, \pi_{112}\} = \mathcal{PP}_{\mathcal{FR}(\Pi)}(\phi_4)$$

for Π_1 and Π_2, respectively. Intuitively, the inaccuracy of potential passability for programs with global formal procedure parameters or for programs with mode depth greater than 2, even if $A = \mathcal{FR}(\Pi)$, is caused by the fact that potential passability implicitly assumes independence of the passability of a procedure identifier from other procedure identifiers. As illustrated in Example 6.2.1 this is in general not true. However, for programs with mode depth 2 without global formal procedure parameters, potential passability and formal passability coincide (cf. Theorem 6.4.1).

Formal Reference Parameters and Aliasing. The notions of formal passability and potential passability can naturally be extended to formal reference parameters. This is important because regarding formal reference parameters as parameterless formal procedures, Equation System 6.3.1 yields directly a characterization of the set of may-aliases of a formal reference parameter. Moreover, it is easy to modify the equation system in order to also obtain a characterization of the set of must-aliases of a reference parameter. The HO-DFA can thus immediately be used for computing alias-information of formal reference parameters. In particular, this also holds in the presence of both formal reference parameters and formal procedure parameters in a program. Conceptually, this approach is significantly different from the traditional approaches for computing the aliases of formal reference parameters (cf. [Ban, Co, CpK2, LH, We]).

6.3.1 Computing Potential Passability

The practical relevance of potential passability is due to the fact that Equation System 6.3.1 directly specifies an iterative procedure for computing it.

Algorithm 6.3.3 (Computing Potential Passability).

Input: A program $\Pi \in Prog$, and a correct (safe) approximation $A \in \mathcal{FR}_{App}(\Pi)$ of formal reachability.

Output: For every procedure identifier $\iota \in \mathcal{I}_{\mathbf{P}}(\Pi)$ occurring in Π the least solution $\mathcal{PP}_A(\iota)$ of Equation System 6.3.1 (stored in $pp[\iota]$).

Remark: The variable workset controls the iterative process, and the variable M stores the most recent approximation for the procedure identifier currently processed.

(Initialization of the annotation array pp and the variable $workset$)
FORALL $\iota \in \mathcal{I}_{\mathbf{P}}(\Pi)$ **DO**
    IF $\iota \in \mathcal{I}_{\mathbf{OP}}(\Pi)$ **THEN** $pp[\iota] := \{\iota\}$ **ELSE** $pp[\iota] := \emptyset$ **FI**
OD;
$workset := \mathcal{I}_{\mathbf{FP}}(\Pi)$;

(Iterative fixed point computation)
WHILE $workset \neq \emptyset$ **DO**
    LET $\iota \in workset$
      BEGIN
        $workset := workset \backslash \{\iota\}$;
        $M := pp[\iota] \cup \bigcup \{\, pp[ParLst(st)\!\downarrow_{pos(\iota)}] \,\mid$
                     $st \in c\text{-}occ_{Stmt(A)}(\{\, \kappa \mid decl(\iota) \in pp[\kappa] \,\}) \,\}$;

        IF $pp[\iota] \subset M$
           THEN
               $pp[\iota] := M$;
               $workset := workset \cup \{\kappa \mid \kappa \in$
                   $\mathcal{I}^d_{\mathbf{FP}}(\{pp[\hat{\imath}] \mid \hat{\imath} \in \{\,CalledProc(st) \mid st \in occ_{Stmt(A)}(\iota)\,\}\})\,\}$
          FI
        END
OD.

In order to simplify the formulation of the central properties of Algorithm 6.3.3, we abbreviate the values of $workset$ and $pp[\iota]$ after the k-th execution of the while-loop by $workset^k$ and $pp^k[\iota]$, respectively. Using this notation, the first part of the following proposition follows immediately from the monotonicity of the union operator, while the second part is a consequence of the first one, and the finiteness of Π, i.e., Π contains only a finite number of procedures.

Proposition 6.3.1.

   1. $\forall \Pi \in Prog \; \forall \iota \in \mathcal{I}_{\mathbf{P}}(\Pi) \; \forall k \in I\!N. \; pp^k[\iota] \subseteq pp^{k+1}[\iota]$
   2. $\forall \Pi \in Prog \; \exists k \in I\!N. \; workset^k = \emptyset$

Note that Proposition 6.3.1(2) guarantees the termination of Algorithm 6.3.3. Moreover, the following theorem shows that it terminates with the least solution $\mathcal{PP}_A$ of Equation System 6.3.1, which defines potential passability.

Theorem 6.3.2 (Algorithm 6.3.3).

$$\forall \Pi \in Prog \; \forall A \in \mathcal{FR}_{App}(\Pi) \; \forall \iota \in \mathcal{I}_{\mathbf{P}}(\Pi). \; \mathcal{PP}_A(\iota) = \bigcup \{pp^k[\iota] \mid k \geq 0\}$$

In particular, for all $\iota \in \mathcal{I}_{\mathbf{P}}(\Pi)$ we have $\mathcal{PP}_A(\iota) = pp[\iota]$ after the termination of Algorithm 6.3.3.

Proof. Let fix be an arbitrary solution of Equation System 6.3.1 with respect to $A \in \mathcal{FR}_{App}(\Pi)$, i.e.,

$$fix(\iota) = \begin{cases} \{\iota\} & \text{if } \iota \in \mathcal{I}_{\mathbf{OP}}(\Pi) \\ \bigcup \{fix(ParLst(st){\downarrow}_{pos(\iota)}) \mid \\ \quad st \in c\text{-}occ_{Stmt(A)}(\{\kappa \mid decl(\iota) \in fix(\kappa)\})\} & \text{otherwise} \end{cases} \quad (6.3)$$

and let throughout the proof M^k denote the value of the variable M after the k-th execution of the while-loop. Then the central step in proving Theorem 6.3.2 is to check the following four invariants of Algorithm 6.3.3:

   1. $\forall k \in I\!N \; \forall \iota \in \mathcal{I}_{\mathbf{P}}(\Pi). \; pp^k[\iota] \subseteq fix(\iota)$
   2. $\forall k \in I\!N \; \forall \iota \in \mathcal{I}_{\mathbf{OP}}(\Pi). \; pp^k[\iota] = \{\iota\} = fix(\iota)$

3. $\forall\, k \in \mathbb{N} \; \forall\, \iota \in \mathcal{I}_{\mathbf{FP}}(\Pi) \backslash workset^k$.
$$pp^k[\iota] = \bigcup \{\, pp^k[ParLst(st)\!\downarrow_{pos(\iota)}]\,|$$
$$st \in c\text{-}occ_{Stmt(A)}(\{\,\kappa\,|\, decl(\iota) \in pp^k[\kappa]\,\})\,\}$$

4. $\forall\, k \in \mathbb{N}.\; workset^k \subseteq \mathcal{I}_{\mathbf{FP}}(\Pi)$

For $k = 0$, the investigation of the initialization part of Algorithm 6.3.3 yields:

a) $\forall\, \iota \in \mathcal{I}_{\mathbf{OP}}(\iota).\; pp^0[\iota] = \{\iota\}$
b) $\forall\, \iota \in \mathcal{I}_{\mathbf{FP}}(\iota).\; pp^0[\iota] = \emptyset$
c) $workset^0 = \mathcal{I}_{\mathbf{FP}}(\Pi)$

Hence, invariant (3) holds trivially because of (c), and the invariants (1), (2), and (4) follow immediately from (a), (b), and (c).

In order to prove the induction step, let $k > 0$, and let ι be the formal procedure identifier chosen from the workset during the k-th execution of the while-loop. Under the induction hypothesis (IH) that the invariants (1) to (4) are satisfied for all $0 \le l < k$, we have to show that the invariants (1) to (4) hold after the k-th execution of the while-loop. We obtain

$$M^k = pp^{k-1}[\iota] \cup \bigcup \{\, pp^{k-1}[ParLst(st)\!\downarrow_{pos(\iota)}]\,|$$
$$st \in c\text{-}occ_{Stmt(A)}(\{\,\kappa\,|\, decl(\iota) \in pp^{k-1}[\kappa]\,\})\,\}$$

Moreover, we have

$$pp^k[\kappa] = \begin{cases} M^k & \text{if } \iota = \kappa \,\wedge\, M^k \backslash pp^{k-1}[\iota] \ne \emptyset \\ pp^{k-1}[\kappa] & \text{otherwise} \end{cases} \tag{6.4}$$

$workset^k =$

$$\begin{cases} (workset^{k-1}\backslash\{\iota\}) \cup \{\,\kappa\,|\,\kappa \in \mathcal{I}^d_{\mathbf{FP}}(pp[\hat{\iota}]\,| & \text{if } M^k\backslash pp^{k-1}[\iota] \\ \quad \hat{\iota} \in \{\, CulledProc(st)\,|\, st \subset occ_{Stmt(A)}(\iota)\,\})\,\} & \ne \emptyset \\ workset^{k-1}\backslash\{\iota\} & \text{otherwise} \end{cases} \tag{6.5}$$

Now, the invariants (2) and (3) follow immediately from equation (6.4) and the induction hypothesis (IH). Similarly, invariant (4) is a consequence of equation (6.5) and the induction hypothesis (IH). Thus, we are left with checking invariant (1). By means of equation (6.4) and the induction hypothesis (IH) it is sufficient to check invariant (1) for ι. If $M^k\backslash pp^{k-1}[\iota] = \emptyset$, invariant (1) is simply a consequence of the induction hypothesis (IH). Without loss of generality we can thus assume that there is a $\pi \in M^k\backslash pp^{k-1}[\iota]$. The induction step then follows from the following sequence of inclusions:

$$\begin{aligned} M^k \;=\; & pp^{k-1}[\iota] \cup \bigcup \{\, pp^{k-1}[ParLst(st)\!\downarrow_{pos(\iota)}]\,| \\ & \qquad st \in c\text{-}occ_{Stmt(A)}(\{\,\kappa\,|\, decl(\iota) \in pp^{k-1}[\kappa]\,\})\,\} \\ ((\text{IH}) \text{ for } (1)) \;\subseteq\; & fix(\iota) \cup \bigcup \{\, fix(ParLst(st)\!\downarrow_{pos(\iota)})\,| \\ & \qquad st \in c\text{-}occ_{Stmt(A)}(\{\,\kappa\,|\, decl(\iota) \in fix(\kappa)\,\})\,\} \\ ((6.3)) \;=\; & fix(\iota) \end{aligned}$$

Theorem 6.3.2 is now an immediate consequence of the invariants (1), (2), and (3), and the emptiness of the workset after the termination of Algorithm 6.3.3, which is guaranteed by Proposition 6.3.1(2).   □

6.3.2 An Efficient Variant

In this section we present an alternative algorithm for computing potential passability. In comparison to Algorithm 6.3.3, the new algorithm organizes the workset more sophisticatedly, which results in an improved estimation of its worst-case time complexity. The point is that whenever an element is added to the workset the global chain length has decreased.

Algorithm 6.3.4 (Computing Potential Passability Efficiently).

Input: A program $\Pi \in Prog$, and a correct (safe) approximation $A \in \mathcal{FR}_{App}(\Pi)$ of formal reachability.

Output: For every procedure identifier $\iota \in \mathcal{I}_{\mathbf{P}}(\Pi)$ occurring in Π the least solution $\mathcal{PP}_A(\iota)$ of Equation System 6.3.1 (stored in $pp[\iota]$).

Remark: The variable $workset$ controls the iterative process, and the variable M stores the most recent approximation for the procedure identifier currently processed.

(Initialization of the annotation array pp and the variable $workset$)
FORALL $\iota \in \mathcal{I}_{\mathbf{P}}(\Pi)$ **DO**
   IF $\iota \in \mathcal{I}_{\mathbf{OP}}(\Pi)$ **THEN** $pp[\iota] := \{\iota\}$ **ELSE** $pp[\iota] := \emptyset$ **FI**
OD;
$workset := \mathcal{I}_{\mathbf{OP}}(\Pi)$;

(Iterative fixed point computation)
WHILE $workset \neq \emptyset$ **DO**
   LET $\iota \in workset$
     BEGIN
       $workset := workset \setminus \{\iota\}$;
       FORALL $\iota' \in pp[\iota] \cup$
          $\bigcup \{ pp[\hat{\iota}] \mid \hat{\iota} \in \{ CalledProc(st) \mid st \in p\text{-}occ_{Stmt(A)}(\iota) \} \}$ **DO**
         FORALL $\kappa \in \mathcal{I}_{\mathbf{FP}}(\iota')$ **DO**
           $M := pp[\kappa] \cup \bigcup \{ pp[ParLst(st)\downarrow_{pos(\kappa)}] \mid$
                    $st \in c\text{-}occ_{Stmt(A)}(\{ \hat{\kappa} \mid decl(\kappa) \in pp[\hat{\kappa}] \}) \}$;
          IF $pp[\kappa] \subset M$
           THEN
             $pp[\kappa] := M$;
             $workset := workset \cup \{ \kappa \}$
          FI
        OD
       OD
     END
OD.

Algorithm 6.3.4 terminates like Algorithm 6.3.3 with the least solution of Equation System 6.3.1. Thus, it also computes potential passability.

Theorem 6.3.3 (Algorithm 6.3.4).

$$\forall \varPi \in Prog \ \forall A \in \mathcal{FR}_{App}(\varPi) \ \forall \iota \in \mathcal{I}_{\mathbf{P}}(\varPi). \ \mathcal{PP}_A(\iota) = \bigcup \{\, pp^k[\iota] \mid k \geq 0 \,\}$$

In particular, for all $\iota \in \mathcal{I}_{\mathbf{P}}(\varPi)$ we have $\mathcal{PP}_A(\iota) = pp[\iota]$ after the termination of Algorithm 6.3.4.

Central for proving this result is Proposition 6.3.2, where $workset^{(k,l,m)}$ and $pp^{(k,l,m)}[\iota]$ denote the values of $workset$ and $pp[\iota]$ after the k-th execution of the while-loop, the l-th execution of the outer for-loop, and the m-th execution of the inner for-loop, respectively. Mpreover, $<_{lex}$ denotes the lexicographic order of elements of $\mathbb{N} \times \mathbb{N} \times \mathbb{N}$.

Proposition 6.3.2.

1. $\forall \varPi \in Prog \ \forall \iota \in \mathcal{I}_{\mathbf{P}}(\varPi) \ \forall k, l, m, k', l', m' \in \mathbb{N}.$
   $(k, l, m) <_{lex} (k', l', m') \Rightarrow pp^{(k,l,m)}[\iota] \subseteq pp^{(k',l',m')}[\iota]$
2. $\forall \varPi \in Prog \ \exists k \in \mathbb{N}. \ workset^k = \emptyset$

Based on Proposition 6.3.2, the proof of Theorem 6.3.3 proceeds along the lines of the proof of Theorem 6.3.2, and is thus omitted. In addition to the induction on the number of executions of the while-loop it requires nested inductions on the number of executions of the outer and the inner for-loop.

6.4 Main Results on Potential Passability

In this section we present the main results concerning correctness (safety), precision, and computational complexity of potential passability.

6.4.1 Correctness and Precision

The Correctness Theorem 6.3.1 and the Passability Theorem 6.2.1 guarantee that potential passability is a correct (safe) approximation of formal passability and formal callability. Moreover, for programs of mode depth 2 without global formal procedure parameters, i.e., for $Prog_{fm(2),ugfpp}$-programs, potential passability and formal passability coincide:

Theorem 6.4.1 ($Prog_{fm(2),ugfpp}$-$\mathcal{FP}$-Precision).

$$\forall \varPi \in Prog_{fm(2),ugfpp} \ \forall \iota \in \mathcal{I}_{\mathbf{FP}}(\varPi). \ \mathcal{PP}_{\mathcal{FR}(\varPi)}(\iota) = \mathcal{FP}(\iota)$$

Proof. As the inclusion "$\supseteq$" is a consequence of the Safety Theorem 6.3.1, we are left with the inclusion "$\subseteq$". According to Theorem 6.3.2 we prove the equivalent formula

$$\forall \iota \in \mathcal{I}_{\mathbf{FP}}(\Pi) \ \forall \pi \in pp^k[\iota]. \ \pi \in \mathcal{FP}(\iota) \tag{6.6}$$

by induction on the number k of executions of the while-loop of Algorithm 6.3.4. Throughout this proof, let M^k denote the value of the variable M after the k-th execution of the while-loop.

The case $k=0$ is trivial according to the initialization of $pp^k[\iota]$, $\iota \in \mathcal{I}_{\mathbf{FP}}(\Pi)$, with $\emptyset$. Thus, let $k > 0$, and consider the k-th execution of the while-loop under the induction hypothesis (IH) that (6.6) holds before the k-th execution of the while-loop. Let ι be the element currently chosen from the workset. Then we have:

$$M^k \quad = \quad pp^{k-1}[\iota] \cup \bigcup \{ pp^{k-1}[ParLst(st)\downarrow_{pos(\iota)}] \mid$$
$$st \in c\text{-}occ_{Stmt(\mathcal{FR}(\Pi))}(\{\kappa \mid decl(\iota) \in pp^{k-1}[\kappa]\}) \}$$

Without loss of generality we can assume that there is a $\pi \in M^k \backslash pp^{k-1}[\iota]$, since otherwise the induction hypothesis (IH) would suffice. This implies that there is a statement $st \in c\text{-}occ_{Stmt(\mathcal{FR}(\Pi))}(\kappa')$ for some $\kappa' \in \mathcal{I}_{\mathbf{P}}(\Pi)$ with $decl(\iota) \in pp^{k-1}[\kappa']$, and $CalledProc(st) = \kappa'$.
Moreover, we have $ParLst(st)\downarrow_{pos(\iota)} = \kappa''$, and $\pi \in pp^{k-1}[\kappa'']$. Since Π is a program with mode depth 2, property (6.1) yields $\kappa' \in \mathcal{I}_{\mathbf{OP}}(\Pi)$. This directly delivers $\kappa' = decl(\iota)$, and therefore $CalledProc(st) = decl(\iota)$. Next we must investigate two cases. First, if $\kappa'' \in \mathcal{I}_{\mathbf{OP}}(\Pi)$, we obtain $\kappa'' = \pi$, and therefore $ParLst(st)\downarrow_{pos(\iota)} = \pi$. Hence, $\pi \in \mathcal{FP}(\iota)$ is a consequence of $st \in c\text{-}occ_{Stmt(\mathcal{FR}(\Pi))}(decl(\iota))$. Second, if $\kappa'' \in \mathcal{I}_{\mathbf{FP}}(\Pi)$, the induction hypothesis (IH) yields $\pi \in \mathcal{FP}(\kappa'')$ because of $\pi \in pp^{k-1}[\kappa'']$. According to Definition 6.2.1, there is a program $\Pi' \in T_\Pi^{stat}$, which contains in the main part of the innermost generated block a statement st' with $CalledProc(st') = decl(\kappa'')$, and $ParLst(st')\downarrow_{pos(\kappa'')} = \pi$. Let Π'' be the successor of Π' in T_Π^{stat}, which results from applying the copy rule to the call statement st' in Π'. Since Π is a program without global formal procedure parameters, the main part of the innermost generated block of Π'' contains a copy st'' of st, in which κ'' is replaced by π, i.e., $CalledProc(st'') = decl(\iota)$, and $ParLst(st'')\downarrow_{pos(\iota)} = \pi$. Thus, Definition 6.2.1 yields $\pi \in \mathcal{FP}(\iota)$, which completes the proof of Theorem 6.4.1. $\qquad\square$

Combining Theorem 6.2.3 and Theorem 6.4.1 we directly obtain that potential passability and formal callability coincide for programs of mode depth 2 without global formal procedure parameters:

Corollary 6.4.1 ($Prog_{fm(2),ugfpp}$-$\mathcal{FC}$-**Precision**).

$$\forall \Pi \in Prog_{fm(2),ugfpp}(\forall \iota \in \mathcal{I}_{\mathbf{FP}}(\Pi).c\text{-}occ_{\mathcal{FR}(\Pi)}(\iota) \neq \emptyset).\mathcal{PP}_{\mathcal{FR}(\Pi)}(\iota) = \mathcal{FC}(\iota)$$

6.4.2 Complexity

The costs of our HO-DFA are the added up costs of computing a safe approximation of formal reachability information, and the costs of computing potential passability accordingly to this information by means of Algorithm 6.3.4. The complexity of the first step depends above all on the degree of precision desired for the approximation. In order to illustrate the range of the complexity of this step, recall that formal reachability is undecidable in general, and P-space hard for finite mode languages [Ar3, La1, Wi2], but that it is always safely approximated by the set of procedures occurring in a program. The complexity of the second step is given by the complexity of Algorithm 6.3.4. Given its input, a program $\Pi \in Prog$, and a safe approximation of formal reachability information, the worst-case time complexity of this algorithm can essentially be estimated by

$$O(|\mathcal{I}_{\mathbf{OP}}(\Pi)| + |\mathcal{I}_{\mathbf{FP}}(\Pi)| * |\mathcal{I}_{\mathbf{P}}(\Pi)|)$$

which reflects the worst-case number of occurrences of procedure identifiers on the workset before Algorithm 6.3.4 terminates. Thus, we have:

Theorem 6.4.2 (ComputationalComplexity of PotentialPassability).
Given a program $\Pi \in Prog$, and a safe approximation of formal reachability information, potential passability is computable in quadratic time.

It is important that for programs of $Prog_{fm(2),ugfpp}$ the proposition of Theorem 6.4.2 can considerably be strengthened. The point here is that formal reachability is decidable in quadratic time for programs with mode depth 2 and a limit on the length of parameter lists by solving a reachability problem in a graph with $|\Pi|$ nodes, and $|Stmt_{call}(\Pi)|$ edges as shown in [Ar3]. Combining this result with Theorem 6.4.1 and Theorem 6.4.2, we obtain:

Theorem 6.4.3 ($Prog_{fm(2),ugfpp}$-Complexity).
For all programs $\Pi \in Prog_{fm(2),ugfpp}$, formal callability is decidable in quadratic time, if there is a limit on the length of parameter lists.

For practical applications, the limit required on the length of parameter lists can be considered harmless. Thus, the results of this section can be summarized as follows. Potential passability is

1. a correct (safe) approximation of formal callability,
2. is efficiently computable for all programs $\Pi \in Prog$, and
3. is precise for formal callability for programs of $Prog_{fm(2),ugfpp}$.

As a consequence, we obtain the following corollary on Wirth's Pascal (cf. [Wth, HW]):

Corollary 6.4.2 (Wirth's Pascal).
Formal callability is decidable in quadratic time for programs of Wirth's Pascal without global formal procedure parameters, if there is a limit on the length of parameter lists.

7. The Interprocedural Setting

In this chapter we complete the setting of our framework for interprocedural program optimization. We first introduce *flow graph systems* and *interprocedural flow graphs* as program representations, and subsequently, describe the interface connecting HO-DFA and IDFA. Central is then the extension of the two-step scheme of optimal intraprocedural program optimization to the interprocedural setting. It turns out that this scheme applies naturally to the interprocedural setting, too. One should note, however, that in contrast to the data flow analyses the transformations based thereon usually require additional care.

7.1 Flow Graph Systems

As usual in interprocedural program optimization we represent a *Prog*-program $\Pi = \langle \pi_{\bar{\omega}_0}, \pi_{\bar{\omega}_1}, \ldots, \pi_{\bar{\omega}_k} \rangle$ by means of a *flow graph system* $S = \langle G_{\bar{\omega}_0}, G_{\bar{\omega}_1}, \ldots, G_{\bar{\omega}_k} \rangle$, $\bar{\omega}_j \in \mathbb{N}^*$. S is a system of *flow graphs* with disjoint sets of nodes and edges, where every procedure π of Π is represented as a *directed flow graph* $G = (N, E, \mathbf{s}, \mathbf{e})$ in the sense of Section 2.1.1. Nodes $n \in N_i$ represent the statements and edges $(n, m) \in E_i$ the nondeterministic (intraprocedural) branching structure of the underlying procedure π_i. In our setting, the nodes represent *parallel assignments* and *procedure calls*. We assume that the fictitious procedure π_0, which stands for the (unspecified) external procedures occurring in the environment of Π (cf. Section 5.3), is represented by the flow graph $G_{\bar{\omega}_0} = (N_0, E_0, \mathbf{s}_0, \mathbf{e}_0)$ with node set $N_0 =_{df} \{\mathbf{s}_0, n_0, \mathbf{e}_0\}$ and edge set $E_0 =_{df} \{(\mathbf{s}_0, n_0), (n_0, \mathbf{e}_0)\}$. External variables and external procedure calls occurring in Π are considered local variables and ordinary procedure calls of G_0. Moreover, $\mathbf{N}^S =_{df} \bigcup\{N_{\bar{\omega}_i} \mid i \in \{0, \ldots, k\}\}$ and $\mathbf{E}^S =_{df} \bigcup\{E_{\bar{\omega}_i} \mid i \in \{0, \ldots, k\}\}$ denote the sets of all nodes and edges of S. Additionally, $\mathbf{N}^S_{oc}$ and $\mathbf{N}^S_{fc}$ denote the sets of ordinary and formal procedure call nodes, and $\mathbf{N}^S_c =_{df} \mathbf{N}^S_{oc} \cup \mathbf{N}^S_{fc}$ the set of all procedure call nodes of S.

Figure 7.1 shows an illustrating flow graph system using the convention that a procedure with name π, formal value parameters $f_1, \ldots, f_q$, formal reference parameters $z_1, \ldots, z_r$, formal procedure parameters $\phi_1, \ldots, \phi_s$, and

J. Knoop: Optimal Interprocedural Program Optimization, LNCS 1428, pp. 99-108, 1998.
© Springer-Verlag Berlin Heidelberg 1998

local variables $v_1, \ldots, v_u$ is denoted by $\pi(f_1, \ldots, f_q : z_1, \ldots, z_r : \phi_1, \ldots, \phi_s) :$ $v_1, \ldots, v_u$.

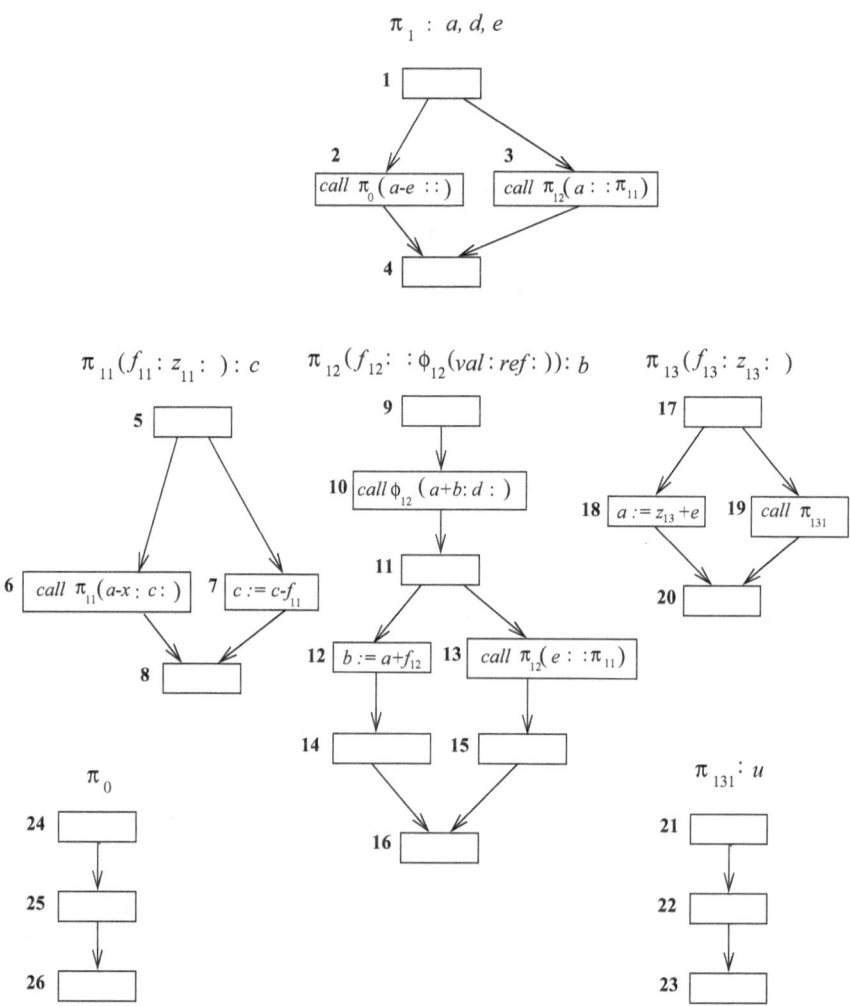

Fig. 7.1. Flow graph system

7.1.1 The Functions *fg*, *callee*, *caller*, *start*, and *end*

For every flow graph system S we define the functions *fg*, *callee*, *caller*, *start*, and *end*. Intuitively, *fg* maps every node of S to the flow graph it is contained in, *callee* maps every procedure call node to the set of procedures it may call, *caller* maps every procedure to the set of call nodes, from which it

may be called, and *start* and *end* map every flow graph to its start node and
end node, respectively. We remark that in the definition of *callee* call nodes
of S are identified with the corresponding call statements of the program Π
underlying S. Thus, *CalledProc*(n), $n \in \mathbf{N}_c^S$, denotes the identifier of the
called procedure.

Concerning the definition of the function *callee*, recall that $\mathcal{FR}_{App}(\Pi) \neq \emptyset$
$\emptyset$ because we always have $\Pi \in \mathcal{FR}_{App}(\Pi)$. Moreover, we recall that formal
reachability is decidable for finite mode languages, and decidable in quadratic
time for programs of mode depth 2 and a limit on the length of parameter
lists (cf. [Ar3]).

---

1. $fg : \mathbf{N}^S \to S$ with $fg(n)=_{df} G_{\bar{\omega}_i}$ iff $n \in N_{\bar{\omega}_i}$
2. $callee : \mathbf{N}_c^S \to \mathcal{P}(S)$ with
$$callee(n)=_{df} \begin{cases} \mathcal{PP}_A(CalledProc(n)) & \text{if } CalledProc(n) \neq G_0 \\ \{G_0\} & \text{otherwise} \end{cases}$$
   where $A \in \mathcal{FR}_{App}(\Pi)$ is assumed to be a correct (safe) approxima-
   tion (i.e., a superset) of the set of formally reachable procedures of
   Π.
3. $caller : S \to \mathcal{P}(\mathbf{N}_c^S)$ with $caller(G_{\bar{\omega}_j})=_{df} \{ n \mid G_{\bar{\omega}_j} \in callee(n) \}$.
4. $start : S \to \{\mathbf{s}_{\bar{\omega}_0}, \ldots, \mathbf{s}_{\bar{\omega}_k}\}$ with $start(G_{\bar{\omega}_j})=_{df} \mathbf{s}_{\bar{\omega}_j}$
$$\text{for all } j \in \{0, \ldots, k\}$$
5. $end : S \to \{\mathbf{e}_{\bar{\omega}_0}, \ldots, \mathbf{e}_{\bar{\omega}_k}\}$ with $end(G_{\bar{\omega}_j})=_{df} \mathbf{e}_{\bar{\omega}_j}$
$$\text{for all } j \in \{0, \ldots, k\}.$$

7.1.2 The Interface Between HO-DFA and IDFA

In this section we present the interface between HO-DFA and IDFA. It is
given by the function *callee*, which imports the results of the HO-DFA, and
allows us to feed them into the subsequent IDFA. It is thus the connecting link
between HO-DFA and IDFA. Technically, it gives us the handle for treating
formal procedure calls as nondeterministic higher-order branch statements
during IDFA (cf. Definition 8.3.2). In Section 7.2 this will be made explicit
by constructing the interprocedural flow graph of a flow graph system (cf.
Algorithm 7.2.1).

7.2 Interprocedural Flow Graphs

In contrast to the intraprocedural control flow, a flow graph system S does
not explicitly represent the interprocedural control flow caused by procedure
calls. As usual, this is achieved by combining the flow graphs of S to an
interprocedural flow graph $G^* = (N^*, E^*, \mathbf{s}^*, \mathbf{e}^*)$, whose start and end node
$\mathbf{s}^*$ and $\mathbf{e}^*$ are given by the start and end node $\mathbf{s}_1$ and $\mathbf{e}_1$ of the main

procedure of the underlying program, respectively (cf. [My, SP]). For every flow graph system S, the interprocedural flow graph G^* corresponding to S is then constructed by means of the three-step procedure of Algorithm 7.2.1, which is applied to all procedure call nodes of S. Note that this algorithm replaces every formal procedure call by a set of ordinary procedure calls, which is given by the set of procedures which are potentially passable to the formal call under consideration.

Algorithm 7.2.1 (Constructing the Interprocedural Flow Graph).
Let S be a flow graph system, and let $\{x_1, \ldots, x_s\}$ be the set of external variables occurring in S. Then, for every procedure call node $n \in \mathbf{N}_c^S$, do:

1. Replace n by a set of nodes containing for every identifier $\iota \in callee(n)$ a pair of new nodes, the *call node* $n_C(\iota)$ and the *return node* $n_R(\iota)$, where $n_C(\iota)$ has the same set of predecessors as n but no successors, and $n_R(\iota)$ has the same set of successors as n but no predecessors.
2. Attach $n_C(\iota)$ with the assignment

$$\begin{cases} (f_1, \ldots, f_q, z_1, \ldots, z_r, v_1, \ldots, v_u) := (t_1, \ldots, t_q, y_1, \ldots, y_r, \Lambda, \ldots, \Lambda) \\ \qquad\qquad\qquad\qquad\qquad\qquad\qquad\qquad\qquad\qquad \text{if } \iota \neq G_0 \\ (f_{01}, \ldots, f_{0q}, z_{01}, \ldots, z_{0r}) := (t_1, \ldots, t_q, y_1, \ldots, y_r) \\ \qquad\qquad\qquad\qquad\qquad\qquad\qquad\qquad\qquad\qquad\quad \text{otherwise} \end{cases}$$

and $n_R(\iota)$ with the assignment

$$\begin{cases} (f_1, \ldots, f_q, z_1, \ldots, z_r, v_1, \ldots, v_u) := (\Lambda, \ldots, \Lambda) & \text{if } \iota \neq G_0 \\ (x_1, \ldots, x_s\}) := (\Lambda, \ldots, \Lambda) & \text{otherwise} \end{cases}$$

where $t_1, \ldots, t_q$ and $y_1, \ldots, y_r$ are the value and reference parameter arguments of n, where $f_1, \ldots, f_q, z_1, \ldots, z_r, v_1, \ldots, v_u$ are the formal parameters and local variables of the called procedure ι for $\iota \neq G_0$, where $f_{01}, \ldots, f_{0q}, z_{01}, \ldots, z_{0r}$ are new identifiers, which are not occurring in Π, for $\iota = G_0$, and where "Λ" denotes the special value "undefined".
3. For every identifier $\iota \in callee(n)$, add an edge from $n_C(\iota)$ to $start(decl(\iota))$, and from $end(decl(\iota))$ to $n_R(\iota)$.

In the following, we denote the sets of *call nodes* and *return nodes* of N^* by N_c^* and N_r^*, respectively. Moreover, we denote the sets of immediate interprocedural predecessors and successors of n by $pred^*(n) =_{df} \{ m \mid (m, n) \in E^* \}$ and $succ^*(n) =_{df} \{ m \mid (n, m) \in E^* \}$, respectively.

Figure 7.2 shows the interprocedural flow graph, which corresponds to the flow graph system of Figure 7.1. For clarity, edges starting in nodes of N_c^* and N_r^* are displayed by dashed and dotted lines, respectively.

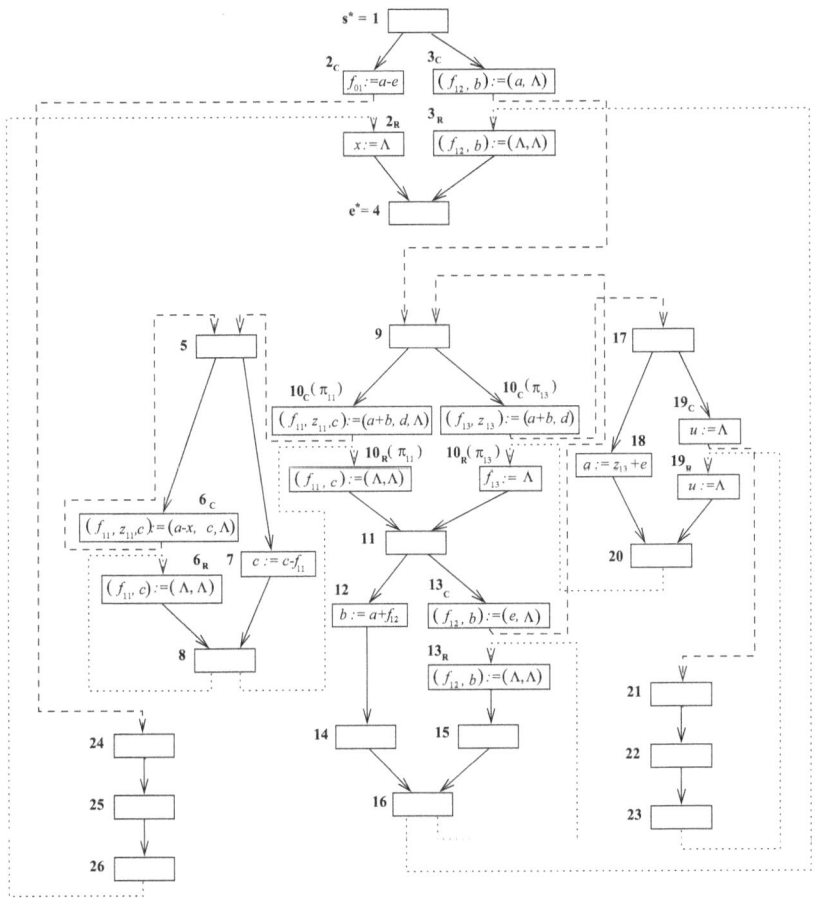

Fig. 7.2. The interprocedural flow graph

7.2.1 Interprocedural Paths

The notion of a finite path introduced in Section 2.1.1 applies to interprocedural flow graphs as well. However, in contrast to the intraprocedural setting, not every finite path of an interprocedural flow graph represents a valid execution. This is because of the special nature of procedure calls: for example, in Figure 7.2 the path $(1, 3_C, 9, 10_C, 5, 7, 8, 10_R)$ is possible, while the path $(1, 3_C, 9, 10_C, 5, 7, 8, 6_R)$ is not. This leads to the notion of interprocedural (or interprocedurally valid) paths, which was originally introduced by Sharir and Pnueli by means of an algorithmic definition (cf. [SP]). Below we present a definition in terms of words of context-free languages, which was also suggested by Sharir and Pnueli, however, without giving details.

Definition 7.2.2 (Path Grammar and Path Language).
Let G^* be an interprocedural flow graph.

1. *The* interprocedural path grammar $\mathcal{G}(G^*)$ *of G^* is the triple (V, T, P), where*
   a) $V =_{df} \{ V_n \mid n \in N^* \}$ *denotes the set of* non-terminal symbols,
   b) $T =_{df} N^*$ *the set of* terminal symbols, *and*
   c) $P =_{df} \{ V_n \to n\, V_m \mid n \notin \{\mathbf{e}_0, \ldots, \mathbf{e}_k\} \wedge m \in succ^*(n) \backslash N_c^* \} \cup$
      $\{ V_n \to n\, V_{m_C(\iota)}\, V_{m_R(\iota)} \mid m_{C(\iota)} \in succ^*(n) \cap N_c^* \} \cup$
      $\{ V_{\mathbf{e}} \to \mathbf{e} \mid \mathbf{e} \in \{\mathbf{e}_0, \ldots, \mathbf{e}_k\} \}$ *the set of context-free* production
      rules.

2. *The* path language *induced by a node $n \in N^* \backslash N_r^*$ is defined by:*

$$\mathcal{L}_n(\mathcal{G}(G^*)) =_{df} \{ p \in T^* \mid \exists q \in (V \cup T)^*.\ V_n \xrightarrow{\;*\;} q \wedge p \text{ is a prefix of } q \}$$

Denoting the set of all finite paths from m to n in an interprocedural flow graph G^* by $\mathbf{P}[m, n]$, we can now define:

Definition 7.2.3 (Interprocedural Paths).
Let G^* be an interprocedural flow graph.

1. *A path $p \in \mathbf{P}[m, n]$ is an* interprocedural path *of G^* if and only if $p \in \mathcal{L}_m(\mathcal{G}(G^*))$.*
2. $\mathbf{IP}[m, n]$ *denotes the set of all* interprocedural paths *from m to n, $\mathbf{IP}[m, n[$ the set of all interprocedural paths from m to a predecessor of n, and $\mathbf{IP}]m, n]$ the set of all interprocedural paths from a successor of m to n.*
3. *An interprocedural path reaching the end node of G^* is called* terminating.

Additionally, we introduce the notion of matching call and return nodes, which simplifies argumentations on interprocedural paths.

Definition 7.2.4 (Matching Call and Return Nodes).
Let G^* be an interprocedural flow graph, and let p be an interprocedural path of G^*. Two occurrences of a call node and a return node on p are called to match *each other, if the corresponding occurrences of their non-terminals in a derivation of a word $q \in \mathcal{L}_m(\mathcal{G}(G^*))$, of which p is a prefix, result from the same application of a production rule of $\mathcal{G}(G^*)$.*

7.2.2 Complete Interprocedural Paths

In addition to interprocedural paths, we need the notion of complete interprocedural paths, which are important for determining the semantics of procedure calls. Complete interprocedural paths are interprocedural paths p from $start(fg(n))$ to n, which are characterized by the fact that all procedure calls occurring on p are completed by a subsequent return. This guarantees that the occurrences of $start(fg(n))$ and n belong to the same procedure incarnation.

Definition 7.2.5 (Complete Interprocedural Paths).

1. *An interprocedural path* $p \in \mathbf{IP}[start(fg(n)), n]$ *is called* complete *if it possesses equally many occurrences of procedure call and return nodes:*

$$| \{i \mid p_i \in N_c^*\} | \ = \ | \{i \mid p_i \in N_r^*\} |$$

2. $\mathbf{CIP}[start(fg(n)), n]$ *and* $\mathbf{CIP}[start(fg(n)), n[$ *denote the set of all complete interprocedural paths from* $start(fg(n))$ *to* n, *and from* $start(fg(n))$ *to a predecessor of* n, *respectively.*

The following property of interprocedural paths expresses that the definition above actually realizes the desired intention. Essentially, this is a consequence of the form of the context-free production rules of $\mathcal{G}(G^*)$.

Lemma 7.2.1. *Let* $p \in \mathbf{IP}[m, n]$ *be an interprocedural path, and let* (p_i, p_j) *and* $(p_{i'}, p_{j'})$ *be two pairs of matching call and return nodes of* p. *Then the integer intervals* $[i : j]$ *and* $[i' : j']$ *are either disjoint or one is included in the other.*

Figure 7.3 illustrates the pattern stated in Lemma 7.2.1, where $\{(n_{C_i}, n_{R_i}) \mid i \in \{1, \ldots, 4\}\}$ are assumed to be pairs of matching call nodes and return nodes of $p \in \mathbf{IP}[m, n]$.

$$p = (m, \ldots, n_{C_1}, \ldots, n_{C_2}, \ldots, n_{R_2}, \ldots, n_{C_3}, \ldots, n_{C_4}, \ldots, n_{R_4}, \ldots, n_{R_3}, \ldots, n_{R_1}, \ldots, n)$$

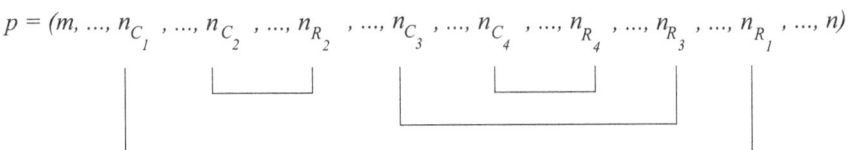

Fig. 7.3. Complete interprocedural paths

The following lemma characterizes another property of matching call and return nodes, which can easily be proved, too.

Lemma 7.2.2. *Let* $s \in \{s_0, \ldots, s_k\}$, *let* $p \in \mathbf{IP}[s, n]$ *and let* (p_i, p_j) *be a pair of matching call and return nodes. Then we have:*

$$p]i, j[\in \mathbf{CIP}[start(callee(p_i)), end(callee(p_i))]$$

Remark 7.2.1. If the underlying program Π consists of a single procedure π only, the flow graph system S and the interprocedural flow graph G^* collapse to the flow graph G of π. In this case the interprocedural framework coincides with the standard framework for intraprocedural optimization of Chapter 2.

Conventions. In the following we restrict our attention to programs of *Prog*, which satisfy the sfmr-property. We recall that this property is decidable for *Prog* [Ka]. In particular, it holds for all programs without static procedure nesting or without formal procedure calls. Additionally, we assume that programs containing formal procedure calls have been analyzed by means of the HO-DFA of Chapter 6. Thus, we have potential passability information for it.

For every program Π satisfying this premise, we denote the flow graph system and the interprocedural flow graph representing Π by S and G^*. Without loss of generality we assume that every node $n \in N^*$ lies on an interprocedural path from s^* to e^*. We denote the call nodes and return nodes of G^* corresponding to a procedure call node $n \in \mathbf{N}_c^S$ of S by $n_C(\iota)$ and $n_R(\iota)$, respectively, where $\iota \in callee(n)$. For ordinary procedure call nodes $n \in \mathbf{N}_{oc}^S$ of S, we usually omit the explicit addition of ι because the procedure called by n is uniquely determined. Conversely, for every call node or return node $n \in N_c^* \cup N_r^*$ of G^* we denote the corresponding procedure call node of S by n_S. Additionally, we identify the set $\mathbf{N}^S$ of nodes of S with the set $N^* \backslash N_r^*$ of nodes of G^* in order to obtain an interpretation independent notion of program point. In particular, we identify every node $n \in \mathbf{N}_{fc}^S$ with the set of nodes $\{n_C(\iota) \mid \iota \in callee(n)\}$. This allows us not only concise notations, e.g.,

$$\forall n \in \mathbf{N}_c^S \; \forall p \in \bigcup \{\mathbf{IP}[s^*, n_C(\iota)[\; \mid \; \iota \in callee(n)\}$$

can be abbreviated by

$$\forall n \in \mathbf{N}_c^S \; \forall p \in \mathbf{IP}[s^*, n[,$$

it is also the key for handling backward analyses in our framework by forward analyses simply by inverting the flow of control (cf. Section 8.7).

7.3 Interprocedural Program Optimization

In this section we can now extend the two-step approach of optimal intraprocedural program optimization to the interprocedural setting. As in the intraprocedural case, we are interested in program transformations, which are provably optimal with respect to *formal optimality criteria*. The central contribution of this section is to demonstrate that *optimal* interprocedural program optimization can be organized by the same two-step approach as its intraprocedural counterpart. In the first step, we fix a class of interprocedural program transformations $\mathcal{T}$, and a formal optimality criterion $\mathcal{O}$. In the second step, we fix a transformation $Tr_{opt} \in \mathcal{T}$, and prove that it is $\mathcal{O}$-optimal. Like intraprocedural optimizations, also interprocedural ones are usually defined in terms of appropriate program properties φ, whose validity must be verified in order to perform the transformation Tr_{opt} under consideration. This is the task of interprocedural DFA (IDFA). As in the intraprocedural setting, the program properties involved must be computed precisely (or at least conservatively, i.e., safely, approximated) by the IDFA in order to guarantee that the transformation induced by its results is $\mathcal{O}$-optimal. This leads us to the notion of φ-*precise* (φ-*correct*) IDFA-algorithms.

In Section 7.3.1 we present the two-step scheme of optimal interprocedural program optimization, and subsequently, we introduce in Section 7.3.2 the notion of precise (correct) IDFA-algorithms.

7.3.1 Provably Optimal Interprocedural Program Transformations

Let S be a flow graph system, let $\mathcal{T}$ be a class of interprocedural program transformations, let $Tr \in \mathcal{T}$ be a transformation of $\mathcal{T}$, and let S_{Tr} denote the flow graph system resulting from the application of Tr to S. Additionally, let $S_{\mathcal{T}} =_{df} \{ S \} \cup \{ S_{Tr} \mid Tr \in \mathcal{T} \}$ denote the set of all programs resulting from a transformation of $\mathcal{T}$ extended by S itself. Following the lines of Section 2.1.2, optimal interprocedural program optimization proceeds along the following two-step procedure:

Step 1: Fix a class of interprocedural program transformations $\mathcal{T}$ and a relation $\leq_{\mathcal{T}} \subseteq S_{\mathcal{T}} \times S_{\mathcal{T}}$.

Intuitively, the relation $\leq_{\mathcal{T}}$ compares the "quality" of transformations $Tr, Tr' \in \mathcal{T}$. It is usually given by a quasi-order or a partial order, and $S_{Tr} \leq_{\mathcal{T}} S_{Tr'}$ can informally be read as "Tr is *better* than Tr'". This induces the interprocedural version of $\mathcal{O}_{\leq_{\mathcal{T}}}$-optimality:

Definition 7.3.1 ($\mathcal{O}_{\leq_{\mathcal{T}}}$-Optimality).
A transformation $Tr \in \mathcal{T}$ is $\mathcal{O}_{\leq_{\mathcal{T}}}$-optimal, if for all $Tr' \in \mathcal{T}$ holds:
$S_{Tr} \leq_{\mathcal{T}} S_{Tr'}$

Step 2: Fix a transformation $Tr_{opt} \in \mathcal{T}$ and prove that it is $\mathcal{O}_{\leq_{\mathcal{T}}}$-optimal.

Note that the two-step scheme above evolves from its intraprocedural counter-part just by replacing the flow graph G, which represents a single procedure of the argument program Π, by the flow graph system S, which represents all its procedures. This analogy can be continued. In particular, the inter-procedural transformations $Tr \in \mathcal{T}$ are also typically defined in terms of a set of program properties Φ, where every $\varphi \in \Phi$ is a pair $(N\text{-}\varphi, X\text{-}\varphi)$ of functions from the set of nodes of S to the set of Boolean truth values $\mathcal{B}$, i.e.,

$$N\text{-}\varphi, X\text{-}\varphi : \mathbf{N}^S \to \mathcal{B}$$

Though in the interprocedural setting the definition of a property φ is usu-ally more complex than in the intraprocedural setting because the effects of procedure calls must be taken into account, the underlying intuition is the same: $N\text{-}\varphi(n)$ and $X\text{-}\varphi(n)$, $n \in \mathbf{N}^S$, indicate whether φ holds at the entry and at the exit of the argument node n, respectively.

Finally, it is worth noting that proving the $\mathcal{O}_{\leq_T}$-optimality of an inter-procedural transformation $Tr_{opt} \in \mathcal{T}$ does not rely on the algorithms used for computing the program properties involved in Tr_{opt}. In fact, this can separately be proved, which structures and simplifies the overall proof like in the intraprocedural case by decomposing it into two independent steps.

7.3.2 Provably Precise Interprocedural Data Flow Analyses

In the context of our two-step approach for optimal interprocedural pro-gram optimization the task of IDFA is to compute the program properties φ, which are involved in the program transformation Tr_{opt}. As in the in-traprocedural case, this requires static analyses of S, which are performed by IDFA-algorithms computing the sets of program points enjoying the program properties φ. This leads directly to the notions of correctness and precision of an IDFA-algorithm. Intuitively, an IDFA-algorithm is φ-correct, if it com-putes a subset of nodes of S enjoying φ, and it is φ-precise, if it computes this set precisely.[1] Once the IDFA-algorithms have been proved precise for the program properties involved in Tr_{opt}, it is usually easy to perform the transformation itself, and the program resulting from this transformation is guaranteed to be $\mathcal{O}_{\leq_T}$-optimal.[2] In the following chapter we will show, how to construct correct and precise IDFA-algorithms. Central will be the stack-based framework for *interprocedural abstract interpretation* of [KS1].

---

[1] φ-correctness and φ-precision are formally defined in Section 8.6.
[2] ϕ-correctness is usually not sufficient to draw this conclusion.

8. Interprocedural Abstract Interpretation

In this chapter we extend the theory of abstract interpretation interprocedurally. The point of this extension, which proceeds essentially along the lines of [KS1], is to mimic the operational behaviour of run-time systems of Algol-like programming languages. Central is the introduction of *data flow analysis stacks* (*DFA-stacks*) and *return functions*. DFA-stacks can be considered the compile-time equivalent of run-time stacks of run-time systems. While the DFA-information of interest is encoded as intraprocedurally by the elements of a lattice, the local semantic functions defining the abstract semantics of elementary statements are enhanced. Interprocedurally, they work on DFA-stacks composed of lattice elements instead of lattice elements only. Return functions, finally, mimic the effect of a return from a (recursive) procedure call on the run-time stack. In comparison to the presentation of [KS1], the development is enhanced in order to handle formal procedure calls and external procedures.

8.1 Data Flow Analysis Stacks

Considering a program with recursive procedures and local variables it is important to note that there are potentially infinitely many copies of the local variables at run-time. In fact, every procedure call occurring in a run-time execution causes the creation of a new copy of the local variables of the procedure called, which are removed after finishing the call. Finishing a recursive call it is important that the local variables of the enclosing, but not yet finished procedure call of the same procedure become valid ("visible") again. Technically, a run-time system achieves this by maintaining a run-time stack recording the part of the history which will become relevant after returning from nested procedure calls. These effects must properly be modeled by an interprocedural abstract interpretation. In essence, this requires to work on stacks composed of lattice elements instead of the lattice elements only, which are assumed to represent the DFA-information of interest. This gives rise to introduce the set of DFA-stacks $STACK$ as the compile-time equivalent of run-time stacks. $STACK$ is the set of all non-empty stacks with entries of $\mathcal{C}$. Like run-time stacks, DFA-stacks record the part of the history which will become relevant after returning from nested procedure calls. They directly

J. Knoop: Optimal Interprocedural Program Optimization, LNCS 1428, pp. 109-140, 1998.
© Springer-Verlag Berlin Heidelberg 1998

reflect the nesting of procedure incarnations according to the current call sequence. We remark that DFA-stacks can be manipulated by means of the typical stack-operations:[1]

$$
\begin{array}{ll}
1. & newstack : \mathcal{C} \to STACK \\
2. & push : STACK \times \mathcal{C} \to STACK \\
3. & pop : STACK \to STACK \\
4. & top : STACK \to \mathcal{C}
\end{array}
$$

Intuitively, $newstack(c)$ creates a new stack with single entry c, $push$ puts a new entry on top of the argument stack, pop removes the top entry, and top delivers the content of the top entry, while not affecting the argument stack.[2] Thus, only the top entries of the stacks can be affected by these operations. As we will see below, this is sufficient for our purposes.

As indicated above, DFA-stacks are an abstract version of the run-time stacks of run-time systems, which are used for maintaining the activation records of different procedure incarnations. Intuitively, the top entry of a DFA-stack contains the data flow information corresponding to the currently valid activation record,[3] while the data flow informations of the remaining stack entries correspond to activation records of preceding but not yet finished procedure calls. In contrast to a concrete run-time stack, however, whose entries are organized by means of static and dynamic link chains, and where variables being global for the currently activated procedure are accessed by means of the static link chain, the entries of a DFA-stack are assumed to contain all the information concerning the current procedure incarnation, i.e., also the information related to global variables. The usual static and dynamic link chains are just a technical means for enhancing the efficiency of run-time systems. In our abstract framework DFA-stacks of potentially unlimited size occur only in the interprocedural meet over all paths approach. This approach, however, is only conceptually important in order to define the specifying solution of an IDFA-problem. In the practically relevant interprocedural maximal fixed point approach only DFA-stacks of at most two entries arise (cf. Remark 8.3.1). This allows us to omit modeling link chains. Moreover, this also allows us to work with local semantic functions, which only affect the top entries of DFA-stacks.

---

[1] A definition of (DFA-) stacks in terms of an abstract data type can be found e.g. in [Gu].

[2] The operation $newstack$ instead of the usual $emptystack : \to STACK$ is considered here in order to exclude empty stacks, which are irrelevant in our framework.

[3] Therefore, we are never dealing with empty stacks.

8.2 Local Abstract Semantics

Basically, the local abstract semantics of an interprocedural flow graph G^* is given by a local semantic functional

$$[\![\ ]\!]' : N^* \to (\mathcal{C} \to \mathcal{C})$$

as in the intraprocedural case. It gives meaning to every node n of G^* in terms of a transformation on $\mathcal{C}$. Without loss of generality we assume that every node $n \in \{\, start(G), end(G) \mid G \in S \,\}$ is associated with the identity on $\mathcal{C}$, i.e., $[\![\, n \,]\!]' = Id_{\mathcal{C}}$. Moreover, we assume that the node n_0 of G_0 representing the fictitious procedure π_0 of the underlying program Π, is associated with the least element of the set of functions on $\mathcal{C}$, denoted by $[\mathcal{C} \to \mathcal{C}]$, i.e., $[\![\, n_0 \,]\!]' = \bot_{[\mathcal{C} \to \mathcal{C}]}$, where $\bot_{[\mathcal{C} \to \mathcal{C}]}(c) =_{df} \bot$ for all $c \in \mathcal{C}$. Intuitively, this means that we do not assume anything about the external procedures occurring in the environment of Π. Note that the effects of variable aliasing caused by reference parameters are not explicitly treated at this stage. At the current level of detail, they are encoded in the semantic functions defined above. They must be made explicit only, when considering a concrete application (cf. [KRS4]).

Next we define a second semantic functional, which works on DFA-stacks. It is induced by a lattice $\mathcal{C}$, a local semantic functional $[\![\ ]\!]'$, and a *return functional* $\mathcal{R} : N_r^* \to (\mathcal{C} \times \mathcal{C} \to \mathcal{C})$, which is described below, and, intuitively, models the effect of returning from a procedure call:

$$[\![\ ]\!]^* : N^* \to (STACK \to STACK)$$

This functional is defined as follows:

$$\forall n \in N^* \ \forall stk \in STACK. [\![\, n \,]\!]^*(stk) =_{df}$$

$$\begin{cases} push(\ pop(stk),\ [\![\, n \,]\!]'(top(stk))\ ) & \text{if } n \in N^* \backslash (N_c^* \cup N_r^*) \\ push(\ stk,\ [\![\, n \,]\!]'(top(stk))\ ) & \text{if } n \in N_c^* \\ push(\ pop(pop(stk)),\ \mathcal{R}(n)(\ top(pop(stk)),\ [\![\, n \,]\!]'(top(stk)))\ ) & \\ & \text{if } n \in N_r^* \end{cases}$$

The intuition behind its definition is as follows:

The execution of an ordinary statement (i.e., $n \in N^* \backslash (N_c^* \cup N_r^*)$) affects only the currently valid activation record. Thus, it can be modeled by simply modifying the top entry of the stack representing the current data flow information.

A procedure call (i.e., $n \in N_c^*$) requires the generation of a new activation record. This is reflected by pushing a new element on the top of the stack, which results from modifying the top entry of the stack according to the parameter transfer.

The treatment of return statements (i.e., $n \in N_r^*$) demonstrates the necessity of introducing stacks into the framework. Returning from a procedure call (i.e., $n \in N_r^*$) requires to remove the activation record belonging to the called procedure and to reactivate its predecessor. Thereby the following observation is important. The effect of a (directly) recursive procedure to a global variable needs to be maintained, whereas the local variables must be reset to their values at call time. Thus we need to consider the data flow information valid immediately before entering the procedure (available in $top(pop(stk))$), as well as the information valid after executing its body (available in $[\![n]\!]'(top(stk))$), in order to compute the data flow information that is valid after returning from the called procedure. The function $\mathcal{R}(n) : \mathcal{C} \times \mathcal{C} \to \mathcal{C}$ models this computation. Thus, popping the top entry of the stack and replacing the subsequent entry by

$$\mathcal{R}(n)(\ top(pop(stk)),\ [\![n]\!]'(top(stk)))$$

reflects the whole process of completing a procedure call. Note that the functions $[\![n]\!]^*$ for nodes $n \in N_r^*$ are only defined for stacks with at least two components. This fact is automatically taken care of in any reasonable analysis context.

8.2.1 The Structure of the Semantic Functions

Let $\mathcal{F} =_{df} [\ STACK \to STACK\ ]$ denote the set of all functions from $STACK$ to $STACK$, let $STACK_{\geq 2}$ denote the set of all DFA-stacks with at least two entries, and let

$$\mathcal{F}_O =_{df} \{\ f \in \mathcal{F} \mid \forall\, stk \in STACK.\ pop(f(stk)) = pop(stk)\ \}$$

$$\mathcal{F}_C =_{df} \{\ f \in \mathcal{F} \mid \forall\, stk \in STACK.\ pop(f(stk)) = stk\ \}$$

$$\mathcal{F}_R =_{df} \{\ f \in \mathcal{F} \mid \forall\, stk \in STACK_{\geq 2}.\ pop(f(stk)) = pop(pop(stk))\ \}$$

Then we have:

Lemma 8.2.1.

1. $\forall n \in N^* \backslash (N_c^* \cup N_r^*).\ [\![n]\!]^* \in \mathcal{F}_O$
2. $\forall n \in N_c^*.\ [\![n]\!]^* \in \mathcal{F}_C$
3. $\forall n \in N_r^*.\ [\![n]\!]^* \in \mathcal{F}_R$

Intuitively, this means that the semantic function of an ordinary statement only affects the top entry of the argument stack, that the semantic function of a call statement adds a new top entry to the argument stack, and that a return statement replaces the upper two entries of the argument stack by a new component. As a consequence we have the following lemma.

Lemma 8.2.2. $\forall f_r \in \mathcal{F}_R\ \forall f_o, f_o' \in \mathcal{F}_O\ \forall f_c \in \mathcal{F}_C.\ f_o \circ f_o',\ f_r \circ f_o \circ f_c \in \mathcal{F}_O$

Next we introduce derived notions of monotonicity and distributivity for functions on stacks. They are required for the formal development of our framework, and are based on the "significant part" of a function of $\mathcal{F}_O$, $\mathcal{F}_C$ and $\mathcal{F}_R$. Given a function $f \in \mathcal{F}_O \cup \mathcal{F}_C \cup \mathcal{F}_R$, its *significant part* f_s, is defined according to the following two cases:

– $f \in \mathcal{F}_O \cup \mathcal{F}_C$: then $f_s : \mathcal{C} \to \mathcal{C}$ is defined by:

$$f_s(c) =_{df} top(f(newstack(c)))$$

– $f \in \mathcal{F}_R$: then $f_s : \mathcal{C} \times \mathcal{C} \to \mathcal{C}$ is defined by:[4]

$$f_s(c_1, c_2) =_{df} top(f(push(newstack(c_1), c_2)))$$

Now we can define:

Definition 8.2.1 (S-Monotonicity, S-Distributivity).
A function $f \in \mathcal{F}_O \cup \mathcal{F}_C \cup \mathcal{F}_R$ is called

1. s-monotonic *if and only if f_s is monotonic*
2. s-distributive *if and only if f_s is distributive*

Intuitively, the significant part of a local semantic function $[\![\, n \,]\!]^*$ is given by the underlying basic local semantic function $[\![\, n \,]\!]$, and, in case of a return node, by the return function $\mathcal{R}(n)$. Thus, we have:

Lemma 8.2.3. *For all $n \in N^*$ we have that $[\![\, n \,]\!]^*$ is s-monotonic (s-distributive) if*

$n \in N_r^* : \quad [\![\, n \,]\!]'$ *and $\mathcal{R}(n)$ are monotonic (distributive)*

$n \notin N_r^* : \quad [\![\, n \,]\!]'$ *is monotonic (distributive)*

This lemma is important because it shows that the effort for checking the premises of the Interprocedural Correctness Theorem 8.4.1 and the Interprocedural Coincidence Theorem 8.4.2 is comparable to the effort necessary for checking the premises of their intraprocedural counterparts (cf. Section 2.2.4). In fact, only the return functions $\mathcal{R}(n)$, $n \in N_r^*$, must additionally be investigated.

Conventions. In the following we consider s-monotonicity and s-distributivity generalizations of the usual monotonicity and distributivity by identifying lattice elements with their unique representations as one-entry stacks. Moreover, we extend the meet operation $\sqcap$ to work on stacks in the following way:

$$\forall\, STK \subseteq STACK.\ \sqcap STK =_{df}\ newstack(\sqcap\{top(stk)\,|\,stk \in STK\})$$

Thus, the meet over a set of stacks is the one-entry stack containing the meet of all the top entries in its single entry.

---

[4] Note that $\mathcal{C} \times \mathcal{C}$ is a lattice, whenever $\mathcal{C}$ is.

8.3 Global Abstract Semantics

The global abstract semantics of an interprocedural flow graph G^* and its underlying flow graph system S results from the interprocedural extensions of the meet over all paths approach and the maximal fixed point approach, respectively.

8.3.1 The Interprocedural Meet Over All Paths Approach

Like its intraprocedural counterpart, the interprocedural meet over all paths ($IMOP$) solution records the effect of all possible program executions reaching a particular program point. To this end the local abstract semantics $[\![\ ]\!]^*$ must be extended to cover finite interprocedural paths. For every path $p \in \mathbf{IP}[m, n]$, we define $[\![\, p\,]\!]^* : STACK \to STACK$ by

$$[\![\, p\,]\!]^* =_{df} \begin{cases} Id_{STACK} & \text{if } p = \varepsilon \\ [\![\, p[2, \lambda_p]\,]\!]^* \circ [\![\, p_1\,]\!]^* & \text{otherwise} \end{cases}$$

Considering an interprocedural path $p \in \mathbf{IP}[\mathbf{s}^*, n[$ and a DFA-stack $stk \in STACK$, it is important to note that the data flow information, which is relevant for node n after executing p, is given by the element $top([\![\, p\,]\!]^*(stk))$. In fact, all other entries of $[\![\, p\,]\!]^*(stk)$ correspond to activation records which are invisible after p. Identifying one-entry stacks with the content of their single entry, the interprocedural meet over all paths solution is formally defined by:[5]

Definition 8.3.1 (The *IMOP*-Solution).
Given an interprocedural flow graph G^*, a complete semi-lattice $\mathcal{C}$, a local abstract semantics $[\![\ ]\!]'$, and a return functional $\mathcal{R}$, the IMOP-solution is defined by:[6]

$$\forall c_s \in \mathcal{C} \ \forall n \in N^* . IMOP_{([\![\ ]\!]^*, c_s)}(n)$$
$$=_{df} N\text{-}IMOP_{([\![\ ]\!]^*, c_s)}(n), X\text{-}IMOP_{([\![\ ]\!]^*, c_s)}(n))$$

where

$$N\text{-}IMOP_{([\![\ ]\!]^*, c_s)}(n) =_{df} \sqcap \{ [\![\, p\,]\!]^*(newstack(c_s)) \mid p \in \mathbf{IP}[\mathbf{s}^*, n[\}$$
$$X\text{-}IMOP_{([\![\ ]\!]^*, c_s)}(n) =_{df} \sqcap \{ [\![\, p\,]\!]^*(newstack(c_s)) \mid p \in \mathbf{IP}[\mathbf{s}^*, n] \}$$

Identifying a node $n \in \mathbf{N}_c^S$ with the set of nodes $\{ n_C(\iota) \mid \iota \in callee(n) \}$, Definition 8.3.1 yields:

$$N\text{-}IMOP_{([\![\ ]\!]^*, c_s)}(n)$$
$$=_{df} \sqcap \{ [\![\, p\,]\!]^*(newstack(c_s)) \mid p \in \mathbf{IP}[\mathbf{s}^*, n_C(\iota)[\ \wedge \ \iota \in callee(n) \}$$

---

[5] As in the intraprocedural case, "N" and "X" stand for entry and exit of a node n.

[6] Recall that $\mathcal{C}$, $[\![\ ]\!]'$, and $\mathcal{R}$ induce the local semantic functional $[\![\ ]\!]^*$.

$$X\text{-}IMOP_{(\llbracket\ \rrbracket^*,c_s)}(n)$$
$$=_{df} \sqcap \{ \, \llbracket\, p\,\rrbracket^*(newstack(c_s)) \mid p \in \mathbf{IP}[\mathbf{s}^*, n_C(\iota)] \wedge \iota \in callee(n) \, \}$$

This is important for nodes of $\mathbf{N}^S_{fc}$, particularly, when dealing with backward analyses, which are treated essentially by inverting the flow of control in our framework (cf. Section 8.7).

8.3.2 The Interprocedural Maximal Fixed Point Approach

In contrast to a flow graph of Chapter 2, which represents a single procedure without procedure calls, a flow graph system, which represents a complete program with procedures and procedure calls, needs a preprocess for determining the meaning of call nodes in terms of the meaning of the called procedures. This requires the introduction of an auxiliary semantic functional $\llbracket\ \rrbracket$, which gives meaning to whole flow graphs. Intuitively, $\llbracket\, n\,\rrbracket$ transforms data flow information, which is assumed to be valid at the entry of the procedure containing n, into the corresponding data flow information, which is valid before an execution of n. The function $\llbracket\, \mathbf{e}_i\,\rrbracket$ is then the meaning function of the i-th procedure.[7] Formally, the full preprocess for determining the meaning $\llbracket\, n\,\rrbracket$ of call nodes $n \in \mathbf{N}^S_c$ is characterized by:

Definition 8.3.2 (Global Semantics of Flow Graphs).
$\llbracket\ \rrbracket : \mathbf{N}^S \to (STACK \to STACK)$ and $\llbracket\ \rrbracket : \mathbf{N}^S \to (STACK \to STACK)$ are defined as the greatest solution of the equation system given by:

$$\llbracket\, n\,\rrbracket = \begin{cases} Id_{STACK} & \text{if } n \in \{\, \mathbf{s}_0, \ldots, \mathbf{s}_k \,\} \\ \sqcap \{ \llbracket\, m\,\rrbracket \circ \llbracket\, m\,\rrbracket \mid m \in pred_{fg(n)}(n) \} & \text{otherwise} \end{cases}$$

and

$$\llbracket\, n\,\rrbracket = \begin{cases} \llbracket\, n\,\rrbracket^* & \text{if } n \in \mathbf{N}^S \backslash \mathbf{N}^S_c \\ \sqcap \{ \llbracket\, n_R(\iota)\,\rrbracket^* \circ \llbracket\, end(\iota)\,\rrbracket \circ \llbracket\, n_C(\iota)\,\rrbracket^* \mid \iota \in callee(n) \} & \text{otherwise} \end{cases}$$

where Id_{STACK} denotes the identity on $STACK$, and $\sqcap$ the "componentwise" meet operation on $\mathcal{F}_O$.[8]

Intuitively, the semantics of a procedure call node $n \in \mathbf{N}^S_c$ is the meet over the effects of all procedures in $callee(n)$. For a single procedure $\iota \in callee(n)$ the effect of calling ι is computed in three steps, which reflect the three phases of executing ι:

---

[7] Recall that $\llbracket\, \mathbf{e}_i\,\rrbracket' =_{df} Id_C$. Thus, we have: $\llbracket\, \mathbf{e}_i\,\rrbracket \circ \llbracket\, \mathbf{e}_i\,\rrbracket = \llbracket\, \mathbf{e}_i\,\rrbracket$.
[8] $\forall f, f' \in \mathcal{F}_O. f \sqcap f' =_{df} f'' \in \mathcal{F}_O$ with $\forall stk \in STACK. top(f''(stk)) = top(f(stk)) \sqcap top(f'(stk))$. As usual, "$\sqcap$" induces an inclusion relation "$\sqsubseteq$" on $\mathcal{F}_O$ by: $f \sqsubseteq f'$ iff $f \sqcap f' = f$.

- *Entering* the called procedure: $[\![\, n_C(\iota)\,]\!]^*$ creates a new activation record by transforming the content of the top entry of the stack according to the semantics of the call node and by pushing it onto the stack. – Usually, the semantics of call nodes reflects the parameter transfer.
- *Evaluating* the call: $[\![\, end(\iota)\,]\!]$ computes the effect of the procedure body. Note that this affects the top entry of the argument stack only.
- *Leaving* the called procedure: $[\![\, n_R(\iota)\,]\!]^*$ removes the activation record of the current procedure call by popping the top entry from the stack, and replacing its subsequent entry by the data flow information representing the effect of the procedure call relatively to its call site.

Applying Lemma 8.2.2, we obtain:

Lemma 8.3.1. $\forall n \in \mathbf{N}^S. \ [\![\, n \,]\!], \ [\![\, n \,]\!] \in \mathcal{F}_O$

After fixing the meaning of call nodes, the functional $[\![\ ]\!]$ plays essentially the same role as the local (abstract) semantic functional of Section 2.2.3. Formally, the interprocedural maximal fixed point approach is characterized by Equation System 8.3.3. Similar to its intraprocedural counterpart, this approach labels every node n of $\mathbf{N}^S$ with a pre-information $\mathbf{pre}(n)$ and a post-information $\mathbf{post}(n)$, whose top entries are the greatest solution of this equation system with respect to a start information $c_s \in \mathcal{C}$.

Equation System 8.3.3.

$$
\mathbf{pre}(n) \;=\; \begin{cases} newstack(c_s) & \text{if } n = \mathbf{s}_1 \\ \bigsqcap\{\, [\![\, m_C(fg(n))\,]\!]^*(\mathbf{pre}(m)) \mid \\ \quad m \in caller(fg(n))\} & \text{if } n \in \{\mathbf{s}_0, \mathbf{s}_2, \ldots, \mathbf{s}_k\} \\ \bigsqcap\{\, \mathbf{post}(m) \mid m \in pred_{fg(n)}(n)\,\} & \text{otherwise} \end{cases}
$$

$$
\mathbf{post}(n) \;=\; [\![\, n \,]\!](\mathbf{pre}(n))
$$

Identifying stacks with a single entry only with the content of this entry, and denoting the greatest solution of Equation System 8.3.3 with respect to the start information c_s by pre_{c_s} and post_{c_s}, respectively, we define analogously to the intraprocedural case:

Definition 8.3.4 (The *IMFP*-Solution).
Given a flow graph system S, a complete semi-lattice $\mathcal{C}$, a local abstract semantics $[\![\ ]\!]'$, and a return functional $\mathcal{R}$, the IMFP-solution is defined by: [9]

$$\forall c_s \in \mathcal{C} \; \forall n \in \mathbf{N}^S.$$

$$IMFP_{([\![\ ]\!]^*, c_s)}(n) =_{df} (\, N\text{-}IMFP_{([\![\ ]\!]^*, c_s)}(n), \, X\text{-}IMFP_{([\![\ ]\!]^*, c_s)}(n)\,)$$

where

$$N\text{-}IMFP_{([\![\ ]\!]^*, c_s)}(n) =_{df} \mathsf{pre}_{c_s}(n) \qquad and \qquad X\text{-}IMFP_{([\![\ ]\!]^*, c_s)}(n) =_{df} \mathsf{post}_{c_s}(n)$$

---

[9] Recall that $\mathcal{C}$, $[\![\ ]\!]'$, and $\mathcal{R}$ induce the local semantic functional $[\![\ ]\!]^*$.

Remark 8.3.1 (Limited Stack Size in the IMFP-Approach).
Equation System 8.3.3 shows that the *IMFP*-solution is based on a one-entry stack attached to the start node s_1 of the argument program. This is important because together with Lemma 8.3.1, this guarantees that all stacks occurring during the iterative computation of the *IMFP*-solution have at most two entries (cf. Algorithm 8.5.2). This allows us to prove termination in the usual way. It also dramatically contrasts the *IMOP*-approach defining the specifying solution of an IDFA-problem. The size of DFA-stacks contributing to the *IMOP*-solution is not limited in general.

In analogy to the intraprocedural case, we consider the *IMOP*-approach as a means for the direct specification of an IDFA, and the *IMFP*-approach as its algorithmic realization. Consequently, this rises the questions of correctness and precision, which are answered by means of the Interprocedural Correctness Theorem 8.4.1 and the Interprocedural Coincidence Theorem 8.4.2.

8.4 *IMOP*-Correctness and *IMOP*-Precision

In this section we present the interprocedural versions of the Correctness and the Coincidence Theorem 2.2.1 and 2.2.2. In analogy to their intraprocedural counterparts, the Interprocedural Correctness Theorem 8.4.1 and the Interprocedural Coincidence Theorem 8.4.2 give sufficient conditions for the correctness and the precision of the *IMFP*-solution with respect to the *IMOP*-solution, respectively. Central for proving these theorems is the Main Lemma 8.4.3, which is presented in the following section.

8.4.1 The Main Lemma

Throughout this section we assume that the semantic functions $[\![\ ]\!]^*$, $n \in N^*$, are s-monotonic or s-distributive. Obviously, the composition and the meet of s-monotonic (s-distributive) functions is again s-monotonic (s-distributive). Thus we have:

Lemma 8.4.1. *The semantic functions $[\![\, n\,]\!]$ and $[\![\, n\,]\!]$, $n \in \mathbf{N}^S$, are s-monotonic (s-distributive) iff the semantic functions $[\![\, m\,]\!]^*$, $m \in N^*$, are s-monotonic (s-distributive).*

Next we define for every node n of G^* a mapping $imop_n : STACK \to STACK$ by

$$imop_n =_{df} \begin{cases} Id_{STACK} & \text{if } n \in \{\, s_0^*, \ldots, s_k^* \,\} \\ \sqcap \{\, [\![\, p\,]\!]^* \mid p \in \mathbf{CIP}[start(fg(n)), n[\, \} & \text{otherwise} \end{cases}$$

We have:

Lemma 8.4.2. *For all $n \in \mathbf{N}^S$, we have, if the semantic functions $[\![\, m\,]\!]^*$, $m \in N^*$, are*

1. *s-monotonic:* $[\![\,n\,]\!] \sqsubseteq imop_n$
2. *s-distributive:* $[\![\,n\,]\!] = imop_n$

Proof.   The first part of Lemma 8.4.2, $[\![\,n\,]\!] \sqsubseteq imop_n$, is an immediate consequence of the formula

$$(*) \quad \forall n \in \mathbf{N}^S \ \forall p \in \mathbf{CIP}[start(fg(n)), n[. \ [\![\,n\,]\!] \sqsubseteq [\![\,p\,]\!]^*$$

which we prove by induction on the length k of path p. Paths of length 0 only reach nodes in $\{\mathbf{s}_0, \mathbf{s}_1, \ldots, \mathbf{s}_k\}$ for which $(*)$ is trivial. Moreover, paths of length 0 are the only complete interprocedural paths ending in a node $\mathbf{s} \in \{\mathbf{s}_0, \mathbf{s}_1, \ldots, \mathbf{s}_k\}$. Thus, let $n \in \mathbf{N}^S \backslash \{\mathbf{s}_0, \mathbf{s}_1, \ldots, \mathbf{s}_k\}$ such that there is a path $p \in \mathbf{CIP}[start(fg(n)), n[$ with $0 < \lambda_p \le k$. Then we must show

$$[\![\,p\,]\!]^* \sqsupseteq [\![\,n\,]\!]$$

under the induction hypothesis

(IH) $\forall m \in \mathbf{N}^S \ (\forall q \in \mathbf{CIP}[start(fg(m)), m[. \ 0 \le \lambda_q < k). \ [\![\,q\,]\!]^* \sqsupseteq [\![\,m\,]\!]$

Let $m \in pred^*(n)$ and $p' \in \mathbf{IP}[start(fg(n)), m[$ such that $p = p';(m)$. If $m \in N^*\backslash(N_c^* \cup N_r^*)$, we have $m \notin \mathbf{N}_c^S$, and $p' \in \mathbf{CIP}[start(fg(n)), m[$. Therefore, we obtain as desired:

$$
\begin{aligned}
[\![\,p\,]\!]^* &= [\![\,m\,]\!]^* \circ [\![\,p'\,]\!]^* \\
(m \notin \mathbf{N}_c^S) &= [\![\,m\,]\!] \circ [\![\,p'\,]\!]^* \\
(\text{IH, s-monotonicity}) &\sqsupseteq [\![\,m\,]\!] \circ [\![\,m\,]\!] \\
(\text{Definition 8.3.2 and } n \notin \{\mathbf{s}_0, \mathbf{s}_1, \ldots, \mathbf{s}_k\}) &\sqsupseteq [\![\,n\,]\!]
\end{aligned}
$$

On the other hand, $m \in N_c^*$ cannot occur because this would imply $n \in \{\mathbf{s}_0, \mathbf{s}_1, \ldots, \mathbf{s}_k\}$ in contradiction to the choice of n. Thus we are left with the case $m \in N_r^*$, which is problematic because here m is not the predecessor of n in $\mathbf{N}^S$, rather it is the return node $\bar{m}_R(\iota)$ for some node $\bar{m} \in pred_{fg(n)}(n)$ with $\iota \in callee(\bar{m})$. This situation, which does not allow the direct application of the induction hypothesis, can be pictured as follows:

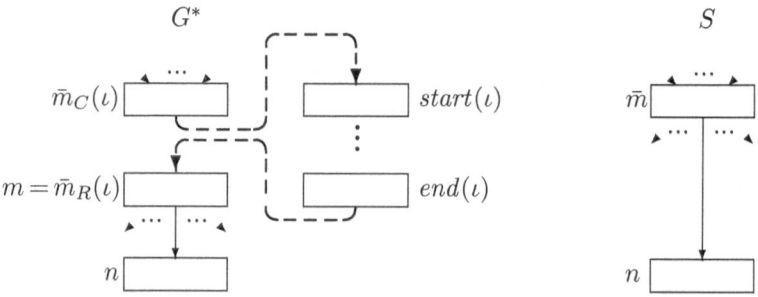

Figure 8.4.1.

Identifying in the situation of Figure 8.4.1 the nodes $\bar{m}_C(\iota)$ and $\bar{m}$ and considering the decomposition of path p with

$$p = \bar{p}; (\bar{m}_C(\iota)); (start(\iota)), \ldots, end(\iota)); (\bar{m}_R(\iota))$$

we obtain by means of Lemma 7.2.2

$$\bar{p} \in \mathbf{CIP}[start(fg(n)), \bar{m}[$$

and

$$(start(\iota), \ldots, end(\iota)) \in \mathbf{CIP}[start(\iota), end(\iota)]$$

The first inclusion can therefore be completed by:[10]

$$
\begin{array}{lll}
[\![\,p\,]\!]^* & = & [\![\,\bar{m}_R(\iota)\,]\!]^* \circ [\![\,(start(\iota), \ldots, end(\iota))\,]\!]^* \circ [\![\,\bar{m}_C(\iota)\,]\!]^* \circ [\![\,\bar{p}\,]\!]^* \\
\text{(IH, s-mon.)} & \sqsupseteq & [\![\,\bar{m}_R(\iota)\,]\!]^* \circ [\![\,end(\iota)\,]\!] \circ [\![\,\bar{m}_C(\iota)\,]\!]^* \circ [\![\,\bar{p}\,]\!]^* \\
\text{(Def. 8.3.2)} & \sqsupseteq & [\![\,\bar{m}\,]\!] \circ [\![\,\bar{p}\,]\!]^* \\
\text{(IH, s-mon.)} & \sqsupseteq & [\![\,\bar{m}\,]\!] \circ [\![\,\bar{m}\,]\!] \\
\text{(Def. 8.3.2)} & \sqsupseteq & [\![\,n\,]\!]
\end{array}
$$

In order to prove the second part of Lemma 8.4.2, we anticipate Algorithm 8.5.1 and Theorem 8.5.1. This, however, does not cause any subleties as they are independent of the results of Section 8.4. The second part of Lemma 8.4.2, $[\![\,n\,]\!] \sqsupseteq imop_n$, is then a consequence of

$$(**) \quad \forall k \geq 0 \, \forall n \in \mathbf{N}^S. \ (1) \ imop_n \sqsubseteq gtr^k[n] \text{ and } (2) \ [\![\,n\,]\!] \sqsubseteq ltr^k[n]$$

which is proved by (simultaneous) induction on the number k of times the while-loop in Algorithm 8.5.1 is executed.[11]

The induction base is an immediate consequence of the initialization part of the algorithm. Thus let $k>0$, and let us consider the k-th iteration of the while-loop under the induction hypothesis (IH) that $(**)$ holds before the k-th execution of the while-loop. To show (1), we only need to consider the node $n \in \mathbf{N}^S$, which belongs to the workset entry (n, f) being processed in the k-th iteration because the gtr-information associated with all the other nodes remains unchanged in this iteration and therefore satisfies $(**)$ according to (IH).

If $n \equiv \mathbf{s} \in \{\mathbf{s}_0, \ldots, \mathbf{s}_k\}$, we have $f = Id_{STACK}$, since

$$\{(\mathbf{s}, Id_{STACK}) \mid \mathbf{s} \in \{\mathbf{s}_0, \ldots, \mathbf{s}_k\}\}$$

is initially a subset of the workset and nodes in $\{\mathbf{s}_0, \ldots, \mathbf{s}_k\}$ are never added again to the workset. Thus, we have as desired

$$imop_\mathbf{s} = Id_{STACK} = gtr^k[\mathbf{s}]$$

---

[10] Remember that $[\![\,end(\iota)\,]\!] = Id_{STACK}$.

[11] We remark that $ltr^k[n]$ and $gtr^k[n]$ denote the values of $ltr[n]$ and $gtr[n]$ after the k-th execution of the while-loop of Algorithm 8.5.1, respectively.

This leaves us with the case $n \in \mathbf{N}^S \setminus \{\mathbf{s}_0, \ldots, \mathbf{s}_k\}$. Thus there exists $m \in \mathbf{N}^S$ and $k > l \geq 0$ such that the pair

$$(n, f) = (n, ltr^l[m] \circ gtr^l[m])$$

was added in the l-th iteration to the workset.[12] This allows us to deduce $imop_n \sqsubseteq f$ by investigating the following two cases:

Case 1. $m \notin \mathbf{N}_c^S$
Here we have:

$$
\begin{array}{lcl}
imop_n & = & \sqcap\{ [\![p]\!]^* \mid p \in \mathbf{CIP}[start(fg(n)), n[\} \\
(m \notin \mathbf{N}_c^S) & \sqsubseteq & \sqcap\{ [\![m]\!]^* \circ [\![p]\!]^* \mid p \in \mathbf{CIP}[start(fg(n)), m[\} \\
\text{(s-distributivity)} & = & [\![m]\!]^* \circ \sqcap\{ [\![p]\!]^* \mid p \in \mathbf{CIP}[start(fg(n)), m[\} \\
\text{(Def. } imop_m) & = & [\![m]\!]^* \circ imop_m \\
\text{(IH, s-monotonicity)} & \sqsubseteq & [\![m]\!]^* \circ gtr^l[m] \\
(m \notin \mathbf{N}_c^S) & = & ltr^l[m] \circ gtr^l[m] \;=\; f
\end{array}
$$

Case 2. $m \in \mathbf{N}_c^S$
In this case we obtain by means of the s-distributivity and the s-monotonicity:[13]

$$
\begin{array}{lcl}
imop_n & = & \sqcap\{ [\![p]\!]^* \mid p \in \mathbf{CIP}[start(fg(n)), n[\} \\
(m \in \mathbf{N}_c^S) & \sqsubseteq & \sqcap\{ [\![m_R(\iota)]\!]^* \circ [\![p']\!]^* \circ [\![m_C(\iota)]\!]^* \circ [\![p]\!]^* \\
& & \quad \mid \iota \in callee(m),\, p' \in \mathbf{CIP}[start(\iota), end(\iota)], \\
& & \quad\quad p \in \mathbf{CIP}[start(fg(m)), m[\} \\
\text{(IH)} & \sqsubseteq & \sqcap\{ [\![m_R(\iota)]\!]^* \circ gtr^l[end(\iota)] \circ [\![m_C(\iota)]\!]^* \circ gtr^l[m] \\
& & \quad \mid \iota \in callee(m) \} \\
\text{(Prop. 8.5.1(3))} & = & ltr^l[m] \circ gtr^l[m] \;=\; f
\end{array}
$$

Thus, in both cases we uniformly have $imop_n \sqsubseteq f$. Together with the induction hypothesis this yields inclusion

(1) $imop_n \sqsubseteq gtr^{k-1}[n] \sqcap f = gtr^k[n]$.

Also the remaining inclusion

(2) $[\![n']\!] \sqsubseteq ltr^k[n'],\ n' \in \mathbf{N}^S$

requires the investigation of two cases depending on the nature of the node $n \in \mathbf{N}^S$ being processed in the k-th iteration.

Case 1. $n \notin \{\mathbf{e}_0, \ldots, \mathbf{e}_k\}$. This guarantees that ltr remains unchanged in the k-th iteration of the while-loop. Thus $[\![n']\!] \sqsubseteq ltr^k[n'],\ n' \in \mathbf{N}^S$, is a direct consequence of the induction hypothesis.

---

[12] $l = 0$ means that (n, f) was added during the initialization of the workset.
[13] Recall that $[\![\mathbf{e}]\!] = Id_{STACK}$ for all nodes $\mathbf{e} \in \{\mathbf{e}_0, \ldots, \mathbf{e}_k\}$.

Case 2. $n \in \{\mathbf{e}_0, \ldots, \mathbf{e}_k\}$. In this case we have

$$ltr^k[l] = \begin{cases} ltr^{k-1}[l] \sqcap [\![l_R(fg(n))]\!]^* \circ gtr^k[n] \circ [\![l_C(fg(n))]\!]^* & \text{if } l \in caller(fg(n)) \\ ltr^{k-1}[l] & \text{otherwise} \end{cases}$$

Thus $[\![n']\!] \sqsubseteq ltr^k[n']$ is a direct consequence of the previously proved inclusion $imop_n \sqsubseteq gtr^k[n]$, Definition 8.3.2, and the induction hypothesis.

$\square$

By means of Lemma 8.4.2 we can now prove the Main Lemma 8.4.3, which is central for proving the Interprocedural Correctness Theorem 8.4.1 and the Interprocedural Coincidence Theorem 8.4.2 (cf. Section 8.4.2 and 8.4.3). In fact, by means of the Main Lemma 8.4.3 their proofs proceed straightforward almost as in the intraprocedural case (cf. [Ki1, Ki2]).

Lemma 8.4.3 (The Main Lemma).
For all $n \in \mathbf{N}_c^S$, we have, if the semantic functions $[\![m]\!]^*$, $m \in N^*$, are

1. *s-monotonic:* $[\![n]\!] \sqsubseteq \sqcap\{ [\![p]\!]^* \mid \iota \in callee(n), \ p \in \mathbf{CIP}[n_C(\iota), n_R(\iota)] \}$
2. *s-distributive:* $[\![n]\!] = \sqcap\{ [\![p]\!]^* \mid \iota \in callee(n), \ p \in \mathbf{CIP}[n_C(\iota), n_R(\iota)] \}$

Proof. Let $n \in \mathbf{N}_c^S$. The first part of Lemma 8.4.3 follows from the subsequent sequence of inequations:

$$\sqcap\{ [\![p]\!]^* \mid \iota \in callee(n), \ p \in \mathbf{CIP}[n_C(\iota), n_R(\iota)] \}$$
$$= \sqcap\{ \sqcap\{ [\![p]\!]^* \mid p \in \mathbf{CIP}[n_C(\iota), n_R(\iota)] \} \mid \iota \in callee(n) \}$$
$$\text{(s-mon.)} \quad \sqsupseteq \sqcap\{ [\![n_R(\iota)]\!]^* \circ \sqcap\{ [\![p]\!]^* \mid p \in \mathbf{CIP}[start(\iota), end(\iota)] \} \circ [\![n_C(\iota)]\!]^*$$
$$\mid \iota \in callee(n) \}$$
$$\text{(L. 8.4.2(1))} \quad \sqsupseteq \sqcap\{ [\![n_R(\iota)]\!]^* \circ [\![end(\iota)]\!] \circ [\![n_C(\iota)]\!]^* \mid \iota \in callee(n) \}$$
$$\text{(Def. 8.3.2)} \quad = [\![n]\!]$$

The second part of Lemma 8.4.3 can be proved analogously:

$$\sqcap\{ [\![p]\!]^* \mid \iota \in callee(n), \ p \in \mathbf{CIP}[n_C(\iota), n_R(\iota)] \}$$
$$= \sqcap\{ \sqcap\{ [\![p]\!]^* \mid p \in \mathbf{CIP}[n_C(\iota), n_R(\iota)] \} \mid \iota \in callee(n) \}$$
$$\text{(s-distr.)} \quad = \sqcap\{ [\![n_R(\iota)]\!]^* \circ \sqcap\{ [\![p]\!]^* \mid p \in \mathbf{CIP}[start(\iota), end(\iota)] \} \circ [\![n_C(\iota)]\!]^*$$
$$\mid \iota \in callee(n) \}$$
$$\text{(L. 8.4.2(2))} \quad = \sqcap\{ [\![n_R(\iota)]\!]^* \circ [\![end(\iota)]\!] \circ [\![n_C(\iota)]\!]^* \mid \iota \in callee(n) \}$$
$$\text{(Def. 8.3.2)} \quad = [\![n]\!]$$

$\square$

8.4.2 The Interprocedural Correctness Theorem

Similar to its intraprocedural counterpart, the *IMFP*-solution is a correct approximation of the *IMOP*-solution, whenever all the local abstract semantic functions are s-monotonic:

Theorem 8.4.1 (Interprocedural Corrrectness Theorem).
Given a flow graph system $S = \langle G_0, G_1, \ldots, G_k \rangle$ *and its derived interprocedural flow graph* $G^* = (N^*, E^*, \mathbf{s}^*, \mathbf{e}^*)$, *the IMFP-solution is a correct approximation of the IMOP-solution, i.e.,*

$$\forall c_s \in \mathcal{C} \; \forall n \in \mathbf{N}^S. \; \mathit{IMFP}_{(\llbracket \; \rrbracket^*, c_s)}(n) \sqsubseteq \mathit{IMOP}_{(\llbracket \; \rrbracket^*, c_s)}(n)$$

if all the semantic functions $\llbracket n \rrbracket^*$, $n \in N^*$, *are s-monotonic.*

Proof. In order to prove Theorem 8.4.1, it is sufficient to prove for all $c_s \in \mathcal{C}$
and $n \in \mathbf{N}^S$ the inclusion

$$N\text{-}\mathit{IMFP}_{(\llbracket \; \rrbracket^*, c_s)}(n) \sqsubseteq N\text{-}\mathit{IMOP}_{(\llbracket \; \rrbracket^*, c_s)}(n) \tag{8.1}$$

because the validity of the second inclusion

$$X\text{-}\mathit{IMFP}_{(\llbracket \; \rrbracket^*, c_s)}(n) \sqsubseteq X\text{-}\mathit{IMOP}_{(\llbracket \; \rrbracket^*, c_s)}(n) \tag{8.2}$$

follows immediately from (8.1), Definition 8.3.2, Equation System 8.3.3, and
the Main Lemma 8.4.3(1).
Throughout the proof we abbreviate $N\text{-}\mathit{IMFP}_{(\llbracket \; \rrbracket^*, c_s)}$ by $N\text{-}\mathit{IMFP}_{c_s}$, and
prove (8.1) by equivalently showing for all $c_s \in \mathcal{C}$:

$(*)$ $\quad \forall n \in \mathbf{N}^S \; \forall p \in \mathbf{IP}[\mathbf{s}^*, n[. \; N\text{-}\mathit{IMFP}_{c_s}(n) \sqsubseteq \llbracket p \rrbracket^*(newstack(c_s))$

Formula $(*)$ is now proved by induction on the length k of path p. The case
$k = 0$ follows from the sequence of equations

$$\llbracket p \rrbracket^*(newstack(c_s)) \; = \; \llbracket \varepsilon \rrbracket^*(newstack(c_s)) \; = \; newstack(c_s) \; = \; \mathsf{pre}_{c_s}(\mathbf{s}_1)$$

Hence, let $k > 0$ and assume that $(*)$ holds for all paths q with $\lambda_q < k$, i.e.,

(IH) $\forall n \in \mathbf{N}^S (\forall q \in \mathbf{IP}[\mathbf{s}^*, n[. \, 0 \leq \lambda_q < k). N\text{-}\mathit{IMFP}_{c_s}(n) \sqsubseteq \llbracket q \rrbracket^*(newstack(c_s))$

Now, given a node $n \in \mathbf{N}^S$, it is sufficient to show for each path $p \in \mathbf{IP}[\mathbf{s}^*, n[$
with $\lambda_p = k$:

$$N\text{-}\mathit{IMFP}_{c_s}(n) \sqsubseteq \llbracket p \rrbracket^*(newstack(c_s))$$

Without loss of generality, we can thus assume that there is such a path p,
which obviously can be rewritten as $p = p'; (m)$ for some $m \in pred^*(n)$ and
$p' \in \mathbf{IP}[\mathbf{s}^*, m[$. Moreover, for $m \notin N_r^*$ we have by induction hypothesis

$$N\text{-}\mathit{IMFP}_{c_s}(m) \sqsubseteq \llbracket p' \rrbracket^*(newstack(c_s))$$

We are now left with the investigation of three cases in order to complete the
proof of formula $(*)$.

Case 1. $m \in N^* \backslash (N_c^* \cup N_r^*)$
In this case we succeed straightforward by considering the following inclusions
resulting from Equation System 8.3.3:

$$
\begin{aligned}
N\text{-}IMFP_{c_s}(n) &= \bigsqcap \{\, \mathsf{post}_{c_s}(l) \mid l \in pred_{fg(n)}(n) \,\} \\
(m \in pred_{fg(n)}(n)) &\sqsubseteq \mathsf{post}_{c_s}(m) \\
(m \notin \mathbf{N}_c^S) &= [\![\, m \,]\!]^*(N\text{-}IMFP_{c_s}(m)) \\
\text{(IH, s-monotonicity)} &\sqsubseteq [\![\, m \,]\!]^*([\![\, p' \,]\!]^*(newstack(c_s))) \\
(p = p';(m)) &= [\![\, p \,]\!]^*(newstack(c_s))
\end{aligned}
$$

Case 2. $m \in N_c^*$

In this case we have $n \in \{s_0, \ldots, s_k\}$, and the existence of a node $\bar{m} \in \mathbf{N}_c^S$ corresponding to $m = \bar{m}_C(fg(n))$ in S. Thus we obtain as above:

$$
\begin{aligned}
N\text{-}IMFP_{c_s}(n) &= \bigsqcap \{\, [\![\, l_C(fg(n)) \,]\!]^*(\mathsf{pre}_{c_s}(l)) \mid l \in caller(fg(n)) \} \\
(\bar{m} \in caller(fg(n)) &\sqsubseteq [\![\, \bar{m}_C(fg(n)) \,]\!]^*(\mathsf{pre}_{c_s}(\bar{m})) \\
&= [\![\, \bar{m}_C(fg(n)) \,]\!]^*(N\text{-}IMFP_{c_s}(\bar{m})) \\
\text{(IH, s-monotonicity)} &\sqsubseteq [\![\, \bar{m}_C(fg(n)) \,]\!]^*([\![\, p' \,]\!]^*(newstack(c_s))) \\
(p = p';(m)) &= [\![\, p \,]\!]^*(newstack(c_s))
\end{aligned}
$$

Case 3. $m \in N_r^*$

Here, there exists a predecessor $\bar{m} \in \mathbf{N}_c^S$ of n in S corresponding to m, i.e., $\bar{m}_R(fg(m)) = m$. Considering now the following decomposition of path p

$$
p = \bar{p}; (\bar{m}_C(fg(m)); (start(fg(m)), \ldots, end(fg(m))); (\bar{m}_R(fg(m)))
$$

and identifying $\bar{m}$ and $\bar{m}_C(fg(m))$, the induction hypothesis yields:[14]

$$
N\text{-}IMFP_{c_s}(\bar{m}_C(fg(m))) \sqsubseteq [\![\, \bar{p} \,]\!]^*(newstack(c_s))
$$

Thus, together with Equation System 8.3.3 we obtain as desired:

$$
\begin{aligned}
N\text{-}IMFP_{c_s}(n) &= \bigsqcap \{\, \mathsf{post}_{c_s}(l) \mid l \in pred_{fg(n)}(n) \,\} \\
(\bar{m} \in pred_{fg(n)}(n)) &\sqsubseteq \mathsf{post}_{c_s}(\bar{m}) \\
&= [\![\, \bar{m} \,]\!](N\text{-}IMFP_{c_s}(\bar{m}_C(fg(m)))) \\
\text{(IH, s-monot.)} &\sqsubseteq [\![\, \bar{m} \,]\!]([\![\, \bar{p} \,]\!]^*(newstack(c_s))) \\
\text{(M.L. 8.4.3(1))} &\sqsubseteq \bigsqcap \{\, [\![\, p' \,]\!]^*([\![\, \bar{p} \,]\!]^*(newstack(c_s))) \mid \\
&\qquad\qquad p' \in \mathbf{CIP}[\bar{m}_C(fg(m)), \bar{m}_R(fg(m))] \,\} \\
\text{(Lemma 7.2.2)} &\sqsubseteq [\![\, \bar{m}_R(fg(m)) \,]\!]^*([\![\, (start(fg(m)), \ldots, end(fg(m))) \,]\!]^* \\
&\qquad ([\![\, \bar{m}_C(fg(m)) \,]\!]^*([\![\, \bar{p} \,]\!]^*(newstack(c_s)))))
\end{aligned}
$$

This completes the proof of the Intraprocedural Correctness Theorem 8.4.1.
□

8.4.3 The Interprocedural Coincidence Theorem

Like its intraprocedural counterpart, the *IMFP*-solution is precise for the *IMOP*-solution, whenever the local abstract semantic functions are s-distributive:

---

[14] The situation is illustrated in Figure 8.4.1.

Theorem 8.4.2 (Interprocedural Coincidence Theorem).
Given a flow graph system $S = \langle G_0, G_1, \ldots, G_k \rangle$ *and its derived interprocedural flow graph* $G^* = (N^*, E^*, \mathbf{s}^*, \mathbf{e}^*)$, *the IMFP-solution is precise for the IMOP-solution, i.e.,*

$$\forall c_s \in \mathcal{C} \ \forall n \in \mathbf{N}^S. \ \mathit{IMFP}_{(\llbracket\ \rrbracket^*, c_s)}(n) = \mathit{IMOP}_{(\llbracket\ \rrbracket^*, c_s)}(n)$$

if all the semantic functions $\llbracket\, n \,\rrbracket^*$, $n \in N^*$, *are s-distributive.*

Proof. The first inclusion, " $\sqsubseteq$ ", is a consequence of the Interprocedural Correctness Theorem 8.4.1. In order to prove the second inclusion, " $\sqsupseteq$ ", we have to show for all $c_s \in \mathcal{C}$ and $n \in \mathbf{N}^S$ the following two inclusions:

$$N\text{-}\mathit{IMFP}_{(\llbracket\ \rrbracket^*, c_s)}(n) \sqsupseteq N\text{-}\mathit{IMOP}_{(\llbracket\ \rrbracket^*, c_s)}(n) \tag{8.3}$$

$$X\text{-}\mathit{IMFP}_{(\llbracket\ \rrbracket^*, c_s)}(n) \sqsupseteq X\text{-}\mathit{IMOP}_{(\llbracket\ \rrbracket^*, c_s)}(n) \tag{8.4}$$

In order to prove (8.3) and (8.4) we anticipate Algorithm 8.5.2 and Theorem 8.5.2. This does not cause any problems because they do not rely on the results of Section 8.4. Moreover, we abbreviate $N\text{-}\mathit{IMOP}_{(\llbracket\ \rrbracket^*, c_s)}$ and $X\text{-}\mathit{IMOP}_{(\llbracket\ \rrbracket^*, c_s)}(n)$ throughout the proof by $N\text{-}\mathit{IMOP}_{c_s}$ and $X\text{-}\mathit{IMOP}_{c_s}$ in order to simplify the notation. Now (8.3) and (8.4) will be proved by proving by induction on k the equivalent formulas:[15]

$$\forall k \geq 0 \ \forall n \in \mathbf{N}^S. \ N\text{-}\mathit{IMOP}_{c_s}(n) \sqsubseteq pre^k[n] \tag{8.5}$$

$$\forall k \geq 0 \ \forall n \in \mathbf{N}^S. \ X\text{-}\mathit{IMOP}_{c_s}(n) \sqsubseteq post^k[n] \tag{8.6}$$

Actually, it is even sufficient to prove (8.5) because of the following two facts. First, for every node $n \in \mathbf{N}^S$ we have:

$$X\text{-}\mathit{IMOP}_{c_s}(n)$$

(Definition 8.3.1)	$=$	$\bigsqcap \{ \llbracket\, p \,\rrbracket^* (newstack(c_s)) \mid p \in \mathbf{IP}[\mathbf{s}^*, n] \}$
(Def. 8.3.2, M.L. 8.4.3(2))	$=$	$\bigsqcap \{ \llbracket\, n \,\rrbracket (\llbracket\, p \,\rrbracket^* (newstack(c_s))) \mid p \in \mathbf{IP}[\mathbf{s}^*, n[\}$
(Lemma 8.4.1)	$=$	$\llbracket\, n \,\rrbracket (\bigsqcap \{ \llbracket\, p \,\rrbracket^* (newstack(c_s)) \mid p \in \mathbf{IP}[\mathbf{s}^*, n[\})$
(Definition 8.3.1)	$=$	$\llbracket\, n \,\rrbracket (N\text{-}\mathit{IMOP}_{c_s}(n))$

Second, an investigation of Algorithm 8.5.2 yields:

$$\forall k \geq 0 \ \forall n \in \mathbf{N}^S. \ post^k[n] = \llbracket\, n \,\rrbracket (pre^k[n])$$

Combining these facts with the distributivity of the local semantic functions, (8.5) implies (8.6) as desired.

---

[15] We remark that $pre^k[n]$ and $post^k[n]$ denote the values of $pre[n]$ and $post[n]$ after the k-th execution of the while-loop of Algorithm 8.5.2, respectively.

In the proof of (8.5) the case $k = 0$ is trivial according to the initialization of $pre[n]$, $n \in \mathbf{N}^S$, with $newstack(\top)$. Thus let $k > 0$, and let us consider the k-th iteration of the while-loop under the induction hypothesis (IH) that (8.5) holds before the k-th execution of the while-loop. Then we only need to consider the node $n \in \mathbf{N}^S$, which belongs to the workset entry (n, stk) which is processed in the k-th iteration because the information associated with all the other nodes remains unchanged in this iteration and therefore satisfies (8.5) according to the induction hypothesis (IH). If $n = \mathbf{s}_1$, we have $stk = newstack(c_s)$, since $(\mathbf{s}_1, newstack(c_s))$ is initially contained in the workset, and $\mathbf{s}_1$ occurs only once in the workset. In this case we obtain

$$N\text{-}IMOP_{c_s}(\mathbf{s}^*) \sqsubseteq [\![\,\varepsilon\,]\!]^*(newstack(c_s)) \;=\; newstack(c_s) \;=\; pre[\mathbf{s}_1]$$

This leaves us with the case $n \in \mathbf{N}^S \backslash \{\mathbf{s}_1\}$, which yields the existence of a node $m \in \mathbf{N}^S$, whose execution in the l-th iteration caused (n, stk) to be added to the workset. Thus we have:[16]

$$stk \;=\; \begin{cases} [\![\, m_C(fg(n))\,]\!]^*(pre^l[m]) & \text{if } n \in \{\mathbf{s}_0, \mathbf{s}_2, \ldots, \mathbf{s}_k\} \\ [\![\, m\,]\!](pre^l[m]) & \text{otherwise} \end{cases}$$

Now the inclusion $N\text{-}IMOP_{c_s}(n) \sqsubseteq stk$ is proved by investigating three cases:

Case 1. $m \in pred_{fg(n)}(n) \backslash \mathbf{N}_c^S$
Here we succeed straightforward:

$$
\begin{aligned}
N\text{-}IMOP_{c_s}(n) &= \sqcap \{[\![\,p\,]\!]^*(newstack(c_s)) \mid p \in \mathbf{IP}[\mathbf{s}^*, n[\,\} \\
(m \in pred_{fg(n)}(n) \backslash \mathbf{N}_c^S) &\sqsubseteq \sqcap \{[\![\,m\,]\!]^*([\![\,p\,]\!]^*(newstack(c_s))) \mid p \in \mathbf{IP}[\mathbf{s}^*, m[\,\} \\
(\text{s-distributivity}) &= [\![\,m\,]\!]^*(\sqcap\{[\![\,p\,]\!]^*(newstack(c_s)) \mid p \in \mathbf{IP}[\mathbf{s}^*, m[\}) \\
(\text{Definition of } N\text{-}IMOP) &= [\![\,m\,]\!]^*(N\text{-}IMOP_{c_s}(m)) \\
(m \notin \mathbf{N}_c^S) &= [\![\,m\,]\!](N\text{-}IMOP_{c_s}(m)) \\
(\text{IH, s-monotonicity}) &\sqsubseteq [\![\,m\,]\!](pre^l[m]) \;=\; stk
\end{aligned}
$$

Case 2. $m \in pred_{fg(n)}(n) \cap \mathbf{N}_c^S$
Here we obtain as required:

$$
\begin{aligned}
N\text{-}IMOP_{c_s}(n) &= \sqcap\{[\![\,p\,]\!]^*(newstack(c_s)) \mid p \in \mathbf{IP}[\mathbf{s}^*, n[\,\} \\
&\sqsubseteq \sqcap\{[\![\,\bar{p}\,]\!]^*([\![\,p\,]\!]^*(newstack(c_s))) \mid p \in \mathbf{IP}[\mathbf{s}^*, m[\,\wedge \\
&\qquad\qquad \iota \in callee(m),\, \bar{p} \in \mathbf{CIP}[m_C(\iota), m_R(\iota)]\,\} \\
(\text{s-distr.}) &= \sqcap\{[\![\,\bar{p}\,]\!]^*(\sqcap\{[\![\,p\,]\!]^*(newstack(c_s)) \mid p \in \mathbf{IP}[\mathbf{s}^*, m[\})| \\
&\qquad\qquad \iota \in callee(m),\, \bar{p} \in \mathbf{CIP}[m_C(\iota), m_R(\iota)]\,\} \\
(\text{Def. } N\text{-}IMOP) &= \sqcap\{[\![\,\bar{p}\,]\!]^*(N\text{-}IMOP_{c_s}(m))| \\
&\qquad\qquad \iota \in callee(m),\, \bar{p} \in \mathbf{CIP}[m_C(\iota), m_R(\iota)]\} \\
(\text{M.L. 8.4.3(2)}) &= [\![\,m\,]\!](N\text{-}IMOP_{c_s}(m)) \\
(\text{IH, s-mon.}) &\sqsubseteq [\![\,m\,]\!](pre^l[m]) \;=\; stk
\end{aligned}
$$

---

[16] $l = 0$ means that m was processed during the initialization part of Algorithm 8.5.2.

Case 3. $m \notin pred_{fg(n)}(n)$

In this case we have $m \in caller(fg(n))$ and $n \in \{\mathbf{s}_0, \ldots, \mathbf{s}_k\}$. Identifying the nodes m and $m_C(fg(n))$ we obtain as desired:

$$
\begin{aligned}
N\text{-}IMOP_{c_s}(n) \quad &= \quad \sqcap\{[\![\,p\,]\!]^*(newstack(c_s)) \mid p \in \mathbf{IP}[\mathbf{s}^*, n[\,\} \\
&\sqsubseteq \quad \sqcap\{[\![\,m_C(fg(n))\,]\!]^*([\![\,p\,]\!]^*(newstack(c_s))) \mid \\
&\qquad\qquad\qquad p \in \mathbf{IP}[\mathbf{s}^*, m_C(fg(n))[\,\} \\
(\text{s-distr.}) \quad &= \quad [\![\,m_C(fg(n))\,]\!]^*(\sqcap\{[\![\,p\,]\!]^*(newstack(c_s)) \mid \\
&\qquad\qquad\qquad p \in \mathbf{IP}[\mathbf{s}^*, m_C(fg(n))[\,\}) \\
(\text{Def. } N\text{-}IMOP) \quad &= \quad [\![\,m_C(fg(n))\,]\!]^*(N\text{-}IMOP_{c_s}(m)) \\
(\text{IH, s-mon.}) \quad &\sqsubseteq \quad [\![\,m_C(fg(n))\,]\!]^*(pre^l[m]) \quad = \quad stk
\end{aligned}
$$

Thus, together with the induction hypothesis, we uniformly have in all three cases as required:

$$
N\text{-}IMOP_{c_s}(n) \sqsubseteq pre^{k-1}[n] \sqcap stk = pre^k[n]
$$

This completes the proof of the Interprocedural Coincidence Theorem 8.4.2. $\square$

It is worth noting that Lemma 8.2.3 allows us to check the s-monotonicity and s-distributivity of the semantic functions $[\![\,n\,]\!]^*$, which are the premises of the Interprocedural Correctness Theorem 8.4.1 and the Interprocedural Coincidence Theorem 8.4.2, simply by checking these properties for the semantic functions $[\![\,n\,]\!]'$ and the return functions $\mathcal{R}(n)$. Thus, in comparison to the intraprocedural setting the only additional effort arises from checking the return functions, which is important for applying the framework in practice.

8.5 The Interprocedural Generic Fixed Point Algorithms

Like its intraprocedural counterpart, the *IMFP*-approach is practically relevant because it induces an iterative procedure for computing the *IMFP*-solution. Interprocedurally, however, the computation proceeds in two steps. First, a preprocess computing the semantics of procedure call nodes, which is described in Section 8.5.1, and second, the main process computing then essentially as in the intraprocedural case the *IMFP*-solution as described in Section 8.5.2. Section 8.5.3, subsequently, presents an alternative algorithm for the main process, which is more efficient in practice.

8.5.1 Computing the Semantics of Procedures

In this section we present a generic algorithm, which computes the semantics of flow graphs according to Definition 8.3.2.

Algorithm 8.5.1 (Computing the Semantic Functionals $[\![\ ]\!]$ and $[\![\ ]\!]$).

Input: A flow graph system $S = \langle G_0, G_1, \ldots, G_k \rangle$, a complete semi-lattice $\mathcal{C}$, a local semantic functional $[\![\ ]\!]' : N^* \to (\mathcal{C} \to \mathcal{C})$ with $[\![\,n\,]\!]' = Id_{\mathcal{C}}$ for all $n \in \{\, start(G),\, end(G) \mid G \in S \,\}$, and a return functional $\mathcal{R} : N_r^* \to (\mathcal{C} \times \mathcal{C} \to \mathcal{C})$.

Output: An annotation of S with functions $[\![\,n\,]\!] : STACK \to STACK$ (stored in gtr, which stands for *global transformation*), and $[\![\,n\,]\!] : STACK \to STACK$ (stored in ltr, which stands for *local transformation*) representing the greatest solution of the equation system of Definition 8.3.2.

Remark: The lattice $\mathcal{C}$, the semantic functions $[\![\,n\,]\!]'$, $n \in N^*$, and the return functions $\mathcal{R}(n)$, $n \in N_r^*$, induce the local semantic functions $[\![\,n\,]\!]^*$, $n \in N^*$, working on stacks of $\mathcal{C}$. $\top_{\mathcal{F}_O} : STACK \to STACK \in \mathcal{F}_O$ denotes the "universal" function which is assumed to "contain" every function $f \in \mathcal{F}_O$, and Id_{STACK} denotes the identity on $STACK$. The variable *workset* controls the iterative process. Its elements are pairs, whose first components are nodes $m \in \mathbf{N}^S$ of the flow graph system S, and whose second components are functions $f : STACK \to STACK \in \mathcal{F}_O$, which specify a new approximation for the function $[\![\,m\,]\!]$ of the node of the first component. Note that due to the mutual dependence of the definitions of $[\![\ ]\!]$ and $[\![\ ]\!]$ the iterative approximation of $[\![\ ]\!]$ is superposed by an interprocedural iteration step, which updates the semantics $[\![\ ]\!]$ of call nodes.

(Initialization of the annotation arrays gtr and ltr and the variable *workset*)
FORALL $m \in \mathbf{N}^S$ **DO**
    $gtr[m] := \top_{\mathcal{F}_O}$;
    IF $m \in \mathbf{N}_c^S$
        THEN $ltr[m] := \sqcap\{\, [\![\, m_R(\iota)\,]\!]^* \circ \top_{\mathcal{F}_O} \circ [\![\, m_C(\iota)\,]\!]^* \mid \iota \in callee(m) \,\}$
        ELSE $ltr[m] := [\![\, m\,]\!]^*$
    FI
OD;
$workset := \{\, (\mathbf{s}, Id_{STACK}) \mid \mathbf{s} \in \{\mathbf{s}_0, \ldots, \mathbf{s}_k\} \,\} \cup$
        $\{\, (n, f) \mid n \in succ_{fg(m)}(m) \wedge f = ltr[m] \circ gtr[m] \sqsubset \top_{\mathcal{F}_O} \,\}$

(Iterative fixed point computation)
WHILE $workset \neq \emptyset$ **DO**
    LET $(m, f) \in workset$
      BEGIN
        $workset := workset \setminus \{\, (m, f) \,\}$;
        IF $gtr[m] \sqsupset gtr[m] \sqcap f$
          THEN
            $gtr[m] := gtr[m] \sqcap f$;

IF $m \in \{\mathbf{e}_i \,|\, i \in \{0, \ldots, k\}\}$
    THEN
        FORALL $l \in caller(fg(m))$ **DO**
        $ltr[l] := ltr[l] \sqcap [\![\, l_R(fg(m)) \,]\!]^* \circ gtr[m] \circ [\![\, l_C(fg(m)) \,]\!]^*;$
        $workset := workset \cup \{(n, ltr[l] \circ gtr[l]) \,|\, n \in succ_{fg(l)}(l)\}$
        OD
    ELSE
        $workset := workset \cup$
                $\{(n, ltr[m] \circ gtr[m]) \,|\, n \in succ_{fg(m)}(m)\}$
  FI
 FI
END
OD.

In order to formulate the central property of this algorithm, we denote the values of the variables $workset$, $ltr[n]$ and $gtr[n]$ after the k-th execution of the while-loop by $workset^k$, $ltr^k[n]$ and $gtr^k[n]$, respectively. We have:

Proposition 8.5.1. *If the semantic functions* $[\![\, n \,]\!]^*$, $n \in N^*$, *are s-monotonic, we have:*

1. $\forall n \in \mathbf{N}^S \; \forall k \in I\!N. \; ltr^k[n] \in \mathcal{F}_O \wedge gtr^k[n] \in \mathcal{F}_O$
2. $\forall n \in \mathbf{N}^S \; \forall k \in I\!N. \; (ltr^{k+1}[n], gtr^{k+1}[n]) \sqsubseteq (ltr^k[n], gtr^k[n])$
3. $\forall n \in \mathbf{N}^S \; \forall k \in I\!N. \; ltr^k[n] = \begin{cases} \sqcap \{\, [\![\, n_R(\iota) \,]\!] \circ gtr^k[end(\iota)] \circ [\![\, n_C(\iota) \,]\!]^* \,| \\ \qquad \iota \in callee(n) \,\} & \text{if } n \in \mathbf{N}_c^S \\ [\![\, n \,]\!]^* & \text{otherwise} \end{cases}$

The first part of Proposition 8.5.1 is a direct consequence of Lemma 8.2.2. The second part follows from the s-monotonicity of the semantic functions $[\![\, n \,]\!]^*$, $n \in N^*$, and the third part can straightforward be proved by an induction on the number k of iterations of the while-loop of Algorithm 8.5.1 (cf. proof of Theorem 8.5.1). By means of Proposition 8.5.1 we can now prove the central result concerning Algorithm 8.5.1:

Theorem 8.5.1 (Algorithm 8.5.1).
If the semantic functions $[\![\, n \,]\!]^*$, $n \in N^*$, *are s-monotonic, we have:*

1. *If* $[\mathcal{C} \to \mathcal{C}]$ *satisfies the descending chain condition, there is a* $k_0 \in I\!N$ *with*

$$\forall k \geq k_0 \; \forall n \in \mathbf{N}^S. \; (gtr^k[n], ltr^k[n]) = (gtr^{k_0}[n], ltr^{k_0}[n])$$

2. $\forall n \in \mathbf{N}^S. \; ([\![n]\!], [\![n]\!]) = (\sqcap\{gtr^k[n] \,|\, k \geq 0\}, \sqcap\{ltr^k[n] \,|\, k \geq 0\})$

Proof. The first part of Theorem 8.5.1 follows easily by means of Proposition 8.5.1(2). In order to prove the second part, let *fix-gtr* and *fix-ltr* denote an arbitrary solution of the equation system of Definition 8.3.2 for $[\![\ ]\!]$ and $[\ ]$, respectively. Then the central step is to prove the following four invariants of Algorithm 8.5.1, which we simultaneously prove by induction on the number k of iterations of the while-loop:

1. $\forall k \in \mathbb{IN} \ \forall n \in \mathbf{N}^S.\ (\text{fix-gtr}[n], \text{fix-ltr}[n]) \sqsubseteq (\text{gtr}^k[n], \text{ltr}^k[n])$
2. $\forall k \in \mathbb{IN} \ \forall n \in \mathbf{N}^S.\ \text{gtr}^k[n] \sqcap \bigsqcap\{\, f \mid (n, f) \in \text{workset}^k \,\} =$

$$\begin{cases} Id_{STACK} & \text{if } n \in \{s_0, \dots, s_k\} \\ \bigsqcap\{\, \text{ltr}^k[m] \circ \text{gtr}^k[m] \mid m \in \text{pred}_{fg(n)}(n) \,\} & \text{otherwise} \end{cases}$$

3. $\forall k \in \mathbb{IN} \ \forall n \in \mathbf{N}^S.\ \text{ltr}^k[n] =$

$$\begin{cases} \bigsqcap\{\, [\![\, n_R(\iota)\,]\!]^* \circ \text{gtr}^k[\text{end}(\iota)] \circ [\![\, n_C(\iota)\,]\!]^* \mid \iota \in \text{callee}(n) \,\} & \text{if } n \in \mathbf{N}^S_c \\ [\![\, n\,]\!]^* & \text{otherwise} \end{cases}$$

4. $\forall (m, f) \in \text{workset}^k.\ \text{fix-gtr}[m] \sqsubseteq f$

For $k = 0$, we obtain by investigating the initialization part of Algorithm 8.5.1:

(a) $\forall n \in \mathbf{N}^S.\ \text{gtr}^0[n] = \top_{\mathcal{F}_O}$
(b) $\forall n \in \mathbf{N}^S.\ \text{ltr}^0[n] =$
$$\begin{cases} \bigsqcap\{\, [\![\, n_R(\iota)\,]\!]^* \circ \text{gtr}^0[\text{end}(\iota)] \circ [\![\, n_C(\iota)\,]\!]^* \mid \iota \in \text{callee}(n) \,\} & \text{if } n \in \mathbf{N}^S_c \\ [\![\, n\,]\!]^* & \text{otherwise} \end{cases}$$
(c) $\text{workset}^0 = \{\, (\mathbf{s}, Id_{STACK}) \mid \mathbf{s} \in \{s_0, \dots, s_k\} \,\} \cup$
$$\{(n, f) \mid \text{ninsucc}_{fg(m)}(m) \wedge f = \text{ltr}^0[m] \circ \text{gtr}^0[m] \sqsubset \top_{\mathcal{F}_O}\}$$

Hence, invariant (1) is an immediate consequence of (a), (b), and Definition 8.3.2; invariant (2) holds because of (a) and (c); invariant (3) is a consequence of (b), and invariant (4), finally, holds because of (c), Definition 8.3.2, and the choice of fix-gtr.

For the induction step let $k > 0$ and let (m, f) be the element currently chosen from the workset. Obviously, we have:

(d) $\text{gtr}^k[n] = \begin{cases} \text{gtr}^{k-1}[n] \sqcap f & \text{if } n = m \wedge \text{gtr}^{k-1}[n] \sqsupset \text{gtr}^{k-1}[n] \sqcap f \\ \text{gtr}^{k-1}[n] & \text{otherwise} \end{cases}$

(e) $\text{ltr}^k[n] = \begin{cases} \text{ltr}^{k-1}[n] \sqcap [\![\, n_R(fg(m))\,]\!]^* \circ \text{gtr}^k[m] \circ [\![\, n_C(fg(m))\,]\!]^* \\ \qquad \text{if } n \in \text{caller}(fg(m)) \wedge m \in \{\mathbf{e}_0, \dots, \mathbf{e}_k\} \wedge \\ \qquad \text{gtr}^k[m] \sqsubset \text{gtr}^{k-1}[m] \\ \text{ltr}^{k-1}[n] \qquad\qquad\qquad\qquad\qquad\qquad \text{otherwise} \end{cases}$

Moreover, the induction hypothesis yields:

(i) $\forall n \in \mathbf{N}^S.\ (\textit{fix-gtr}[n], \textit{fix-ltr}[n]) \sqsubseteq (gtr^{k-1}[n], ltr^{k-1}[n])$

(ii) $\textit{fix-gtr}[m] \sqsubseteq f$ and

(iii) $\forall n \in \mathbf{N}^S.\ ltr^{k-1}[n] =$

$$\begin{cases} \bigsqcap\{\,[\![\,n_R(\iota)\,]\!]^* \circ gtr^{k-1}[end(\iota)] \circ [\![\,n_C(\iota)\,]\!]^* \mid \iota \in callee(n)\,\} \\ \qquad\qquad\qquad\qquad \text{if } n \in \mathbf{N}^S_c \\ [\![\,n\,]\!]^* \qquad\qquad\qquad\qquad \text{otherwise} \end{cases}$$

Together this directly proves invariants (1) and (3).

During the induction step for the remaining two invariants (2) and (4), we can assume

$$gtr^k[m] = gtr^{k-1}[m] \sqcap f \sqsubseteq gtr^{k-1}[m]$$

because otherwise, they trivially hold by induction hypothesis.

Considering invariant (2) first, the induction step is an immediate consequence of (d) and the induction hypothesis, if $n = m$. On the other hand, if $m \in \{e_0, \ldots, e_k\}$ and $n \in \bigcup\{\,succ_{fg(l)}(l) \mid l \in caller(fg(m))\,\}$, or if $n \in succ_{fg(m)}(m)$, invariant (2) follows from the induction hypothesis and the update of the workset during the $k-th$ iteration of the while-loop. For the remaining nodes invariant (2) is a trivial consequence of the induction hypothesis.

This leaves us with proving the induction step for invariant (4). Here we have to investigate two cases. If $m \notin \{e_0, \ldots, e_k\}$, we have to show

(∗) $\forall n \in succ_{fg(m)}(m).\ \textit{fix-gtr}[n] \sqsubseteq ltr^k[m] \circ gtr^k[m]$

and if $m \in \{e_0, \ldots, e_k\}$, we have to show

(∗∗) $\forall l \in caller(fg(m))\ \forall n \in succ_{fg(l)}(l).\ \textit{fix-gtr}[n] \sqsubseteq ltr^k[l] \circ gtr^k[l]$

According to the choice of $\textit{fix-gtr}$ and $\textit{fix-ltr}$ and Definition 8.3.2, we have in the first case

$$\forall n \in succ_{fg(m)}(m).\ \textit{fix-gtr}[n] \sqsubseteq \textit{fix-ltr}[m] \circ \textit{fix-gtr}[m]$$

and in the second one

$$\forall l \in caller(fg(m))\ \forall n \in succ_{fg(l)}(l).\ \textit{fix-gtr}[n] \sqsubseteq \textit{fix-ltr}[l] \circ \textit{fix-gtr}[l]$$

Thus, (∗) and (∗∗) follow immediately from invariant (1) and the s-monotonicity of all semantic functions. This completes the proof of the remaining invariant (4).

Having now proved all four invariants, the second part of Theorem 8.5.1 is a consequence of Proposition 8.5.1(2), the invariants (1), (2), and (3), and the equations

$$\bigsqcap\{gtr^k[n] \mid k \geq 0\} = \bigsqcap\{f \mid k>0 \wedge (n,f) \in workset^k\}$$

and

$$\sqcap \{ ltr^k[n] \mid k \geq 0 \} =$$

$$\begin{cases} \sqcap \{ [\![n_R(\iota)]\!]^* \circ gtr^k[end(\iota)] \circ [\![n_C(\iota)]\!]^* \mid \iota \in callee(n) \} & \text{if } n \in \mathbf{N}_c^S \\ [\![n]\!]^* & \text{otherwise} \end{cases}$$

which hold due to the commutativity and associativity of $\sqcap$.   □

As a corollary of Theorem 8.5.1 we get:

Corollary 8.5.1 (Algorithm 8.5.1).
If the semantic functions $[\![n]\!]^*$, $n \in N^*$, are s-monotonic, we have:

1. *Algorithm 8.5.1 terminates, if $[\mathcal{C} \to \mathcal{C}]$ satisfies the descending chain condition.*

2. *After the termination of Algorithm 8.5.1 holds:*
   $\forall n \in \mathbf{N}^S. \ ([\![n]\!], [\![n]\!]) \ = \ (gtr[n], ltr[n])$

8.5.2 Computing the *IMFP*-Solution

In this section we present a generic algorithm which computes the *IMFP*-solution. It is based on the output of Algorithm 8.5.1.

Algorithm 8.5.2 (Computing the *IMFP*-Solution).

Input: A flow graph system $S = \langle G_0, G_1, \ldots, G_k \rangle$, a complete semi-lattice $\mathcal{C}$, the local semantic functional $[\![\ ]\!] =_{df} ltr$ with respect to $\mathcal{C}$ (computed by Algorithm 8.5.1), for every node $m \in \mathbf{N}_c^S$ the functions $[\![m_C(\iota)]\!]'$, $\iota \in callee(m)$, and a start information $c_s \in \mathcal{C}$.

Output: An annotation of S with data flow informations, i.e., an annotation with pre-informations (stored in *pre*) and post-informations (stored in *post*) of one-entry stacks which characterize valid data flow information at the entry and at the exit of every node, respectively.

Remark: The lattice $\mathcal{C}$ and the semantic functions $[\![m_C(\iota)]\!]'$ induce the semantic functions $[\![m_C(\iota)]\!]^*$ working on DFA-stacks. *newstack*($\top$) denotes the "universal" data flow information, which is assumed to "contain" every data flow information. The variable *workset* controls the iterative process. Its elements are pairs, whose first components are nodes $m \in \mathbf{N}^S$ of the flow graph system S, and whose second components are elements of *STACK* specifying a new approximation for the pre-information of the node of the first component. Recall that $\mathbf{s}_1$ denotes the start node of the main procedure.

(Initialization of the annotation arrays pre and $post$, and the variable $workset$)
FORALL $m \in \mathbf{N}^S$ **DO**

$\quad (pre[m], post[m]) := (newstack(\top), [\![m]\!](newstack(\top)))$ **OD**;

$workset := \{ (\mathbf{s}_1, newstack(c_s)) \} \cup$

$\qquad\qquad \{ (n, stk) \mid n \in succ_{fg(m)}(m) \wedge stk = post[m] \sqsubset newstack(\top) \} \cup$

$\qquad\qquad \{ (n, stk) \mid m \in \mathbf{N}_c^S \wedge \iota \in callee(m) \wedge n = start(\iota) \wedge$

$\qquad\qquad\qquad stk = [\![m_C(\iota)]\!]^*(pre[m]) \sqsubset newstack(\top) \};$

(Iterative fixed point computation)
WHILE $workset \neq \emptyset$ **DO**

$\quad$ **LET** $(m, stk) \in workset$

$\qquad$ **BEGIN**

$\qquad\quad workset := workset \setminus \{ (m, stk) \};$

$\qquad\quad$ **IF** $pre[m] \sqsupset pre[m] \sqcap stk$

$\qquad\qquad$ **THEN**

$\qquad\qquad\quad pre[m] := pre[m] \sqcap stk;$

$\qquad\qquad\quad post[m] := [\![m]\!](pre[m]);$

$\qquad\qquad\quad workset := workset \cup \{ (n, post[m]) \mid n \in succ_{fg(m)}(m) \};$

$\qquad\qquad\quad$ **IF** $m \in \mathbf{N}_c^S$

$\qquad\qquad\qquad$ **THEN**

$\qquad\qquad\qquad\quad workset := workset \cup$

$\qquad\qquad\qquad\qquad\qquad \{(start(\iota), [\![m_C(\iota)]\!]^*(pre[m])) \mid \iota \in callee(m) \}$

$\qquad\qquad$ **FI**

$\qquad$ **FI**

$\quad$ **END**

OD.

As in the previous section, we denote the values of the variables $workset$, $pre[n]$, and $post[n]$ after the k-th execution of the while-loop by $workset^k$, $pre^k[n]$, and $post^k[n]$, respectively. In analogy to Proposition 8.5.1 and Theorem 8.5.1 we can prove:

Proposition 8.5.2. *If the semantic functions* $[\![n]\!]$, $n \in \mathbf{N}^S$, *and* $[\![m_C(\iota)]\!]^*$, $m \in \mathbf{N}_c^S$ $\iota \in callee(m)$, *are s-monotonic, we have:*

1. $\forall n \in \mathbf{N}^S \; \forall k \in I\!N. \; pop(pre^k[n]) = emptystack \quad \wedge$
$\qquad\qquad\qquad\qquad\qquad pop(post^k[n]) = emptystack$
2. $\forall n \in \mathbf{N}^S \; \forall k \in I\!N. \; (pre^{k+1}[n], post^{k+1}[n]) \sqsubseteq (pre^k[n], post^k[n])$

Intuitively, the first part of Proposition 8.5.2 states that the DFA-stacks stored in the variables $pre[n]$ and $post[n]$, $n \in \mathbf{N}_c^S$, always have a single entry only; the second part states that these values decrease monotonicly. Together, this allows us to prove:

Theorem 8.5.2 (Algorithm 8.5.2).
If the semantic functions $[\![\, n \,]\!]$, $n \in \mathbf{N}^S$, *and* $[\![\, m_C(\iota) \,]\!]^*$, $m \in \mathbf{N}_c^S$ *and*
$\iota \in callee(m)$, *are s-monotonic, we have:*

1. *If* C *satisfies the descending chain condition, there is a* $k_0 \in I\!N$ *with*

$$\forall k \geq k_0 \; \forall n \in \mathbf{N}^S. \; (pre^k[n], post^k[n]) = (pre^{k_0}[n], post^{k_0}[n])$$

2. $\forall n \in \mathbf{N}^S.IMFP_{([\![\,]\!]^*, c_s)}(n) = (\sqcap\{pre^k[n] \mid k \geq 0\}, \sqcap\{post^k[n] \mid k \geq 0\})$

Proof. The first part of Theorem 8.5.2 is a simple consequence of Proposition 8.5.2(2). Thus, we are left with proving the second part. To this end let *fix-pre* and *fix-post* denote an arbitrary solution of Equation System 8.3.3 with respect to $newstack(c_s) \in STACK$. As in the proof of Theorem 8.5.1(2), the essential step is to prove a number of invariants for Algorithm 8.5.2 by simultaneous induction on the number k of iterations of the while-loop.

1. $\forall k \in I\!N \; \forall n \in \mathbf{N}^S. \; (fix\text{-}pre[n], fix\text{-}post[n]) \sqsubseteq (pre^k[n], post^k[n])$
2. $\forall k \in I\!N \; \forall n \in \mathbf{N}^S. \; pre^k[n] \sqcap \sqcap\{stk \mid (n, stk) \in workset^k\} =$

$$\begin{cases} newstack(c_s) & \text{if } n = s_1 \\ \sqcap\{[\![\, m_C(fg(n)) \,]\!]^*(pre^k[m]) \mid m \in caller(fg(n))\} & \text{if } n \in \{s_0, s_2, \ldots, s_k\} \\ \sqcap\{post^k[m] \mid m \in pred_{fg(n)}(n)\} & \text{otherwise} \end{cases}$$

3. $\forall k \in I\!N \; \forall n \in \mathbf{N}^S. \; post^k[n] = [\![\, n \,]\!](pre^k[n])$
4. $\forall (m, stk) \in workset^k. \; fix\text{-}pre[m] \sqsubseteq stk$

For $k = 0$, the investigation of the initialization part of Algorithm 8.5.2 yields:

(a) $\forall n \in \mathbf{N}^S. \; (pre^0[n], post^0[n]) = (newstack(\top), [\![\, n \,]\!](newstack(\top)))$ and
(b) $workset^0 =$
$$\{(s_1, newstack(c_s))\} \cup$$
$$\{(n, stk) \mid n \in succ_{fg(m)}(m) \wedge stk = post^0[m] \sqsubset newstack(\top)\} \cup$$
$$\{(n, stk) \mid m \in \mathbf{N}_c^S \wedge \iota \in callee(m) \wedge n = start(\iota) \wedge$$
$$stk = [\![\, m_C(\iota) \,]\!]^*(pre^0[m]) \sqsubset newstack(\top)\}$$

Thus, invariant (1) is an immediate consequence of (a) and Equation System 8.3.3; invariant (2) follows from (a) and (b); invariant (3) holds because of (a); invariant (4), finally, because of (b), Equation System 8.3.3, and the choice of *fix-pre*.

In order to prove the induction step let $k > 0$ and let (m, stk) be the element currently chosen from the workset. Obviously, we have

(c) $pre^k[n] = \begin{cases} pre^{k-1}[n] \sqcap stk & \text{if } n = m \wedge pre^{k-1}[n] \sqsupset pre^{k-1}[n] \sqcap stk \\ pre^{k-1}[n] & \text{otherwise} \end{cases}$

(d) $post^k[n] = \begin{cases} [\![\, n \,]\!](pre^k[n]) & \text{if } n = m \wedge pre^{k-1}[n] \sqsupset pre^{k-1}[n] \sqcap stk \\ post^{k-1}[n] & \text{otherwise} \end{cases}$

Moreover, the induction hypothesis yields:

(i) $\forall n \in \mathbf{N}^S.\ (\textit{fix-pre}[n], \textit{fix-post}[n]) \sqsubseteq (\textit{pre}^{k-1}[n], \textit{post}^{k-1}[n])$
(ii) $\textit{fix-pre}[m] \sqsubseteq stk$ and
(iii) $\forall n \in \mathbf{N}^S.\ \textit{post}^{k-1}[n] = [\![\, n \,]\!](\textit{pre}^{k-1}[n])$

Together this proves immediately the induction step for the invariants (1) and (3).

For the proof of the induction step of the remaining two invariants (2) and (4), we can assume

$$(\textit{pre}^k[m], \textit{post}^k[m]) = (\textit{pre}^{k-1}[m] \sqcap stk, [\![\, m \,]\!](\textit{pre}^{k-1}[m] \sqcap stk))$$
$$\sqsubseteq (\textit{pre}^{k-1}[m], \textit{post}^{k-1}[m])$$

because otherwise they would simply hold by induction hypothesis. Starting with invariant (2), we obtain the induction step in case of $n = m$ as an immediate consequence of (c) and the induction hypothesis. Otherwise, if $n \in \textit{succ}_{fg(m)}(m)$, or if $m \in \mathbf{N}_c^S$ and $n = start(\iota)$ for some $\iota \in \textit{callee}(m)$, invariant (2) follows from the induction hypothesis and the update of the workset during the $k - th$ iteration of the while-loop. For the remaining nodes invariant (2) is a trivial consequence of the induction hypothesis.

We are thus left with proving the induction step for invariant (4). Here we have to show

$(*)$ $\forall n \in \textit{succ}_{fg(m)}(m).\ \textit{fix-pre}[n] \sqsubseteq \textit{post}^k[m]$

and, in case of $m \in \mathbf{N}_c^S$, additionally

$(**)\ \forall \iota \in \textit{callee}(m).\ \textit{fix-pre}[start(\iota)] \sqsubseteq [\![\, m_C(\iota) \,]\!]^*(\textit{pre}^k[m])$

According to the choice of *fix-pre* and Equation System 8.3.3, we have

$$\forall n \in \textit{succ}_{fg(m)}(m).\ \textit{fix-pre}[n] \sqsubseteq \textit{fix-post}[m]$$

and in case of $m \in \mathbf{N}_c^S$, additionally

$$\forall \iota \in \textit{callee}(m).\ \textit{fix-pre}[start(\iota)] \sqsubseteq [\![\, m_C(\iota) \,]\!]^*(\textit{fix-pre}[m])$$

Thus, $(*)$ and $(**)$ follow immediately from invariant (1) and the s-monotonicity of all semantic functions. This completes the proof of the remaining invariant (4).

The second part of Theorem 8.5.2 is now a consequence of Proposition 8.5.2(2), the previously proved invariants (1) and (2), and equation

$$\sqcap \{\textit{pre}^k[n] \mid k \geq 0\} = \sqcap \{c \mid k > 0 \wedge (n, c) \in \textit{workset}^k\}$$

which holds due to the commutativity and associativity of $\sqcap$.   □

As a corollary of Theorem 8.5.2 we obtain:

Corollary 8.5.2 (Algorithm 8.5.2).
If the semantic functions $[\![\, n \,]\!]$, $n \in \mathbf{N}^S$, and $[\![\, m_C(\iota) \,]\!]^*$, $m \in \mathbf{N}_c^S$ and $\iota \in callee(m)$, are s-monotonic, we have:

1. *Algorithm 8.5.2 terminates, if $\mathcal{C}$ satisfies the descending chain condition.*

2. *After the termination of Algorithm 8.5.2 holds:*
   $\forall\, n \in \mathbf{N}^S.\ \mathit{IMFP}_{([\![\ ]\!]^*, c_s)}(n) = (\mathit{pre}\,[n], \mathit{post}\,[n])$

8.5.3 An Efficient Variant for Computing the *IMFP*-Solution

In this section we present an alternative algorithm for computing the *IMFP*-solution, which is more efficient than Algorithm 8.5.2 because only the start nodes of the procedures of a program take part in the fixed point iteration. After the fixed point is reached, the data flow information of each of the remaining nodes $n \in \mathbf{N}^S \backslash \{\, start(G)\,|\, G \in S\,\}$ is computed in a single step by applying the semantic function $[\![\, n \,]\!]$ to the data flow information $\mathit{pre}\,[start(fg(n))]$ valid at the entry of the start node of the procedure containing n. Thus, the global chain lengths, which determine the worst-case time complexities of Algorithm 8.5.3 and Algorithm 8.5.2, can be estimated by $O(\mathbf{p}*\mathbf{l}+\mathbf{n})$ and $O(\mathbf{n}*\mathbf{l})$, respectively, where $\mathbf{p}$ and $\mathbf{n}$ denote the number of procedures and statements in a program, and $\mathbf{l}$ the length of a maximal chain in $\mathcal{C}$.

Algorithm 8.5.3 (Computing the *IMFP*-Solution Efficiently).

Input: A flow graph system $S = \langle G_0, G_1, \ldots, G_k \rangle$, a complete semi-lattice $\mathcal{C}$, and the semantic functionals $[\![\ ]\!] =_{df} gtr$ and $[\![\ ]\!] =_{df} ltr$ with respect to $\mathcal{C}$ (computed by Algorithm 8.5.1), a local semantic functional $[\![\ ]\!]'$: $N^* \to (\mathcal{C} \to \mathcal{C})$, and a return functional $\mathcal{R}$. Additionally, for every node $m \in \mathbf{N}_c^S$ the functions $[\![\, m_C(\iota) \,]\!]'$, $\iota \in callee(m)$, and a start information $c_s \in \mathcal{C}$.

Output: An annotation of S with data flow informations, i.e., an annotation with pre-informations (stored in *pre*) and post-informations (stored in *post*) of one-entry stacks which characterize valid data flow information at the entry and at the exit of every node, respectively.

Remark: The lattice $\mathcal{C}$, and the semantic functions $[\![\, m_C(\iota) \,]\!]'$ induce the semantic functions $[\![\, m_C(\iota) \,]\!]^*$. $newstack(\top)$ denotes the "universal" data flow information, which is assumed to "contain" every data flow information. The variable *workset* controls the iterative process, and the variable A is a temporary storing the most recent approximation. Recall that $\mathbf{s}_1$ denotes the start node of the main procedure.

(Initialization of the annotation arrays *pre* and *post*, and the variable *workset*)
FORALL $\mathbf{s} \in \{\mathbf{s}_i \,|\, i \in \{0, \ldots, k\}\}$ **DO**
    IF $\mathbf{s} = \mathbf{s}_1$ **THEN** $pre[\mathbf{s}] := newstack(c_s)$ **ELSE** $pre[\mathbf{s}] := newstack(\top)$
FI OD;
$workset := \{\mathbf{s}_i \,|\, i \in \{0, 2, \ldots, k\}\}$;

(Iterative fixed point computation)
WHILE $workset \neq \emptyset$ **DO**
    LET $\mathbf{s} \in workset$
      BEGIN
        $workset := workset \backslash \{\mathbf{s}\}$;
        $A := pre[\mathbf{s}] \sqcap$
               $\sqcap \{ [\![\, n_C(fg(\mathbf{s}))\,]\!] \circ [\![\, n\,]\!] (pre[start(fg(n))]) \,|\, n \in caller(fg(\mathbf{s})) \}$;
        IF $pre[\mathbf{s}] \sqsupset A$
          THEN
            $pre[\mathbf{s}] := A$;
            $workset := workset \cup$
                      $\{start(callee(n)) \,|\, n \in \mathbf{N}_c^S. \ fg(n) = fg(\mathbf{s})\}$
FI
      END
OD;

(Postprocess)
FORALL $n \in \mathbf{N}^S \backslash \{\mathbf{s}_i \,|\, i \in \{0, \ldots, k\}\}$ **DO**
    $pre[n] := [\![\, n\,]\!] (pre[start(fg(n))])$ **OD**;
FORALL $n \in \mathbf{N}^S$ **DO** $post[n] := [\![\, n\,]\!] (pre[n])$ **OD**.

Denoting the values of *workset*, $pre[n]$, and $post[n]$ after the k-th execution of the while-loop by $workset^k$, $pre^k[n]$, and $post^k[n]$, respectively, we obtain similar to Proposition 8.5.2, Theorem 8.5.2, and Corollary 8.5.2:

Proposition 8.5.3. *If the semantic functions* $[\![\, n\,]\!]$ *and* $[\![\, n\,]\!]$, $n \in \mathbf{N}^S$, *and* $[\![\, m_C(\iota)\,]\!]^*$, $m \in \mathbf{N}_c^S$ *and* $\iota \in callee(m)$, *are s-monotonic, we have:*

1. $\forall n \in \mathbf{N}^S \ \forall k \in I\!N. \ pop(pre^k[n]) = emptystack \ \land$
                  $pop(post^k[n]) = emptystack$
2. $\forall n \in \mathbf{N}^S \ \forall k \in I\!N. \ (pre^{k+1}[n], post^{k+1}[n]) \sqsubseteq (pre^k[n], post^k[n])$

Theorem 8.5.3 (Algorithm 8.5.3).
If the semantic functions $[\![\, n\,]\!]$ *and* $[\![\, n\,]\!]$, $n \in \mathbf{N}^S$, *and* $[\![\, m_C(\iota)\,]\!]^*$, $m \in \mathbf{N}_c^S$ *and* $\iota \in callee(m)$, *are s-monotonic, we have:*

1. *If* C *satisfies the descending chain condition, there is a* $k_0 \in I\!N$ *with*

$$\forall k \geq k_0 \ \forall n \in \mathbf{N}^S. \ (pre^k[n], post^k[n]) = (pre^{k_0}[n], post^{k_0}[n])$$

2. $\forall n \in \mathbf{N}^S. IMFP_{([\![\,]\!]^*, c_s)}(n) = (\sqcap \{pre^k[n] \,|\, k \geq 0\}, \sqcap \{post^k[n] \,|\, k \geq 0\})$

Corollary 8.5.3 (Algorithm 8.5.3).
If the semantic functions $[\![\, n\,]\!]$ and $[\![\, n\,]\!]$, $n \in \mathbf{N}^S$, and $[\![\, m_C(\iota)\,]\!]^*$, $m \in \mathbf{N}_c^S$ and $\iota \in callee(m)$, are s-monotonic, we have:

1. *Algorithm 8.5.3 terminates, if C satisfies the descending chain condition.*

2. *After the termination of Algorithm 8.5.3 holds:*
   $\forall\, n \in \mathbf{N}^S.\ \mathit{IMFP}_{([\![\,]\!]^*, c_s)}(n) = (pre[n], post[n])$

8.6 Formal Specification of IDFA-Algorithms

Summarizing the presentation of the previous sections, an IDFA $\mathcal{A}$ is specified by a quadruple consisting of a lattice $\mathcal{C}$, a local semantic functional $[\![\ ]\!]'$, a return functional $\mathcal{R}$, and a start information c_s. In comparison to the intraprocedural setting only the return functional is new. Moreover, it is important that the specification of an IDFA $\mathcal{A}$ can directly be fed into the generic Algorithms 8.5.1 and 8.5.2, which yields the pair of IDFA-algorithms for the preprocess and the main process of computing the *IMFP*-solution induced by $\mathcal{A}$.

Definition 8.6.1 (Specification of an IDFA-Algorithm).
The specification of an IDFA $\mathcal{A}$ is a quadruple $(\mathcal{C}, [\![\ ]\!]', \mathcal{R}, c_s)$, where

1. *$\mathcal{C} = (\mathcal{C}, \sqcap, \sqsubseteq, \bot, \top)$ is a complete semi-lattice,*
2. *$[\![\ ]\!]' : N^* \to (\mathcal{C} \to \mathcal{C})$ a local semantic functional,*
3. *$\mathcal{R} : N_r^* \to (\mathcal{C} \times \mathcal{C} \to \mathcal{C})$ a return functional, and*
4. *$c_s \in \mathcal{C}$ a start information.*

The pair of IDFA-algorithms induced by $\mathcal{A}$ results from instantiating the generic Algorithms 8.5.1 and 8.5.2 with $(\mathcal{C}, [\![\ ]\!]', \mathcal{R})$ and $(\mathcal{C}, ltr, [\![\ ]\!]'|_{N_c^*})$, respectively, where ltr results from Algorithm 8.5.1. The induced pair of IDFA-algorithms is denoted by $Alg(\mathcal{A}) =_{df} (Alg_1(\mathcal{A}), Alg_2(\mathcal{A}))$. The IMOP-solution of $\mathcal{A}$ and the IMFP-solution of $Alg(\mathcal{A})$ are the specifying and the algorithmic solution of $\mathcal{A}$, respectively.[17]

As in the intraprocedural case the gap between an IDFA $\mathcal{A}$, which expresses the information of interest in terms of lattice elements, and a program property φ, which is a Boolean predicate, is closed by means of an interpretation function, which interprets the lattice elements in the set of Boolean truth values. This leads to the interprocedural versions of φ-correctness and φ-precision.

Definition 8.6.2 (φ-Correctness and φ-Precision of an IDFA).
Let φ be a program property, $\mathcal{A} = (\mathcal{C}, [\![\ ]\!]', \mathcal{R}, c_s)$ an IDFA, and $Int : \mathcal{C} \to \mathcal{B}$ an interpretation of $\mathcal{C}$ in $\mathcal{B}$. Then $\mathcal{A}$ is

---

[17] Recall that $\mathcal{C}$, $[\![\ ]\!]'$, and $\mathcal{R}$ induce the local semantic functional $[\![\ ]\!]^*$.

1. φ-correct *if and only if* (i) $Int \circ N\text{-}IMOP_{([\![\ ]\!]^*,c_s)} \Rightarrow N\text{-}\varphi$
(ii) $Int \circ X\text{-}IMOP_{([\![\ ]\!]^*,c_s)} \Rightarrow X\text{-}\varphi$
2. φ-precise *if and only if* (i) $Int \circ N\text{-}IMOP_{([\![\ ]\!]^*,c_s)} \Longleftrightarrow N\text{-}\varphi$
(ii) $Int \circ X\text{-}IMOP_{([\![\ ]\!]^*,c_s)} \Longleftrightarrow X\text{-}\varphi$

The notions of φ-correctness and φ-precision relate the specifying solution of an IDFA to a specific program property φ. In order to close the gap between the algorithmic solution of $\mathcal{A}$ and φ, we introduce the interprocedural versions of *MOP*-correctness and *MOP*-precision, which like their intraprocedural counterparts relate the algorithmic solution to the specifying solution of $\mathcal{A}$. Additionally, we also introduce the notion of a terminating IDFA. Together, this allows us to prove the algorithmic solution of an IDFA $\mathcal{A}$ to be precise (correct) for a property φ essentially as in the intraprocedural case: the proof reduces to checking the premises of the Interprocedural Coincidence Theorem 8.4.2 (Interprocedural Correctness Theorem 8.4.1) and of the termination of $\mathcal{A}$. This is important because the proof of precision does not require any knowledge about the generic algorithms computing the *IMFP*-solution.

Definition 8.6.3 (*IMOP*-Correctness, *IMOP*-Precision, Termination).

An IDFA $\mathcal{A} = (\mathcal{C}, [\![\ ]\!]', \mathcal{R}, c_s)$ *is*

1. *IMOP*-correct *if and only if* $IMFP_{([\![\ ]\!]^*,c_s)} \sqsubseteq IMOP_{([\![\ ]\!]^*,c_s)}$
2. *IMOP*-precise *if and only if* $IMFP_{([\![\ ]\!]^*,c_s)} = IMOP_{([\![\ ]\!]^*,c_s)}$
3. terminating, *if its induced pair of IDFA-algorithms* $Alg(\mathcal{A})$ *terminates.*

As in the intraprocedural case, *IMOP*-correctness, *IMOP*-precision, and termination of an IDFA can usually be proved straightforward by a few substeps. This is a consequence of Theorem 8.6.1, which follows from Lemma 8.2.3, the Interprocedural Correctness Theorem 8.4.1, the Interprocedural Coincidence Theorem 8.4.2, Corollary 8.5.1 and Corollary 8.5.2, and gives sufficient conditions guaranteeing these properties of an IDFA.

Theorem 8.6.1 (*IMOP*-Correctness, *IMOP*-Precision, Termination).

An IDFA $\mathcal{A} = (\mathcal{C}, [\![\ ]\!]', \mathcal{R}, c_s)$ *is*

1. *IMOP-correct, if all semantic functions* $[\![\ n\ ]\!]'$, $n \in N^*$, *and all return functions* $\mathcal{R}(n)$, $n \in N_r^*$, *are monotonic.*
2. *IMOP-precise, if all semantic functions* $[\![\ n\ ]\!]'$, $n \in N^*$, *and all return functions* $\mathcal{R}(n)$, $n \in N_r^*$, *are distributive.*
3. *terminating, if* (i) $[\mathcal{C} \to \mathcal{C}]$ *satisfies the descending chain condition,*
(ii) *all semantic functions* $[\![\ n\ ]\!]'$, $n \in N^*$, *are monotonic,*
(iii) *all return functions* $\mathcal{R}(n)$, $n \in N_r^*$, *are monotonic.*

Note that for $\mathcal{C}$ itself the descending chain condition, though belonging to the premises of Corollary 8.5.2, need not explicitly be checked because of:

Lemma 8.6.1. *If* $[\mathcal{C} \to \mathcal{C}]$ *satisfies the descending chain condition, then* $\mathcal{C}$ *satisfies the descending chain condition as well.*

Note that the converse implication of Lemma 8.6.1 is in general invalid. For convenience we introduce as in the intraprocedural setting a notion which expresses both the termination of an IDFA and its φ-correctness (φ-precision) for a given program property φ.

Definition 8.6.4 (Correctness and Precision of an IDFA).
Let φ *be a program property and* $\mathcal{A}$ *an IDFA. Then* $\mathcal{A}$ *is called* correct *(*precise*) for* φ *if and only if* $\mathcal{A}$ *is (i) terminating and (ii)* φ-correct *(*φ-precise*).*

8.7 Forward, Backward, and Bidirectional IDFA-Algorithms

Like their intraprocedural counterparts, also interprocedural DFA-algorithms can be grouped into *forward*, *backward*, and *bidirectional* analyses according to the direction of information flow (cf. Section 2.2.7). In this chapter we developed our framework for interprocedural abstract interpretation for forward analyses. Backward analyses, however, can be dealt with by forward analyses like in the intraprocedural counterpart of our framework essentially after inverting the flow of control. Central is to identify the set of nodes $\mathbf{N}^S$ of S with the set of nodes $N^* \backslash N_r^*$ of G^*, and to identify every node $n \in \mathbf{N}_{fc}^S$ with the set of nodes $\{ n_C(\iota) \mid \iota \in callee(n) \}$. As a consequence of inverting the flow of control, the return functions must be associated with call nodes instead of return nodes. Bidirectional problems are in contrast to forward and backward problems more difficult to handle because of the lack of a natural operational (or *IMOP-*) interpretation. As in the intraprocedural case this problem can elegantly be overcome by decomposing bidirectional analyses into sequences of unidirectional ones. In Chapter 10 we illustrate this by means of the interprocedural extensions of the computationally and lifetime optimal algorithms for busy and lazy code motion of Chapter 3. The interprocedural algorithm for busy code motion decomposes the originally bidirectional flow of data flow information (cf. [Mo, MR2]) into a sequence of a backward analysis followed by a forward analysis. Though computationally optimal results are in general impossible in the interprocedural setting, we show that it generates interprocedurally computationally optimal programs if it is canonic. Moreover, like its intraprocedural counterpart the algorithm can then be extended to achieve *interprocedurally computationally* and *lifetime* *optimal* results. This requires only two further unidirectional analyses. The resulting algorithm for lazy interprocedural code motion is the first algorithm which meets these optimality criteria.

9. A Cookbook for Optimal Interprocedural Program Optimization

In this chapter we present the interprocedural counterpart of the intraprocedural cookbook for program optimization. To this end we summarize the presentation of the Chapters 5, 6, 7, and 8 for constructing an interprocedural program optimization from the designer's point of view. As in the intraprocedural setting, the point is to provide the designer of a program optimization with concise guidelines which structure and simplify the construction process, and simultaneously hide all details of the framework which are irrelevant for its application. Following the guidelines the construction and the corresponding optimality and precision proofs of the transformations and the IDFA-algorithms, respectively, can be done like in the intraprocedural setting in a cookbook style.

9.1 Optimal Interprocedural Program Optimization

9.1.1 Fixing the Program Transformations and the Optimality Criterion

According to the interprocedural version of our two-step approach to optimal program optimization (cf. Section 7.3.1), we first have to fix the class of program transformations and the optimality criterion of interest. This requires:

Define ...

1. a set of appropriate program properties Φ
2. the class of program transformations $\mathcal{T}$ of interest in terms of a subset $\Phi_C \subseteq \Phi$
3. a relation $\leq_{\mathcal{T}} \subseteq S_{\mathcal{T}} \times S_{\mathcal{T}},$[1] which induces the optimality criterion of interest

---

The optimality criterion induced by $\leq_{\mathcal{T}}$ is the criterion of $\mathcal{O}_{\leq_{\mathcal{T}}}$-optimality in the sense of Definition 7.3.1, i.e.:

A transformation $Tr \in \mathcal{T}$ is $\mathcal{O}_{\leq_{\mathcal{T}}}$-optimal, if for all $Tr' \in \mathcal{T}$ holds:
$$S_{Tr} \leq_{\mathcal{T}} S_{Tr'}$$

---

[1] In general, $\leq_{\mathcal{T}}$ will be a pre-order.

J. Knoop: Optimal Interprocedural Program Optimization, LNCS 1428, pp. 141-144, 1998.
© Springer-Verlag Berlin Heidelberg 1998

9.1.2 Fixing the Optimal Program Transformation

Next, the (optimal) program transformation of interest must be defined. Similar to the class of program transformations $\mathcal{T}$, it is defined in terms of a subset of the properties of Φ, i.e.:

Define ...

4. the program transformation Tr_{opt} of interest in terms of a subset $\Phi_T \subseteq \Phi$

Like in the intraprocedural case, we have to prove that the transformation Tr_{opt} is a member of the transformation class under consideration and satisfies the optimality criterion of interest. Thus, we have to prove the following two steps:

Prove ...

5. $Tr_{opt} \in \mathcal{T}$
6. Tr_{opt} is $\mathcal{O}_{\leq_T}$-optimal

9.2 Precise Interprocedural Data Flow Analysis

After proving the optimality of Tr_{opt}, we must define for every property $\varphi \in \Phi_T$ involved in the definition of Tr_{opt} an IDFA $\mathcal{A}_\varphi$, whose induced IDFA-algorithms compute the set of program points enjoying φ. Without loss of generality, we thus consider an arbitrary, but fixed property φ of Φ_T in the following.

9.2.1 Specifying the IDFA $\mathcal{A}_\varphi$

According to Section 8.6 the specification of the IDFA $\mathcal{A}_\varphi$, and the proof of its φ-precision requires the following components:

Specify ...

7. a complete semi-lattice $(\mathcal{C}, \sqcap, \sqsubseteq, \bot, \top)$
8. a local semantic functional $[\![\ ]\!]' : N^* \to (\mathcal{C} \to \mathcal{C})$
9. a return functional $\mathcal{R} : N_r^* \to (\mathcal{C} \times \mathcal{C} \to \mathcal{C})$
10. a start information $c_s \in \mathcal{C}$
11. an interpretation $Int : \mathcal{C} \to \mathcal{B}$

As in the intraprocedural case, the lattice $\mathcal{C}$ represents the data flow information of interest, the local semantic functional gives meaning to the elementary statements of the argument program, and the start information c_s represents the data flow information which is assumed to be valid immediately before the execution of the argument program starts. New is the return functional, which is the handle to properly deal with local variables and value parameters of recursive procedures. The function Int, finally, interprets like in the intraprocedural case the elements of $\mathcal{C}$ as Boolean truth values, and therefore, closes the gap between the data flow information computed and the program property φ of interest.

Handling Backward Analyses. We recall that in our framework backward analyses can be dealt with by means of forward analyses after inverting the flow of control (cf. Section 8.7). The role of call nodes and return nodes is then interchanged. Hence, for backward analyses the functionality of the return functional is $\mathcal{R} : N_{\mathcal{C}}^* \to (\mathcal{C} \times \mathcal{C} \to \mathcal{C})$. This is demonstrated in the applications of Section 11.1 and Section 11.4.

9.2.2 Proving Precision of $\mathcal{A}_\varphi$

Next, we have to show that $\mathcal{A}_\varphi$ is precise for φ in the sense of Definition 8.6.2. According to Theorem 8.6.1 the following proof steps are sufficient:

Prove . . .

12. the function lattice $[\mathcal{C} \to \mathcal{C}]$ satisfies the descending chain condition
13. the local semantic functions $[\![n]\!]'$, $n \in N^*$, are distributive
14. the return functions $\mathcal{R}(n)$, $n \in N_r^*$, are distributive
15. the specifying solution of $\mathcal{A}_\varphi$ is φ-precise, i.e.:

        (i) $Int \circ N\text{-}IMOP_{([\![\,]\!]^*, c_s)} \iff N\text{-}\varphi$

        (ii) $Int \circ X\text{-}IMOP_{([\![\,]\!]^*, c_s)} \iff X\text{-}\varphi$

Combining Definition 8.6.2, Theorem 8.6.1, and and the propositions of the steps 12, 13, 14, and 15 we obtain the desired precision result:

Theorem 9.2.1 ($\mathcal{A}_\varphi$-Precision).
$\mathcal{A}_\varphi$ is precise for φ, i.e., $\mathcal{A}_\varphi$ is terminating and φ-precise.

After proving Theorem 9.2.1 for all IDFAs $\mathcal{A}_\varphi$, $\varphi \in \Phi_T$, we obtain that the transformation Tr_{opt} and the transformation $Tr_{\{\mathcal{A}_\varphi \mid \varphi \in \Phi_T\}}$ induced by the algorithmic solutions of the IDFA-algorithms $\mathcal{A}_\varphi$, $\varphi \in \Phi_T$, coincide. Hence, we have the desired optimality result:

Theorem 9.2.2 ($\mathcal{O}$-Optimality).
The transformation $Tr_{\{\mathcal{A}_\varphi \mid \varphi \in \Phi_T\}}$ is $\mathcal{O}_{\leq_T}$-optimal.

Monotonic IDFA-Problems: Additional Proof Obligations. For a monotonic IDFA-problem, i.e., an IDFA, whose local semantic and return functions are monotonic (but not distributive), the Interprocedural Correctness Theorem 8.4.1 still guarantees *IMOP*-correctness of $\mathcal{A}_\varphi$. Combining this with the proposition of step 15, this even implies φ-correctness of $\mathcal{A}_\varphi$. In general, however, this is not sufficient in order to guarantee that the program $S_{Tr_{\{\mathcal{A}_\varphi \mid \varphi \in \Phi_T\}}}$ resulting from the transformation $Tr_{\{\mathcal{A}_\varphi \mid \varphi \in \Phi_T\}}$ is correct or even $\mathcal{O}_{\leq_T}$-optimal. Similarly, this holds if in step 15 only φ-correctness of the specifying solution of $\mathcal{A}_\varphi$ could be proved instead of φ-precision. In both cases the following two proof obligations must additionally be verified in order to guarantee correctness and profitability of the induced transformation:

Prove ...

16. $Tr_{\{\mathcal{A}_\varphi \mid \varphi \in \Phi_T\}} \in \mathcal{T}$

17. $S_{Tr_{\{\mathcal{A}_\varphi \mid \varphi \in \Phi_T\}}} \leq_T S$

Application: Interprocedural Code Motion. Similar to Section 2.3, we conclude this chapter with an outlook to the application considered in Chapter 10, *interprocedural code motion*. Like for its intraprocedural counterpart, the set of program properties Φ required is basically given by the interprocedural predicates for *safety, correctness, down-safety, earliestness, latestness,* and *isolation*. The class of program transformations $\mathcal{T}$ is given by the set of *interprocedurally admissible code motion transformations*, which are defined in terms of the interprocedural predicates for *safety* and *correctness*. Under a natural side-condition, the interprocedural predicates for *down-safety* and *earliestness* specify the computationally optimal transformation of interprocedural *busy* code motion, and the interprocedural predicates for *latestness* and *isolation* the computationally and lifetime optimal transformation of interprocedural *lazy* code motion.

10. Optimal Interprocedural Code Motion: The Transformations

In this chapter we illustrate our two-step approach for optimal interprocedural program optimization considering interprocedural code motion as application. At first sight, the very same strategies as in the intraprocedural setting seem to apply in order to avoid unnecessary recomputations of values. However, as we are going to show there is a fundamental difference to the intraprocedural setting: computationally optimal results are in general impossible. Consequently, every code motion transformation must fail for some programs to yield computationally optimal results. Intraprocedurally successful strategies, however, can even exhibit severe anomalies interprocedurally. This applies to the interprocedural counterparts of busy and lazy code motion, too. In the interprocedural setting, the strategies of placing computations as early as possible or as late as possible, which are the guarantors of computationally and lifetime optimal results in the intraprocedural setting, can fail to be strict in the sense of [CLZ], and thus fail to guarantee even profitability. In essence, this is caused by the failure of an intraprocedural decomposition theorem for safety (cf. Safety Lemma 3.2.1). As a consequence, the conjunction of down-safety and earliestness does not imply profitability of an insertion. Insertions at down-safe earliest program points can even fail to cover any original computation.

Revealing these differences and demonstrating their impact onto interprocedural code motion is a major contribution of this chapter. Going beyond, we additionally propose a natural constraint, which is sufficient in order to guarantee the computational and lifetime optimality of the interprocedural counterparts of busy and lazy code motion, denoted as *IBCM*- and *ILCM*-transformation, for a large class of programs.

The constraint, we propose, is *canonicity* (cf. Definition 3.2.3): whenever the *IBCM*-transformation is *canonic* for a program, its result is computationally optimal, and the result of the *ILCM*-transformation is lifetime optimal. Intuitively, this constraint means that every insertion of the *IBCM*-transformation is required, i.e., it is used on every program continuation without a preceding modification or insertion of the computation under consideration. This is quite a natural requirement for an optimization based on code motion. In fact, in the intraprocedural setting, it is even necessary for computational optimality (cf. Theorem 3.2.1).

J. Knoop: Optimal Interprocedural Program Optimization, LNCS 1428, pp. 147-207, 1998.
© Springer-Verlag Berlin Heidelberg 1998

Moreover, the introduction of this constraint allows us to capture the primary goal of this chapter: illustrating the two-step approach of our framework for optimal interprocedural program optimization, and showing how to apply the cookbook of Chapter 9. In fact, one should note that the problems encountered in interprocedural code motion are not caused by the underlying data flow analyses. These can rather straightforward be deduced from their intraprocedural counterparts in order to compute the interprocedural versions of the properties their intraprocedural counterparts are designed for. The subtleties encountered in interprocedural code motion are caused by the optimization itself.

In Section 10.1 we investigate and illustrate the essential differences between the intraprocedural and interprocedural setting concerning code motion. Subsequently, we informally propose canonicity as a natural sufficient constraint for the computational and liftetime optimality of the *IBCM*- and *ILCM*-transformation. Afterwards, we introduce in Sections 10.2 and 10.3 the basic definitions required for defining interprocedural code motion transformations together with some technical lemmas simplifying the reasoning about their properties. Central is then Section 10.4, in which we present the specification of the *IBCM*-transformation together with its proof of *interprocedural computational optimality* under the premise of its canonicity for the program under consideration. Under the same premise, we subsequently present in Section 10.5 the specification of the *ILCM*-transformation together with its proof of *interprocedural lifetime optimality*. It turns out that both optimality results can be proved by means of the same techniques as in the intraprocedural case (cf. [KRS2]). Only the treatment of local variables and formal parameters of recursive procedures requires some technical refinements. In the absence of procedures, the interprocedural transformations of busy and lazy code motion reduce to their intraprocedural counterparts of Chapter 3.

10.1 Essential Differences to the Intraprocedural Setting

10.1.1 Computational Optimality

In the intraprocedural setting, every program has a computationally optimal counterpart. Moreover, canonicity is necessary for computational optimality, i.e., computationally optimal transformations are always canonic. Both facts do not carry over to the interprocedural setting as illustrated by the examples of Figure 10.1 and Figure 10.5.

In the example of Figure 10.1, the computations of $a + b$ at the nodes **12** and **24** are partially redundant with respect to the computations of $a + b$ at the nodes **7** and **23**.

Investigating this example in more detail reveals that there are only two admissible code motion transformations eliminating some of these redundan-

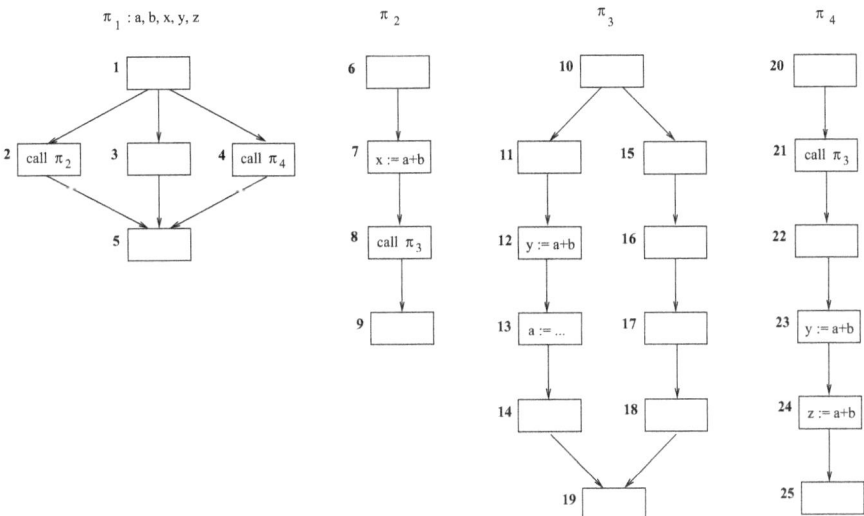

Fig. 10.1. The original program Π_1

cies and generating a "significantly" different and computationally better program than Π_1. Their results are shown in Figure 10.2 and Figure 10.3.

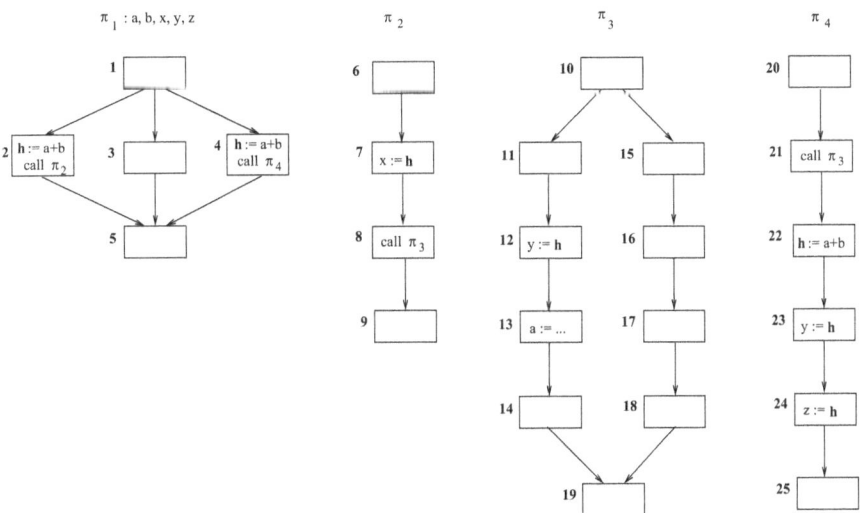

Fig. 10.2. Π_1': computationally minimal, but not computationally optimal

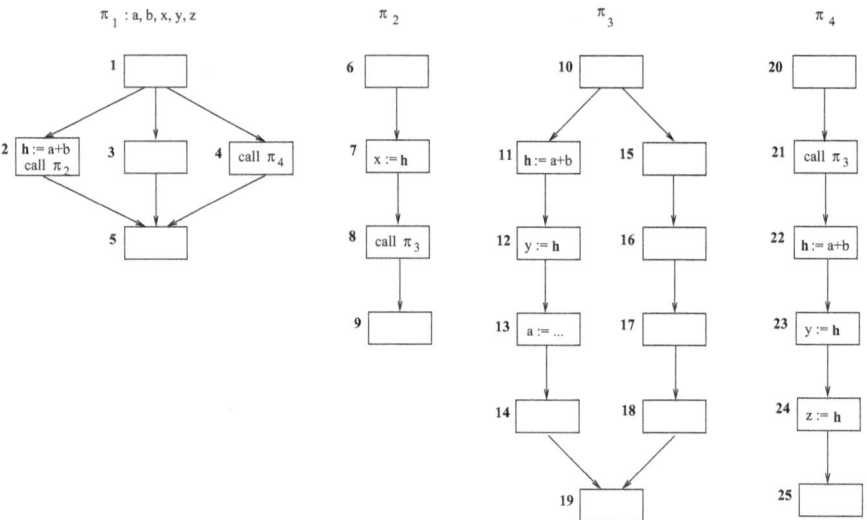

Fig. 10.3. Π_1'': computationally minimal, but not computationally optimal

Note that Π_1' and Π_1'' are both computationally better than Π_1, but are themselves incomparable with respect to this relation; a fact, which can easily be checked by means of the subsequent table summarizing the number of computations executed in Π, Π_1', and Π_1'', respectively.

Program	paths via π_2		paths via π_4	
	"left" path	"right" path	"left" path	"right" path
Π_1	2	1	3	2
Π_1'	1	1	2	2
Π_1''	2	1	2	1

Calling procedure π_3 via π_2 in Π_1', there is a single computation of $a+b$ on every program path; calling it via π_4, there are two computations of $a+b$ on each path. This contrasts with Π_1'', where independently of calling π_3 via π_2 or π_4, there is a path containing two computations of $a+b$ and another one containing only one. Hence, both programs are computationally better than Π_1. However, as one can easily see, there is no computationally optimal counterpart of Π_1.

Consider next the program of Figure 10.5. It shows the result of an admissible code motion transformation applied to the program of Figure 10.4. Note that the program of Figure 10.5 is computationally optimal. However, it is not canonic because the insertion at node **8** is not used along program continuations passing nodes **9** and **22**. In fact, computationally optimal results can only be achieved for this example if one is prepared for dropping the request for canonicity. The result of any canonic code motion transformation for the program of Figure 10.4 is computationally worse than the program of Figure 10.5.

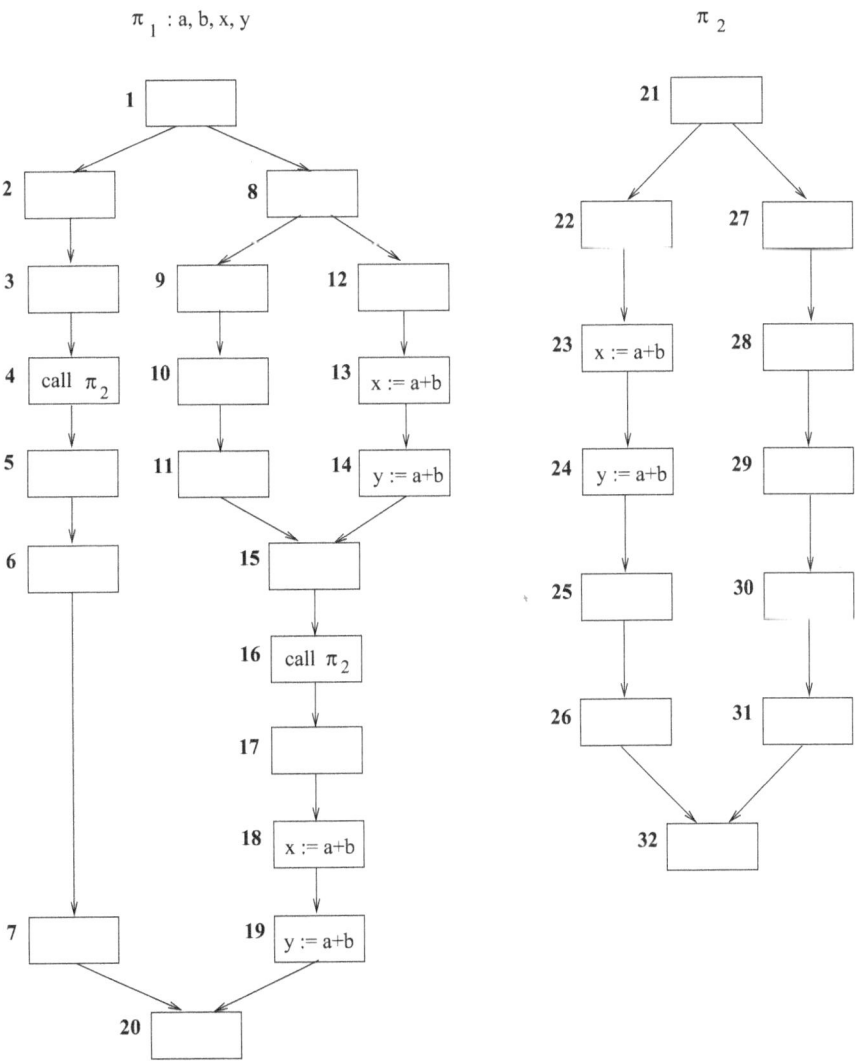

Fig. 10.4. The original program Π_2

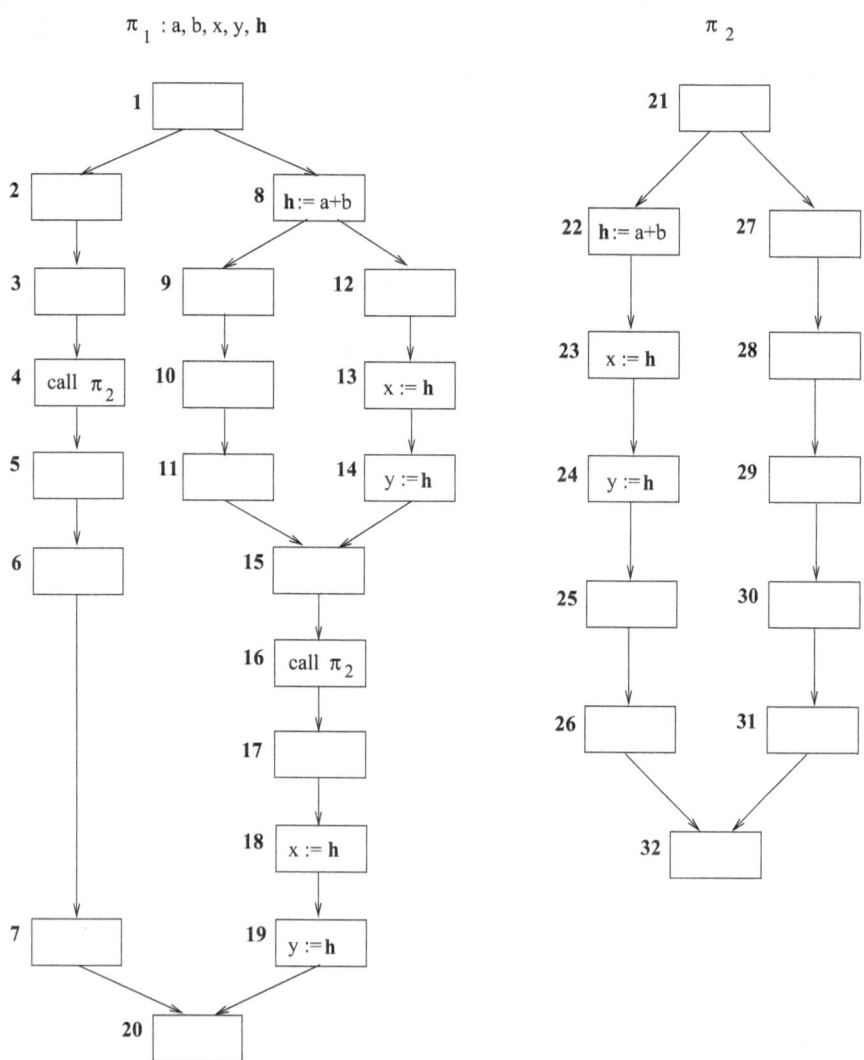

Fig. 10.5. Transf. program Π_2': computationally optimal, but not canonic

As a consequence of these examples we have:

Theorem 10.1.1 (Computational Optimality).
In the interprocedural *setting,*

1. *computational optimality is in general impossible,*
2. *canonicity is not necessary for computational optimality.*

10.1.2 Safety

In the intraprocedural setting, safety can be decomposed into up-safety and down-safety: a program point, which is safe, is always up-safe or down-safe. In the interprocedural setting, safety cannot be decomposed this way in general. Program points can be safe, though they are neither up-safe nor down-safe. This is demonstrated by the program of Figure 10.6. All nodes of procedure π_2 are safe, but none of them is up-safe or down-safe with respect to the computation of $a + b$.

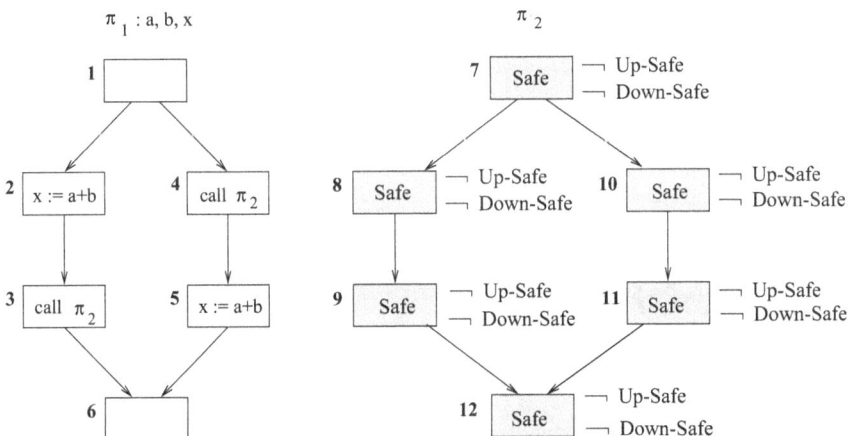

Fig. 10.6. Safe though neither up-safe nor down-safe

Figure 10.7 shows the interprocedural flow graph of the program of Figure 10.6, and illustrates the difference to the intraprocedural setting in more detail. The point of this example is that all interprocedurally valid paths passing a node of π_2 satisfy that $a + b$ has been computed before entering π_2 or that it will be computed after leaving it. Together, this implies safety of all program points of π_2. In fact, all paths of the interprocedural flow graph lacking a computation of $a + b$ are interprocedurally invalid because they do not respect the call/return-behaviour of procedure calls, and thus do not represent legal program paths as illustrated by the highlighted paths in Figure 10.7. Intraprocedurally, i.e., considering the graph of Figure 10.7 an intraprocedural flow graph, the highlighted paths would be valid excluding safety for any of the nodes **7** to **12**. Thus, in contrast to the intraprocedural setting we have:

Theorem 10.1.2 (Safety).
In the interprocedural setting, the disjunction of up-safety and down-safety is not necessary for safety.

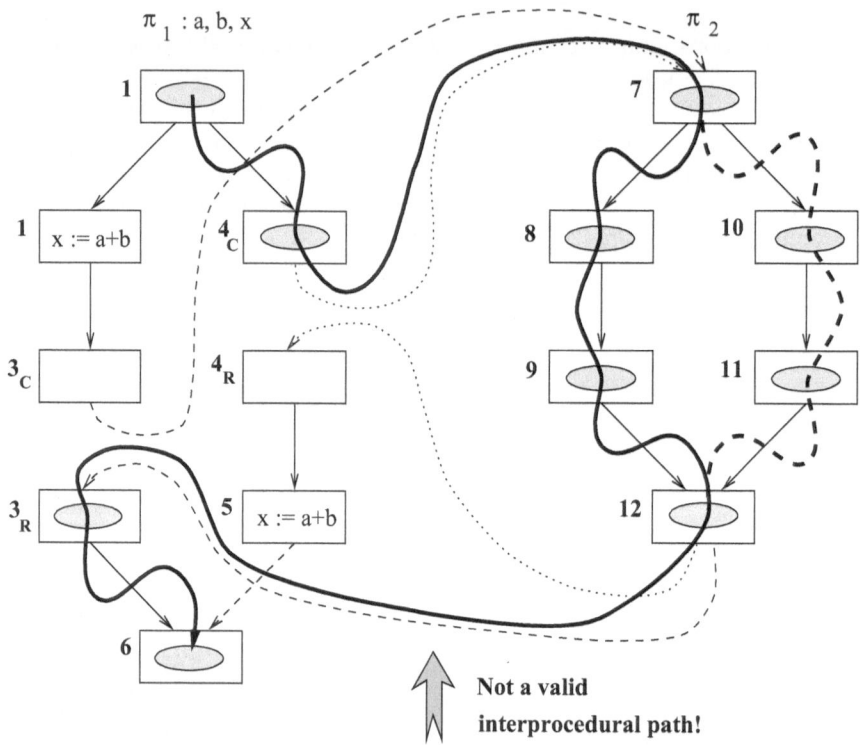

Fig. 10.7. Interprocedural flow graph of the program of Figure 10.6

10.1.3 Down-Safety

In the intraprocedural setting, down-safe program points are always candidates of a "canonic" insertion. This means, whenever a program point n is down-safe, there is an admissible code motion transformation inserting at n, and the value computed and stored at n reaches on *every* program continuation a use site without an intervening modification of any of the operands of the computation under consideration or an insertion of the same value. Moreover, every node lying on a path from a down-safe node to a node containing an original computation without an intervening modification of one of its operands is down-safe, too. Both facts do not carry over to the interprocedural setting as illustrated by the example of Figure 10.8.

Note that the computation of $a + b$ at node **10** is down-safe. Nonetheless, there is no admissible code motion transformation inserting a computation at node **10**, such that this value can be used on some program continuation for replacing an original computation. In essence, this is a consequence of the interplay of the call site of π_2 at node **4**, and the assignment to a at node **25** modifying the value of $a + b$. Together this prevents the insertion of $a + b$ at

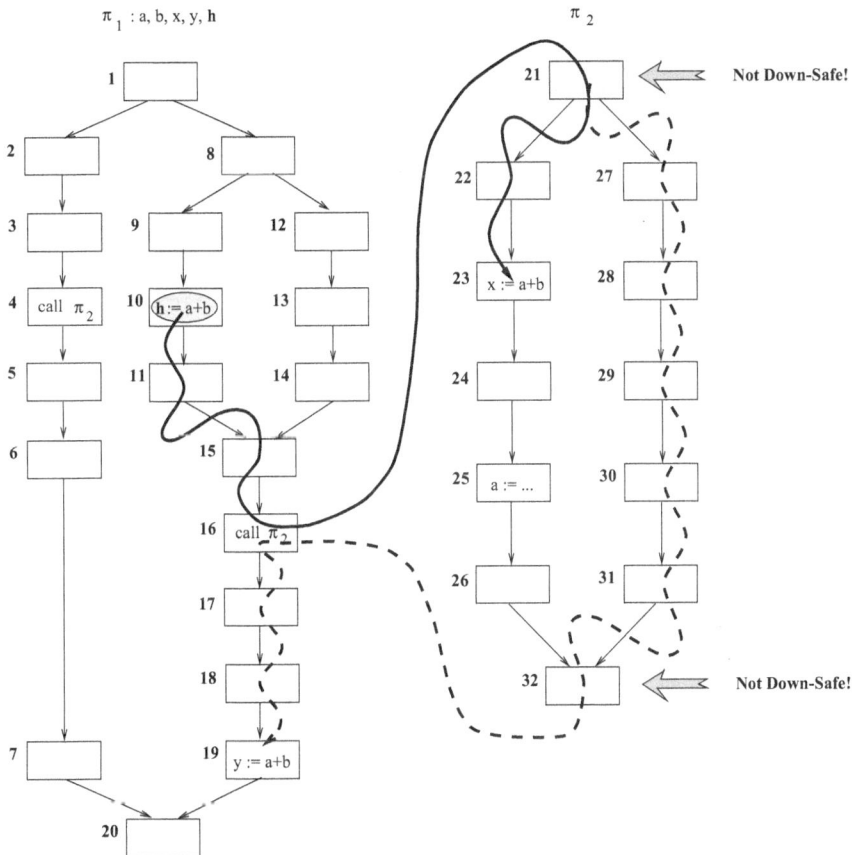

Fig. 10.8. Down-safe, but unusable

node **26**. Moreover, note that every program path from node **10** to node **23** or node **19**, passes node **21** or **32**, respectively, containing a computation of $a + b$. Nonetheless, neither node **21** nor node **32** are down-safe.

Summarizing, we therefore have:

Theorem 10.1.3 (Down-Safety).

In the interprocedural *setting,*

1. *down-safety of a program point n does not imply the existence of a canonic code motion transformation inserting at n, such that the temporary initialized at n reaches on every program continuation a use site,*

2. *nodes lying on a path from a down-safe node to a node containing an original computation are not necessarily down-safe, even if there is no intervening modification of any of its operands.*

Figure 10.9 illustrates the impact of Theorem 10.1.3. It shows a program, which is only slightly different from the program of Figure 10.8. Though node **8** is down-safe (and even earliest), a temporary initialized at node **8** cannot contribute to the elimination of any (partially) redundant computation. This is an important difference to the intraprocedural setting, where down-safe earliest program points are the insertion points of the computationally optimal *BCM*-transformation.

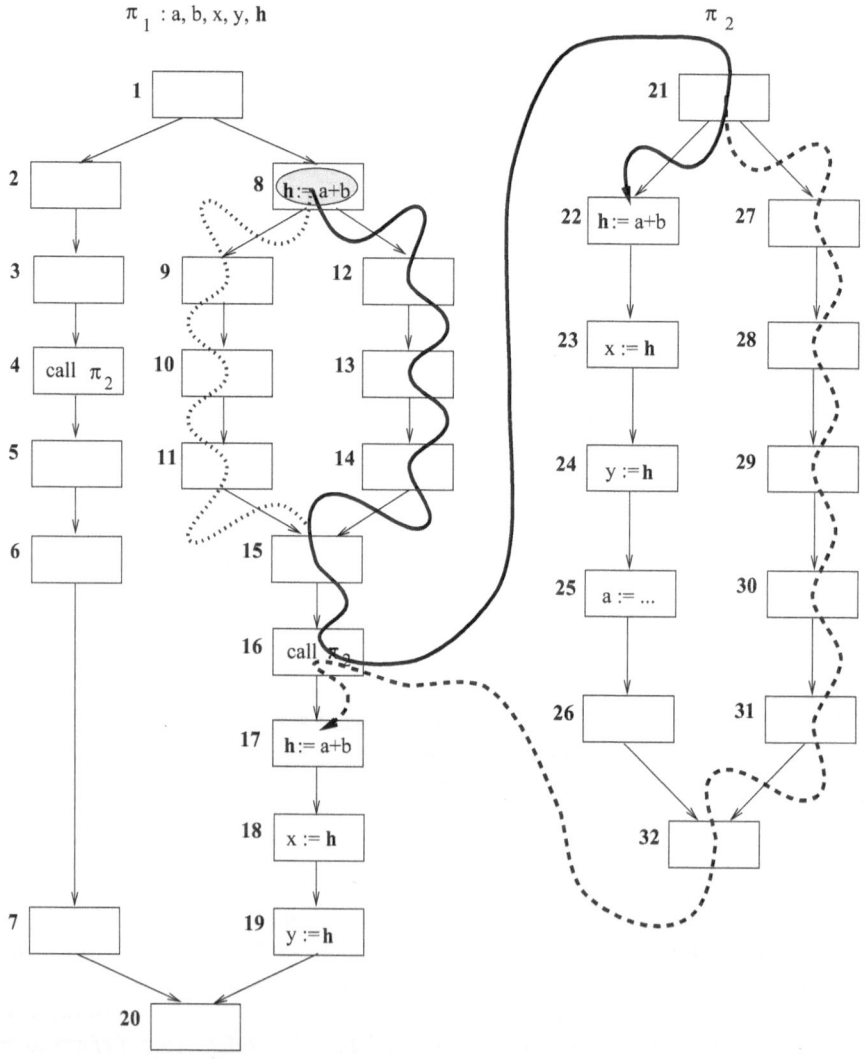

Fig. 10.9. Down-safe and earliest, but unusable

10.1.4 Canonicity: The Key to Computational and Lifetime Optimality

Theorem 10.1.1 excludes computational optimality in general. The failure of the decomposability of safety into up-safety and down-safety, the backbone of computationally and lifetime optimal intraprocedural code motion, turns out to be the source of placing anomalies showing up when adapting intraprocedural placing strategies interprocedurally. This applies to the as-early-as-possible and as-late-as-possible placing strategies underlying busy and lazy code motion, too.

However, as we are going to show, under the premise of canonicity the interprocedural counterpart of busy code motion is computationally optimal, and the interprocedural counterpart of lazy code motion is computationally and lifetime optimal. Moreover, as in the intraprocedural setting, the latter transformation is unique in satisfying both optimality criteria. Canonicity is a natural constraint as it requires that insertions are used on every program continuation. It can easily be checked, and characterizes for a large class of interprocedural programs a situation where there is no difference to the intraprocedural setting.

This is illustrated by the example of Figure 10.10. It shows a program, for which the *IBCM*-transformation is canonic as shown in Figure 10.11, where for convenience the set of interprocedurally down-safe and earliest program points are highlighted. Note that the program of Figure 10.11 is indeed computationally optimal.

10.2 Preliminaries

After the introductory discussion of the previous section on interprocedural code motion, we now present the basic definitions required for a formal treatment. As in the intraprocedural setting we develop the *IBCM*- and *ILCM*-transformation with respect to an arbitrary, but fixed pair of a program $\Pi \in Prog$ and a program term $t \in \mathbf{T}$ allowing a simpler and unparameterized notation. We denote the flow graph system and the interprocedural flow graph representing Π by S and G^*, respectively. Without loss of generality, we can dispense with reference parameters, which according to Chapter 6 can be considered parameterless formal procedure parameters. This allows us to compute alias-information for reference parameters which can subsequently be used in a block-box fashion along the lines of [KRS4] for code motion (cf. Section 12.2.2). In the following we thus assume that Π is free of reference parameters. If Π contains formal procedure calls and satisfies the sfmr-property, we assume that it was analyzed by means of the HO-DFA of Chapter 6.[1] We thus assume that the function *callee* yields for

---

[1] Recall that the sfmr-property is decidable. In particular, it holds for all programs being free of formal procedure calls, or of statically nested procedures.

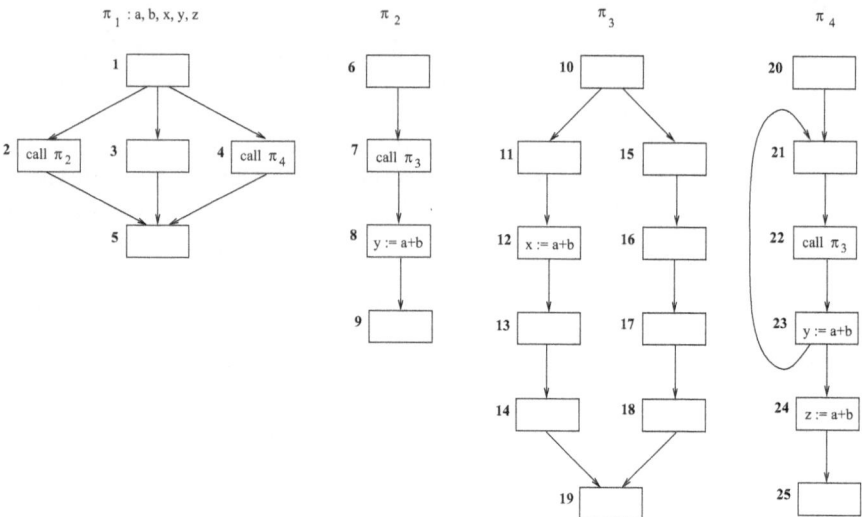

Fig. 10.10. The original program Π_3

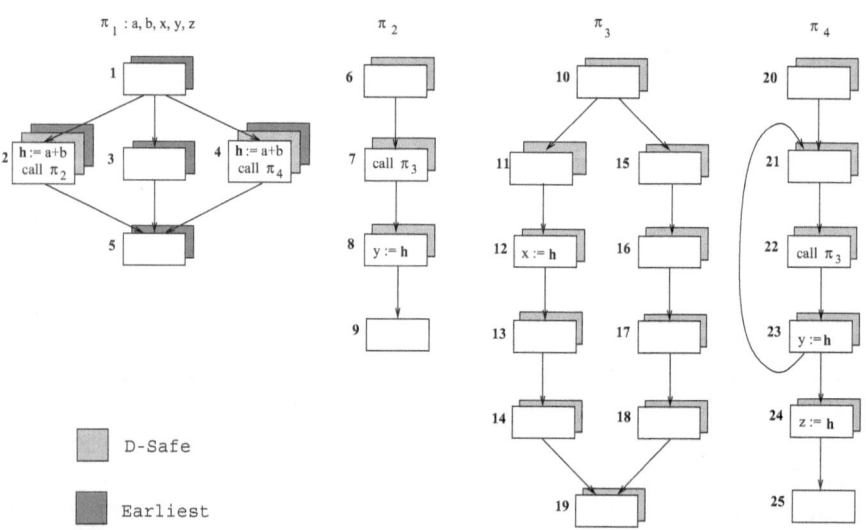

Fig. 10.11. Canonic and hence comp. optimal result of the *IBCM*-transf.

every (formal) procedure call the set of procedures it can potentially call. If the sfmr-property is violated, formal procedure calls are treated like external procedure calls. Without loss of generality, we finally assume that every formal procedure call node n has a unique predecessor and successor. If necessary, this situation can easily be achieved by appropriately inserting a new predecessor p and successor s of n as illustrated in Figure 10.12.

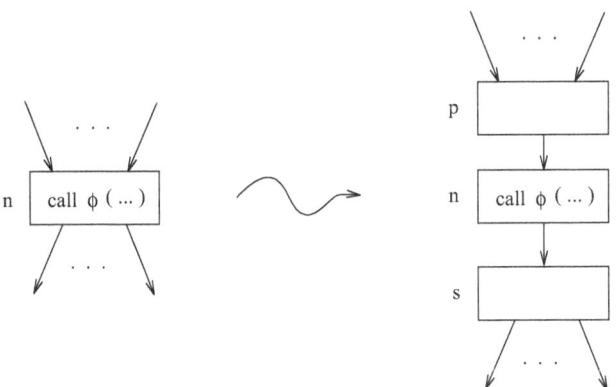

Fig. 10.12. Unique predecessors (successors) of formal procedure call nodes

As in the intraprocedural case, the process of code motion can be blocked in completely arbitrary graph structures. The flow graph system S must therefore slightly be modified in order to avoid any blocking (cf. Section 3.1). In a first step, every formal procedure call node n with $|callee(n)| \geq 2$ is replaced by a set of nodes $M =_{df} \{ n(\pi) \mid \pi \in callee(n) \}$ representing pairwise disjoint ordinary procedure calls of a procedure $\pi \in callee(n)$, and having all the same predecessor and successor as n. After this modification, every procedure call node m in S represents an ordinary procedure call, and satisfies $|callee(m)| = 1$ as illustrated in Figure 10.13.

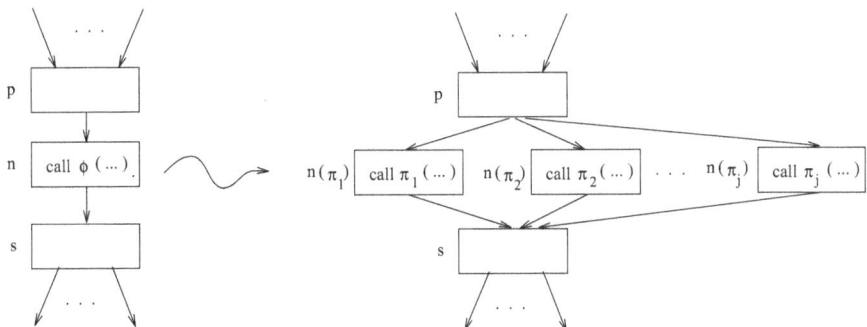

Fig. 10.13. "Unfolding" formal procedure calls

In a second step, all edges in S (and hence also in G^* except for edges starting in nodes of N_c^*) leading to a node with more than one incoming edge are split by inserting a synthetic node. Figure 10.14 illustrates this transformation for the program fragment of Figure 10.13.

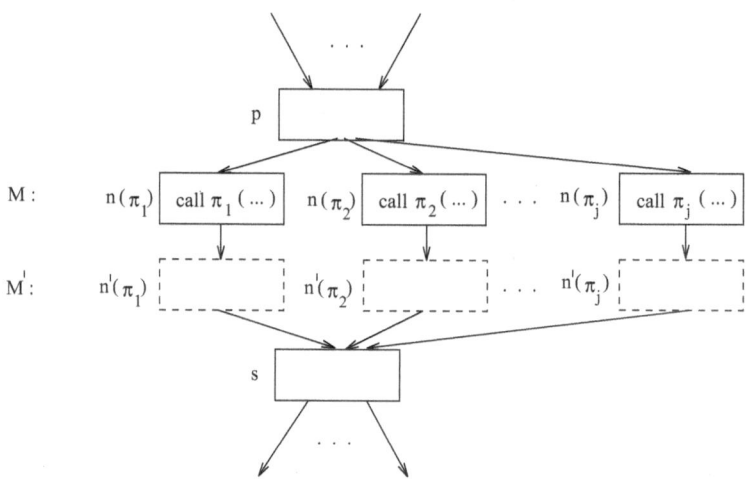

Fig. 10.14. Splitting of edges

As in the intraprocedural case, the splitting of edges and the replacing of formal procedure calls by their associated sets of ordinary procedure calls excludes any blocking of the process of code motion. In addition, it simplifies this process because computations can uniformly be moved to node entries (cf. Section 3.1). On the other hand, it enlarges the argument program. Thus, it is worth to be noted that formal procedure calls are reestablished after the code motion transformation. Analogously, synthetic nodes, which are not used for an insertion of the code motion transformation under consideration, are removed afterwards, too.

10.2.1 Basic Definitions

Global and Local Variables, and the Polymorphic Function *Var*.
For every procedure $\pi \in \Pi$, let $Loc\,Var(\pi)$ denote the set of local variables and value parameters of π:

$$\forall\, \pi \in \Pi.\ Loc\,Var(\pi) =_{df} \mathcal{I}^d_{\mathbf{LV},\mathbf{VP}}(\pi)$$

Analogously, let $Glob\,Var(\pi)$ denote the set of variables which are global for π:

$$\forall\, \pi \in \Pi.\ Glob\,Var(\pi) =_{df} Ext_{\mathbf{V}}(\Pi) \cup \mathcal{I}^d_{\mathbf{LV},\mathbf{VP}}(StatPred^+(\pi))$$

In addition, let *Var* be an abbreviation of $\mathcal{I}_{\mathbf{LV},\mathbf{VP}}$ in the following.

Range of Terms. Given a term t', its *range* is the set of nodes, where all variables of $Var(t')$ are bound according to the binding rules of *Prog*. Intuitively, the range of t' is the set of all program points where a placement of t' can safely be placed with respect to the static semantics of *Prog*. For example, in the program of Figure 7.1 the range of the terms $a+b$ and $z_{13}+e$ are the nodes $\mathbf{9},\ldots,\mathbf{16}$ and $\mathbf{17},\ldots,\mathbf{23}$, respectively. We define:

$$\forall t' \in \mathbf{T}.\ Range(t') =_{df} \{\, n \in N^* \mid \forall v \in Var(t').\ decl(v) \in StatPred^*(fg(n)) \,\}$$

The function fg is here extended to nodes of N_c^* and N_r^* according to the following convention:

$$\forall n \in (N_c^* \cup N_r^*).\ fg(n) =_{df} \begin{cases} fg(n_S) & \text{if } n \in N_c^* \\ fg(pred^*(n)) & \text{if } n \in N_r^* \end{cases}$$

We recall that n_S denotes the procedure call node of S corresponding to n (cf. Section 7.2.2).

Incarnations of Variables and Terms. Interprocedurally, there are potentially infinitely many incarnations of local variables of recursive procedures. In order to formally deal with this phenomenon, we define for every occurrence of a node m on a path $p \in \mathbf{IP}[s^*,n]$, $n \in N^*$, two functions $RhsLev_p$ and $LhsLev_p$, which map every variable to a natural number giving the nesting level of its *right-hand side incarnation* and its *left-hand side incarnation*, respectively, when m is reached on p. Right-hand side and left-hand side here refer to the "sides" of an assignment statement. For every $p \in \bigcup \{\mathbf{IP}[s^*,n] \mid n \in N^*\}$, we define the function

$$RhsLev_p : \{1,\ldots,\lambda_p\} \to (Var(\Pi) \to \mathbb{N}_0)$$

by

$$\forall i \in \{1,\ldots,\lambda_p\}\ \forall v \in Var(\Pi).\ RhsLev_p^v(i) =_{df}$$

$$\begin{cases} 1 & \text{if } i=1 \ \wedge\ v \in Ext_{\mathbf{V}}(\Pi) \cup LocVar(\pi_1) \\ 0 & \text{if } i=1 \ \wedge\ v \in LocVar(\Pi\backslash\{\pi_1\}) \\ RhsLev_p^v(i-1)+1 & \text{if } p_i = start(decl(v)) \\ RhsLev_p^v(i-1)-1 & \text{if } p_i \in succ^*(N_r^*) \ \wedge\ p_{i-2} = end(decl(v)) \\ RhsLev_p^v(i-1) & \text{otherwise} \end{cases}$$

Intuitively, $RhsLev_p^v(i) = 0$ means that currently there is no storage allocated for v. By means of $RhsLev_p$ we can now analogously define the function

$$LhsLev_p : \{1,\ldots,\lambda_p\} \to (Var(\Pi) \to \mathbb{N}_0)$$

by

$$\forall i \in \{1,\ldots,\lambda_p\}\ \forall v \in Var(\Pi).\ LhsLev_p^v(i) =_{df}$$

$$\begin{cases} RhsLev_p^v(i) + 1 & \text{if } p_i \in N_c^* \wedge succ^*(p_i) = start(decl(v)) \\ RhsLev_p^v(i) & \text{otherwise} \end{cases}$$

The notion of an incarnation of a variable carries over to terms: whenever a new incarnation of a variable is generated, simultaneously a new incarnation of all terms is created containing this variable as an operand. For interprocedural code motion it is necessary to distinguish the incarnations of terms being valid at different points of a program path (see e.g., Definition 10.4.1). Considering the term t, which we have fixed as code motion candidate, this is conveniently achieved by means of the predicate $SameInc$ defined below. Intuitively, for $p \in \bigcup \{ \mathbf{IP}[\mathbf{s}^*, n] \mid n \in N^* \}$, and $1 \leq i \leq j \leq \lambda_p$, the predicate $SameInc_p[i, j]$ indicates, whether the same incarnation of the term t is involved at the nodes p_i and p_j on p.

$$SameInc_p[i,j] \quad =_{df} \quad RhsLev_p^{Var(t)}(i) = LhsLev_p^{Var(t)}(j) \wedge$$
$$\forall i \leq k \leq j. \ RhsLev_p^{Var(t)}(i) \leq RhsLev_p^{Var(t)}(k)$$

$$SameInc_p[i,j[\quad =_{df} \quad RhsLev_p^{Var(t)}(i) = RhsLev_p^{Var(t)}(j) \wedge$$
$$\forall i \leq k < j. \ RhsLev_p^{Var(t)}(i) \leq RhsLev_p^{Var(t)}(k)$$

$$SameInc_p]i,j[\quad =_{df} \quad LhsLev_p^{Var(t)}(i) = RhsLev_p^{Var(t)}(j) \wedge$$
$$\forall i < k < j. \ RhsLev_p^{Var(t)}(i) \leq RhsLev_p^{Var(t)}(k)$$

We remark that

$$RhsLev_p^{Var(t)}(i) = LhsLev_p^{Var(t)}(j) \quad \text{and} \quad RhsLev_p^{Var(t)}(i) = RhsLev_p^{Var(t)}(j)$$

are used as abbreviations of

$$\forall v \in Var(t). \ RhsLev_p^v(i) = LhsLev_p^v(j)$$

and

$$\forall v \in Var(t). \ RhsLev_p^v(i) = RhsLev_p^v(j)$$

respectively.

Local Predicates *Comp** **and** *Transp**, **and the Function** *ModLev.* The predicates *Comp** and *Transp** are the counterparts of the intraprocedural predicates *Comp* and *Transp*. They are the basic properties for the specification of the *IBCM*- and *ILCM*-transformation, and their definitions reflect the existence of different, potentially even infinitely many incarnations of the code motion candidate t in the interprocedural setting. In fact, the incarnation of the term t, which is computed or modified by a node n, depends on the context of the program execution n occurs in. This is in contrast to the intraprocedural setting, where only a single incarnation of every term exists. As a consequence, one does not need to deal with incarnation information intraprocedurally. For every path $p \in \mathbf{IP}[\mathbf{s}^*, \mathbf{e}^*]$ we define:

$$Comp^*_{(p,i)}(p_j) =_{df} Comp(p_j) \wedge SameInc_p[i,j[$$

and

$$Transp^*_{(p,i)}(p_j) =_{df} RhsLev_p^{Var_{\mathrm{Lhs}\mathrm{Var}(p_j)}(t)}(i) \neq LhsLev_p^{Var_{\mathrm{Lhs}\mathrm{Var}(p_j)}(t)}(j) \; \vee$$
$$\exists\, i \leq l \leq j \; \exists\, v \in Var(t).\; RhsLev_p^v(l) < RhsLev_p^v(i)$$

where

$$RhsLev_p^{Var_{\mathrm{Lhs}\mathrm{Var}(p_j)}(t)}(i) \neq LhsLev_p^{Var_{\mathrm{Lhs}\mathrm{Var}(p_j)}(t)}(j)$$

is a shorthand for

$$\forall\, v \in Var_{\mathrm{Lhs}\,Var(p_j)}(t).\; RhsLev_p^v(i) \neq LhsLev_p^v(j)$$

Intuitively, the predicate $Comp^*_{(p,i)}(p_j)$ holds if and only if t is computed in p_j (i.e., $Comp(p_j)$), and if the incarnation of t valid in p_j on p is the same, which is valid at p_i (i.e., $SameInc_p[i,j[$). Similarly, the predicate $Transp^*_{(p,i)}(p_j)$ is true if the variables of t modified by p_j concern other incarnations of these variables than those, which are valid at p_i on p (i.e., $RhsLev_p^{Var_{\mathrm{Lhs}\mathrm{Var}(p_j)}(t)}(i) \neq LhsLev_p^{Var_{\mathrm{Lhs}\mathrm{Var}(p_j)}(t)}(j)$), or if the incarnation of t valid at p_i is not valid at p_j, and will never become valid again (i.e., $\exists\, i \leq l \leq j \; \exists\, v \in Var(t).\; RhsLev_p^v(l) < RhsLev_p^v(i)$).

By means of the definitions of $Comp^*$ and $Transp^*$, we obtain immediately:

Lemma 10.2.1.

1. $\forall\, p \in \mathbf{IP}[\mathbf{s}^*, \mathbf{e}^*] \; \forall\, 1 \leq i \leq \lambda_p.\; Comp^*_{(p,i)}(p_i) \iff Comp(p_i)$
2. $\forall\, p \in \mathbf{IP}[\mathbf{s}^*, \mathbf{e}^*] \; \forall\, 1 \leq i \leq \lambda_p \; \forall\, i \leq j \leq \lambda_p.\; Transp(p_j) \Rightarrow Transp^*_{(p,i)}(p_j)$

In addition to the predicates $Comp^*$ and $Transp^*$, the specification of the IDFA-algorithms involved in the *IBCM*-transformation requires the function *ModLev* : $N^* \rightarrow \mathcal{N}$, which stands for *modified level*. Here, $\mathcal{N} =_{df} \mathbf{IN} \cup \{\infty\}$ denotes the disjoint union of $\mathbf{IN}$ and $\{\infty\}$, which forms together with the *minimum* function as meet-operation the chain-like lattice $\mathbf{IN}_\infty$ of natural numbers with least element 0 and greatest element ∞:

$$\mathbf{IN}_\infty =_{df} (\mathcal{N}, Min, \leq, 0, \infty)$$

Intuitively, $ModLev(n)$ yields of all variables of t which are modified by n the lowest of the statical levels some of these variables are declared on, i.e., $ModLev(n)$ yields the statical level of those variables of t modified by n, which are "most globally" declared.

$ModLev$: $N^* \rightarrow \mathcal{N}$ defined by
$$\forall\, n \in N^*.\; ModLev(n) =_{df} Min(\{\, StatLevel(v) \mid v \in Var_{\mathrm{Lhs}\,Var(n)}(t) \,\})$$

where the function $StatLevel : \mathbf{V} \to \mathrm{I\!N}$ is assumed to map its arguments to the statical level they are declared on.

Convention: For a predicate $Predicate$ and an interprocedural path $p \in \mathbf{IP}[m, n]$ of G^*, we introduce in analogy to the intraprocedural setting the following abbreviations (cf. Section 3.1):

- $Predicate^{\forall}(p) \iff \forall 1 \leq i \leq \lambda_p. \ Predicate(p_i)$
- $Predicate^{\exists}(p) \iff \exists 1 \leq i \leq \lambda_p. \ Predicate(p_i)$

Note that $\neg Predicate^{\forall}(p)$ and $\neg Predicate^{\exists}(p)$ are then abbreviations of the formulas $\exists 1 \leq i \leq \lambda_p. \ \neg Predicate(p_i)$ and $\forall 1 \leq i \leq \lambda_p. \ \neg Predicate(p_i)$, respectively.

Global Transparency. Based on the predicate $Transp^*$, we additionally introduce the predicate $GlobTransp$, which generalizes the notion of transparency uniformly to all nodes of the flow graph system S.

$$\forall n \in \mathbf{N}^S. \ GlobTransp(n) =_{df}$$

$$
\left\{
\begin{array}{ll}
Transp(n) & \text{if } n \in \mathbf{N}^S \backslash \mathbf{N}_c^S \\
\forall p \in \mathbf{IP}[s^*, e^*] \ \forall \iota \in callee(n) \ \forall i, j. \\
\quad (\, p_i = n_C(\iota) \wedge p_j = n_R(\iota) \wedge p]i, j[\in \mathbf{CIP}[p_{i+1}, p_{j-1}]\,) \\
\quad \Rightarrow Transp^{*\forall}_{(p,i)}(p[i,j]) & \text{otherwise}
\end{array}
\right.
$$

10.2.2 First Results

In this section we present some technical and easily to prove lemmas, which are helpful for establishing the optimality of the $IBCM$- and $ILCM$-transformation.

The first lemma follows from the fact that all edges in S leading to nodes with more than one incoming edge have been split by inserting a synthethic node. This holds analogously for the corresponding edges of G^*. For the remaining edges of G^* starting in nodes of N_c^* the lemma is trivial because the start node of the called procedure is their unique successor.

Lemma 10.2.2 (Interprocedural Control Flow).

1. a) $\forall n \in \mathbf{N}^S. \ |pred_{fg(n)}(n)| \geq 2 \Rightarrow succ_{fg(n)}(pred_{fg(n)}(n)) = \{\,n\,\}$
   b) $\forall n \in \mathbf{N}^S. \ |succ_{fg(n)}(n)| \geq 2 \Rightarrow pred_{fg(n)}(succ_{fg(n)}(n)) = \{\,n\,\}$
2. a) $\forall n \in N^*. \ |pred^*(n)| \geq 2 \Rightarrow succ^*(pred^*(n)) = \{\,n\,\}$
   b) $\forall n \in N^*. \ |succ^*(n)| \geq 2 \Rightarrow pred^*(succ^*(n)) = \{\,n\,\}$

Synthetic nodes represent the empty statement "skip". Thus, as a corollary of the Control Flow Lemma 10.2.2 we get:

Corollary 10.2.1.

1. $\forall n \in \mathbf{N}^S. \; |\mathit{pred}_{fg(n)}(n)| \geq 2 \Rightarrow$
$$\mathit{pred}_{fg(n)}(n) \subseteq \mathbf{N}^S \backslash \mathbf{N}_c^S \wedge \prod_{m \in \mathit{pred}_{fg(n)}(n)} \mathit{Transp}\,(m)$$

2. $\forall n \in N^* \backslash \{\mathit{start}(G) \,|\, G \in S\}.$
$$|\mathit{pred}^*(n)| \geq 2 \Rightarrow \mathit{pred}^*(n) \subseteq N^* \backslash N_r^* \wedge \prod_{m \in \mathit{pred}^*(n)} \mathit{Transp}\,(m)$$

The next two lemmas follow by means of the definitions of *RhsLev* and *LhsLev*.

Lemma 10.2.3. *Let* $p \in \mathbf{IP}[\mathbf{s}^*, \mathbf{e}^*]$, *and* $i \in \{1, \ldots, \lambda_p\}$. *We have:*

1. $p_i \in N^* \backslash (N_c^* \cup N_r^*) \Rightarrow \mathit{RhsLev}_p^{\mathit{Var}(\Pi)}(i) = \mathit{RhsLev}_p^{\mathit{Var}(\Pi)}(i+1)$
2. $p_i \in N_c^* \Rightarrow \forall v \in \mathit{Var}(\Pi). \; \mathit{RhsLev}_p^v(i) =$
$$\begin{cases} \mathit{RhsLev}_p^v(i+1) - 1 & \text{if } v \in \mathit{LocVar}(fg(\mathit{succ}^*(p_i))) \\ \mathit{RhsLev}_p^v(i+1) & \text{otherwise} \end{cases}$$
3. $p_i \in N_r^* \Rightarrow \forall v \in \mathit{Var}(\Pi). \; \mathit{RhsLev}_p^v(i) =$
$$\begin{cases} \mathit{RhsLev}_p^v(i+1) + 1 & \text{if } v \in \mathit{LocVar}(fg(\mathit{pred}^*(p_i))) \\ \mathit{RhsLev}_p^v(i+1) & \text{otherwise} \end{cases}$$

Lemma 10.2.4. *Let* $p \in \mathbf{IP}[\mathbf{s}^*, \mathbf{e}^*]$, *and* $i \in \{1, \ldots, \lambda_p\}$. *We have:*

1. $p_i \in N^* \backslash N_c^* \Rightarrow \mathit{RhsLev}_p^{\mathit{Var}(\Pi)}(i) = \mathit{LhsLev}_p^{\mathit{Var}(\Pi)}(i)$
2. $p_i \in N_c^* \Rightarrow \forall v \in \mathit{Var}(\Pi).$
$$\mathit{RhsLev}_p^v(i) = \begin{cases} \mathit{LhsLev}_p^v(i) - 1 & \text{if } v \in \mathit{LocVar}(fg(\mathit{succ}^*(p_i))) \\ \mathit{LhsLev}_p^v(i) & \text{otherwise} \end{cases}$$

The call nodes and return nodes of G^* modify the local variables and value parameters of the called procedure. Thus, we have:

Lemma 10.2.5.

1. $\forall n \in N_c^*. \; \mathit{Transp}\,(n) \Longleftrightarrow \mathit{Var}(t) \cap \mathit{LocVar}(fg(\mathit{succ}^*(n))) = \emptyset$
2. $\forall n \in N_r^*. \; \mathit{Transp}\,(n) \Longleftrightarrow \mathit{Var}(t) \cap \mathit{LocVar}(fg(\mathit{pred}^*(n))) = \emptyset$

The following lemma is essentially a consequence of the fact that intervals of call nodes and return nodes on interprocedural paths are either disjoint or one is included in the other (cf. Lemma 7.2.1).

Lemma 10.2.6. *Let* $p \in \mathbf{IP}[\mathbf{s}^*, \mathbf{e}^*]$, *and* $i, j \in \{1, \ldots, \lambda_p\}$ *such that* $p_i \in N_c^*$ *and* $p_j \in N_r^*$ *are a pair of matching call and return nodes of* p. *We have:*

1. $\forall i < l \leq j. \; \mathit{RhsLev}_p^{\mathit{LocVar}(fg(\mathit{succ}^*(p_i)))}(i) < \mathit{RhsLev}_p^{\mathit{LocVar}(fg(\mathit{succ}^*(p_i)))}(l)$
2. $\mathit{RhsLev}_p^{\mathit{Var}(\Pi)}(i) = \mathit{RhsLev}_p^{\mathit{Var}(\Pi)}(j+1)$

Recalling that t is the fixed program term under consideration, we obtain by means of Lemma 10.2.6 and the definition of $Comp^*$:

Lemma 10.2.7. *Let $p \in \mathbf{IP}[\mathbf{s}^*, \mathbf{e}^*]$, and $i, j \in \{1, \ldots, \lambda_p\}$ such that $p_i \in N_c^*$ and $p_j \in N_r^*$ are a pair of matching call and return nodes of p. Then we have:*

$$Var(t) \nsubseteq GlobVar(fg(succ^*(p_i))) \Rightarrow$$

$$(\forall i < l \leq j. \; \neg Comp^*_{(p,i)}(p_l) \; \wedge \; \neg SameInc_p[i, l[)$$

10.3 Interprocedural Code Motion Transformations

In essence, and quite similar to the intraprocedural case an interprocedural code motion transformation is characterized by a three-step procedure:

1. Declare a new temporary $\mathbf{h}$ in the statically most deeply nested procedure of Π containing a defining occurrence of a variable of $Var(t)$, or in the main procedure of Π, if all variables of $Var(t)$ are free in Π.
2. Insert assignments of the form $\mathbf{h} := t$ at some nodes in $Range(t)$.
3. Replace some of the original computations of t by $\mathbf{h}$.

Note that the first step is commonly shared by all interprocedural code motion transformations. Thus, the specification of a specific interprocedural code motion transformation ICM can be completed by defining two predicates $Insert_{ICM}$ and $Replace_{ICM}$, which denote the sets of program points where an initialization must be inserted and an original computation must be replaced. As in the intraprocedural setting, we assume that $Replace_{ICM}$ implies $Comp$, and that the conjunction of $Insert_{ICM}$ and $Comp$ implies $Replace_{ICM}$. This avoids transformations keeping an original computation even after an insertion into the node it occurs in making it locally redundant. Obviously, this does not impose any restrictions to our approach.

- *Declare a new temporary $\mathbf{h}$ in procedure π: π is the statically most deeply nested procedure of Π containing a defining occurrence of a variable of $Var(t)$, or the main procedure of Π, if all variables of $Var(t)$ are free in Π.*
- *Insert at the entry of every node satisfying $Insert_{ICM}$ the assignment $\mathbf{h} := t$.*
- *Replace every original computation of t in nodes satisfying $Replace_{ICM}$ by $\mathbf{h}$.*

Table 10.1: Scheme of interprocedural code motion transformations

Note that the static semantics of *Prog* requires that the predicate $Insert_{ICM}$ obeys the following implication:

$$\forall\, n \in \mathbf{N}^S.\ Insert_{ICM}(n) \Rightarrow n \in Range(t)$$

In the following we denote the set of all interprocedural code motion transformations with respect to t, i.e., the set of all transformations matching the scheme of Table 10.1, by $\mathcal{ICM}$.

10.3.1 Admissible Transformations

A code motion transformation *ICM* is *admissible*, if it preserves the semantics of its argument program. Intuitively, this requires that *ICM* is *safe* and *correct*. "Safe" means that there is no program path, on which the computation of a new value is introduced, and "correct" means that **h** always represents the same value as t, when it is replaced by **h**. This is reflected in the following definition, which defines when inserting and replacing a computation of t is interprocedurally *safe* and *correct* in a node $n \in N^*$. Additionally, it introduces the notion of *strongly safe* program points, which we are going to show reveals an important difference to the intraprocedural setting.

Definition 10.3.1 (Safety and Correctness).
For all nodes $n \in N^*$ we define:

1. Safety: $Safe(n) \Longleftrightarrow_{df}$
   $\forall\, p \in \mathbf{IP}[\mathbf{s}^*, \mathbf{e}^*]\ \forall\, i.\ (p_i = n) \Rightarrow$
   $\qquad a)\ \exists\, j < i.\ Comp\,(p_j) \wedge SameInc_p[j, i[\wedge Transp^*{}^{\vee}_{(p,j)}(p[j, i[)\ \vee$
   $\qquad b)\ \exists\, j \geq i.\ Comp^*{}_{(p,i)}(p_j) \wedge Transp^*{}^{\vee}_{(p,i)}(p[i, j[)$
2. Strong Safety: $S\text{-}Safe(n) \Longleftrightarrow_{df} N\text{-}USafe^*(n) \vee N\text{-}DSafe^*(n)$, *where*
   $\qquad a)\ N\text{-}USafe^*(n) \Longleftrightarrow_{df}$
   $\qquad\quad \forall\, p \in \mathbf{IP}[\mathbf{s}^*, \mathbf{e}^*]\ \forall\, i.\ (p_i = n) \Rightarrow$
   $\qquad\qquad \exists\, j < i.\ Comp\,(p_j) \wedge SameInc_p[j, i[\wedge Transp^*{}^{\vee}_{(p,j)}(p[j, i[)$
   $\qquad b)\ N\text{-}DSafe^*(n) \Longleftrightarrow_{df}$
   $\qquad\quad \forall\, p \in \mathbf{IP}[\mathbf{s}^*, \mathbf{e}^*]\ \forall\, i.\ (p_i = n) \Rightarrow$
   $\qquad\qquad \exists\, j \geq i.\ Comp^*{}_{(p,i)}(p_j) \wedge Transp^*{}^{\vee}_{(p,i)}(p[i, j[)$
3. Correctness: *Let $ICM \in \mathcal{ICM}$. Then:*
   $Correct_{ICM}(n) \Longleftrightarrow_{df}$
   $\forall\, p \in \mathbf{IP}[\mathbf{s}^*, n]\, \exists\, i.Insert_{ICM}(p_i) \wedge SameInc_p[i, \lambda_p[\wedge Transp^*{}^{\vee}_{(p,i)}(p[i, \lambda_p[)$

Obviously, we have:

Lemma 10.3.1.
$\forall\, n \in N^*.\ Safe(n) \Rightarrow n \in Range(t)$

By means of the predicates of safety and correctness we can now define the set of *admissible* interprocedural code motion transformations.

Definition 10.3.2 (Admissible Interprocedural Code Motion).
An interprocedural code motion transformation $ICM \in \mathcal{ICM}$ is admissible if and only if every node $n \in \mathbf{N}^S$ satisfies the following two conditions:

1. $Insert_{ICM}(n) \Rightarrow Safe(n)$
2. $Replace_{ICM}(n) \Rightarrow Correct_{ICM}(n)$

We denote the set of all admissible interprocedural code motion transformations by $\mathcal{ICM}_{Adm}$.

For admissible code motion transformations we can prove:

Lemma 10.3.2 (Correctness Lemma).

$$\forall ICM \in \mathcal{ICM}_{Adm} \ \forall n \in N^*. \ Correct_{ICM}(n) \Rightarrow Safe(n)$$

Proof. Let $ICM \in \mathcal{ICM}_{Adm}$, and $n \in N^*$ satisfying $Correct_{ICM}$. Then the following sequence of implications proves Lemma 10.3.2, where the last one follows easily by means of Definition 10.3.1(1) and a case analysis on j:

$$Correct_{ICM}(n)$$

(Def. 10.3.1(3)) $\Rightarrow$ $\forall p \in \mathbf{IP}[\mathbf{s}^*, \mathbf{e}^*] \ \forall k. \ p_k = n. \ \exists i \leq k.$
$$Insert_{ICM}(p_i) \land SameInc_p[i, k[\land Transp^*{}^{\forall}_{(p,i)}(p[i, k[)$$

($ICM \in \mathcal{ICM}_{Adm}$) $\Rightarrow$ $\forall p \in \mathbf{IP}[\mathbf{s}^*, \mathbf{e}^*] \ \forall k. \ p_k = n. \ \exists i \leq k.$
$$Safe(p_i) \land SameInc_p[i, k[\land Transp^*{}^{\forall}_{(p,i)}(p[i, k[)$$

(Def. 10.3.1(1)) $\Rightarrow$ $\forall p \in \mathbf{IP}[\mathbf{s}^*, \mathbf{e}^*] \ \forall k. \ p_k = n. \ \exists i \leq k.$
$$(\exists j < i. Comp(p_j) \land SameInc_p[j, i[\land Transp^*{}^{\forall}_{(p,j)}(p[j, i[)$$
$$\lor (\exists j \geq i. \ Comp^*{}_{(p,i)}(p_j) \land Transp^*{}^{\forall}_{(p,i)}(p[i, j[)) \land$$
$$SameInc_p[i, k[\land Transp^*{}^{\forall}_{(p,i)}(p[i, k[))$$

(Def. 10.3.1(1)) $\Rightarrow$ $Safe(n)$

$\square$

Up to now, the analogy to the intraprocedural setting seems to be complete at first sight. However, there is an essential difference between safety and strong safety interprocedurally. Whereas intraprocedurally both properties are equivalent (cf. Lemma 3.2.1), interprocedurally only the (trivial) implication posed by Lemma 10.3.3 holds.

Lemma 10.3.3 (Interprocedural Safety).

$$\forall n \in N^*. \ S\text{-}Safe(n) \Rightarrow Safe(n)$$

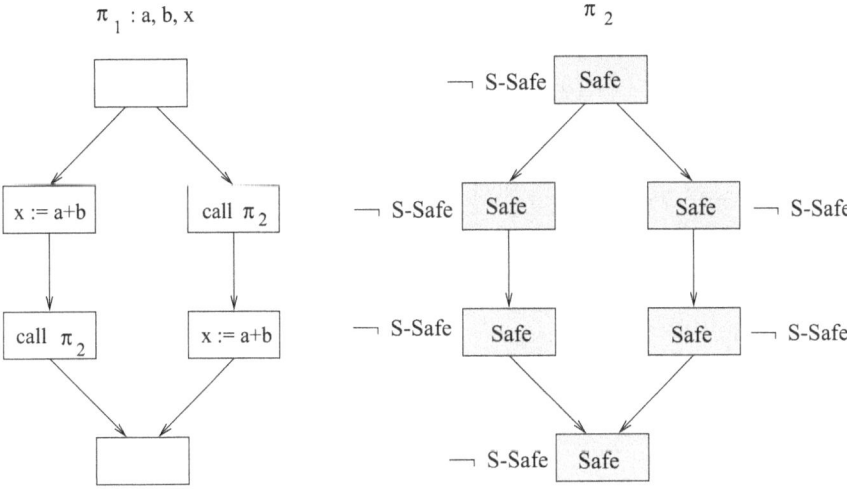

Fig. 10.15. Safety does not imply strong safety

The backward implication of Lemma 10.3.3 is in fact in general invalid as already previously illustrated by the program fragment of Figure 10.6. For convenience, Figure 10.15 recalls the essential part of this example. Note that all nodes of procedure π_2 are safe, though none of them is up-safe or down-safe.

Thus, the interprocedural version of the correctness lemma is weaker than its intraprocedural counterpart because intraprocedurally safety and strong safety coincide. In fact, the stronger implication

$$Correct_{ICM}(n) \Rightarrow S\text{-}Safe(n)$$

is in general invalid. This can be proved by means of Figure 10.15, too. Note that the start node of procedure π_2 is safe. After inserting an initialization at this node all nodes of π_2 satisfy the predicate *Correct* without that any of these nodes is strongly safe.

In the following we focus on canonic code motion transformations. Canonicity is sufficient for the computational optimality of the *IBCM*-transformation.

Definition 10.3.3 (Canonic Transformations).
An admissible interprocedural code motion transformation $ICM \in \mathcal{ICM}_{Adm}$ is canonic if and only if for every node $n \in \mathbf{N}^S$ the following condition holds:

$Insert_{ICM}(n) \Rightarrow$

$\forall p \in \mathbf{IP}[\mathbf{s}^*, \mathbf{e}^*] \, \forall k. \, p_k = n. \, \exists k \leq i \leq \lambda_p. \, SameInc_p[k, i[\, \wedge \, Replace_{ICM}(p_i) \, \wedge$

$$(\forall k + 1 \leq j \leq i. \, Insert_{ICM}(p_j) \Rightarrow \neg SameInc_p[k, j[)$$

We denote the set of all canonic interprocedural code motion transformations by $\mathcal{ICM}_{Can}$. A program resulting from a transformation of $\mathcal{ICM}_{Can}$ will be called canonic, too.

10.3.2 Computationally Optimal Transformations

Technically, the intraprocedural criterion of computational optimality can easily be extended to the interprocedural setting: a code motion transformation $ICM \in \mathcal{ICM}_{Adm}$ is *computationally better*[2] than a code motion transformation $ICM' \in \mathcal{ICM}_{Adm}$ if and only if

$$\forall \, p \in \mathbf{IP}[\mathbf{s}^*, \mathbf{e}^*]. \, | \, \{i \, | \, Comp_{ICM}(p_i)\} \, | \, \leq \, | \, \{i \, | \, Comp_{ICM'}(p_i)\} \, |$$

Note that $Comp_{ICM}$ denotes a local predicate, which is true for nodes containing a computation of t after applying the code motion transformation it is annotated with, i.e.:

$$Comp_{ICM}(n) =_{df} Insert_{ICM}(n) \vee (Comp(n) \wedge \neg Replace_{ICM}(n))$$

This allows us to define:

Definition 10.3.4 (Comp. Optimal Interprocedural Code Motion).

An admissible interprocedural code motion transformation $ICM \in \mathcal{ICM}_{Adm}$ is computationally optimal *if and only if it is computationally better than any other admissible interprocedural code motion transformation. We denote the set of all computationally optimal interprocedural code motion transformations by $\mathcal{ICM}_{CmpOpt}$.*

Intraprocedurally, $\mathcal{ICM}_{CmpOpt}$ is never empty: each program has a computationally (and even a lifetime) optimal counterpart (cf. Corollary 3.4.1). Moreover, canonicity is necessary for computational optimality (cf. Theorem 3.2.1). As shown in Section 10.1.1, these theorems do not carry over to the interprocedural setting (cf. Theorem 10.1.1). We have:

Theorem 10.3.1 (InterproceduralComp.OptimalityandCanonicity).

1. *There are programs, for which $\mathcal{ICM}_{CmpOpt}$ is empty.*
2. *In general, $\mathcal{ICM}_{CmpOpt}$ is not a subset of $\mathcal{ICM}_{Can}$.*

---

[2] Note that this relation is reflexive like its intraprocedural counterpart.

10.3.3 Lifetime Optimal Transformations

In this section we extend the notion of lifetime optimality to the interprocedural setting. Central is the introduction of the interprocedural notion of a lifetime range. In essence, interprocedural lifetime ranges are like their intraprocedural counterparts paths from insertion to replacement points. However, we have to take different incarnations of terms into account: nodes where relatively to the insertion point n a different incarnation of the term under consideration is valid, do not belong to a lifetime range starting in n, and must be excluded from the underlying path. Technically, this is accomplished by defining the set of (maximal) segments of a path, which are characterized by the fact that at all nodes of the segments the same incarnation of t is valid.

Definition 10.3.5 (Interprocedural Path Segments).
We define:

$$\forall\, p \in \mathbf{IP}[\mathbf{s}^*, \mathbf{e}^*] \ \forall\, 1 \leq i \leq j \leq \lambda_p.$$
$$Segments_{(i,j)}(p) =_{df} \{\, p[i',j'] \mid (i \leq i' \leq j' \leq j) \,\wedge$$
$$(\forall\, i' \leq l \leq j'. \ SameInc_p[i, l[\,) \,\wedge$$
$$(i' > i \Rightarrow \neg SameInc_p[i, i'-1[\,) \,\wedge$$
$$(j' < j \Rightarrow \neg SameInc_p[i, j'+1[\,)\,\}$$

This allows us to introduce the definition of interprocedural lifetime ranges.

Definition 10.3.6 (Interprocedural Lifetime Ranges).
Let $ICM \in \mathcal{ICM}_{Adm}$. We define:

$$LtRg\,(ICM) =_{df}$$
$$\{\,Segments_{(i,j)}(p) \mid\ p \in \mathbf{IP}[\mathbf{s}^*, \mathbf{c}^*] \,\wedge$$
$$1 \leq i \leq j \leq \lambda_p.\ Insert_{ICM}(p_i) \wedge SameInc_p[i, j[\ \wedge Replace_{ICM}(p_j) \,\wedge$$
$$(\forall\, i < l \leq j.\ Insert_{ICM}(p_l) \Rightarrow \neg SameInc_p[i, l[\,\}$$

By means of interprocedural lifetime ranges we can now define the interprocedural variant of the relation "lifetime better". An interprocedural code motion transformation $ICM \in \mathcal{ICM}_{Adm}$ is *lifetime better* than an interprocedural code motion transformation $ICM' \in \mathcal{ICM}_{Adm}$ if and only if

$$\forall\, P \in LtRg\,(ICM)\ \exists\, Q \in LtRg\,(ICM').\ P \sqsubseteq Q$$

where $\sqsubseteq$ denotes the inclusion relation on sets of paths (cf. Section 2.1.1). Summarizing, we define:

Definition 10.3.7 (Lifetime Optimal Interprocedural Code Motion).
A computationally optimal interprocedural code motion transformation $ICM \in \mathcal{ICM}_{CmpOpt}$ is lifetime optimal if and only if it is lifetime better than any other computationally optimal interprocedural code motion transformation. We denote the set of all lifetime optimal interprocedural code motion transformations by $\mathcal{ICM}_{LtOpt}$.

Obviously, we have (cf. Theorem 10.3.1(1)):

Theorem 10.3.2 (Interprocedural Lifetime Optimality).
There are programs, for which $\mathcal{ICM}_{LtOpt}$ is empty.

This is in contrast to the intraprocedural case. However, the following facts carry over to the interprocedural setting: if $\mathcal{ICM}_{CmpOpt} \neq \emptyset$, then there is usually more than one computationally optimal transformation, i.e., $|\mathcal{ICM}_{CmpOpt}| \geq 1$. Lifetime optimality, however, can at most be achieved by a single transformation (cf. Section 3.2.3). Note that the corresponding theorem relies only on properties of lifetime ranges and of computational optimality. Canonicity is not required.

Theorem 10.3.3 (Uniqueness of Lifetime Optimal Interproc. CM).

$$|\mathcal{ICM}_{LtOpt}| \leq 1$$

Proof. Let $ICM, ICM' \in \mathcal{ICM}_{LtOpt}$. Then we have to prove two equivalences:

$$\forall n \in \mathbf{N}^S.\ Insert_{ICM}(n) \iff Insert_{ICM'}(n) \tag{10.1}$$

$$\forall n \in \mathbf{N}^S.\ Replace_{ICM}(n) \iff Replace_{ICM'}(n) \tag{10.2}$$

For symmetry reasons it is sufficient to prove only one direction of these equivalences. Starting with (10.1), the computational optimality of *ICM* guarantees

$$\forall n \in \mathbf{N}^S.\ Insert_{ICM}(n) \Rightarrow$$
$$\exists m \in \mathbf{N}^S\ \exists p \in \mathbf{IP}[\mathbf{s}^*, \mathbf{e}^*]\ \exists i, j.$$
$$p_i = n \wedge p_j = m \wedge Segments_{(i,j)}(p) \in LtRg(ICM)$$

Moreover, the lifetime optimality of *ICM* yields that there are indexes i' and j' with

$$i' \leq i \leq j \leq j'$$

and

$$Segments_{(i,j)}(p) \sqsubseteq Segments_{(i',j')}(p) \in LtRg(ICM')$$

Suppose $i' < i$. Since *ICM'* is also lifetime optimal, there must be indexes i'' and j'' with

$$i'' \leq i' < i \leq j \leq j' \leq j''$$

and

$$Segments_{(i,j)}(p) \sqsubseteq Segments_{(i',j')}(p) \sqsubseteq Segments_{(i'',j'')}(p) \in LtRg(ICM)$$

In particular, we have

$$Segments_{(i,j)}(p), Segments_{(i'',j'')}(p) \in LtRg(ICM)$$

and

$$Segments_{(i,j)}(p) \sqsubseteq Segments_{(i'',j'')}(p)$$

Hence, Definition 10.3.6 delivers

$$\neg Insert_{ICM}(n)$$

This, however, is a contradiction to the premise of the implication under consideration. Thus, we have as desired $Insert_{ICM'}(n)$.

In order to prove (10.2), let $n \in \mathbf{N}^S$. Then (10.2) is a consequence of the following chain of implications:

$$
\begin{aligned}
& & Replace_{ICM}(n) \\
(ICM \in \mathcal{ICM}_{Adm}) & \Rightarrow & Comp(n) \wedge Correct_{ICM}(n) \\
(10.1) & \Rightarrow & Comp(n) \wedge Correct_{ICM'}(n) \\
(ICM' \in \mathcal{ICM}_{CmpOpt}) & \Rightarrow & Replace_{ICM'}(n)
\end{aligned}
$$

$\square$

Continuing the analogy to the intraprocedural setting, we introduce next the notion of *interprocedural first-use-lifetime ranges*, which is important for the optimality proofs of the *IBCM*- and *ILCM*-transformation.

Definition 10.3.8 (Interprocedural First-Use-Lifetime Ranges).
Let $ICM \in \mathcal{ICM}_{Adm}$. *We define*

$$FU\text{-}LtRg(ICM) =_{df} \{P \in LtRg(ICM) \mid \forall Q \in LtRg(ICM).Q \sqsubseteq P \Rightarrow Q = P\}$$

We have:

Lemma 10.3.4 (Interprocedural First-Use-Lifetime Range Lemma).

Let $ICM \in \mathcal{ICM}_{Adm}$, $p \in \mathbf{IP}[\mathbf{s}^*, \mathbf{e}^*]$, *and* $Q_1, Q_2 \in FU\text{-}LtRg(ICM)$ *with* $Q_1 \sqsubseteq p$ *and* $Q_2 \sqsubseteq p$. *Then either*

- $Q_1 = Q_2$ *or*
- Q_1 *and* Q_2 *are disjoint, i.e., they do not have any node occurrence in common.*

10.4 The *IBCM*-Transformation

In this section we present the interprocedural version of the busy code motion transformation called *IBCM*-transformation. Like its intraprocedural counterpart, it is based on the properties of down-safety and earliestness. We will prove that it is always admissible, and that it is computationally optimal, whenever it is canonic for the program under consideration.

10.4.1 Specification

Intuitively, a node n is *interprocedurally down-safe* at its entry, if on every terminating program path starting in n the first modification of t is preceded by a computation of t. Analogously, it is *interprocedurally down-safe* at its exit, if on every terminating path starting in a successor of n the first modification of t is preceded by a computation of t. Note that the definition of the corresponding intraprocedural property relies on the same intuition. However, the definition of interprocedural down-safety must be refined in order take care of the fact that there are different incarnations of t (cf. Definition 3.3.1).

Definition 10.4.1 (Interprocedural Down-Safety).
Let $n \in N^*$. n is interprocedurally

1. entry-down-safe $[\,in\ signs:\ N\text{-}DSafe^*\,(n)\,]$ $\iff_{df}$
   $\forall p \in \mathbf{IP}[\mathbf{s}^*, \mathbf{e}^*]\ \forall i.\ p_i = n \Rightarrow$
   $$\exists i \le j \le \lambda_p.\ Comp^*_{(p,i)}(p_j) \wedge Transp^{*\vee}_{(p,i)}(p[i,j[)$$
2. exit-down-safe $[\,in\ signs:\ X\text{-}DSafe^*\,(n)\,]$ $\iff_{df}$
   $\forall p \in \mathbf{IP}[\mathbf{s}^*, \mathbf{e}^*]\ \forall i.\ p_i = n \Rightarrow$
   $$\exists i < j \le \lambda_p.\ Comp\,(p_j) \wedge SameInc_p]i,j[\wedge Transp^{*\vee}_{(p,i+1)}(p]i,j[)$$

Note that the program point, which corresponds to the entry of a return node n of G^* in S, is the entry point of the unique successor of n. This implies that the entry of a return node of G^* must not be an insertion point of any interprocedural code motion transformation. This is automatically taken care of by the IDFA-algorithms of the *IBCM*-transformation. The specification here, however, requires a slightly modified version of the predicate $N\text{-}DSafe^*$, denoted by $I\text{-}DSafe$. A node $n \in N^*$ is *interprocedurally down-safe*, if it satisfies the predicate $I\text{-}DSafe$ defined by

$$\forall n \in N^*.\ I\text{-}DSafe\,(n) =_{df} \begin{cases} N\text{-}DSafe^*\,(n) & \text{if } n \notin N_r^* \\ N\text{-}DSafe^*\,(pred^*(n)) & \text{otherwise} \end{cases}$$

Considering a return node n, the predicates $I\text{-}DSafe$ and $N\text{-}DSafe^*$ coincide if all "siblings" of n have the same truth value. Using $I\text{-}DSafe$ instead of $N\text{-}DSafe^*$ guarantees that return nodes never satisfy the predicate "earliest", and therefore do not occur as insertion points of the *IBCM*-transformation.

Definition 10.4.2 (Interprocedural Earliestness).
Let $n \in Range(t)$. n is interprocedurally

1. entry-earliest $[\,in\ signs:\ N\text{-}Earliest^*\,(n)\,]$ $\iff_{df}$
   $\exists p \in \mathbf{IP}[\mathbf{s}^*, n]\ \forall 1 \le i < \lambda_p.\ I\text{-}DSafe\,(p_i) \wedge SameInc_p[i,\lambda_p[\Rightarrow$
   $$\neg Transp^{*\vee}_{(p,i)}(p[i,\lambda_p[)$$
2. exit-earliest $[\,in\ signs:\ X\text{-}Earliest^*\,(n)\,]$ $\iff_{df}$
   $\exists p \in \mathbf{IP}[\mathbf{s}^*, n]\ \forall 1 \le i \le \lambda_p.\ I\text{-}DSafe\,(p_i) \wedge SameInc_p[i,\lambda_p] \Rightarrow$
   $$\neg Transp^{*\vee}_{(p,i)}(p[i,\lambda_p])$$

Abbreviating *N-Earliest** by *I-Earliest*, Lemma 10.4.1 yields that the *IBCM*-transformation does not insert a computation into a return node or into the fictious procedure G_0 representing the external procedures of the program under consideration. This lemma follows immediately from the definition of the predicate *I-DSafe* and the local abstract semantics of end nodes and return nodes being a successor of the end node of G_0.[3] A dual lemma holds for the *ILCM*-transformation. For the *IBCM*-transformation it is as follows:

Lemma 10.4.1. $\forall n \in N^*.\ I\text{-}DSafe(n) \wedge I\text{-}Earliest(n) \Rightarrow$
$$n \in N^* \setminus (N_r^* \cup \{\mathbf{s_0}, n_0, \mathbf{e_0}\})$$

Table 10.2 now presents the definitions of the predicates $Insert_{IBCM}$ and $Replace_{IBCM}$, which define the *IBCM*-transformation.

- $\forall n \in \mathbf{N}^S.\ Insert_{IBCM}(n) =_{df} I\text{-}DSafe(n) \wedge I\text{-}Earliest(n)$
- $\forall n \in \mathbf{N}^S.\ Replace_{IBCM}(n) =_{df} Comp(n)$

Table 10.2: The *IBCM*-transformation

The *IBCM*-transformation is admissible. We prove this property next, though it requires to anticipate the second part of the *IBCM*-Lemma 10.4.2. However, this does not cause any subtleties as it is independent of the admissibility theorem. We have:

Theorem 10.4.1 (*IBCM*-Admissibility).

$$IBCM \in \mathcal{ICM}_{Adm}$$

Proof. In order to prove $IBCM \in \mathcal{ICM}_{Adm}$, we must show that all insertions and replacements are safe and correct, respectively. The safety of insertions is a consequence of:

$$
\begin{array}{rcl}
 & & Insert_{IBCM} \\
(\text{Def. } Insert_{IBCM}) & \Rightarrow & I\text{-}DSafe \\
(\text{Def. } I\text{-}DSafe) & \Rightarrow & N\text{-}DSafe^* \\
(\text{Def. } S\text{-}Safe) & \Rightarrow & S\text{-}Safe \\
(\text{Lemma } 10.3.3) & \Rightarrow & Safe
\end{array}
$$

The correctness of replacements follows from:

---

[3] Recall that nodes $\mathbf{e} \in \{\mathbf{e_0}, \mathbf{e_1}, \dots, \mathbf{e_k}\}$ represent the empty statement "skip".

$$Replace_{IBCM}$$

$$
\begin{aligned}
(\text{Def. } Replace_{IBCM}) \;&\Rightarrow\; Comp \\
(\text{Def. } N\text{-}DSafe^*) \;&\Rightarrow\; N\text{-}DSafe^* \\
(\text{Def. } S\text{-}Safe) \;&\Rightarrow\; S\text{-}Safe \\
(\text{Lemma } 10.3.3) \;&\Rightarrow\; Safe \\
(\text{Lemma } 10.4.2(2)) \;&\Rightarrow\; Correct_{IBCM}
\end{aligned}
$$

$\square$

Reestablishing Formal Procedure Calls. In this section we discuss how to reestablish the formal procedure calls in S after the $IBCM$-transformation, a step, which is necessary because formal procedure calls have been unfolded before the transformation (cf. Section 10.2). We illustrate this procedure by means of Figure 10.14. In order to fix the setting, let $M =_{df} \{ n(\pi) \mid \pi \in callee(n) \}$ be the set of nodes introduced for replacing a formal procedure call node n, and let $M' =_{df} \{ n'(\pi) \mid \pi \in callee(n) \}$ be the set of immediate successors of nodes of M. According to the splitting of edges leading to nodes with more than one predecessor, all nodes of M' are synthetic and represent the empty statement "skip". In particular, for every $\pi \in callee(n)$, we assume that $n'(\pi)$ denotes the unique successor of $n(\pi)$, and $n(\pi)$ the unique predecessor of $n'(\pi)$. Moreover, we have $|\, pred_{fg(M)}(M)\,| = |\, succ_{fg(M')}(M')\,| = 1$. In this situation the formal procedure call is reestablished as displayed in Figure 10.16: the sets M and M' of nodes are replaced by the original node n and a new node n', respectively. Correspondingly, the set of edges reaching a node in M is replaced by a single edge from the unique predecessor p of the nodes of M to n, and the set of edges leaving a node of M is replaced by a single edge from n to n'. Moreover, the set of edges leaving a node of M' is replaced by a single edge from n' to the unique successor s of the nodes of M' (cf. Figure 10.16(a)). Having settled the graph structure, we are left with fixing the predicates $Insert$ and $Replace$ for n and n' with respect to the predicate values applying to nodes of M and M'. Starting with the predicate $Insert$, this is straightforward, if all or if none of the nodes of M and M', respectively, satisfy the predicate $Insert_{IBCM}$, i.e., if the following equalities $|\{ Insert_{IBCM}(n(\pi)) \mid \pi \in callee(n) \}| = |\{ Insert_{IBCM}(n'(\pi)) \mid \pi \in callee(n) \}| = 1$ hold. In these cases we define

$$
Insert_{IBCM}(m) =_{df}
\begin{cases}
\displaystyle\prod_{\pi \in callee(n)} Insert_{IBCM}(n(\pi)) & \text{if } m = n \\[2ex]
\displaystyle\prod_{\pi \in callee(n)} Insert_{IBCM}(n'(\pi)) & \text{if } m = n'
\end{cases}
$$

The remaining cases are slightly more complicated:
If $|\{ Insert_{IBCM}(n(\pi)) \mid \pi \in callee(n) \}| = 2$, a new edge must be introduced between n and its unique predecessor p, which is split by a new node $\bar{n}$ as illustrated in Figure 10.16(b). In this case, $Insert_{IBCM}(n)$ is set

to *false* and *Insert*$_{IBCM}(\bar{n})$ to *true*. Note that the new branch in p is deterministic, i.e., the branch to $\bar{n}$ is taken if and only if the argument procedure bound to the parameter procedure of node n is an element of $\{\pi \in$ *callee*$(n) \mid$ *Insert*$_{IBCM}(n(\pi))\}$. Analogously, a new branch must be inserted at the end of node n' in case of $|\{$ *Insert*$_{IBCM}(n'(\pi)) \mid \pi \in$ *callee*$(n)\}| = 2$.

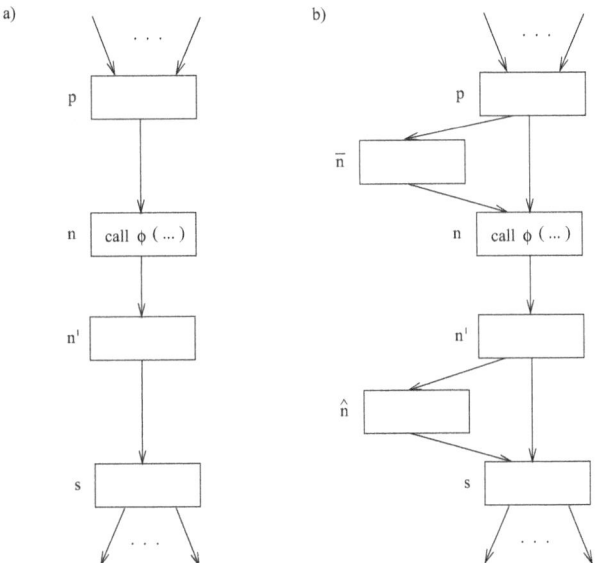

Fig. 10.16. Reestablishing formal procedure calls after the *IBCM*-transf.

Finally, the predicates *Replace*$_{IBCM}(n)$ and *Replace*$_{IBCM}(n')$ have to be set as follows:[4]

$$Replace_{IBCM}(m) =_{df} \begin{cases} \prod\limits_{\pi \in callee(n)} Replace_{IBCM}(n(\pi)) & \text{if } m = n \\ false & \text{if } m = n' \end{cases}$$

Note that the number of computations on a program path of $\mathbf{IP}[\mathbf{s}^*, \mathbf{e}^*]$ is invariant under the restoration of formal procedure calls. Without loss of generality we can thus prove the computational optimality of the *IBCM*-transformation before their reconstruction.

Checking Canonicity. The *IBCM*-transformation is always admissible (cf. Theorem 10.4.1). Under the premise of canonicity it is also computationally optimal; a condition, which can easily be checked by investigating the insertion points. For a specific insertion this can be accomplished in time linear to the number of nodes of the program by a simple marking algorithm,

---

[4] Note that n' represents the empty statement "skip", which implies $\neg Comp(n')$.

which, starting at the insertion point under consideration, recursively marks all nodes reachable from it until it either stops at a use site or a reinsertion of the computation under consideration of the same incarnation. The insertion is canonic, if the marking stops at use sites only. Note that even in the presence of recursive procedure calls the algorithm does not have to visit nodes twice: if the term contains a variable being local to the callee, the call can simply be skipped as entering the callee activates a new incarnation of the term. Thus, as a consequence of the down-safety of the insertion point under consideration, we obtain that the use site justifying down-safety follows the recursive call. Alternatively and more efficiently, canonicity of the *IBCM*-transformation can also be checked in the style of the "unusability" analysis of Section 10.5.1 using the dual version of this property.

10.4.2 Proving Computational Optimality

In this section we assume that the *IBCM*-transformation is canonic for the program under consideration. Under this premise, we will prove that it is interprocedurally computationally optimal (cf. *IBCM*-Optimality Theorem 10.4.2). In essence, this can be proved as in the intraprocedural case. Central is the *IBCM*-Lemma 10.4.2. Note that only its third part, which intuitively states that every insertion of the *IBCM*-insertion is used on every program continuation without a preceding modification or reinsertion, relies on the canonicity of the *IBCM*-transformation. This, in fact, is crucial for the proof of computational optimality.

Lemma 10.4.2 (*IBCM*-Lemma).

1. $\forall\, n \in \mathbf{N}^S.\ Insert_{IBCM}(n) \iff S\text{-}Safe(n) \land$

$$
\begin{cases}
\displaystyle\prod_{m\in caller(fg(n))} \neg Transp(m_C) & \text{if } n \in \{\mathbf{s}_1,\ldots,\mathbf{s}_k\} \\[2ex]
\displaystyle\prod_{m\in pred_{fg(n)}(n)} (\neg GlobTransp(m) \lor \neg Safe(m)) \\
\quad\quad\quad \text{if } \emptyset \neq pred_{fg(n)}(n) \subseteq \mathbf{N}^S\backslash\mathbf{N}_c^S\ \lor \\
\quad\quad\quad\quad (pred_{fg(n)}(n) = \{m\} \subseteq \mathbf{N}_c^S\ \land \\
\quad\quad\quad\quad\ Var(t) \not\subseteq GlobVar(callee(m))) \\[1ex]
(\neg GlobTransp(m) \lor \neg Safe(m))\ \land \\
\neg Safe(end(callee(m))) \quad\quad \text{if } pred_{fg(n)}(n) = \{m\} \subseteq \mathbf{N}_c^S\ \land \\
\quad\quad\quad\quad\quad\quad\quad\quad\quad\ Var(t) \subseteq GlobVar(callee(m))
\end{cases}
$$

2. $\forall\, n \in \mathbf{N}^S.\ Correct_{IBCM}(n) \iff Safe(n)$
3. If $IBCM \in \mathcal{ICM}_{Can}$, then we have:

$$\forall\, p \in \mathbf{IP}[\mathbf{s}^*,\mathbf{e}^*]\ \forall\, i.\ Insert_{IBCM}(p_i) \Rightarrow$$
$$\exists\, j \geq i.\ Segments_{(i,j)}(p) \in FU\text{-}LtRg(IBCM)$$

4. $\forall\, ICM \in \mathcal{ICM}_{Adm} \forall\, p \in \mathbf{IP}[\mathbf{s}^*,\mathbf{e}^*](\forall\, i,j.\ Segments_{(i,j)}(p) \in LtRg(IBCM)).$
$$\neg Replace_{ICM}(p_j) \lor \exists\, i \leq l \leq j.\ Insert_{ICM}(p_l) \land (p_l) \sqsubseteq Segments_{(i,j)}(p)$$

Proof. Part 1). Starting with the proof of the first implication, "$\Rightarrow$", we have that $Insert_{IBCM}$ implies *I-DSafe*, and *I-DSafe* implies *S-Safe*. Thus, we are left with showing the implication

$$Insert_{IBCM}(n) \Rightarrow$$

$$\begin{cases} \displaystyle\prod_{m \in caller(fg(n))} \neg Transp(m_C) & \text{if } n \in \{\mathbf{s}_1, \ldots, \mathbf{s}_k\} \\[2ex] \displaystyle\prod_{m \in pred_{\mathbf{fg}(n)}(n)} (\neg GlobTransp(m) \vee \neg Safe(m)) \\[1ex] \qquad\qquad \text{if } \emptyset \neq pred_{fg(n)}(n) \subseteq \mathbf{N}^S \backslash \mathbf{N}_c^S \vee \\[0.5ex] \qquad\qquad\quad (pred_{fg(n)}(n) = \{m\} \subseteq \mathbf{N}_c^S \wedge \\[0.5ex] \qquad\qquad\quad Var(t) \not\subseteq GlobVar(callee(m))) \\[1ex] (\neg GlobTransp(m) \vee \neg Safe(m)) \wedge \\[0.5ex] \neg Safe(end(callee(m))) \\[1ex] \qquad\qquad \text{if } pred_{fg(n)}(n) = \{m\} \subseteq \mathbf{N}_c^S \wedge \\[0.5ex] \qquad\qquad\quad Var(t) \subseteq GlobVar(callee(m)) \end{cases} \tag{10.3}$$

As the main procedure cannot be called, we have $caller(fg(\mathbf{s}_1)) = \emptyset$. This directly implies the validity of implication (10.3) for $n = \mathbf{s}_1$. Next, let $n \in \{\mathbf{s}_2, \ldots, \mathbf{s}_k\}$, and assume that

$$\prod_{m \in caller(fg(n))} \neg Transp(m_C)$$

is invalid. As all procedure calls in S are ordinary, this assumption implies

$$\prod_{m \in caller(fg(n))} Transp(m_C)$$

which yields

$$\forall p \in \mathbf{IP}[\mathbf{s}^*, n].\ SameInc_p[\lambda_p - 1, \lambda_p[$$

Combining this with *I-DSafe*(n) we get

$$\prod_{m \in caller(fg(n))} \text{*I-DSafe*}(m)$$

and therefore by means of Definition 10.4.2 $\neg$*I-Earliest*(n), which is a contradiction to $Insert_{IBCM}(n)$.

We are now left with proving implication (10.3) for $n \in \mathbf{N}^S \backslash \{\mathbf{s}_1, \ldots, \mathbf{s}_k\}$. First, we show that n has a unique predecessor, which is accomplished by proving the contrapositive of

$$\forall n \in \mathbf{N}^S \backslash \{\mathbf{s}_1, \ldots, \mathbf{s}_k\}.\ Insert_{IBCM}(n) \Rightarrow |pred_{fg(n)}(n)| = 1 \tag{10.4}$$

Thus, let $n \in \mathbf{N}^S \backslash \{\mathbf{s}_1, \ldots, \mathbf{s}_k\}$, and suppose that $|pred_{fg(n)}(n)| \geq 2$. Lemma 10.2.2(1a) and Corollary 10.2.1(1) then yield

$$succ_{fg(n)}(pred_{fg(n)}(n)) = \{n\} \quad \wedge \prod_{m \in pred_{\mathbf{fg}(n)}(n)} Transp(m)$$

Moreover, we have

$$\forall\, p \in \mathbf{IP}[\mathbf{s}^*, n].\ SameInc_p[\lambda_p - 1, \lambda_p[$$

Hence, $I\text{-}DSafe\,(n)$ implies

$$\prod_{m \in pred_{\mathrm{fg}(n)}(n)} I\text{-}DSafe\,(m) \tag{10.5}$$

By means of (10.5), Definition 10.4.2 yields

$$\neg I\text{-}Earliest\,(n)$$

This directly implies $\neg Insert_{IBCM}(n)$ as desired. Thus, n has a unique predecessor, which we denote by m.

In order to complete the proof of implication (10.3), we must investigate three cases. Without loss of generality we can assume that m satisfies the predicate $GlobTransp(m)$.

Case 1. $m \in \mathbf{N}^S \backslash \mathbf{N}_c^S$

In this case $GlobTransp(m)$ is equivalent to $Transp\,(m)$. Moreover, for all $p \in \mathbf{IP}[\mathbf{s}^*, n]$ we have $SameInc_p[\lambda_p - 1, \lambda_p[$. Suppose that m satisfies the predicate $Safe$. According to Definition 10.3.1 this implies

$$\forall\, p \in \mathbf{IP}[\mathbf{s}^*, \mathbf{e}^*]\ \forall\, i.\ (p_i = m) \Rightarrow$$
$$a)\ \exists\, j < i.\ Comp\,(p_j) \wedge SameInc_p[j, i[\, \wedge\, Transp^{*\vee}_{(p,j)}(p[j, i[)\ \vee \tag{10.6}$$
$$b)\ \exists\, j \geq i.\ Comp^*_{(p,i)}(p_j) \wedge Transp^{*\vee}_{(p,i)}(p[i, j[)$$

The proof proceeds now by showing that $I\text{-}Earliest\,(n)$ does not hold, which as desired yields a contradiction to $Insert_{IBCM}(n)$. This can be achieved by considering each path passing node n separately. Thus, let $p \in \mathbf{IP}[\mathbf{s}^*, \mathbf{e}^*]$ and let $i \in \{1, \ldots, \lambda_p\}$ with $p_i = n$. If there is an index $j < i$ satisfying condition a) of (10.6), i.e., in case of a)

$$\exists\, j < i.\ Comp\,(p_j) \wedge SameInc_p[j, i[\, \wedge\, Transp^{*\vee}_{(p,j)}(p[j, i[)$$

we immediately get the equivalent formula

$$\exists\, j < i.\ I\text{-}DSafe\,(p_j) \wedge SameInc_p[j, i[\, \wedge\, Transp^{*\vee}_{(p,j)}(p[j, i[)$$

According to Definition 10.4.2, p cannot be used for justifying the predicate $I\text{-}Earliest\,(n)$. Thus, we are left with the case of condition b), i.e.,

$$\exists\, j \geq i.\ Comp^*_{(p,i)}(p_j) \wedge Transp^{*\vee}_{(p,i)}(p[i, j[)$$

Without loss of generality we can assume

$$\forall\, l < i.\ Comp\,(p_l) \Rightarrow \neg(SameInc_p[l, i[\, \wedge\, Transp^{*\vee}_{(p,l)}(p[l, i[)) \tag{10.7}$$

because otherwise we succeed as above. Moreover, without loss of generality we can additionally assume that

$$\forall l < i. \ I\text{-}DSafe\,(p_l) \Rightarrow \neg(SameInc_p[l,i[\wedge Transp^{*\,\vee}_{(p,l)}(p[l,i[)) \qquad (10.8)$$

because the existence of an index l violating (10.8) would exclude according to Definition 10.4.2 the usage of p for justifying *I-Earliest*(n). Together, (10.7) and (10.8), however, imply the existence of a path p passing node m violating both constraint a) and b) of (10.6). This, however, is a contradiction to the safety of m, which finishes the proof of Case 1.

Case 2. $m \in \mathbf{N}_c^S \wedge Var(t) \nsubseteq GlobVar(callee(m))$
In this case Lemma 10.2.6(2) yields for all paths $p \in \mathbf{IP}[\mathbf{s}^*,n]$ with

$$p[i,\lambda_p-2] \in \mathbf{CIP}[start(callee(m)), end(callee(m))]$$

that the predicate $SameInc_p[i-1,\lambda_p[$ is satisfied. Additionally, $GlobTransp(m)$ implies

$$Transp^{*\,\vee}_{(p,i-1)}(p[i-1,\lambda_p[)$$

Thus, as in Case 1, the assumption that m satisfies the predicate *Safe*, implies $\neg I\text{-}Earliest\,(n)$, and therefore a contradiction to $Insert_{IBCM}(n)$, which completes the proof of Case 2.

Case 3. $m \in \mathbf{N}_c^S \wedge Var(t) \subseteq GlobVar(callee(m))$
Here we have to prove the conjunction

$$\neg Safe(m) \wedge \neg Safe(end(callee(m)))$$

Clearly, $\neg Safe(m)$ holds for the same reasons as in Case 2. Thus, we are left with showing $\neg Safe(end(callee(m)))$. Suppose that $end(callee(m))$ satisfies the predicate *Safe*. This yields

$$\forall p \in \mathbf{IP}[\mathbf{s}^*,\mathbf{e}^*] \ \forall i. \ (p_i = end(callee(m))) \Rightarrow$$
$$a) \ \exists j < i. \ Comp\,(p_j) \wedge SameInc_p[j,i[\wedge Transp^{*\,\vee}_{(p,j)}(p[j,i[) \ \vee \ (10.9)$$
$$b) \ \exists j \geq i. \ Comp^*_{(p,i)}(p_j) \wedge Transp^{*\,\vee}_{(p,i)}(p[i,j[)$$

and the proof can now be completed as in Case 1 using $end(callee(m))$ instead of m.

The converse implication, "$\Leftarrow$", is proved as follows. If $n = \mathbf{s}_1$, $S\text{-}Safe(n)$ is equivalent to $N\text{-}DSafe^*\,(n)$. This directly implies $I\text{-}DSafe\,(n)$ and $t \in Range(n)$. Moreover, Definition 10.4.2 yields $N\text{-}Earliest^*\,(n)$, which is equivalent to $I\text{-}Earliest\,(n)$. Hence, we obtain as desired

$$Insert_{IBCM}(\mathbf{s}_1)$$

Let now $n \in \{\mathbf{s}_2,\dots,\mathbf{s}_k\}$. Then

$$\prod_{m \in caller(fg(n))} \neg\, Transp\,(m_C) \qquad (10.10)$$

yields

$$N\text{-}DSafe^*\,(n)$$

Since $n \in \{s_2, \ldots, s_k\}$ this is equivalent to $I\text{-}DSafe(n)$. Moreover, this yields $t \in Range(n)$. Thus, we are left with showing that $I\text{-}Earliest(n)$ holds, too. Clearly, (10.10) yields

$$\forall p \in \mathbf{IP}[\mathbf{s}^*, n] \; \forall i < \lambda_p. \; \neg SameInc_p[i, \lambda_p[$$

Hence, applying Definition 10.4.2(1) we get as desired $I\text{-}Earliest(n)$.

We are now left with the case $n \in \mathbf{N}^S \backslash \{s_1, \ldots, s_k\}$. Similar to the first implication, we prove that n has exactly one predecessor. This is done by showing the contrapositive of

$$
\begin{aligned}
&\forall n \in \mathbf{N}^S \backslash \{s_1, \ldots, s_k\}. \\
&\quad S\text{-}Safe(n) \; \wedge \prod_{m \in pred_{fg(n)}(n)} (\neg GlobTransp(m) \vee \neg Safe(m)) \\
&\quad \Rightarrow |pred_{fg(n)}(n)| = 1
\end{aligned}
\tag{10.11}
$$

To this end let $n \in \mathbf{N}^S \backslash \{s_1, \ldots, s_k\}$, and suppose that

$$|pred_{fg(n)}(n)| \geq 2$$

Lemma 10.2.2(1a) and Corollary 10.2.1(1) then yield

$$succ_{fg(n)}(pred_{fg(n)}(n)) = \{n\} \quad \wedge \prod_{m \in pred_{fg(n)}(n)} Transp(m)$$

In particular, we therefore have

$$\prod_{m \in pred_{fg(n)}(n)} GlobTransp(m)$$

Without loss of generality we can assume (recall that n satisfies $S\text{-}Safe$)

$$N\text{-}USafe^*(n) \; \wedge \; \neg N\text{-}DSafe^*(n) \tag{10.12}$$

because $N\text{-}DSafe^*(n)$ and the transparency of n's predecessors yield

$$\prod_{m \in pred_{fg(n)}(n)} S\text{-}Safe(m)$$

This implies

$$\prod_{m \in pred_{fg(n)}(n)} Safe(m)$$

and therefore as desired the negation of the premise of (10.11). (10.12) now implies

$$\prod_{m \in pred_{fg(n)}(n)} N\text{-}USafe^*(m) \vee Comp(m)$$

Clearly, *Comp* implies *N-DSafe**. Hence, we obtain

$$\prod_{m \in pred_{\mathrm{fg}(n)}(n)} N\text{-}USafe^*\,(m) \vee N\text{-}DSafe^*\,(m)$$

and therefore

$$\prod_{m \in pred_{\mathrm{fg}(n)}(n)} S\text{-}Safe(m)$$

implying

$$\prod_{m \in pred_{\mathrm{fg}(n)}(n)} Safe(m)$$

as well. This yields as desired the negation of the premise of (10.11). Hence, n has a unique predecessor, which we denote by m. Next, we must investigate the following three cases.

Case 1. $m \in \mathbf{N}^S \backslash \mathbf{N}_c^S$
In this case the predicates *GlobTransp* and *Transp* are equivalent for m. Additionally, we have:

$$\forall\, p \in \mathbf{IP}[\mathbf{s}^*, n].\ SameInc_p[\lambda_p - 1, \lambda_p[\tag{10.13}$$

Moreover, we also have

$$N\text{-}USafe^*\,(n)\ \vee N\text{-}DSafe^*\,(n)$$

because n satisfies the predicate *S-Safe*. Suppose now that n satisfies *N-USafe**. Applying the definition of *N-USafe** we obtain

$$\forall\, p \in \mathbf{IP}[\mathbf{s}^*, n]\ \exists\, j < \lambda_p.$$
$$Comp\,(p_j) \wedge SameInc_p[j, \lambda_p[\wedge Transp^{*\vee}_{(p,j)}(p[j, \lambda_p[) \tag{10.14}$$

Together with (10.13) this implies *Transp* (m). Thus, by means of the premise of "$\Leftarrow$" we get

$$\neg Safe(m) \tag{10.15}$$

In particular, this yields $\neg Comp\,(m)$. Hence, (10.14) is equivalent to

$$\forall\, p \in \mathbf{IP}[\mathbf{s}^*, m]$$
$$\exists\, j < \lambda_p - 1.\ Comp\,(p_j) \wedge SameInc_p[j, \lambda_p - 1[\wedge Transp^{*\vee}_{(p,j)}(p[j, \lambda_p - 2[)$$

which directly yields

$$N\text{-}USafe^*\,(m)$$

and hence

$$Safe(m)$$

This, however, is a contradiction to (10.15). Thus, we have *N-DSafe** (n), and therefore also *I-DSafe* (n). Hence, we are left with showing *I-Earliest* (n). If *Transp* (m) is invalid, *I-Earliest* (n) holds trivially by means of (10.13) and

Definition 10.4.2(1). Otherwise, i.e., if $Transp\,(m)$ and $\neg Safe(m)$ hold, the assumption $\neg I\text{-}Earliest\,(n)$ implies $N\text{-}USafe^*\,(m)$. This, however, yields a contradiction to the premise $\neg Safe(m)$. Together, this implies $Insert_{IBCM}\,(n)$ as desired.

Case 2. $m \in \mathbf{N}_c^S \wedge Var(t) \not\subseteq GlobVar(callee(m))$

Suppose that $S\text{-}Safe(n)$ does not imply $N\text{-}DSafe^*\,(n)$, i.e., suppose we have

$$N\text{-}USafe^*\,(n) \wedge \neg N\text{-}DSafe^*\,(n)$$

Applying the definition of $N\text{-}USafe^*$ and Lemma 10.2.6(2) we obtain

$$\forall p \in \mathbf{IP}[\mathbf{s}^*, n] \; \exists j \leq i'.$$
$$Comp\,(p_j) \wedge SameInc_p[j, \lambda_p[\wedge Transp^{*\forall}_{(p,j)}(p[j, \lambda_p[) \tag{10.16}$$

where $p_{i'}$ is the matching call node to $p_{\lambda_p - 1}$ on p. Together with Lemma 10.2.7 this delivers

$$N\text{-}USafe^*\,(p_{i'}) \vee Comp\,(p_{i'})$$

Since $Comp$ implies $N\text{-}DSafe^*$ we obtain

$$N\text{-}USafe^*\,(p_{i'}) \vee N\text{-}DSafe^*\,(p_{i'})$$

Thus, we have

$$S\text{-}Safe(p_{i'})$$

and therefore

$$S\text{-}Safe(m)$$

which implies

$$Safe(m)$$

Moreover, (10.16) yields directly

$$GlobTransp(m)$$

This, however, is a contradiction to the premise of "$\Leftarrow$". Thus, we have $N\text{-}DSafe^*\,(n)$, and therefore also $I\text{-}DSafe\,(n)$. Now, $I\text{-}Earliest\,(n)$ remains to be verified. If $GlobTransp(m)$ does not hold, $I\text{-}Earliest\,(n)$ holds trivially according to Definition 10.4.2(1). Otherwise, i.e., if $GlobTransp(m)$ and $\neg Safe(m)$ hold, the assumption $\neg I\text{-}Earliest\,(n)$ directly yields $N\text{-}USafe^*\,(m)$, and therefore a contradiction to the premise $\neg Safe(m)$. Thus, we obtain $Insert_{IBCM}\,(n)$ as desired.

Case 3. $m \in \mathbf{N}_c^S \wedge Var(t) \subseteq GlobVar(callee(m))$

Similar to Case 2, the assumption

$$N\text{-}USafe^*\,(n) \wedge \neg N\text{-}DSafe^*\,(n)$$

leads to a contradiction to the premise that $end(callee(m))$ does not satisfy the predicate $Safe$. Thus, we have $N\text{-}DSafe^*\,(n)$, and therefore also $I\text{-}DSafe\,(n)$. Additionally, if

$$\neg Safe(end(callee(m))) \wedge \neg GlobTransp(m)$$

is satisfied, Definition 10.4.2(1) yields directly *I-Earliest*(n). Otherwise, i.e., if

$$\neg Safe(end(callee(m))) \ \wedge \ \neg Safe(m)$$

holds, the assumption $\neg I\text{-}Earliest(n)$ implies $N\text{-}USafe^*(end(callee(m)))$, and therefore a contradiction to the premise $\neg Safe(end(callee(m)))$. Hence, in both cases we obtain as desired $Insert_{IBCM}(n)$.

Part 2). The first implication, "$\Rightarrow$", holds by means of the Correctness Lemma 10.3.2. Thus, we are left with showing the second implication, "$\Leftarrow$",

$$\forall n \in \mathbf{N}^S. \ Safe(n) \Rightarrow Correct_{IBCM}(n) \qquad (10.17)$$

This is equivalent to

$$
\begin{aligned}
(\forall p \in \mathbf{IP}[\mathbf{s}^*, \mathbf{e}^*] \ \forall i. \ (p_i = n) \Rightarrow & \\
a) \ \exists j < i. \ Comp(p_j) \wedge SameInc_p[j,i[\wedge Transp^{*\vee}_{(p,j)}(p[j,i[) \ \vee & \\
b) \ \exists j \geq i. \ Comp^*_{(p,i)}(p_j) \wedge Transp^{*\vee}_{(p,i)}(p[i,j[) \ ) & \\
\Rightarrow \ \exists l < i. \ Insert_{IBCM}(p_l) \wedge SameInc_p[l,i[\wedge Transp^{*\vee}_{(p,l)}(p[l,i[) &
\end{aligned}
\qquad (10.18)
$$

Implication (10.18) is now proved by investigating every path p separately by a case analysis on the size of j. If there is an index j satisfying condition a) of (10.18), condition a) is because of the fact that *Comp* implies *I-DSafe* equivalent to

$$\exists j < i. \ I\text{-}DSafe(p_j) \wedge SameInc_p[j,i[\wedge Transp^{*\vee}_{(p,j)}(p[j,i[) \qquad (10.19)$$

Thus, the index l_p

$$l_p =_{df} Min(\{\, j \mid I\text{-}DSafe(p_j) \wedge SameInc_p[j,i[\wedge Transp^{*\vee}_{(p,j)}(p[j,i[)\,\}) \quad (10.20)$$

is well-defined. Together with Definition 10.4.2(1) we then obtain

$$I\text{-}DSafe(p_{l_p}) \ \wedge \ I\text{-}Earliest(p_{l_p})$$

and therefore

$$Insert_{IBCM}(p_{l_p}) \qquad (10.21)$$

Combining (10.20) and (10.21), we have:

$$Insert_{IBCM}(p_{l_p}) \wedge SameInc_p[l_p, \lambda_p[\wedge Transp^{*\vee}_{(p,l_p)}(p[l_p,i[)$$

Hence, $Correct_{IBCM}(n)$ holds on p as desired.

If there is no index j satisfying condition a) of (10.18), but condition b), we obtain

$$I\text{-}DSafe(p_j)$$

and hence, as in the previous case, the index l_p

$$l_p =_{df} Min(\{\, j \mid \textit{I-DSafe}\,(p_j) \wedge \textit{SameInc}_p[j, i[\wedge \textit{Transp}^{*\vee}_{(p,j)}(p[j, i[)\}) \quad (10.22)$$

is well-defined for path p. In particular, we have

$$l_p \leq i$$

because $l_p > i$ yields a contradiction to the safety of node n. Thus, the proof can now be completed as in Case 1.

Part 3). Let $p \in \mathbf{IP}[\mathbf{s}^*, \mathbf{e}^*]$ and $i \in \{1, \ldots, \lambda_p\}$ with $\textit{Insert}_{IBCM}(p_i)$. Clearly, we have $p_i \in N^* \setminus N_r^*$. Moreover, we also have $\textit{I-DSafe}\,(p_i)$, and therefore $\textit{N-DSafe}^*\,(p_i)$ as well. This yields

$$\exists\, i \leq j \leq \lambda_p.\ \textit{Comp}^*_{(p,i)}(p_j) \ \wedge \ \textit{Transp}^{*\vee}_{(p,i)}(p[i, j[) \quad (10.23)$$

In particular,

$$j_p =_{df} Min(\{\, j \mid i \leq j \leq \lambda_p.\ \textit{Comp}^*_{(p,i)}(p_j) \ \wedge \ \textit{Transp}^{*\vee}_{(p,i)}(p[i, j[)\,\})$$

is well-defined. Hence, the canonicity of $IBCM$ yields

$$\forall\, i < l \leq j_p.\ \textit{SameInc}_p[i, l[\ \Rightarrow \ \neg\textit{Insert}_{IBCM}(p_l) \quad (10.24)$$

and therefore

$$\textit{Segments}_{(i, j_p)}(p) \in \textit{FU-LtRg}\,(IBCM)$$

as desired.

Part 4). Let $ICM \in \mathcal{ICM}_{Adm}$, $p \in \mathbf{IP}[\mathbf{s}^*, \mathbf{e}^*]$, and $\textit{Segments}_{(i,j)}(p) \in \textit{LtRg}\,(IBCM)$. Without loss of generality we can assume that the original computation in p_j is replaced, i.e., $\textit{Replace}_{ICM}(p_j)$ holds. The admissibility of ICM then guarantees

$$\textit{Correct}_{ICM}(p_j) \quad (10.25)$$

Moreover, $\textit{Segments}_{(i,j)}(p) \in \textit{LtRg}\,(IBCM)$ yields $\textit{Insert}_{IBCM}(p_i)$. Thus, by means of Lemma 10.4.2(1) we have

$$\begin{cases} \displaystyle\prod_{m \in caller(fg(p_i))} \neg\,\textit{Transp}\,(m_C) & \text{if } p_i \in \{\mathbf{s}_1, \ldots, \mathbf{s}_k\} \\[2ex] \displaystyle\prod_{m \in pred_{fg(p_i)}(p_i)} (\neg\,\textit{GlobTransp}(m) \vee \neg\textit{Safe}(m)) & \\[1ex] & \text{if } \emptyset \neq pred_{fg(p_i)}(p_i) \subseteq \mathbf{N}^S \setminus \mathbf{N}_c^S \ \vee \\ & \quad (pred_{fg(p_i)}(p_i) = \{m\} \subseteq \mathbf{N}_c^S \ \wedge \\ & \quad \textit{Var}(t) \not\subseteq \textit{GlobVar}(callee(m))) \\[1ex] (\neg\,\textit{GlobTransp}(m) \vee \neg\textit{Safe}(m)) \ \wedge & \\ \neg\textit{Safe}(end(callee(m))) & \text{if } pred_{fg(p_i)}(p_i) = \{m\} \subseteq \mathbf{N}_c^S \ \wedge \\ & \quad \textit{Var}(t) \subseteq \textit{GlobVar}(callee(m)) \end{cases}$$

The Correctness Lemma 10.3.2 now implies

$$
\begin{cases}
\displaystyle\prod_{m\in caller(fg(p_i))} (\neg Transp\,(m_C)\vee\neg Correct_{ICM}(m_C)) & \text{if } p_i\in\{\mathbf{s}_0,\mathbf{s}_1,\dots,\mathbf{s}_k\}\\[2mm]
\displaystyle\prod_{m\in pred_{fg(p_i)}(p_i)} (\neg GlobTransp(m)\vee\neg Correct_{ICM}(m)) & \\
\qquad\qquad \text{if } \emptyset\neq pred_{fg(p_i)}(p_i)\subseteq \mathbf{N}^S\backslash\mathbf{N}^S_c\ \vee\\
\qquad\qquad (pred_{fg(p_i)}(p_i)=\{m\}\subseteq \mathbf{N}^S_c\ \wedge\\
\qquad\qquad\quad Var(t)\not\subseteq GlobVar(callee(m)))\\[2mm]
(\neg GlobTransp(m)\vee\neg Correct_{ICM}(m))\ \wedge\\
\neg Correct_{ICM}(end(callee(m))) \qquad \text{if } pred_{fg(p_i)}(p_i)=\{m\}\subseteq \mathbf{N}^S_c\ \wedge\\
\qquad\qquad\qquad\qquad\qquad Var(t)\subseteq GlobVar(callee(m))
\end{cases}
$$

This yields

$$\neg Correct_{ICM}(p_i)\vee Insert_{ICM}(p_i)$$

A straightforward induction now delivers the validity of the formula

$$\exists i\le l\le j.\ Insert_{ICM}(p_l)\ \wedge\ (p_l)\sqsubseteq Segments_{(i,j)}(p)$$

which completes the proof of part 4. $\qquad\qquad\qquad\qquad\qquad\qquad\qquad\square$

Before proving the main result of this section, we demonstrate that canonicity is indeed essential for the validity of the third part of the *IBCM*-Lemma 10.4.2. Tho this end we consider the example of Figure 10.17. It shows the result of the *IBCM*-transformation for a program, whose original computations of $a + b$ have been replaced by **h**. Note that the insertion at node **6** is perfectly down-safe because of the original computations of $a+b$ at the nodes **8**, **9**, **14**, and **15**. Nonetheless, it is not used along the program continuation passing node **12** of procedure π_2. This can easily be verified by considering the relevant lifetime ranges of this example, which, for convenience, are highlighted. Note that the light-shadowed lifetime range prefix starting in node **6** cannot be extended to a first-use-lifetime range because of the insertion at node **13**.

However, under the premise of canonicity of the *IBCM*-transformation, and thus by means of the *IBCM*-Lemma 10.4.2 we can prove the main result of this section:

Theorem 10.4.2 (*IBCM*-Optimality).
If the IBCM-transformation is canonic for the program under consideration, then it is computationally optimal, i.e.,

$$IBCM\in \mathcal{ICM}_{Can}\ \Rightarrow\ IBCM\in \mathcal{ICM}_{CmpOpt}$$

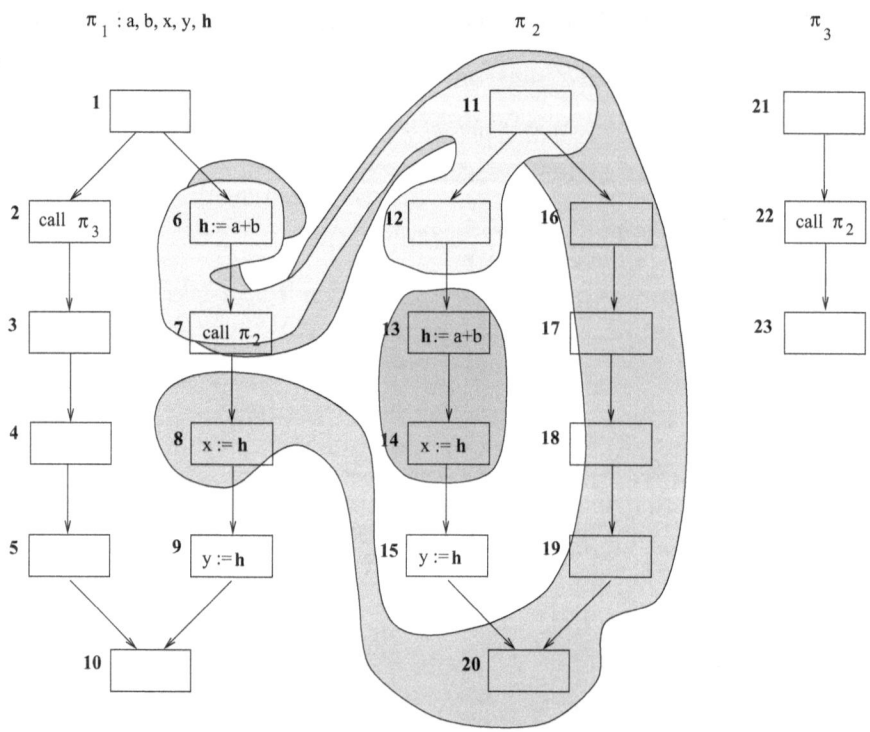

Fig. 10.17. The impact of canonicity on part 3 of *IBCM*-Lemma 10.4.2

Proof. The admissibility of the *IBCM*-transformation is guaranteed by Theorem 10.4.1. Thus, we are left with showing its computational optimality, i.e., with proving $IBCM \in \mathcal{ICM}_{CmpOpt}$. To this end let $ICM \in \mathcal{ICM}_{Adm}$, and $p \in \mathbf{IP}[\mathbf{s}^*, \mathbf{e}^*]$. Then we have as desired:

$$
\begin{aligned}
& Comp_{IBCM}(p) \\
\text{(Def. } IBCM\text{)} \quad = \quad & |\{i \mid Insert_{IBCM}(p_i)\}| \\
\text{(Canon., Lem. 10.3.4, 10.4.2(3))} \quad = \quad & |\{i \mid Segments_{(i,j)}(p) \\
& \qquad \in FU\text{-}LtRg(IBCM)\}| \\
\text{(Lem. 10.4.2(4))} \quad \leq \quad & |\{i \mid Insert_{ICM}(p_i)\}| + \\
& |\{i \mid Comp(p_i) \wedge \neg Replace_{ICM}(p_i)\}| \\
= \quad & Comp_{ICM}(p)
\end{aligned}
$$

$\square$

The *IBCM*-transformation is interprocedurally computationally optimal, whenever it is canonic. The converse implication is in general invalid, i.e., canonicity is not necessary for the computational optimality of the *IBCM*-transformation. For a proof reconsider the program of Figure 10.5, which shows the result of the *IBCM*-transformation for the program of Figure 10.4. It is computationally optimal, but not canonic. Thus, we have:

Theorem 10.4.3 (Canonicity).
Canonicity of the IBCM-transformation for the program under consideration is sufficient for its interprocedural computational optimality, but not necessary.

For the example of Figure 10.5 the *IBCM*-transformation works perfectly without being canonic. In general, however, if the *IBCM*-transformation fails the canonicity constraint, it violates strictness in the sense of [CLZ], i.e., profitability is in general not guaranteed. An extreme example is displayed in Figure 10.18. It shows a program, which is free of any partially redundant computation. Hence, it is computationally optimal. Figure 10.19 shows the result of the *IBCM*-transformation for this program. It inserts a computation inside the loop impairing the program dramatically.

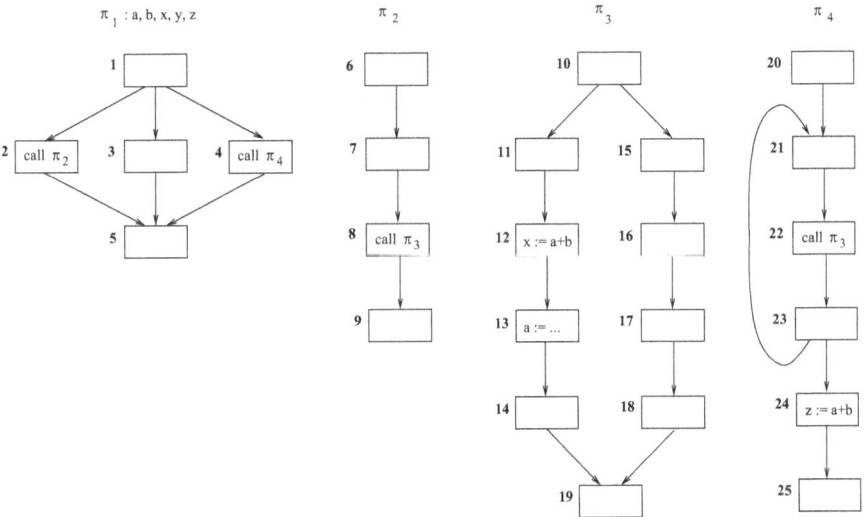

Fig. 10.18. The original program Π_4

10.5 The *ILCM*-Transformation

As in the previous section, we assume that the *IBCM*-transformation is canonic for the program under consideration. According to the *IBCM*-Optimality Theorem 10.4.2 it is thus computationally optimal. However, like

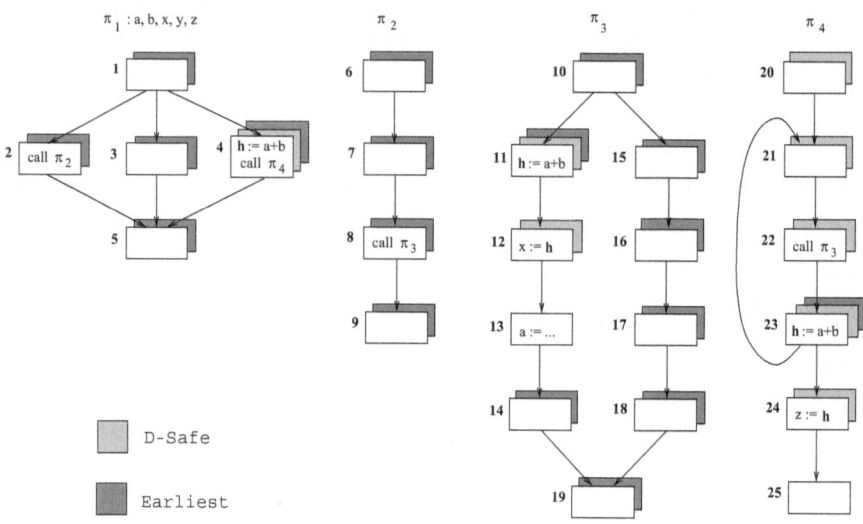

Fig. 10.19. Failure of canonicity causes in general failure of strictness

its intraprocedural counterpart, it does not take the lifetimes of temporaries into account. Lemma 10.5.2 yields that the lifetimes of temporaries introduced by the *IBCM*-transformation are even maximal in this situation, a fact, which can be proved by means of Lemma 10.5.1.

Lemma 10.5.1 (*IBCM*-First-Use-Lifetime Range Lemma).

$\forall\, ICM \in \mathcal{ICM}_{CmpOpt}\; \forall\, p \in \mathbf{IP}[\mathbf{s}^*, \mathbf{e}^*]\; \forall\, l \leq \lambda_p.$
$\quad Comp_{ICM}(p_l) \Rightarrow \exists\, i \leq l \leq j.\; (p_l) \sqsubseteq Segments_{(i,j)}(p) \in FU\text{-}LtRg(IBCM)$

Proof. Let $ICM \in \mathcal{ICM}_{CmpOpt}$, $p \in \mathbf{IP}[\mathbf{s}^*, \mathbf{e}^*]$, and let l be an index with

$$Comp_{ICM}(p_l)$$

Suppose that

$$\forall\, i \leq l \leq j.\; (p_l) \sqsubseteq Segments_{(i,j)}(p) \notin FU\text{-}LtRg(IBCM)$$

Then we obtain according to the premise of the canonicity of the *IBCM*-transformation the following sequence of inequations:

$$
\begin{array}{rl}
 & |\,\{i\,|\, Comp_{ICM}(p_i)\}\,| \\
\text{(Lem. 10.3.4 \& 10.4.2(4))} \geq & |\,\{i\,|\, Segments_{(i,j)}(p) \\
 & \quad\in FU\text{-}LtRg(IBCM)\}\,| + 1 \\
\text{(Canon. \& Lem. 10.3.4 \& 10.4.2(3))} = & |\,\{i\,|\, Insert_{IBCM}(p_i)\}\,| + 1 \\
> & |\,\{i\,|\, Insert_{IBCM}(p_i)\}\,| \\
= & |\,\{i\,|\, Comp_{IBCM}(p_i)\}\,|
\end{array}
$$

This, however, is a contradiction to the computational optimality of *ICM* completing the proof of Lemma 10.5.1.   □

Using this lemma we can now prove:

Lemma 10.5.2 (*IBCM*-Lifetime Range Lemma).
$\forall ICM \in \mathcal{ICM}_{CmpOpt} \ \forall P \in LtRg(ICM) \ \exists Q \in LtRg(IBCM). \ P \sqsubseteq Q$

Proof. Let $ICM \in \mathcal{ICM}_{CmpOpt}$, $p \in \mathbf{IP}[\mathbf{s}^*, \mathbf{e}^*]$, and $Segments_{(i,j)}(p) \in LtRg(ICM)$. By means of Definition 10.3.6 we obtain

$$\forall i < l \leq j \ \forall q \in Segments_{(i,j)}(p). \ (p_l) \sqsubseteq q \Rightarrow \neg Insert_{ICM}(p_l)$$

Additionally, we also have $Replace_{IBCM}(p_j)$. The *IBCM*-Lemma 10.4.2(4) thus yields

$$\forall i < l \leq j \ \forall q \in Segments_{(i,j)}(p). \ (p_l) \sqsubseteq q \Rightarrow \neg Insert_{IBCM}(p_l)$$

Lemma 10.5.1 yields the existence of an index l' with $l' \leq i$ and

$$Segments_{(l',i)}(p) \sqsubseteq P'$$

for some $P' \in FU\text{-}LtRg(IBCM)$. In particular, we therefore have

$$Insert_{IBCM}(p_{l'}) \ \wedge \ \forall i' \in \{l'+1, \ldots, i\}. \ (p_{i'}) \sqsubseteq P' \Rightarrow \neg Insert_{IBCM}(p_{i'})$$

Summarizing, we have as desired

$$Segments_{(i,j)}(p) \sqsubseteq Segments_{(l',j)}(p) \in LtRg(IBCM)$$

    □

10.5.1 Specification

In this section we present the interprocedural extension of the *LCM*-transformation called *ILCM*-transformation. It enhances the *IBCM*-transformation by minimizing the lifetimes of temporaries. Like its intraprocedural counterpart, the *ILCM*-transformation is based on the properties of latestness and isolation.

Definition 10.5.1 (Interprocedural Delayability).
Let $n \in N^*$. n *is* interprocedurally

1. entry-delayable [*in signs: N-Delayable** (n)] $\Longleftrightarrow_{df}$
   $\forall p \in \mathbf{IP}[\mathbf{s}^*, n] \ \exists 1 \leq i \leq \lambda_p. \ Insert_{IBCM}(p_i) \wedge SameInc_p[i, \lambda_p[\ \wedge$
   $\qquad\qquad \neg Comp^{*\exists}_{(p,i)}(p[i, \lambda_p[).$
2. exit-delayable [*in signs: X-Delayable** (n)] $\Longleftrightarrow_{df}$
   $\forall p \in \mathbf{IP}[\mathbf{s}^*, n] \ \exists 1 \leq i \leq \lambda_p. \ Insert_{IBCM}(p_i) \wedge SameInc_p[i, \lambda_p] \ \wedge$
   $\qquad\qquad \neg Comp^{*\exists}_{(p,i)}(p[i, \lambda_p]).$

Interprocedural delayability induces the notion of interprocedurally latest computation points. Intuitively, these are the "maximally delayed" program points, which allow a computationally optimal placement of the program term under consideration. The definition requires the function $Nodes :$ $S \rightarrow \mathcal{P}(\mathbf{N}^S)$, which maps a flow graph G to its node set enlarged by the node sets of flow graphs (indirectly) invoked by call statements of G. Formally, it is defined by:

$$\forall G \in S. \; Nodes(G) =_{df} N_G \cup \bigcup \{\, Nodes(callee(n)) \mid n \in \mathbf{N}_c^S \cap N_G \,\}$$

where $N_G =_{df} \{\, n \in \mathbf{N}^S \mid fg(n) = G \,\}$ denotes the set of nodes of the flow graph G.

Definition 10.5.2 (Interprocedural Latestness).
A node $n \in \mathbf{N}^S$ is interprocedurally latest, if it satisfies the predicate I-Latest defined by

$$I\text{-}Latest(n) =_{df} N\text{-}Delayable^*(n) \wedge (\; Comp(n) \vee$$

$$\begin{cases} \neg \displaystyle\prod_{m \in succ_{fg(n)}(n)} N\text{-}Delayable^*(m) & \text{if } n \in \mathbf{N}^S \backslash \mathbf{N}_c^S \vee (n \in \mathbf{N}_c^S \wedge \\ & Var(t) \not\subseteq GlobVar(callee(n))) \\[2ex] \neg N\text{-}Delayable^*(start(callee(n))) \; \wedge \\ \quad Required(start(callee(n))) & \text{otherwise} \end{cases}$$

where

$$Required(start(callee(n))) =_{df} \sum_{m \in Nodes(fg(start(callee(n))))} Comp(m)$$

For nodes outside of $\mathbf{N}_c^S$ the definition of latestness is straightforward and coincides with its intraprocedural counterpart. For procedure call nodes, it needs some more explanation.

If the term t under consideration contains local variables of the called procedure (i.e., $Var(t) \not\subseteq GlobVar(callee(m))$), the incarnation of t, which is valid before entering the procedure is invalid as long as the call is not finished because entering the procedure activates a new incarnation of t. Hence, the original computations of t having led to the insertions of the *IBCM*-transformation, which are now responsible for the delayability of t at the entry of n, are located on program continuation parts starting at the exit of n. As a side-effect we thus obtain that the called procedure is transparent for t, i.e., it does not modify global variables of t, since otherwise the hoisting of t across the call by the *IBCM*-transformation would have been blocked. Together this implies that n blocks the sinking of t only if it is passed as a parameter, i.e., if $Comp(n)$ holds. Thus, the call node can be treated like an ordinary node in this case.

In the remaining case, i.e., if all variables of t are global for the procedure called by n (i.e., $Var(t) \subseteq GlobVar(callee(m)))$, latestness of n depends on properties of the start node of the called procedure. The point here is that entering the procedure does not activate a new incarnation of t. The start node, therefore, takes the role of the successors of n in this case, which explains the term $\neg N\text{-}Delayable^*$ $(start(callee(n)))$ occurring in the definition of latestness. However, this condition and entry-delayability of n are not sufficient in order to imply latestness of n. In addition, this requires that the value of t is required for capturing a use site of t inside the called procedure, i.e., before finishing the call. This requirement, whose equivalent is automatically satisfied for ordinary nodes and call nodes involving local variables, must explicitly be checked. This is reflected by the predicate *Required* indicating whether there is an occurrence of t inside the called procedure. Checking this predicate, which does not require a data flow analysis, is sufficient because of the postulated canonicity of the *IBCM*-transformation.

After defining latestness, we introduce next the interprocedural version of the predicate "unusable". Like its intraprocedural counterpart, it indicates, whether an initialization of **h** at a specific program point would be unusable because of the lack of a terminating program continuation containing a further computation of the same incarnation of t without a preceding reinitialization of the same incarnation of **h**.

Definition 10.5.3 (Interprocedural Unusability).
Let $n \in N^*$. n *is* interprocedurally

1. entry-unusable $[\textit{in signs: } N\text{-}Unusable^*(n)]$ $\Longleftrightarrow_{df}$
   $\forall p \in \mathbf{IP}[\mathbf{s}^*, \mathbf{e}^*]\ \forall i.\ p_i = n \Rightarrow$
   $(\forall i \leq j \leq \lambda_p.\ Comp^*_{(p,i)}(p_j) \Rightarrow$
   $\qquad\qquad\qquad\qquad \exists i \leq l \leq j.\ l\text{-}Latest(p_l) \wedge SameInc_p[i, l[).$

2. exit-unusable $[\textit{in signs: } X\text{-}Unusable^*(n)]$ $\Longleftrightarrow_{df}$
   $\forall p \in \mathbf{IP}[\mathbf{s}^*, \mathbf{e}^*]\ \forall i.\ p_i = n \Rightarrow$
   $(\forall i < j \leq \lambda_p.\ Comp(p_j) \wedge SameInc_p]i, j[\Rightarrow$
   $\qquad\qquad\qquad\qquad \exists i < l \leq j.\ l\text{-}Latest(p_l) \wedge SameInc_p]i, l[).$

Unusability allows us to identify isolated program points. Intuitively, a node n is interprocedurally isolated, if a computation inserted at its entry could only be used in n itself, i.e., for transferring the value to the statement of node n. In essence, interprocedural isolation is therefore given by interprocedural exit-unusability. However, similar to the definition of latestness procedure call nodes require special care. For a procedure call node unusability after the parameter transfer is decisive for the validity of the isolation property, i.e., exit-unusability at the node n_C. This node, however, is not included in the set of nodes of the flow graph system, and hence, exit-unusability at n_C is not computed as a part of the *IMFP*-solution. Fortunately, this information can easily be computed for every procedure call node after computing the *IMFP*-

solution of the underlying data flow problem. Important are the semantic functions computed in the preprocess of the fixed point approach:

$$\forall\, n \in \mathbf{N}_c^S.\; X\text{-}Unusable^*(n_C) =$$
$$top(\llbracket\, start(callee(n))\,\rrbracket^* \circ \llbracket\, start(callee(n))\,\rrbracket \circ \llbracket\, n_R\,\rrbracket^*(X\text{-}Unusable^*(n))))$$

In essence, the correctness of this step is a consequence of the Main Lemma 8.4.3, and the precision of the *IMFP*-solution of the IDFA-algorithm for unusability proved in the following chapter. Note also that the application of $\llbracket\, start(callee(n))\,\rrbracket^*$ can actually be dropped here because of our assumption that start nodes of procedures represent the empty statement "skip". The definition of interprocedural isolation is now as follows.

Definition 10.5.4 (Interprocedural Isolation).
A node $n \in \mathbf{N}^S$ is interprocedurally isolated, if it satisfies the predicate I-Isolated defined by

$$\forall\, n \in \mathbf{N}^S.\; I\text{-}Isolated\,(n) =_{df} \begin{cases} X\text{-}Unusable^*(n) & \text{if } n \in \mathbf{N}^S \backslash \mathbf{N}_c^S \vee (n \in \mathbf{N}_c^S \wedge \\ & Var(t) \not\subseteq GlobVar(callee(n))\,) \\[2ex] X\text{-}Unusable^*(n_C)\,\text{otherwise} \end{cases}$$

By means of latestness and isolation we can now fix the insertion and replacement points of the *ILCM*-transformation. Table 10.3 shows the definition of the corresponding predicates $Insert_{ILCM}$ and $Replace_{ILCM}$, which specify the *ILCM*-transformation completely.

- $\forall\, n \in \mathbf{N}^S.\; Insert_{ILCM}(n) =_{df} I\text{-}Latest\,(n) \wedge \neg I\text{-}Isolated\,(n)$
- $\forall\, n \in \mathbf{N}^S.\; Replace_{ILCM}(n) =_{df} Comp\,(n) \wedge$
$$\neg(\, I\text{-}Latest\,(n) \wedge I\text{-}Isolated\,(n)\,)$$

Table 10.3: The *ILCM*-transformation

Reestablishing Formal Procedure Calls. In this section we discuss how to reestablish formal procedure calls after the *ILCM*-transformation. In essence, this can be done along the lines of Section 10.4.1. Thus, we only discuss a special case here, which does not occur for the *IBCM*-transformation. This case is illustrated in Figure 10.20. It is characterized by the equation $|\{\, Replace_{ILCM}(n(\pi))\,|\,\pi \in callee(n)\,\}| = 2$, where $M =_{df} \{\, n(\pi)\,|\,\pi \in callee(n)\,\}$ is the set of nodes introduced for replacing the formal procedure call node n (cf. Section 10.2, Figure 10.14). As a consequence of the equality $|\{\, Replace_{ILCM}(n(\pi))\,|\,\pi \in callee(n)\,\}| = 2$, we obtain

$$\prod_{\pi \in callee(n)} Comp\,(n_C(\pi))$$

together with the existence of two procedures π' and π'' in *callee(n)* such that $n(\pi')$ and $n(\pi'')$ satisfy $\neg Replace_{ILCM}(n(\pi'))$ and $Replace_{ILCM}(n(\pi''))$, respectively. In particular, this means that $n(\pi')$ satisfies the conjunction *I-Latest* $\wedge$ *I-Isolated*, whereas $n(\pi'')$ does not. According to the construction of S we have $|pred_{fg(n)}(M)| = 1$ (cf. Section 10.2, Figure 10.12). Together with $\prod_{\pi \in callee(n)} Comp(n_C(\pi))$ and *I-Latest* $(n(\pi'))$, this yields

$$\prod_{\pi \in callee(n)} \text{*I-Latest*}(n(\pi))$$

Thus, $n(\pi'')$ satisfies the predicate *I-Latest*, but not the predicate *I-Isolated*. Consequently, node n is not isolated after coalescing the nodes of M to n. Therefore, we define

$$Insert_{ILCM}(n) =_{df} Replace_{ILCM}(n) =_{df} true$$

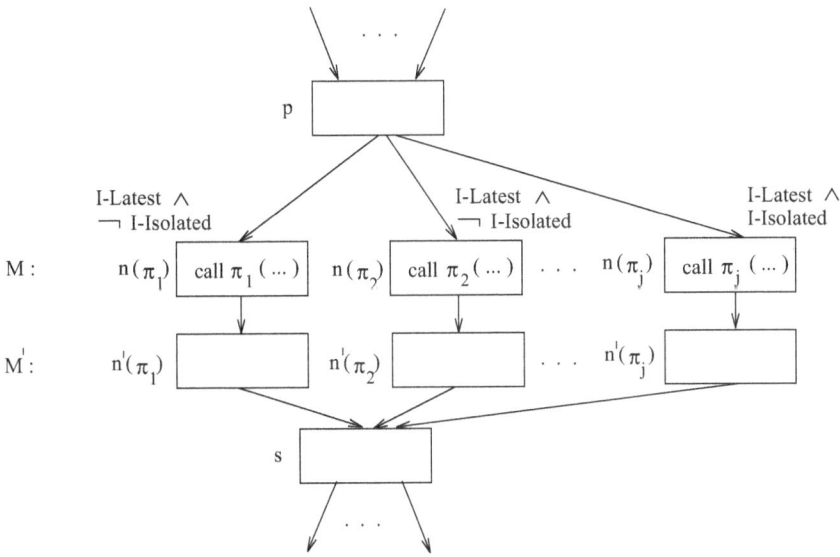

Fig. 10.20. Reestablishing formal procedure calls after the *ILCM*-transf.

Note that reestablishing formal procedure calls does neither affect the number of computations on a program path from $\mathbf{s}^*$ to $\mathbf{e}^*$ nor the lifetimes of temporaries except for the trivial lifetime ranges which are unavoidably introduced for program continuations calling a procedure for which the computation was isolated before coalescing the call nodes. Without loss of generality we can therefore prove the lifetime optimality of the *ILCM*-transformation for the program before the reconstruction of formal procedure calls.

10.5.2 Proving Lifetime Optimality

In this section we prove that the $ILCM$-transformation is (computationally and) lifetime optimal (cf. $ILCM$-Optimality Theorem 10.5.1). Central for proving this result is the following lemma, whose proof relies again on the canonicity of the $IBCM$-transformation.

Lemma 10.5.3 ($ILCM$-Lemma).

1. $\forall n \in N^*.\ N\text{-}Delayable^*(n) \Rightarrow I\text{-}DSafe(n)$
2. $\forall p \in \mathbf{IP}[\mathbf{s}^*, \mathbf{e}^*]\ \forall l.\ N\text{-}Delayable^*(p_l)\ \exists i \le l \le j.$
   $(p_l) \sqsubseteq Segments_{(i,j)}(p) \in FU\text{-}LtRg(IBCM)$
3. $\forall p \in \mathbf{IP}[\mathbf{s}^*, \mathbf{e}^*]\ \forall\, Segments_{(i,j)}(p) \in FU\text{-}LtRg(IBCM)$
   $\exists i \le l \le j.\ I\text{-}Latest(p_l) \wedge (p_l) \sqsubseteq Segments_{(i,j)}(p)$
4. $\forall p \in \mathbf{IP}[\mathbf{s}^*, \mathbf{e}^*]\ \forall\, Segments_{(i,j)}(p) \in LtRg(IBCM)$
   $\forall i \le l \le j.\ I\text{-}Latest(p_l) \wedge (p_l) \sqsubseteq Segments_{(i,j)}(p)$
   $\Rightarrow (\forall l < l' \le j.\ (p_{l'}) \sqsubseteq Segments_{(i,j)}(p)).\ \neg N\text{-}Delayable^*(p_{l'})$
5. $\forall\, ICM \in \mathcal{ICM}_{CmpOpt}\ \forall n \in \mathbf{N}^S.\ Comp_{ICM}(n) \Rightarrow N\text{-}Delayable^*(n)$
6. $\forall p \in \mathbf{IP}[\mathbf{s}^*, \mathbf{e}^*]\ \forall\, Segments_{(i,i)}(p) \in LtRg(ILCM).$
   $\exists p' \in \mathbf{IP}[\mathbf{s}^*, \mathbf{e}^*].p[1,i] = p'[1,i] \wedge \exists j > i.\ Segments_{(i,j)}(p') \in LtRg(ILCM)$

Proof. Part 1). Let $n \in N^*$ satisfying the predicate $N\text{-}Delayable^*$. Then we have

$$N\text{-}Delayable^*(n)$$

$$\begin{aligned}
\text{(Def. 10.5.1(1))} \quad &\Rightarrow\quad \forall p \in \mathbf{IP}[\mathbf{s}^*, n]\ \exists 1 \le i \le \lambda_p.\ Insert_{IBCM}(p_i) \wedge \\
&\qquad SameInc_p[i, \lambda_p[\ \wedge \neg Comp^{*\,\exists}_{(p,i)}(p[i, \lambda_p[) \\
\text{(Def. } Insert_{IBCM}) \quad &\Rightarrow\quad \forall p \in \mathbf{IP}[\mathbf{s}^*, n]\ \exists 1 \le i \le \lambda_p.\ I\text{-}DSafe(p_i) \wedge \\
&\qquad SameInc_p[i, \lambda_p[\ \wedge \neg Comp^{*\,\exists}_{(p,i)}(p[i, \lambda_p[) \\
(p_i \in N^* \setminus N_r^*) \quad &\Rightarrow\quad \forall p \in \mathbf{IP}[\mathbf{s}^*, n]\ \exists 1 \le i \le \lambda_p.\ N\text{-}DSafe^*(p_i) \wedge \\
&\qquad SameInc_p[i, \lambda_p[\ \wedge \neg Comp^{*\,\exists}_{(p,i)}(p[i, \lambda_p[) \\
\text{(Def. 10.3.1(2b))} \quad &\Rightarrow\quad N\text{-}DSafe^*(n) \\
&\Rightarrow\quad I\text{-}DSafe(n)
\end{aligned}$$

The last implication needs some explanation. If $n \in N^* \setminus N_r^*$, it is trivially satisfied. Otherwise, i.e., if $n \in N_r^*$, it follows from the validity of $N\text{-}DSafe^*(n)$ and $N\text{-}Delayable^*(n)$, and the definition of $I\text{-}DSafe$.

Part 2). Let $p \in \mathbf{IP}[\mathbf{s}^*, \mathbf{e}^*]$, and let l be an index with $N\text{-}Delayable^*(p_l)$. Then Definition 10.5.1(1) guarantees the existence of an index i with

$$Insert_{IBCM}(p_i) \wedge SameInc_p[i, l[\ \wedge \neg Comp^{*\,\exists}_{(p,i)}(p[i, l[) \tag{10.26}$$

By means of (10.26) the *IBCM*-Lemma 10.4.2(3) guarantees that there is an index j with $j \geq l$ and

$$(p_l) \sqsubseteq Segments_{(i,j)}(p) \in FU\text{-}LtRg\,(IBCM)$$

which completes the proof of part 2.

Part 3). Let $p \in \mathbf{IP}[\mathbf{s}^*, \mathbf{e}^*]$ and $Segments_{(i,j)}(p) \in FU\text{-}LtRg\,(IBCM)$. This implies

$$Insert_{IBCM}(p_i) \wedge Replace_{IBCM}(p_j)$$

Additionally, Definition 10.5.1(1) and $Replace_{IBCM}(p_j)$ yield

$$N\text{-}Delayable^*\,(p_i)$$

and

$$Comp\,(p_j)$$

respectively. Thus,

$$l' =_{df} Max(\{\, l \mid i \leq l \leq j.\ N\text{-}Delayable^*\,(p_l)\})$$

is well-defined. Moreover, by means of Definition 10.5.1(1) it can easily be shown

$$p_{l'} \in N^* \setminus N_r^*$$

If $l' = j$, Definition 10.5.2 directly yields

$$I\text{-}Latest\,(p_{l'}) \wedge (p_{l'}) \sqsubseteq Segments_{(i,j)}(p)$$

Otherwise, i.e., if $l' < j$, $I\text{-}Latest\,(p_{l'})$ is proved by a simple case analysis on the type of node $p_{l'}$ using Definition 10.5.1(1), Definition 10.5.2, and the maximality of l'.

Part 4). Let $p \in \mathbf{IP}[\mathbf{s}^*, \mathbf{e}^*]$, $Segments_{(i,j)}(p) \in LtRg\,(IBCM)$, and l be an index with $I\text{-}Latest\,(p_l)$ and $(p_l) \sqsubseteq Segments_{(i,j)}(p)$. In particular, this implies $p_l \in N^* \setminus N_r^*$. Without loss of generality we can assume $l < j$. Definition 10.3.6 then yields

$$(\forall l < l' \leq j.\ (p_{l'}) \sqsubseteq Segments_{(i,j)}(p)).\ \neg Insert_{IBCM}(p_{l'})$$

Let now $\hat{l} > l$ with

$$(p_{\hat{l}}) \sqsubseteq Segments_{(i,j)}(p) \ \wedge\ \forall l < l'' < \hat{l}.\ (p_{l''}) \not\sqsubseteq Segments_{(i,j)}(p)$$

Then we obtain by means of Definition 10.5.1(1) and Definition 10.5.2

$$\neg N\text{-}Delayable^*\,(p_{\hat{l}})$$

A straightforward induction now yields the desired result.

Part 5). Let $ICM \in \mathcal{ICM}_{CmpOpt}$ and $n \in \mathbf{N}^S$ with

$$Comp_{ICM}(n)$$

Then the following sequence of implications proves part 5:

$$Comp_{ICM}(n)$$

(Def. $Comp_{ICM}$) $\Rightarrow$ $Comp(n) \wedge \neg Replace_{ICM}(n) \vee Insert_{ICM}(n)$

(Lemma 10.5.1) $\Rightarrow$ $\forall p \in \mathbf{IP}[\mathbf{s}^*, \mathbf{e}^*] \; \forall l \leq \lambda_p. \; p_l = n$

$\Rightarrow \exists i \leq l \leq j. \; (p_l) \sqsubseteq Segments_{(i,j)}(p)$

$\in FU\text{-}LtRg(IBCM)$

(Def. $LtRg(IBCM)$) $\Rightarrow$ $\forall p \in \mathbf{IP}[\mathbf{s}^*, \mathbf{e}^*] \; \forall l \leq \lambda_p. \; p_l = n$

$\Rightarrow \exists i \leq l \leq j. \; Insert_{IBCM}(p_i) \wedge \neg Comp^{*\exists}_{(p,i)}(p]i, l[)$

(Def. 10.5.1(1)) $\Rightarrow$ $N\text{-}Delayable^*(n)$

Part 6). Let $p \in \mathbf{IP}[\mathbf{s}^*, \mathbf{e}^*]$, and let i be an index with $Segments_{(i,i)}(p) \in LtRg(ILCM)$. Thus, we have $Insert_{ILCM}(p_i)$, and therefore

$$I\text{-}Latest(p_i) \wedge \neg I\text{-}Isolated(p_i) \tag{10.27}$$

Suppose now that

$$(\forall p' \in \mathbf{IP}[\mathbf{s}^*, \mathbf{e}^*]. \; p[1, i] = p'[1, i]) \; \forall j > i. \; Segments_{(i,j)}(p') \notin LtRg(ILCM)$$

Then Definition 10.5.3(2) and Definition 10.5.4 yield

$$I\text{-}Isolated(p_i)$$

This, however, is a contradiction to conjunction (10.27), which proves part 6.

$\square$

This suffices to prove the central theorem of this section:

Theorem 10.5.1 ($ILCM$-Optimality).
If the $IBCM$-transformation is canonic for the program under consideration, the $ILCM$-transformation is computationally and lifetime optimal, i.e.,

$$IBCM \in \mathcal{ICM}_{Can} \Rightarrow ILCM \in \mathcal{ICM}_{LtOpt}$$

Proof. The proof of Theorem 10.5.1 is decomposed into three steps. First, proving that the $ILCM$-transformation is admissible; second, that it is computationally optimal; and third, that it is lifetime optimal.

In order to prove $ILCM \in \mathcal{ICM}_{Adm}$, it must be shown that all insertions and replacements are safe and correct, i.e., it must be shown

i) $Insert_{ILCM} \Rightarrow Safe$

ii) $Replace_{ILCM} \Rightarrow Correct_{ILCM}$

Insert$_{ILCM}$ is defined by

$$\forall\, n \in \mathbf{N}^S.\ Insert_{ILCM}(n) =_{df} I\text{-}Latest(n) \wedge \neg I\text{-}Isolated(n)$$

In order to prove i) we show even stronger

$$\forall\, n \in \mathbf{N}^S.\ I\text{-}Latest(n) \Rightarrow S\text{-}Safe(n)$$

Thus, let $n \in \mathbf{N}^S$ satisfying the predicate *I-Latest*. Definition 10.5.2 then yields

$$N\text{-}Delayable^*\,(n)$$

Hence, the first part of the *ILCM*-Lemma 10.5.3 delivers *I-DSafe* (n), which implies *N-DSafe** (n), and hence, *S-Safe*(n). By means of Definition 10.3.1, we then obtain as desired

$$Safe(n)$$

In order to prove ii), consider a node $n \in \mathbf{N}^S$ satisfying *Replace*$_{ILCM}(n)$. Obviously, this guarantees *Comp* (n). In order to complete the proof, we must investigate the following two cases.

Case 1. *I-Latest* (n)
In this case, we have $\neg I\text{-}Isolated(n)$. This directly implies *Insert*$_{ILCM}(n)$. Clearly, for all paths $p \in \mathbf{IP}[\mathbf{s}^*, n]$ the predicate $SameInc_p[\lambda_p, \lambda_p[$ is satisfied, and therefore *Correct*$_{ILCM}(n)$ holds trivially.

Case 2. $\neg I\text{-}Latest(n)$
Obviously, we have *Correct*$_{IBCM}(n)$ because the *IBCM*-transformation is admissible. Moreover, we have $\neg Insert_{IBCM}(n)$, since *Insert*$_{IBCM}(n)$ would directly imply *I-Latest*(n) in contradiction to the premise of Case 2. Thus, we have

$$\forall p \in \mathbf{IP}[\mathbf{s}^*, n] \exists i < \lambda_p.Insert_{IBCM}(p_i) \wedge SameInc_p[i, \lambda_p[\wedge Transp^{*\forall}_{(p,i)}(p[i, \lambda_p[)$$

In particular,

$$i_{p'} =_{df}$$
$$Max(\{i \mid i < \lambda_p \wedge Insert_{IBCM}(p_i) \wedge SameInc_p[i, \lambda_p[\wedge Transp^{*\forall}_{(p,i)}(p[i, \lambda_p[)\})$$

is well-defined. Moreover, the *IBCM*-Lemma 10.4.2(3) delivers the existence of an index $j_{p'}$ with

$$i_{p'} \le j_{p'}$$

such that

$$Segments_{(i_{p'}, j_{p'})}(p) \in FU\text{-}LtRg\,(IBCM)$$

The *ILCM*-Lemma 10.5.3(3) now yields

$$\exists\, i_{p'} \le l \le j_{p'}.\ I\text{-}Latest(p_l) \wedge (p_l) \sqsubseteq Segments_{(i_{p'}, j_{p'})}(p)$$

Clearly, we have

$$l < \lambda_p$$

Thus, by means of Definition 10.5.3(2) and Definition 10.5.4 we obtain

$$\neg\textit{I-Isolated}(p_l)$$

and therefore also

$$\textit{Insert}_{ILCM}(p_l)$$

Hence, we have as desired

$$\textit{Insert}_{ILCM}(p_l) \wedge \textit{SameInc}_p[l, \lambda_p[\wedge \textit{Transp}^{*\forall}_{(p,l)}(p[l, \lambda_p[)$$

which proves ii).

The second step, i.e., proving $ILCM \in \mathcal{ICM}_{CmpOpt}$, is a consequence of the following sequence of inequations, which guarantees that the $ILCM$-transformation causes at most as many computations on a path $p \in \mathbf{IP}[\mathbf{s}^*, \mathbf{e}^*]$ during run-time as the computationally optimal $IBCM$-transformation (cf. Theorem 10.4.2).

$$
\begin{aligned}
& \quad |\{i \mid \textit{Comp}_{ILCM}(p_i)\}| \\
(\text{Def. } \textit{Comp}_{ILCM}) \quad = \quad & |\{i \mid \textit{Insert}_{ILCM}(p_i)\}| + \\
& |\{i \mid \textit{Comp}(p_i) \wedge \neg\textit{Replace}_{ILCM}(p_i)\}| \\
(\text{Def. } ILCM) \quad = \quad & |\{i \mid \textit{I-Latest}(p_i) \wedge \neg\textit{I-Isolated}(p_i)\}| + \\
& |\{i \mid \textit{Comp}(p_i) \wedge \textit{I-Latest}(p_i) \wedge \\
& \qquad\qquad\qquad\qquad \textit{I-Isolated}(p_i)\}| \\
\leq \quad & |\{i \mid \textit{I-Latest}(p_i)\}| \\
(\text{Lem. } 10.3.4, 10.5.3(2,4)) \quad = \quad & |\{i \mid \textit{Segments}_{(i,j)}(p) \in \textit{FU-LtRg}(IBCM)\}| \\
(\text{Canon. \& Lem. } 10.3.4) \quad = \quad & |\{i \mid \textit{Insert}_{IBCM}(p_i)\}| \\
(\text{Def. } IBCM) \quad = \quad & |\{i \mid \textit{Comp}_{IBCM}(p_i)\}|
\end{aligned}
$$

In order to prove the third step, i.e., in order to prove $ILCM \in \mathcal{ICM}_{LtOpt}$, it must be shown

$$\forall\, ICM \in \mathcal{ICM}_{CmpOpt} \ \forall P \in LtRg(ILCM) \ \exists Q \in LtRg(ICM). \ P \sqsubseteq Q$$

Thus, let $ICM \in \mathcal{ICM}_{CmpOpt}$, $p \in \mathbf{IP}[\mathbf{s}^*, \mathbf{e}^*]$, and $P =_{df} \textit{Segments}_{(i,j)}(p) \in LtRg(ILCM)$. Obviously, we have

$$\neg\textit{I-Isolated}(p_i)$$

Thus, if $i = j$, Lemma 10.5.3(6) yields the existence of a path $p' \in \mathbf{IP}[\mathbf{s}^*, \mathbf{e}^*]$ with $p[1, i] = p'[1, i]$ and of an index l with $j < l$, and

$$\textit{Segments}_{(i,j)}(p') \sqsubseteq \textit{Segments}_{(i,l)}(p') \in LtRg(ILCM)$$

Without loss of generality we can thus assume that

$$i < j$$

Then we obtain as desired

$$P \in LtRg(ILCM)$$

$$
\begin{aligned}
\text{(Lemma 10.5.2)} \quad &\Rightarrow\quad \exists Q \in LtRg(IBCM).\ P \sqsubseteq Q \\
\text{(Lemma 10.5.3(4))} \quad &\Rightarrow\quad (\forall\, i < l \leq j.\ (p_l) \sqsubseteq P).\ \neg N\text{-}Delayable^*(p_l) \\
(i < j \ \&\ \text{Lemma 10.5.3(5)}) \quad &\Rightarrow\quad (\forall\, i < l \leq j.\ (p_l) \sqsubseteq P).\ \neg Insert_{ICM}(p_l)\ \wedge \\
& \qquad\qquad (\neg Comp(p_l) \vee Replace_{ICM}(p_l)) \\
(ICM \in \mathcal{ICM}_{Adm}) \quad &\Rightarrow\quad \exists Q \in LtRg(ICM).\ P \sqsubseteq Q
\end{aligned}
$$

$\square$

As a corollary of Theorem 10.3.3 and Theorem 10.5.1 we get:

Corollary 10.5.1. $IBCM \in \mathcal{ICM}_{Can} \Rightarrow \mathcal{ICM}_{LtOpt} = \{\, ILCM \,\}$

10.6 An Example

In this section we illustrate under the premise of canonicity the power of the $IBCM$- and $ILCM$-transformation. To this end we consider the program Π of Figure 10.21, which is complex enough in order to illustrate the essential features of the two transformations. Synthetic nodes, which are not relevant for the transformations because they are not required for inserting computations, are omitted in order to keep the example as small as possible. Analogously, this holds for the formal procedure call at node **9**, which is not (explicitly) replaced by the set of ordinary procedure calls it can invoke.

Note that Π is in $Prog_{fm(2),ugfpp}$, and satisfies the sfmr-property. Whereas the first proposition is obvious, when inspecting the program of Figure 10.21, the second proposition needs some more explanation because Π is composed of statically nested procedures. The point here is that the static predecessor of all procedures, which are passed as an argument, is the main procedure π_1.

Since Π is of mode depth 2, we know that the set of formally reachable procedures of Π is effectively computable by an algorithm of quadratic time complexity [Ar3]. The algorithm yields:

$$\mathcal{FR}(\Pi) = \{\pi_0, \pi_1, \pi_{11}, \pi_{111}, \pi_{12}, \pi_{13}\}$$

Moreover, Π is free of global procedure parameters. Thus, by means of Corollary 6.4.1 and Theorem 6.4.3 we know that formal callability and potential passability coincide on Π, and can be computed by the algorithm of the HO-DFA of Chapter 6, which is also of quadratic time complexity. Parameterized with the set of formally reachable procedures of Π, this algorithm yields:

$$\mathcal{PP}_{\mathcal{FR}(\Pi)}(\phi_{11}) = \{\, \pi_{12}, \pi_{13} \,\} = \mathcal{FC}(\phi_{11})$$

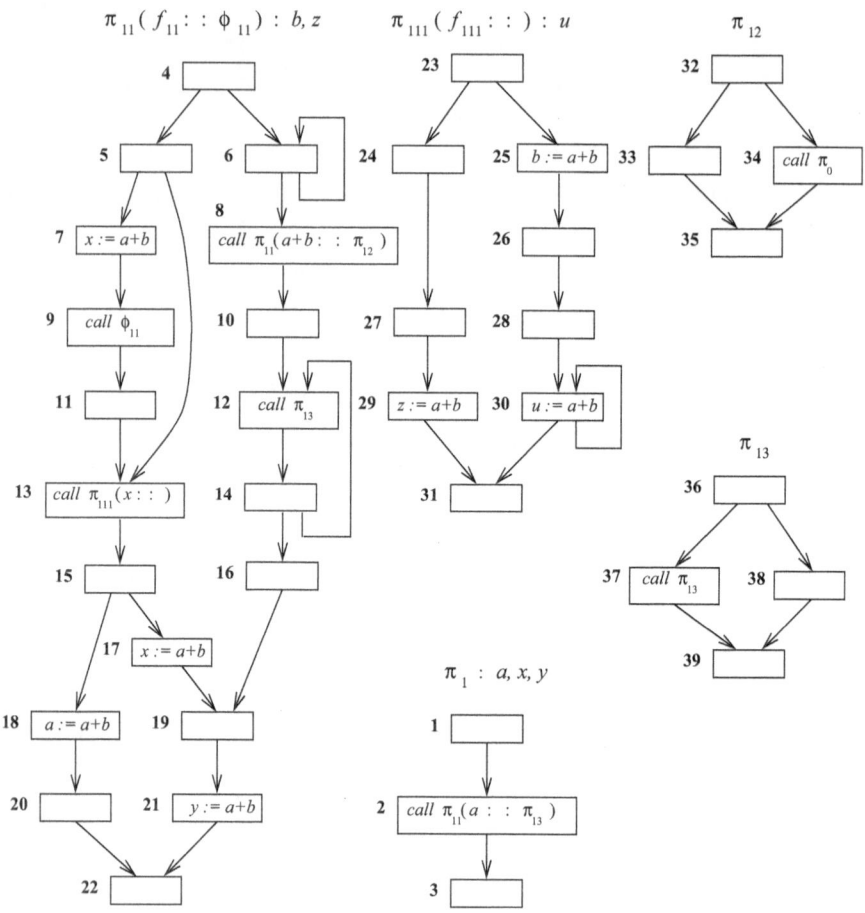

Fig. 10.21. A complex example: the interprocedural argument program

By means of the function *callee* the results of the HO-DFA are made available for the subsequent IDFAs. This implies that the IDFA-algorithms for computing the program properties involved in the *IBCM-* and *ILCM-*transformation treat the formal procedure call statement at node **9** as a higher order branch statement, i.e., it is assumed to nondeterministically call the procedures π_{12} and π_{13}.

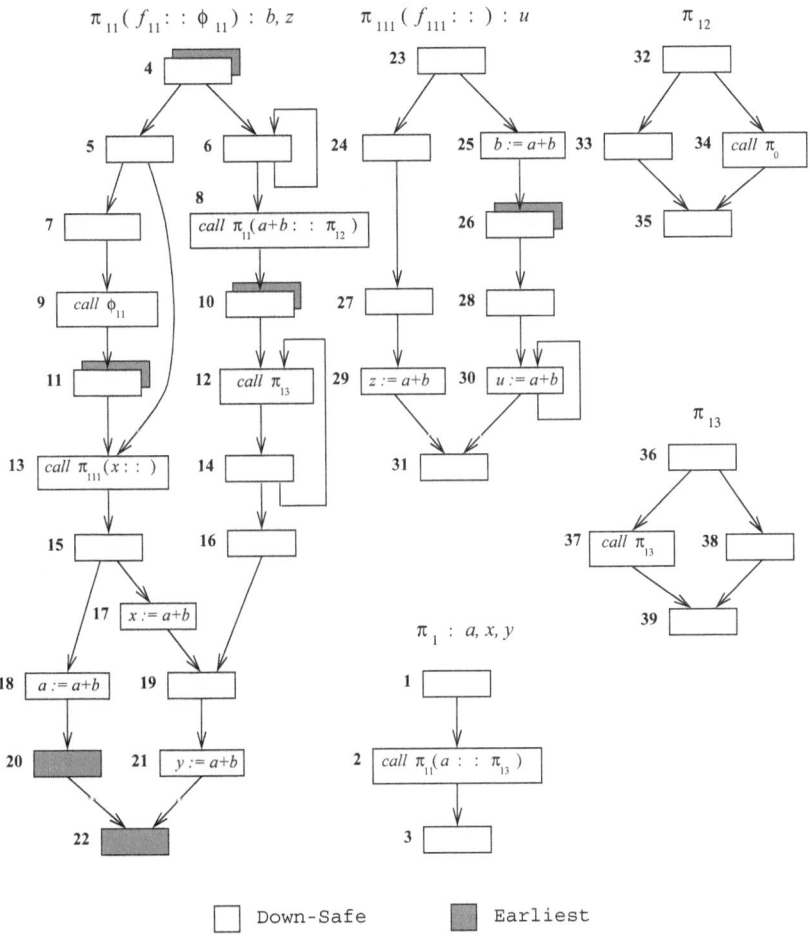

Fig. 10.22. Interprocedurally *down-safe* and *earliest* program points

After these preliminary considerations, Figure 10.22 shows the result of computing the sets of interprocedurally down-safe and earliest program points. They induce the insertion points of the *IBCM*-transformation, whose result is shown in Figure 10.23. Note that the flow graph system of Figure 10.23 is canonic. Hence, Theorem 10.4.2 is applicable and yields that the program of Figure 10.23 is interprocedurally computationally optimal; a fact, which can easily be checked by inspecting this program.

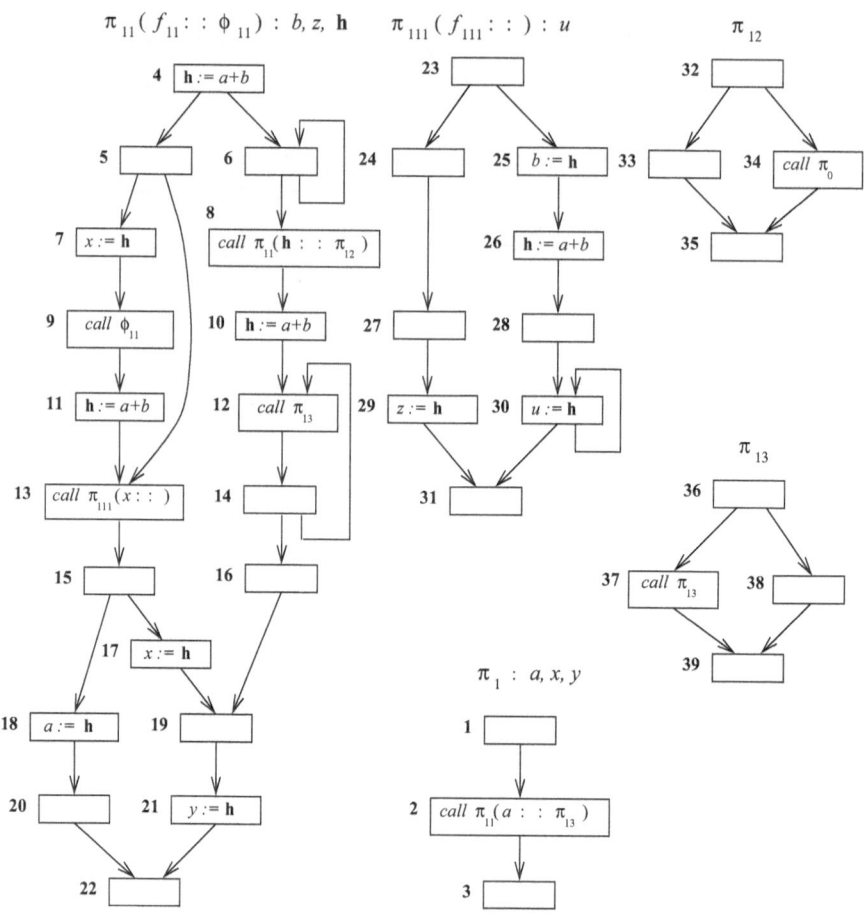

Fig. 10.23. The result of the *IBCM*-transformation

The canonicity of the *IBCM*-transformation implies the computational and lifetime optimality of the *ILCM*-transformation. Figure 10.24 and Figure 10.25 show the results of computing the sets of interprocedurally delayable and latest, and of latest and isolated program points, respectively. Analogously to the intraprocedural setting, the latest and isolated program points induce the computation points of the interprocedural version of the lazy code motion transformation, the *ILCM*-transformation. Figure 10.26 shows the result of this transformation.

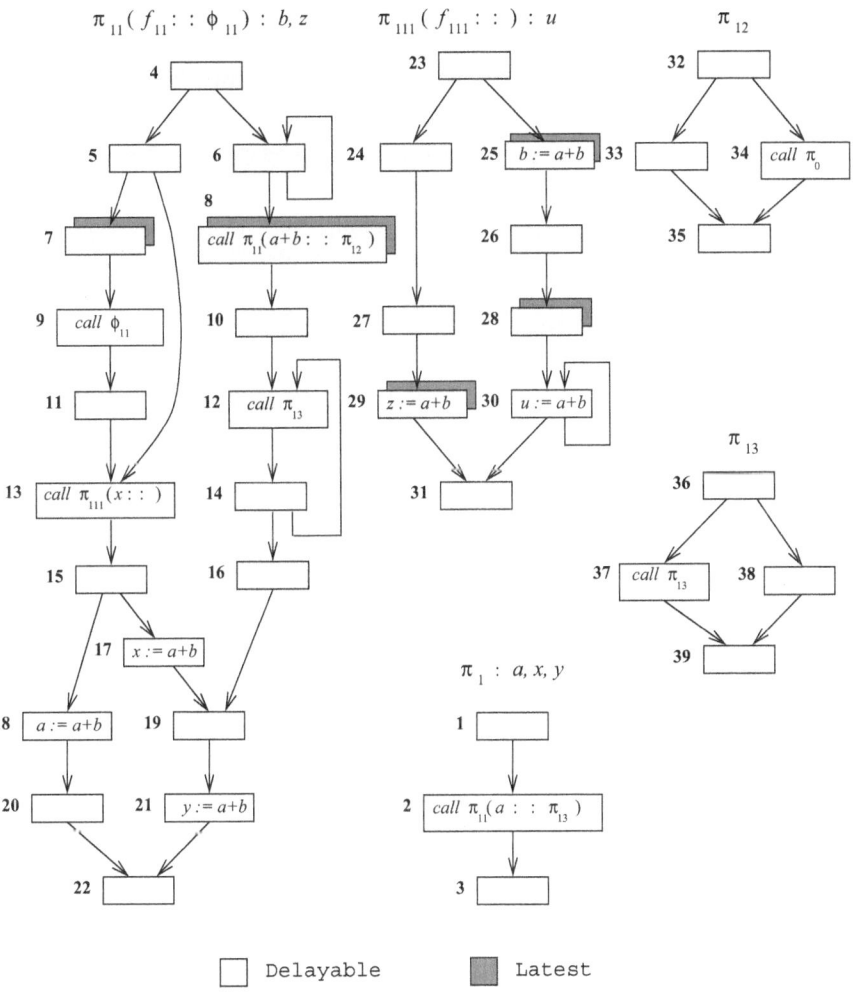

Fig. 10.24. Interprocedurally *delayable* and *latest* program points

Considering this example, the *ILCM*-transformation is exceptional because it eliminates the partially redundant computations of $a + b$ in the nodes **17**, **18**, **21**, **29**, and **30** by moving them to the nodes **16**, **28**, and **29**, but it does not touch the computations of $a + b$ in the nodes **7**, **8**, and **25**, which cannot be moved with run-time gain. This confirms that computations are only moved when it is profitable. In fact, the flow graph system of Figure 10.26 is interprocedurally computationally and lifetime optimal.

Note that no previously proposed transformation for interprocedural partial redundancy elimination would succeed on this example.

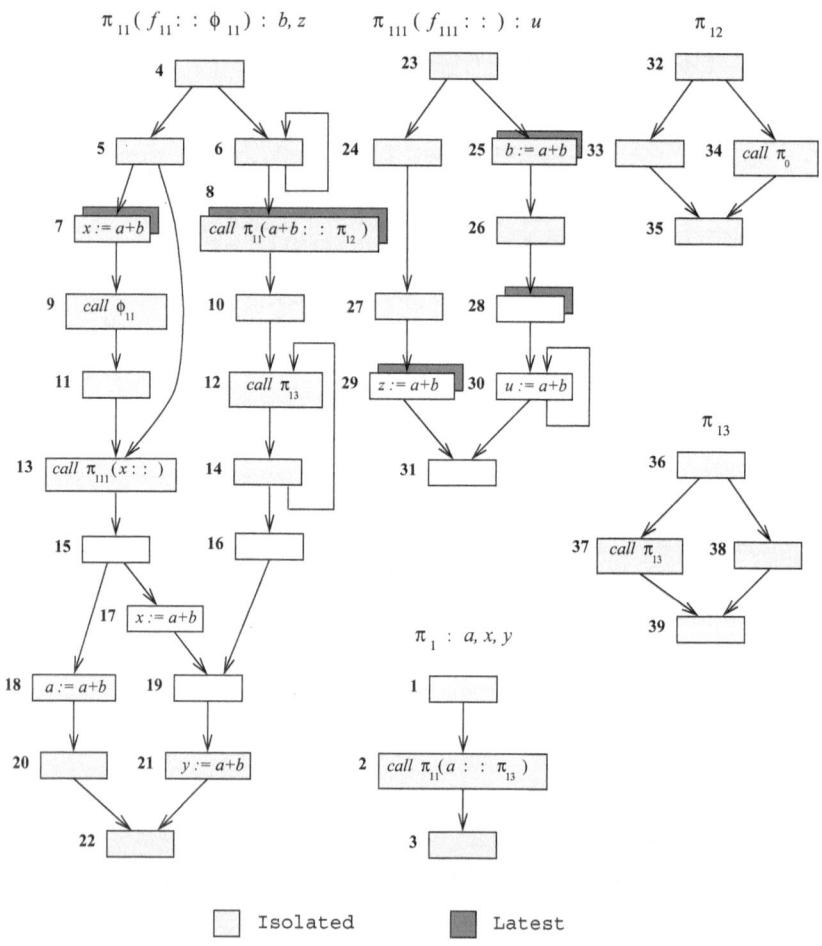

Fig. 10.25. Interprocedurally *latest* and *isolated* program points

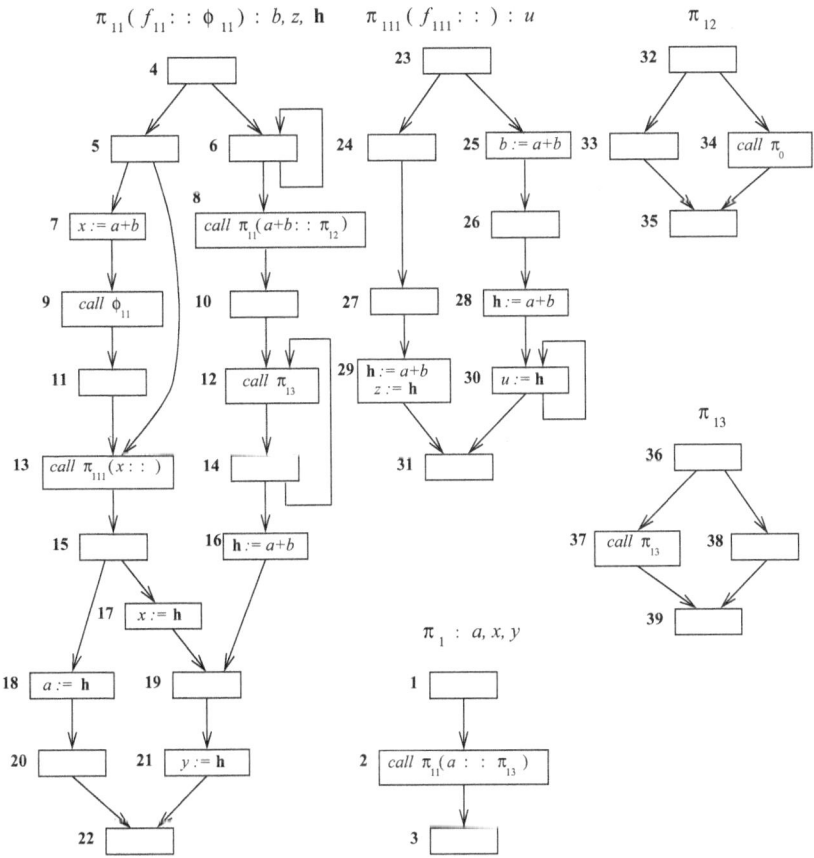

Fig. 10.26. The result of the *ILCM*-transformation

11. Optimal Interprocedural Code Motion: The IDFA-Algorithms

In this chapter we present the interprocedural counterparts of the DFA-algorithms of Chapter 4. For every program property involved in the *IBCM*-transformation and *ILCM*-transformation we specify an IDFA-algorithm and prove it to be precise for the respective property. The specifications and the proofs of being precise follow the cookbook style of Section 9.2. Hence, the specifications consist of a lattice of data flow information, a local semantic functional, a return functional, a start information, and an interpretation of the lattice elements in the set of Boolean truth values. The proofs of being precise consist of four steps. Proving that the function lattice satisfies the descending chain condition, that the local semantic functions and the return functions are distributive, and finally, that the interprocedural meet over all paths solution is precise for the program property under consideration. All proofs are given in full detail in order to illustrate the similarities to their intraprocedural counterparts. For convenience, we identify throughout Chapter 11 the specification of an IDFA with the algorithm it induces (cf. Definition 8.6.1).

11.1 IDFA-Algorithm $\mathcal{A}_{ds}$: Interprocedural Down-Safety

In this section we present the IDFA-algorithm $\mathcal{A}_{ds}$ for computing the set of interprocedurally down-safe program points.[1] The main result applying to this algorithm is the $\mathcal{A}_{ds}$-Precision Theorem 11.1.2. It guarantees that $\mathcal{A}_{ds}$ is precise for this property: it terminates with the set of program points, which are interprocedurally down-safe in the sense of Definition 10.4.1.

We recall that the computation of interprocedurally down-safe program points requires a backward analysis of S (cf. Section 8.7 and Section 9.2.1). Thus, the roles of call nodes and return nodes in the definitions of the local semantic functions (cf. Section 11.1.1) and the return functions (cf. Section 11.1.1) are interchanged. Similarly, the start information is attached to the end node of the program (cf. Section 11.1.1).

---

[1] The index ds stands for down-safety.

J. Knoop: Optimal Interprocedural Program Optimization, LNCS 1428, pp. 209-248, 1998.
© Springer-Verlag Berlin Heidelberg 1998

11.1.1 Specification

Data Flow Information. The domain of data flow information of $\mathcal{A}_{ds}$ is given by the lattice

$$(\mathcal{C}, \sqcap, \sqsubseteq, \bot, \top) =_{df} (\mathcal{B} \times \mathcal{N}, Min, \leq, (false, 0), (true, \infty))$$

We recall that $\mathcal{B}$ denotes the set of Boolean truth values $\{true, false\}$ with $false \leq true$. New is the second component $\mathcal{N}$. It denotes the set of natural numbers enriched by a new element ∞, which is assumed to be the top element of $\mathcal{N}$ with respect to the minimum function. The minimum function Min and the relation $\leq$ are defined pointwise, where Min and $\leq$ are generalized to $\mathcal{B}$ in the natural way.

The structure of this lattice is more complicated than that of its intraprocedural counterpart. This is necessary for being able of dealing with different incarnations of a term during the analysis. Recall that in the intraprocedural setting there exists only a single *incarnation* of each program term. Interprocedurally, however, there are potentially infinitely many incarnations of a term in the presence of recursive procedures with local variables. This requires the safety analysis to distinguish between modifications of global and local variables. Technically, this is achieved by considering the product lattice defined above as the domain of data-flow information. The first component of a data-flow information attached to a program point expresses, whether a placement of t is interprocedurally down-safe at this point. The second component keeps track on the static level of variables of t, which have been modified in the current procedure call. Whenever an operand of t is modified by a statement, and the static level this operand is declared on is lower than that of previously modified operands of t, the second component is updated accordingly, i.e., with the level this operand is declared on. Intuitively, this means that the second component always stores the static level of the "most globally" declared variable which was modified in the most recent procedure call. The special element ∞ expresses that in the call under consideration no operands of t have been modified.

For the effectivity of the analysis, it is important that for a fixed program $\Pi \in Prog$ only a finite subset of $\mathcal{N}$ is relevant for $\mathcal{A}_{ds}$, namely $\mathcal{N}_{\Pi} =_{df} \{0, \ldots, Max(\{StatLevel(\pi) \mid \pi \in \Pi\})\} \cup \{\infty\}$, where Max denotes the maximum function. The finiteness of this subset guarantees the termination of $\mathcal{A}_{ds}$ (cf. Section 11.1.2).

Local Semantic Functional. The local semantic functional $[\![\ ]\!]'_{ds} : N^* \to (\mathcal{B} \times \mathcal{N} \to \mathcal{B} \times \mathcal{N})$ of $\mathcal{A}_{ds}$ is defined by

$$\forall n \in N^* \ \forall (b, z) \in \mathcal{B} \times \mathcal{N}. \ [\![n]\!]'_{ds}(b, z) =_{df} (b', z')$$

where
$$b' =_{df} Comp(n) \vee (Transp(n) \wedge b)$$

$$z' =_{df} \begin{cases} Min(\{z, ModLev(n)\}) & \text{if } n \in N^* \setminus N_r^* \\ \infty & \text{otherwise} \end{cases}$$

Note that the functions $[\![n]\!]'_{ds}$, $n \in N^*$, manipulate the two components of an argument independently of each other. In particular, the first component is treated as by the corresponding intraprocedural function. The treatment of the second component reflects the bookkeeping on the static levels of variables of t, which have been modified.

Return Functional. The return functional $\mathcal{R}_{ds} : N_c^* \rightarrow ((\mathcal{B} \times \mathcal{N})^2 \rightarrow \mathcal{B} \times \mathcal{N})$ of A_{ds} is defined by

$$\forall\, n \in N_c^* \; \forall\, ((b_1, z_1), (b_2, z_2)) \in (\mathcal{B} \times \mathcal{N})^2. \; \mathcal{R}_{ds}(n)((b_1, z_1), (b_2, z_2)) =_{df} (b', z')$$

where
$$b' =_{df} \begin{cases} b_2 & \text{if } Var(t) \subseteq GlobVar(fg(succ^*(n))) \\ Comp(n) \vee & \\ (b_1 \wedge (z_2 \geq StatLevel(fg(succ^*(n))))) & \text{otherwise} \end{cases}$$

$$z' =_{df} Min(\{z_1, z_2\})$$

Intuitively, if all variables of t are global with respect to the called procedure, entering a procedure is essentially the same as traversing an ordinary edge, i.e., t is down-safe before the call (i.e., $b' = true$), if it is down-safe immediately before entering the procedure (i.e., $b_2 = true$). Otherwise, i.e., if t contains local variables of the called procedure, it is down-safe before the call, if it occurs as an actual parameter (i.e., $Comp(n)$), or if it is down-safe after the call (i.e., $b_1 = true$), and none of its operands, which are global for the procedure called are modified by it (i.e., $z_2 \geq StatLevel(fg(succ^*(n)))$).

Start Information. The start information of A_{ds} is given by the element

$$(false, \infty) \in \mathcal{B} \times \mathcal{N}$$

Recall that down-safety requires a backward analysis. Thus, the start information is attached to the end node of S. Intuitively, the first component of the start information expresses that t cannot be used after the termination of the argument program. Similarly, the second component expresses that no variables of t can be modified after the termination.

Interpretation. The interpretation of lattice elements in $\mathcal{B}$ is given by the function $Int_{ds} : \mathcal{B} \times \mathcal{N} \rightarrow \mathcal{B}$ defined by

$$\forall\, (b, z) \in \mathcal{B} \times \mathcal{N}. \; Int_{ds}(b, z) =_{df} b$$

11.1.2 Proving Precision

We first present two lemmas which simplify the proof of the ds-Precision Theorem 11.1.1. The first one is essentially a consequence of Lemma 7.2.1, which guarantees that the intervals of call nodes and return nodes on a program path are either disjoint or one is included in the other. This lemma can be proved by a straightforward induction on the length of program paths. The second lemma is the interprocedural version of Lemma 4.1.3. It follows from the definitions of the local semantic functional $[\![\ ]\!]'_{ds}$ and the return functional $\mathcal{R}_{ds}$.

Lemma 11.1.1. *Let* $p \in \mathbf{IP}[\mathbf{s}^*, \mathbf{e}^*]$, *and* $i, j \in \{1, \dots, \lambda_p\}$ *such that* $p_i \in N_c^*$ *and* $p_j \in N_r^*$ *are a pair of matching call and return nodes of* p. *We have:*

$$Transp^{*\vee}_{(p,i)}(p[i,j]) \Longleftrightarrow$$

$$top([\![\widetilde{p]i, \lambda_p}]\!]^*_{ds}(newstack(false, \infty)))\!\downarrow_2 \geq StatLevel(fg(succ^*(p_i)))$$

Lemma 11.1.2.

1. $\forall n \in N^* \setminus N_c^* \ \forall stk \in STACK.$
   a) $Comp(n) \Rightarrow top([\![n]\!]^*_{ds}(stk))\!\downarrow_1 = true$
   b) $\neg Comp(n) \Rightarrow (top([\![n]\!]^*_{ds}(stk))\!\downarrow_1 = true \Longleftrightarrow$
      $$Transp(n) \wedge top(stk)\!\downarrow_1 = true)$$
2. $\forall n \in N_c^* \ \forall stk \in STACK_{\geq 2}.$
   a) $Comp(n) \Rightarrow top([\![n]\!]^*_{ds}(stk))\!\downarrow_1 = true$

   b) $\neg Comp(n) \Rightarrow (top([\![n]\!]^*_{ds}(stk))\!\downarrow_1 = true \Longleftrightarrow$
      $$\left(\begin{array}{ll} top(stk)\!\downarrow_1 = true & \text{if } Var(t) \subseteq GlobVar(fg(succ^*(n))) \\ top(pop(stk))\!\downarrow_1 = true \ \wedge & \\ top(stk)\!\downarrow_2 \geq StatLevel(fg(succ^*(n))) & \text{otherwise} \end{array} \right)$$

Descending Chain Condition. Note that neither the lattice $\mathcal{B} \times \mathcal{N}$ nor its induced function lattice satisfies the descending chain condition. Fortunately, however, only their finite sublattices $\mathcal{B} \times \mathcal{N}_\Pi$ and $[(\mathcal{B} \times \mathcal{N}_\Pi) \rightarrow (\mathcal{B} \times \mathcal{N}_\Pi)]$ are relevant for $\mathcal{A}_{ds}$ (cf. Section 11.1.1). This is important because the finiteness of a lattice carries over to the corresponding function lattice. Thus, we have the following lemma, which is sufficient for our application.

Lemma 11.1.3 (Descending Chain Condition).
The function lattice $[(\mathcal{B} \times \mathcal{N}_\Pi) \rightarrow (\mathcal{B} \times \mathcal{N}_\Pi)]$ *satisfies the descending chain condition.*

Distributivity. We have:

Lemma 11.1.4 ($[\![\,]\!]'_{ds}$,$\mathcal{R}_{ds}$-Distributivity).

1. *The local semantic functions* $[\![\,n\,]\!]'_{ds}$, $n \in N^*$, *are distributive.*
2. *The return functions* $\mathcal{R}_{ds}(n)$, $n \in N_c^*$, *are distributive.*

Proof. The first part of Lemma 11.1.4 is essentially a consequence of its intraprocedural counterpart Lemma 4.1.5 because the functions $[\![\,n\,]\!]'_{ds}$, $n \in N^*$, treat the components of an argument independently of each other. Hence, it suffices to show that the local semantic functions are distributive in their second components, a fact, which follows immediately from the distributivity of *Min*. Thus, we are left with the second part of Lemma 11.1.4. Abbreviating elements $((b_1, z_1), (b_2, z_2))$ of $(\mathcal{B} \times \mathcal{N})^2$ by **s**, we have to show

$$\forall n \in N_c^* \ \forall S \subseteq (\mathcal{B} \times \mathcal{N})^2. \ \mathcal{R}_{ds}(n)(\sqcap S) = \\ \sqcap\{\mathcal{R}_{ds}(n)((b_1, z_1), (b_2, z_2)) \mid \mathbf{s} \in S\} \tag{11.1}$$

To this end let $n \in N_c^*$, and $S \subseteq (\mathcal{B} \times \mathcal{N})^2$. Then Equation 11.1 is proved by investigating two cases.

Case 1. $Var(t) \subseteq GlobVar(fg(succ^*(n)))$
In this case we obtain the following sequence of equalities proving Case 1.

$$
\begin{aligned}
&&& \mathcal{R}_{ds}(n)(Min(S)) \\
&&=& \mathcal{R}_{ds}(n)(Min(\{((b_1, z_1), (b_2, z_2)) \mid \mathbf{s} \in S\})) \\
&\text{(Def. "meet" in } (\mathcal{B} \times \mathcal{N})^2) &=& \mathcal{R}_{ds}(n)((Min(\{(b_1, z_1) \mid \mathbf{s} \in S\}), \\
&&& \qquad Min(\{(b_2, z_2) \mid \mathbf{s} \in S\}))) \\
&\text{(Def. "meet" in } \mathcal{B} \times \mathcal{N}) &=& \mathcal{R}_{ds}(n)(\\
&&& ((Min(\{b_1 \mid \mathbf{s} \in S\}), Min(\{z_1 \mid \mathbf{s} \in S\})), \\
&&& (Min(\{b_2 \mid \mathbf{s} \in S\}), Min(\{z_2 \mid \mathbf{s} \in S\})))) \\
&\text{(Def. } \mathcal{R}_{ds}(n)) &=& (Min(\{b_2 \mid \mathbf{s} \in S\}), \\
&&& \quad Min(\{Min(\{z_1 \mid \mathbf{s} \in S\}), \\
&&& \qquad Min(\{z_2 \mid \mathbf{s} \in S\})\})) \\
&\text{(Def. "meet" in } \mathcal{N}) &=& (Min(\{b_2 \mid \mathbf{s} \in S\}), \\
&&& \quad Min(\{Min(\{z_1, z_2\} \mid \mathbf{s} \in S\})\})) \\
&\text{(Def. "meet" in } \mathcal{B} \times \mathcal{N}) &=& Min(\{(b_2, Min(\{z_1, z_2\})) \mid \mathbf{s} \in S\}) \\
&\text{(Def. } \mathcal{R}_{ds}(n)) &=& Min(\{\mathcal{R}_{ds}(n)((b_1, z_1), (b_2, z_2)) \mid \mathbf{s} \in S\})
\end{aligned}
$$

Case 2. $Var(t) \nsubseteq GlobVar(fg(succ^*(n)))$
Abbreviating $StatLevel(fg(succ^*(n)))$ by l we obtain:

$$\mathcal{R}_{ds}(n)(Min(S))$$

$$= \mathcal{R}_{ds}(n)(Min(\{((b_1, z_1), (b_2, z_2))\,|\,\mathbf{s} \in S\}))$$

(Def. "meet" in $(\mathcal{B} \times \mathcal{N})^2$) $\quad = \quad \mathcal{R}_{ds}(n)((Min(\{(b_1, z_1)\,|\,\mathbf{s} \in S\}),$
$$Min(\{(b_2, z_2)\,|\,\mathbf{s} \in S\})))$$

(Def. "meet" in $\mathcal{B} \times \mathcal{N}$) $\quad = \quad \mathcal{R}_{ds}(n)($
$$((Min(\{b_1\,|\,\mathbf{s} \in S\}), Min(\{z_1\,|\,\mathbf{s} \in S\})),$$
$$(Min(\{b_2\,|\,\mathbf{s} \in S\}), Min(\{z_2\,|\,\mathbf{s} \in S\}))))$$

(Def. $\mathcal{R}_{ds}(n)$) $\quad = \quad (Comp\,(n) \vee (Min(\{b_1\,|\,\mathbf{s} \in S\}) \wedge$
$$Min(\{z_2\,|\,\mathbf{s} \in S\}) \geq l),$$
$$Min(\{Min(\{z_1\,|\,\mathbf{s} \in S\}),$$
$$Min(\{z_2\,|\,\mathbf{s} \in S\})\}))$$

(Def. "meet" in $\mathcal{B}$) $\quad = \quad (Comp\,(n) \vee Min(\{Min(\{b_1\,|\,\mathbf{s} \in S\}),$
$$Min(\{z_2\,|\,\mathbf{s} \in S\}) \geq l\}),$$
$$Min(\{Min(\{z_1, z_2\,|\,\mathbf{s} \in S\})\}))$$

(Def. "meet" in $\mathcal{N}$) $\quad = \quad (Min(\{Comp\,(n) \vee (b_1 \wedge (z_2 \geq l))\,|\,\mathbf{s} \in S\},$
$$Min(\{Min(\{z_1, z_2\,|\,\mathbf{s} \in S\})\}))$$

(Def. "meet" in $\mathcal{B} \times \mathcal{N}$) $\quad = \quad Min(\{((Comp\,(n) \vee Min(\{b_1, z_2 \geq l\}),$
$$Min(\{z_1, z_2\}))\,|\,\mathbf{s} \in S\})$$

(Def. $\mathcal{R}_{ds}(n)$) $\quad = \quad Min(\{\mathcal{R}_{ds}(n)((b_1, z_1), (b_2, z_2))\,|\,\mathbf{s} \in S\})$

This proves Case 2, and completes the proof of the second part of Lemma 11.1.4. □

ds-Precision. The last step, which is necessary in order to verify the precision of $\mathcal{A}_{ds}$ is to prove that it is ds-precise. This means that interprocedural down-safety in the sense of Definition 10.4.1 coincides with the interprocedural meet over all paths solution of $\mathcal{A}_{ds}$. Without loss of generality, we will only prove the first part of this theorem because it is the relevant one for the definition of the *IBCM*-transformation. The second part can be proved analogously.

Theorem 11.1.1 (ds-Precision).
For all nodes $n \in N^*$ we have:

1. *N-$DSafe^*(n)$ if and only if $Int_{ds}(X\text{-}IMOP_{([\![\,]\!]_{ds}^*,\,(false,\infty))})(n)$*
2. *X-$DSafe^*(n)$ if and only if $Int_{ds}(N\text{-}IMOP_{([\![\,]\!]_{ds}^*,\,(false,\infty))})(n)$*

Proof. As mentioned above, we will only prove the first part of Theorem 11.1.1. For convenience, we use X-$IMOP$ and stk_0 as abbreviations of $Int_{ds} \circ X\text{-}IMOP_{([\![\,]\!]_{ds}^*,\,(false,\infty))}$ and $newstack(false, \infty)$ throughout the proof.

The first implication, "$\Rightarrow$",

$$\forall n \in N^*.\ N\text{-}DSafe^*(n) \Rightarrow X\text{-}IMOP(n)$$

is proved by showing the even stronger implication

$$\forall\, p \in \mathbf{IP}[\mathbf{s}^*, \mathbf{e}^*]\ \forall\, i \le \lambda_p.\ p_i = n \Rightarrow$$
$$(\exists\, i \le j \le \lambda_p.\ \mathit{Comp}^*{}_{(p,i)}(p_j) \wedge \mathit{Transp}^*{}^{\vee}_{(p,i)}(p[i,j[)\ \ (11.2)$$
$$\Rightarrow\ top(\llbracket\, \widetilde{p[i,\lambda_p]}\, \rrbracket^*_{ds}(stk_0))\!\downarrow_1 = true\ )$$

We prove this implication simultaneously for all nodes $n \in N^*$ by induction on the length $k =_{df} (\lambda_p - i + 1)$ of the postfix-paths $p[i,\lambda_p]$ for all paths $p \in \mathbf{IP}[\mathbf{s}^*, \mathbf{e}^*]$ and indexes $i \in \{1, \ldots, \lambda_p\}$ satisfying

$$p_i = n\ \wedge\ \exists\, i \le j \le \lambda_p.\ \mathit{Comp}^*{}_{(p,i)}(p_j) \wedge \mathit{Transp}^*{}^{\vee}_{(p,i)}(p[i,j[)\ \ (11.3)$$

Obviously, the case $k = 0$ does not occur, since we are dealing with inter-procedural entry-down-safety. Thus, let $p[i,\lambda_p]$ be a postfix-path of length $k = 1$. This implies $p[i,\lambda_p] = (p_i)$, $p_i = \mathbf{e}^*$, and therefore $p_i \in N^* \backslash N^*_c$. In this case, (11.3) yields

$$\mathit{Comp}^*{}_{(p,i)}(p_i)$$

Applying Lemma 10.2.1(1) this is equivalent to

$$\mathit{Comp}\,(p_i)$$

Hence, Lemma 11.1.2(1a) yields as desired

$$top(\llbracket\, \widetilde{p[i,\lambda_p]}\, \rrbracket^*_{ds}(stk_0))\!\downarrow_1 = top(\llbracket\, p_i\, \rrbracket^*_{ds}(stk_0))\!\downarrow_1 = true$$

In order to prove the induction step, let $k > 1$, and assume that (11.2) holds for all postfix-paths $q[i,\lambda_q]$ with $\lambda_{q[i,\lambda_q]} < k$, i.e.,

(IH) $(\forall\, q \in \mathbf{IP}[\mathbf{s}^*, \mathbf{e}^*].\ 1 \le \lambda_{q[i,\lambda_q]} < k).\ q_i = n \Rightarrow$
$$(\exists\, i \le j \le \lambda_q.\ \mathit{Comp}^*{}_{(q,i)}(q_j) \wedge \mathit{Transp}^*{}^{\vee}_{(q,i)}(q[i,j[)$$
$$\Rightarrow\ top(\llbracket\, \widetilde{q[i,\lambda_q]}\, \rrbracket^*_{ds}(stk_0))\!\downarrow_1 = true\ )$$

It is sufficient to show that for every path $p \in \mathbf{IP}[\mathbf{s}^*, \mathbf{e}^*]$ with $p_i = n$ and $\lambda_{p[i,\lambda_p]} = k$ satisfying (11.3) holds

$$top(\llbracket\, \widetilde{p[i,\lambda_p]}\, \rrbracket^*_{ds}(stk_0))\!\downarrow_1 = true$$

Without loss of generality we can therefore assume that there is such a postfix-path $p[i,\lambda_p]$, which can be rewritten as $p[i,\lambda_p] = (p_i);p'$ with $p' = p]i,\lambda_p]$. Next, we must investigate two cases depending on the type of node p_i.

Case 1. $p_i \in N^* \backslash N^*_c$
If p_i satisfies the predicate Comp, Lemma 11.1.2(1a) yields as desired

$$top(\llbracket\, \widetilde{p[i,\lambda_p]}\, \rrbracket^*_{ds}(stk_0))\!\downarrow_1 = top(\llbracket\, p_i\, \rrbracket^*_{ds}(\llbracket\, \tilde{p}'\, \rrbracket^*_{ds}(stk_0)))\!\downarrow_1 = true$$

If p_i does not satisfy the predicate $Comp$, (11.3) guarantees the existence of an index j with $i + 1 \leq j \leq \lambda_p$ such that

$$Comp^*{}_{(p,i)}(p_j) \tag{11.4}$$

and

$$Transp^*{}_{(p,i)}^{\forall}(p[i, j[) \tag{11.5}$$

are valid. Together with Lemma 10.2.4(1), (11.5) delivers

$$Transp\,(p_i) \tag{11.6}$$

Moreover, due to (11.6) and Lemma 10.2.5(2), the first and third part of Lemma 10.2.3 yield

$$RhsLev_p^{Var(t)}(i) = RhsLev_p^{Var(t)}(i + 1) \tag{11.7}$$

Combining (11.4), (11.5), and (11.7), we obtain

$$Comp^*{}_{(p,i+1)}(p_j) \ \wedge \ Transp^*{}_{(p,i+1)}^{\forall}(p]i, j[)$$

Hence, the induction hypothesis (IH) yields

$$top(\llbracket\, \tilde{p}'\, \rrbracket_{ds}^*(stk_0))\!\downarrow_1 = true \tag{11.8}$$

Combining (11.6) and (11.8), we obtain by means of Lemma 11.1.2(1b)

$$top(\llbracket\, \widetilde{p[i, \lambda_p]}\, \rrbracket_{ds}^*(stk_0))\!\downarrow_1 = top(\llbracket\, p_i\, \rrbracket_{ds}^*(\llbracket\, \tilde{p}'\, \rrbracket_{ds}^*(stk_0)))\!\downarrow_1 = true$$

which completes the proof of Case 1.

Case 2. $n_i \in N_c^*$
Similar to Case 1, we first assume that p_i satisfies the predicate $Comp$. In this case the desired sequence of equations

$$top(\llbracket\, \widetilde{p[i, \lambda_p]}\, \rrbracket_{ds}^*(stk_0))\!\downarrow_1 = top(\llbracket\, p_i\, \rrbracket_{ds}^*(\llbracket\, \tilde{p}'\, \rrbracket_{ds}^*(stk_0)))\!\downarrow_1 = true$$

is an immediate consequence of Lemma 11.1.2(2a). Thus, we are left with the case that p_i does not satisfy the predicate $Comp$. In this case we have to distinguish, whether t contains local variables of $fg(succ^*(p_i))$ or not. This leads us to the following case analysis.

Case 2.1. $Var(t) \subseteq GlobVar(fg(succ^*(p_i)))$
In this case, Lemma 10.2.3(2) yields

$$RhsLev_p^{Var(t)}(i) = RhsLev_p^{Var(t)}(i + 1) \tag{11.9}$$

Moreover, as in the previous case, (11.3) guarantees the existence of an index j with $i + 1 \leq j \leq \lambda_p$ such that the conjunction

$$Comp^*{}_{(p,i)}(p_j) \ \wedge \ Transp^*{}_{(p,i)}^{\forall}(p[i, j[) \tag{11.10}$$

holds. From (11.9) and (11.10) we obtain

$$Comp^*_{(p,i+1)}(p_j) \wedge Transp^{*\forall}_{(p,i+1)}(p[i,j[)$$

The induction hypothesis (IH) now yields

$$top([\![\tilde{p}']\!]^*_{ds}(stk_0))\downarrow_1 = true \tag{11.11}$$

By means of (11.11), Lemma 11.1.2(2b) yields now as desired

$$top([\![\widetilde{p[i,\lambda_p]}]\!]^*_{ds}(stk_0))\downarrow_1 = top([\![p_i]\!]^*_{ds}([\![\tilde{p}']\!]^*_{ds}(stk_0)))\downarrow_1 = true$$

which completes the proof of Case 2.1.

Case 2.2. $Var(t) \not\subseteq GlobVar(fg(succ^*(p_i)))$
In this case, we obviously have

$$Var(t) \cap LocVar(fg(succ^*(p_i))) \neq \emptyset \tag{11.12}$$

Let now $p_{i'}$ be the matching return node of p_i on p, i.e., $p_i \in N^*_c$, $p_{i'} \in N^*_r$, and $p[i,i'[\in \mathbf{CIP}[succ^*(p_i), pred^*(p_{i'})]$. Because of (11.12), Lemma 10.2.7 delivers

$$\neg Comp^{*\exists}_{(p,i)}(p[i,i']) \tag{11.13}$$

Moreover, by means of (11.13) and (11.3) we obtain the existence of an index j with $i' + 1 \leq j \leq \lambda_p$ such that

$$Comp^*_{(p,i)}(p_j) \wedge Transp^{*\forall}_{(p,i)}(p[i,j[) \tag{11.14}$$

holds. Additionally, Lemma 10.2.6(2) yields

$$RhsLev_p^{Var(t)}(i) = RhsLev_p^{Var(t)}(i' + 1) \tag{11.15}$$

Together (11.14) and (11.15) imply

$$Comp^*_{(p,i'+1)}(p_j) \wedge Transp^{*\forall}_{(p,i'+1)}(p[i',j[) \tag{11.16}$$

Abbreviating the path $p[i', \lambda_p]$ by p'', the induction hypothesis (IH) yields

$$top([\![\tilde{p}'']\!]^*_{ds}(stk_0))\downarrow_1 = true \tag{11.17}$$

This implies

$$top(pop([\![\tilde{p}']\!]^*_{ds}(stk_0))) = top([\![\tilde{p}'']\!]^*_{ds}(stk_0)) \tag{11.18}$$

since intervals of call nodes and return nodes on interprocedural paths are either disjoint or one is included in the other (cf. Lemma 7.2.1). Combining (11.17) and (11.18) we get

$$top(pop([\![\tilde{p}']\!]^*_{ds}(stk_0)))\downarrow_1 = true \tag{11.19}$$

Moreover, by means of (11.14), Lemma 11.1.1 yields

$$top([\![\, \tilde{p'} \,]\!]^*_{ds}(stk_0))\!\downarrow_2 \geq StatLevel(fg(succ^*(p_i))) \qquad (11.20)$$

Now, the desired sequence of equalities

$$top([\![\, \widetilde{p[i,\lambda_p]} \,]\!]^*_{ds}(stk_0))\!\downarrow_1 = top([\![\, p_i \,]\!]^*_{ds}([\![\, \tilde{p'} \,]\!]^*_{ds}(stk_0)))\!\downarrow_1 = true$$

follows from (11.19), (11.20), and Lemma 11.1.2(2b). This completes the proof of the first implication.

The second implication, "$\Leftarrow$",

$$\forall\, n \in N^*. \ X\text{-}IMOP(n) \Rightarrow N\text{-}DSafe^*(n)$$

is proved by showing the even stronger implication

$$\forall\, p \in \mathbf{IP}[\mathbf{s^*},\mathbf{e^*}]\ \forall\, i \leq \lambda_p.\ p_i = n \Rightarrow (top([\![\, \widetilde{p[i,\lambda_p]} \,]\!]^*_{ds}(stk_0))\!\downarrow_1 = true \atop \Rightarrow \exists\, i \leq j \leq \lambda_p.\ Comp^*_{(p,i)}(p_j) \wedge Transp^{*\vee}_{(p,i)}(p[i,j[)} \qquad (11.21)$$

We prove this implication simultaneously for all nodes $n \in N^*$ by induction on the length $k =_{df} (\lambda_p - i + 1)$ of the postfix-paths $p[i,\lambda_p]$ for all paths $p \in \mathbf{IP}[\mathbf{s^*},\mathbf{e^*}]$ and indexes $i \in \{1,\dots,\lambda_p\}$ satisfying

$$p_i = n \ \wedge \ top([\![\, \widetilde{p[i,\lambda_p]} \,]\!]^*_{ds}(stk_0))\!\downarrow_1 = true \qquad (11.22)$$

Like in the proof of the first implication, the case $k = 0$ does not occur, since we are dealing with interprocedural entry-down-safety. Thus, we start with considering a postfix-path $p[i,\lambda_p]$ of length $k = 1$. This implies $p[i,\lambda_p] = (p_i) = (\mathbf{e^*})$, and therefore $p_i \in N^* \backslash N^*_c$. Moreover, (11.22) yields

$$top([\![\, \widetilde{p[i,\lambda_p]} \,]\!]^*_{ds}(stk_0))\!\downarrow_1 = top([\![\, p_i \,]\!]^*_{ds}(stk_0))\!\downarrow_1 = true$$

Additionally, we have
$$top(stk_0)\!\downarrow_1 = false$$

Hence, by means of Lemma 11.1.2(1) we obtain

$$Comp\,(p_i)$$

According to Lemma 10.2.1(1) this is equivalent to

$$Comp^*_{(p,i)}(p_i)$$

Thus, the induction basis follows for $j = i$.

In order to prove the induction step, let $k > 1$, and assume that (11.21) holds for all postfix-paths $q[i,\lambda_q]$ with $\lambda_{q[i,\lambda_q]} < k$, i.e.,

(IH) $(\forall q \in \mathbf{IP}[\mathbf{s}^*, \mathbf{e}^*].\ 1 \le \lambda_{q[i,\lambda_q]} < k).\ q_i = n \Rightarrow$

$$(top(\llbracket \widetilde{q[i, \lambda_q]} \rrbracket_{ds}^* (stk_0)) \downarrow_1 = true \Rightarrow$$
$$\exists i \le j \le \lambda_q.\ Comp^*_{(q,i)}(q_j) \wedge Transp^{*\vee}_{(q,i)}(q[i,j[)\,)$$

It is sufficient to show that for every path $p \in \mathbf{IP}[\mathbf{s}^*, \mathbf{e}^*]$ with $p_i = n$ and $\lambda_{p[i,\lambda_p]} = k$ satisfying (11.22) holds

$$\exists i \le j \le \lambda_p.\ Comp^*_{(p,i)}(p_j) \wedge Transp^{*\vee}_{(p,i)}(p[i,j[)$$

Thus, without loss of generality we can assume that there is such a postfix-path $p[i, \lambda_p]$, which then can be rewritten as $p[i, \lambda_p] = (p_i);p'$ with $p' = p]i, \lambda_p]$. Similar to the proof of the first implication we have to investigate two cases depending on the type of node p_i.

Case 1. $p_i \in N^* \backslash N_c^*$
If p_i satisfies the predicate $Comp$, the induction step follows immediately for $j = i$. Thus, we are left with the case that p_i does not satisfy the predicate $Comp$. In this case Lemma 11.1.2(1b) delivers

$$Transp\,(p_i) \wedge top(\llbracket \tilde{p}' \rrbracket_{ds}^*(stk_0)) \downarrow_1 = true \tag{11.23}$$

Applying the induction hypothesis (IH) to p' we obtain the existence of an index $j_{p'}$ with $i + 1 \le j_{p'} \le \lambda_p$ and

$$Comp^*_{(p,i+1)}(p_{j_{p'}}) \wedge Transp^{*\vee}_{(p,i+1)}(p]i, j_{p'}[) \tag{11.24}$$

Moreover, due to $Transp\,(p_i)$, the first and third part of Lemma 10.2.3 imply

$$RhsLev_p^{Var(t)}(i) = RhsLev_p^{Var(t)}(i + 1) \tag{11.25}$$

Combining (11.23), (11.24), (11.25), we obtain

$$Comp^*_{(p,i)}(p_{j_{p'}}) \wedge Transp^{*\vee}_{(p,i)}(p]i, j_{p'}[)$$

Hence, the induction step follows for $j = j_{p'}$.

Case 2. $p_i \in N_c^*$
Similar to Case 1, if p_i satisfies the predicate $Comp$, the induction step follows trivially for $j = i$. If p_i does not satisfy the predicate $Comp$, we have to distinguish, whether t contains local variables of $fg(succ^*(p_i))$ or not. This leads us to the following case analysis.

Case 2.1. $Var(t) \subseteq GlobVar(fg(succ^*(p_i)))$
In this case, we obtain by means of Lemma 11.1.2(2b)

$$top(\llbracket \tilde{p}' \rrbracket_{ds}^*(stk_0)) \downarrow_1 = true \tag{11.26}$$

and additionally by means of Lemma 10.2.5(1)

$$Transp\,(p_i)$$

According to Lemma 10.2.1(2) $Transp(p_i)$ implies

$$Transp^*_{(p,i)}(p_i) \tag{11.27}$$

By means of (11.26) and the induction hypothesis (IH) we therefore obtain the existence of an index $j_{p'}$ with $i + 1 \leq j_{p'} \leq \lambda_p$ such that

$$Comp^*_{(p,i+1)}(p_{j_{p'}}) \wedge Transp^{*\vee}_{(p,i+1)}(p]i, j_{p'}[) \tag{11.28}$$

holds. Moreover, Lemma 10.2.3(2) yields

$$RhsLev_p^{Var(t)}(i) = RhsLev_p^{Var(t)}(i + 1) \tag{11.29}$$

Now, (11.27), (11.28) and (11.29) deliver

$$Comp^*_{(p,i)}(p_{j_{p'}}) \wedge Transp^{*\vee}_{(p,i)}(p]i, j_{p'}[)$$

Thus, the induction step follows for $j = j_{p'}$ in Case 2.1.

Case 2.2. $Var(t) \not\subseteq GlobVar(fg(succ^*(p_i)))$
Here we have

$$Var(t) \cap LocVar(fg(succ^*(p_i))) \neq \emptyset$$

Let $p_{i'}$ be the matching return node of p_i on p, i.e., $p_i \in N_c^*$, $p_{i'} \in N_r^*$, and $p]i, i'[\in \mathbf{CIP}[succ^*(p_i), pred^*(p_{i'})]$. As a consequence of

$$top(\llbracket \widetilde{p[i, \lambda_p]} \rrbracket_{ds}^*(stk_0))\downarrow_1 = top(\llbracket \tilde{p_i} \rrbracket_{ds}^*(\llbracket \tilde{p'} \rrbracket_{ds}^*(stk_0)))\downarrow_1 = true$$

Lemma 11.1.2(2b) yields

$$top(pop(\llbracket \tilde{p'} \rrbracket_{ds}^*(stk_0)))\downarrow_1 = true \tag{11.30}$$

and

$$top(\llbracket \tilde{p'} \rrbracket_{ds}^*(stk_0))\downarrow_2 \geq StatLevel(fg(succ^*(p_i))) \tag{11.31}$$

Since intervals of call nodes and return nodes on interprocedural paths are either disjoint or one is included in the other (cf. Lemma 7.2.1), we obtain by means of (11.30)

$$top(\llbracket \tilde{p''} \rrbracket_{ds}^*(stk_0))\downarrow_1 = true \tag{11.32}$$

where $p'' =_{df} p]i', \lambda_p]$. The induction hypothesis (IH), therefore, yields the existence of an index $j_{p''}$ with $i' + 1 \leq j_{p''} \leq \lambda_p$ and

$$Comp^*_{(p,i'+1)}(p_{j_{p''}}) \wedge Transp^{*\vee}_{(p,i'+1)}(p]i', j_{p''}[) \tag{11.33}$$

Moreover, (11.31) and Lemma 11.1.1 deliver

$$Transp^{*\vee}_{(p,i)}(p[i, i']) \tag{11.34}$$

and Lemma 10.2.6(2) yields

$$RhsLev_p^{Var(t)}(i) = RhsLev_p^{Var(t)}(i' + 1) \tag{11.35}$$

Combining (11.33), (11.34), and (11.35), we now obtain

$$Comp^*{}_{(p,i)}(p_{j_{p''}}) \ \wedge \ Transp^*{}_{(p,i)}^{\forall}(p[i,j_{p''}])$$

Thus, the induction step follows for $j = j_{p''}$. This completes the proof of the second implication, and finishes the proof of the relevant part of Theorem 11.1.1. □

Combining Lemma 11.1.3, Lemma 11.1.4, and Theorem 11.1.1, we obtain the central result of this section: $\mathcal{A}_{ds}$ is precise for interprocedural down-safety. This guarantees that the *IMFP*-solution computed by $\mathcal{A}_{ds}$ coincides with the set of all program points which are interprocedurally down-safe in the sense of Definition 10.4.1.

Theorem 11.1.2 ($\mathcal{A}_{ds}$-Precision).
$\mathcal{A}_{ds}$ is precise for interprocedural down-safety, i.e., $\mathcal{A}_{ds}$ is terminating and ds-precise.

11.2 IDFA-Algorithm $\mathcal{A}_{ea}$: Interprocedural Earliestness

In this section we present the IDFA-algorithm $\mathcal{A}_{ea}$ for computing the set of interprocedurally earliest program points.[2] The main result of this section, the $\mathcal{A}_{ea}$-Precision Theorem 11.2.2, guarantees that $\mathcal{A}_{ea}$ is precise for this property: it terminates with the set of all program points, which are interprocedurally earliest in the sense of Definition 10.4.2.

11.2.1 Specification

Data Flow Information. The domain of data flow information of $\mathcal{A}_{ea}$ is given by the product lattice

$$(\mathcal{C}, \sqcap, \sqsubseteq, \bot, \top) =_{df} (\mathcal{B} \times \mathcal{N}, (Max, Min), (\geq, \leq), (true, 0), (false, \infty))$$

where *Max* denotes the maximum function, which on $\mathcal{B}$ corresponds to the logical disjunction. In comparison to the down-safety analysis we use a slightly different lattice for the earliestness analysis. This is caused by the fact that the algorithms of Chapter 8.5 are tailored for computing the greatest solution of an equation system, whereas the straightforward specification of the earliestness analysis requires the computation of the least solution.

Intuitively, the first component of a data flow information, which is attached to a program point indicates, whether a placement of t is earliest at this point. The second component has the same meaning as in the down-safety analysis. It stores the static level of the "most globally" declared variable of

---

[2] The index *ea* stands for earliestness.

t, which has been modified in the current procedure call. Hence, like for the down-safety analysis only the finite sublattice $\mathcal{B} \times \mathcal{N}_\Pi$ of $\mathcal{B} \times \mathcal{N}$ is relevant for $\mathcal{A}_{ea}$.

Local Semantic Functional. The local semantic functional $[\![\ ]\!]'_{ea} : N^* \rightarrow (\mathcal{B} \times \mathcal{N} \rightarrow \mathcal{B} \times \mathcal{N})$ of $\mathcal{A}_{ea}$ is defined by

$$\forall n \in N^* \ \forall (b, z) \in \mathcal{B} \times \mathcal{N}. \ [\![\, n\,]\!]'_{ea}(b, z) =_{df} (b', z')$$

where

$$b' =_{df} \neg Transp(n) \ \vee \ (\neg I\text{-}DSafe(n) \wedge b)$$

$$z' =_{df} \begin{cases} Min(\{z, ModLev(n)\}) & \text{if } n \in N^* \setminus N_c^* \\ \infty & \text{otherwise} \end{cases}$$

Return Functional. The return functional $\mathcal{R}_{ea} : N_r^* \rightarrow ((\mathcal{B} \times \mathcal{N})^2 \rightarrow \mathcal{B} \times \mathcal{N})$ of $\mathcal{A}_{ea}$ is defined by

$$\forall n \in N_r^* \ \forall ((b_1, z_1), (b_2, z_2)) \in (\mathcal{B} \times \mathcal{N})^2. \ \mathcal{R}_{ea}(n)((b_1, z_1), (b_2, z_2)) =_{df} (b', z')$$

where

$$b' =_{df} \begin{cases} b_2 \wedge \neg I\text{-}DSafe(n) & \text{if } Var(t) \subseteq GlobVar(fg(pred^*(n))) \\ (\neg I\text{-}DSafe(n_S) \wedge b_1) \ \vee & \\ (z_2 < StatLevel(fg(pred^*(n)))) & \text{otherwise} \end{cases}$$

$$z' =_{df} Min(\{z_1, z_2\})$$

We remark that the definitions of the functionals $[\![\ ]\!]'_{ea}$ and $\mathcal{R}_{ea}$ rely on essentially the same intuitions as the definitions of their counterparts of the down-safety analysis.

Start Information. The start information of $\mathcal{A}_{ea}$ is given by the element

$$(\mathbf{s}_1 \in Range(t), \infty) \in \mathcal{B} \times \mathcal{N}$$

Intuitively, the first component of the start information expresses that t is earliest at the beginning of the argument program if and only if the start node of Π belongs to the range of t. The second component reflects that no variable of t is assumed of having been modified before the execution of the first statement of Π.

Interpretation. The interpretation of lattice elements in $\mathcal{B}$ is given by the function $Int_{ea} : \mathcal{B} \times \mathcal{N} \rightarrow \mathcal{B}$ defined by

$$\forall (b, z) \in \mathcal{B} \times \mathcal{N}. \ Int_{ea}(b, z) =_{df} b$$

11.2.2 Proving Precision

Similar to Section 11.1.2, we first present two lemmas, which are useful for the proof of the *ea*-Precision Theorem 11.2.1. Both lemmas can easily be proved by means of the definitions of the functionals $[\![\ ]\!]'_{ea}$ and $\mathcal{R}_{ea}$.

Lemma 11.2.1. *Let* $p \in \mathbf{IP}[\mathbf{s}^*, \mathbf{e}^*]$, *and* $i, j \in \{1, \ldots, \lambda_p\}$ *such that* $p_i \in N^*_c$ *and* $p_j \in N^*_r$ *are a pair of matching call and return nodes of* p. *We have:*

$$Transp^{*\vee}_{(p,i)}(p[i,j]) \Longleftrightarrow$$
$$top([\![\,p[1,j[\,]\!]^*_{ea}(newstack(\mathbf{s}_1 \in Range(t), \infty)))\downarrow_2 \geq StatLevel(fg(pred^*(p_j)))$$

Lemma 11.2.2.

1. $\forall\, n \in N^* \setminus N^*_r\ \forall\, stk \in STACK.$
   a) $\neg Transp(n) \Rightarrow top([\![\,n\,]\!]^*_{ea}(stk))\downarrow_1 = true$
   b) $Transp(n) \Rightarrow (\, top([\![\,n\,]\!]^*_{ea}(stk))\downarrow_1 = true \Longleftrightarrow$
   $$\neg I\text{-}DSafe(n)\, \wedge\, top(stk)\downarrow_1 = true\,)$$

2. $\forall\, n \in N^*_r\ \forall\, stk \in STACK_{\geq 2}.$
   a) $\neg Transp(n) \Rightarrow (\, top([\![\,n\,]\!]^*_{ea}(stk))\downarrow_1 = true \Longleftrightarrow$
   $$(\,(\neg I\text{-}DSafe(n_S) = top(pop(stk))\downarrow_1 = true)\ \vee$$
   $$(top(stk)\downarrow_2 < StatLevel(fg(pred^*(n))))\,)\,)$$

   b) $Transp(n) \Rightarrow (\, top([\![\,n\,]\!]^*_{ea}(stk))\downarrow_1 = true \Longleftrightarrow$
   $$\neg I\text{-}DSafe(n)\, \wedge\, top(stk)\downarrow_1 = true\,)$$

It is worth noting that in the second part of Lemma 11.2.2 the premise *Transp* implies that all variables occurring in t are global with respect to the procedure $fg(pred^*(n))$. Correspondingly, $\neg Transp(n)$ implies that t contains at least one local variable or formal value parameter of $fg(pred^*(n))$. In the context of interprocedural paths, $\neg Transp(n)$ implies also that a recursive procedure call is finished.

Descending Chain Condition. Like for A_{ds}, also for A_{ea} only the finite sublattices $\mathcal{B} \times \mathcal{N}_{\Pi}$ and $[(\mathcal{B} \times \mathcal{N}_{\Pi}) \to (\mathcal{B} \times \mathcal{N}_{\Pi})]$ of $\mathcal{B} \times \mathcal{N}$ and $[(\mathcal{B} \times \mathcal{N}) \to (\mathcal{B} \times \mathcal{N})]$ are relevant. Thus, we immediately get the following lemma, which is sufficient for our application.

Lemma 11.2.3 (Descending Chain Condition).
The function lattice $[(\mathcal{B} \times \mathcal{N}_{\Pi}) \to (\mathcal{B} \times \mathcal{N}_{\Pi})]$ *satisfies the descending chain condition.*

Distributivity. The distributivity of the local semantic functions and the return functions for earliestness can be proved along the lines of Lemma 11.1.1. We have:

Lemma 11.2.4 ($[\![\ ]\!]'_{ea}, \mathcal{R}_{ea}$-Distributivity).

1. *The local semantic functions $[\![\, n\,]\!]'_{ea}$, $n \in N^*$, are distributive.*
2. *The return functions $\mathcal{R}_{ea}(n)$, $n \in N_r^*$, are distributive.*

ea-**Precision.** Finally, we must prove the coincidence of interprocedural earliestness in the sense of Definition 10.4.2 with the interprocedural meet over all paths solution induced by $\mathcal{A}_{ea}$ as stated by Theorem 11.2.1. Without loss of generality we only prove the first part of this theorem because it is the relevant one for the definition of the *IBCM*-transformation. We remark that the second part can be proved analogously. We have:

Theorem 11.2.1 (*ea*-Precision).
For all nodes $n \in N^*$ we have:

1. *N-Earliest* (n) if and only if $Int_{ea}(N\text{-}IMOP_{([\![\ ]\!]^*_{ea}, (\mathbf{s}_1 \in Range(t), \infty))}(n))$*
2. *X-Earliest* (n) if and only if $Int_{ea}(X\text{-}IMOP_{([\![\ ]\!]^*_{ea}, (\mathbf{s}_1 \in Range(t), \infty))}(n))$*

Proof.
As mentioned before, we will only consider the first part of Theorem 11.2.1 in detail. For convenience, we abbreviate $Int_{ea} \circ N\text{-}IMOP_{([\![\ ]\!]^*_{ea}, (\mathbf{s}_1 \in Range(t), \infty))}$ and $newstack(\mathbf{s}_1 \in Range(t), \infty)$ by $N\text{-}IMOP$ and stk_0 throughout the proof.

The first implication, "$\Rightarrow$",

$$\forall n \in N^*. \ N\text{-}Earliest^* (n) \Rightarrow N\text{-}IMOP(n)$$

is proved by equivalently showing

$$\forall p \in \mathbf{IP}[\mathbf{s}^*, n]. \ (\forall 1 \leq i < \lambda_p.$$
$$I\text{-}DSafe\,(p_i) \wedge SameInc_p[i, \lambda_p[\ \Rightarrow\ \neg Transp^{*\vee}_{(p,i)}(p[i, \lambda_p[) \quad (11.36)$$
$$\Rightarrow\ top([\![\, p[1, \lambda_p[\,]\!]^*_{ea}(stk_0))\downarrow_1 = true\,)$$

We prove (11.36) simultaneously for all nodes $n \in N^*$ by induction on the length k of path $p[1, \lambda_p[$ for all paths $p \in \mathbf{IP}[\mathbf{s}^*, n]$ satisfying

$$\forall 1 \leq i < \lambda_p. I\text{-}DSafe\,(p_i) \wedge SameInc_p[i, \lambda_p[\Rightarrow \neg Transp^{*\vee}_{(p,i)}(p[i, \lambda_p[) \quad (11.37)$$

If $k = 0$, we obtain $n = \mathbf{s}^*$ and $p[1, \lambda_p[= \varepsilon$. Moreover, combining (11.37) and Lemma 10.3.1 we obtain $n \in Range(t)$. Hence, the desired sequence of equalities

$$top([\![\, p[1, \lambda_p[\,]\!]^*_{ea}(stk_0))\downarrow_1 = top([\![\, \varepsilon\,]\!]^*_{ea}(stk_0))\downarrow_1 = stk_0\downarrow_1 = true$$

holds trivially.

In order to prove the induction step, let $k > 0$, and assume that (11.36) holds for all paths q with $\lambda_{q[1, \lambda_q[} < k$, i.e.,

(IH) $(\forall q \in \mathbf{IP}[\mathbf{s}^*, n].\ 0 \leq \lambda_{q[1,\lambda_q[} < k)$.

$(\forall 1 \leq i < \lambda_q.\ \textit{I-DSafe}(q_i) \wedge \textit{SameInc}_q[i, \lambda_q[\Rightarrow \neg \textit{Transp}^{*\vee}_{(q,i)}(q[i, \lambda_q[))$

$\Rightarrow top([\![\, q[1, \lambda_q[\,]\!]^*_{ea}(stk_0))\!\downarrow_1 = \textit{true}\,)$

Now it is sufficient to show that for every path $p \in \mathbf{IP}[\mathbf{s}^*, n]$ with $\lambda_{p[1,\lambda_p[} = k$ satisfying (11.37) holds

$$top([\![\, p[1, \lambda_p[\,]\!]^*_{ea}(stk_0))\!\downarrow_1 = \textit{true}$$

Without loss of generality we can assume that there is such a path p, which then can be rewritten as $p = p';(m);(n)$ with $p' = p[1, k[$ and $m = p_k \in pred^*(n)$. Next, we must investigate two cases depending on the type of node m.

Case 1. $m \in N^* \setminus N_r^*$
If $\textit{Transp}(m)$ does not hold,

$$top([\![\, p[1, \lambda_p[\,]\!]^*_{ea}(stk_0))\!\downarrow_1 = top([\![\, m\,]\!]^*_{ea}([\![\, p'\,]\!]^*_{ea}(stk_0)))\!\downarrow_1 = \textit{true}$$

follows immediately by means of Lemma 11.2.2(1a). Thus, we are left with the case that m satisfies the predicate $\textit{Transp}$. According to the choice of p satisfying (11.37) we directly obtain

$$\neg \textit{I-DSafe}(m) \tag{11.38}$$

Thus, we have

$$\forall 1 \leq i < k.\ \textit{I-DSafe}(p_i) \wedge \textit{SameInc}_p[i, \lambda_p[\Rightarrow \neg \textit{Transp}^{*\vee}_{(p,i)}(p[i, k[)$$

Applying the induction hypothesis (IH) to $p[1, \lambda_p[= p';(m)$, we get

$$top([\![\, p'\,]\!]^*_{ea}(stk_0))\!\downarrow_1 = \textit{true} \tag{11.39}$$

Combining (11.38) and (11.39) with Lemma 11.2.2(1b) we obtain as desired

$$top([\![\, p[1, \lambda_p[\,]\!]^*_{ea}(stk_0))\!\downarrow_1 = top([\![\, m\,]\!]^*_{ea}([\![\, p'\,]\!]^*_{ea}(stk_0)))\!\downarrow_1 = \textit{true}$$

Case 2. $m \in N_r^*$
If $\textit{Transp}(m)$ holds, the proof proceeds as in the corresponding situation of Case 1. Thus, we can assume that $\textit{Transp}(m)$ does not hold. Together with $n \in succ^*(m)$ and $t \in \textit{Range}(n)$, this implies that we are finishing a recursive procedure call, and that

$$\textit{Var}(t) \cap \textit{LocVar}(fg(pred^*(m))) \neq \emptyset$$

Let $\bar{m} =_{df} p_s$ be the matching call node of m on p'. We first consider the case

$$\textit{I-DSafe}(\bar{m})$$

By means of Lemma 10.2.6 we get

$$SameInc_p[s, \lambda_p[$$

According to the choice of p satisfying (11.37), there is an index j with $\lambda_p > j \geq s$ and

$$\neg Transp^*_{(p,\lambda_p)}(p_j)$$

Applying Lemma 11.2.1 we obtain

$$top(\llbracket p' \rrbracket^*_{ea}(stk_0))\downarrow_2 < StatLevel(fg(pred^*(m))) \tag{11.40}$$

Now

$$top(\llbracket p \rrbracket^*_{ea}(stk_0))\downarrow_1 = true$$

follows immediately from (11.40) and Lemma 11.2.2(2a).

Hence, we are left with the case that $I\text{-}DSafe(\bar{m})$ does not hold. Without loss of generality we can assume

$$top(\llbracket p' \rrbracket^*_{ea}(stk_0))\downarrow_2 \geq StatLevel(fg(pred^*(m))).$$

According to the choice of p satisfying (11.37) and due to Lemma 10.2.6(1) we therefore have

$$\forall\, 1 \leq s < r.\ I\text{-}DSafe(p_s) \wedge SameInc_p[s, \lambda_p[\Rightarrow \neg Transp^{*\vee}_{(p,s)}(p[s,r[)$$

Applying the induction hypothesis (IH) to $p'' = p[1, r]$ yields

$$top(\llbracket p''[1, r[\,\rrbracket^*_{ea}(stk_0))\downarrow_1 = true$$

Hence, the application of Lemma 11.2.2(2a) completes the proof of the first implication.

The second implication, "$\Leftarrow$",

$$\forall\, n \in N^*.\ N\text{-}IMOP(n) \Rightarrow N\text{-}Earliest^*(n)$$

is proved by showing the equivalent formula

$$\forall\, p \in \mathbf{IP}[s^*, n].\quad top(\llbracket p[1, \lambda_p[\,\rrbracket^*_{ea}(stk_0))\downarrow_1 = true \Rightarrow$$
$$(\forall\, 1 \leq i < \lambda_p.\, I\text{-}DSafe(p_i) \wedge SameInc_p[i, \lambda_p[\Rightarrow \neg Transp^{*\vee}_{(p,i)}(p[i, \lambda_p[)\,) \tag{11.41}$$

We prove (11.41) simultaneously for all nodes $n \in N^*$ by induction on the length k of path $p[1, \lambda_p[$ for all paths $p \in \mathbf{IP}[s^*, n]$ satisfying

$$top(\llbracket p[1, \lambda_p[\,\rrbracket^*_{ea}(stk_0))\downarrow_1 = true \tag{11.42}$$

If $k = 0$, we obtain $p[1, \lambda_p[= \varepsilon$. Hence, we have

$$top(\llbracket p[1, \lambda_p[\,\rrbracket^*_{ea}(stk_0))\downarrow_1 = top(\llbracket \varepsilon \rrbracket^*_{ea}(stk_0))\downarrow_1 = stk_0\downarrow_1 = true$$

Additionally, we obtain $n = \mathbf{s}^*$, and therefore $\mathbf{s}^* \in Range(t)$. Thus, (11.41) holds trivially.

In order to prove the induction step, let $k > 0$, and assume that (11.41) holds for all paths q with $\lambda_{q[1,\lambda_q[} < k$, i.e.,

(IH) $\forall q \in \mathbf{IP}[\mathbf{s}^*, n].\ 0 \leq \lambda_{q[1,\lambda_q[} < k).$
$$top(\llbracket q[1, \lambda_q[\rrbracket_{ea}^*(stk_0))\downarrow_1 = true \Rightarrow$$
$$(\forall 1 \leq i < \lambda_q.\ I\text{-}DSafe(q_i) \wedge SameInc_q[i, \lambda_q[\Rightarrow \neg Transp^{*\forall}_{(q,i)}(q[i, \lambda_q[))$$

It is sufficient to show that for every path $p \in \mathbf{IP}[\mathbf{s}^*, n]$ with $\lambda_{p[1,\lambda_p[} = k$ satisfying (11.42) holds

$$\forall 1 \leq i < \lambda_p.\ I\text{-}DSafe(p_i) \wedge SameInc_p[i, \lambda_p[\Rightarrow \neg Transp^{*\forall}_{(p,i)}(p[i, \lambda_p[)$$

Thus, we can assume that there is such a path p, which then can be rewritten as $p = p';(m);(n)$ with $p' = p[1, k[$, and $m = p_k \in pred^*(n)$. Similar to the proof of the first implication we must now investigate two cases depending on the type of node m.

Case 1. $m \in N^* \setminus N_r^*$
We first assume that $Transp(m)$ does not hold. If $m \in N_c^*$, the induction step holds trivially, since there is no r with $1 \leq r \leq k$ such that the predicate $SameInc_p[r, \lambda_p[$ is satisfied. Otherwise, i.e., if $m \notin N_c^*$, we have

$$SameInc_p[k, \lambda_p[$$

Thus, for all $1 \leq r \leq k$ with $I\text{-}DSafe(p_r)$ and $SameInc_p[r, \lambda_p[$ we also have

$$SameInc_p[r, \lambda_p[$$

Together with $\neg Transp(p_k)$ this directly implies for all such r as desired

$$\neg Transp^*_{(p,r)}(p_k)$$

Hence, we are left with the case that $Transp(m)$ holds. Applying Lemma 11.2.2(1b) we get
$$\neg I\text{-}DSafe(m)$$
and
$$top(\llbracket p' \rrbracket_{ea}^*(stk_0))\downarrow_1 = true$$
Moreover, $Transp(m)$ implies
$$SameInc_p[k, \lambda_p[$$

Hence, we obtain

$$I\text{-}DSafe(r) \wedge SameInc_p[r, \lambda_p[\Rightarrow I\text{-}DSafe(r) \wedge SameInc_p[r, k[\Rightarrow 1 \leq r < k$$

The induction step now follows from applying the induction hypothesis (IH) to p'.

Case 2. $m \in N_r^*$

If $Transp(m)$ holds, we have

$$SameInc_p[k, \lambda_p[$$

and by means of Lemma 11.2.2(2b) we get

$$\neg I\text{-}DSafe(m) \wedge top(\llbracket p' \rrbracket_{ea}^*(stk_0))\downarrow_1 = true$$

In this case the induction step follows from applying the induction hypothesis (IH) to p' as above. Thus, we are left with the case that $Transp(m)$ does not hold. Since p is an interprocedurally valid path, there is a call node $\bar{m} =_{df} p_s$ on p which matches the return node $m = p_k$. According to Lemma 10.2.6(1)&(2) we have

$$\forall s < j \leq k. \ \neg SameInc_p[s, j]$$

Additionally, Lemma 10.2.6(2) yields

$$SameInc[s, k[$$

Consequently, for all $1 \leq j \leq s$ with $SameInc_p[j, \lambda_p[$, we have

$$SameInc_p[j, s[$$

Now we first assume

$$top(\llbracket p' \rrbracket_{ea}^*(stk_0))\downarrow_2 < StatLevel(fg(pred^*(m)))$$

Then, by means of Lemma 11.2.1 there is an index u with $s \leq u \leq k$ and

$$\neg Transp^*_{(p,s)}(p_u)$$

In this case the induction step follows for $j = u$. Otherwise, i.e., whenever

$$top(\llbracket p' \rrbracket_{ea}^*(stk_0))\downarrow_2 \geq StatLevel(fg(pred^*(m)))$$

holds, Lemma 11.2.2(2a) yields

$$\neg I\text{-}DSafe(p_{\lambda_p}) = top(\llbracket p'' \rrbracket_{ea}^*(stk_0))\downarrow_1 = true$$

where $p'' = p[1, s]$. The application of Lemma 10.2.6 and of the induction hypothesis (IH) to $p''[1, s[$ delivers now the induction step for the last case. This finishes the proof of the relevant part of Theorem 11.2.1. □

Combining now Lemma 11.2.3, Lemma 11.2.4, and Theorem 11.2.1 we obtain the main result of this section: $\mathcal{A}_{ea}$ is precise for interprocedural earliestness. This guarantees that the *IMFP*-solution computed by $\mathcal{A}_{ea}$ coincides with the set of all program points being interprocedurally earliest in the sense of Definition 10.4.2.

Theorem 11.2.2 ($\mathcal{A}_{ea}$-Precision).
$\mathcal{A}_{ea}$ *is precise for interprocedural earliestness, i.e., $\mathcal{A}_{ea}$ is terminating and ea-precise.*

11.3 IDFA-Algorithm A_{dl}: Interprocedural Delayability

In this section we present the IDFA-algorithm A_{dl} for computing the set of interprocedurally delayable program points.[3] The main result of this section, the A_{dl}-Precision Theorem 11.3.2, yields that it is precise for this property: it terminates with the set of all program points, which are interprocedurally delayable in the sense of Definition 10.5.1.

11.3.1 Specification

Data Flow Information. The domain of data flow information of A_{dl} is given by the lattice

$$(\mathcal{C}, \sqcap, \sqsubseteq, \bot, \top) =_{df} (\mathcal{B}, \wedge, \leq, \textit{false}, \textit{true})$$

Intuitively, a data flow information attached to a program point expresses, whether an insertion of t by the $IBCM$-transformation can be delayed to this point. In contrast to the down-safety and the earliestness analysis it is not necessary to work on a product lattice in order to keep track on the static level of modified variables. This information is encoded in the down-safety and earliestness information the delayability analysis relies on.

Local Semantic Functional. The local semantic functional $[\![\ ]\!]'_{dl} : N^* \rightarrow (\mathcal{B} \rightarrow \mathcal{B})$ of A_{dl} is defined by

$$\forall\, n \in N^* \ \forall\, b \in \mathcal{B}. \ [\![\, n\,]\!]'_{dl}(b) =_{df} b'$$

where

$$b' =_{df} \begin{cases} (b \vee \textit{Insert}_{IBCM}(n)) \wedge \neg Comp(n) \\ \qquad \text{if } n \in N^* \backslash N_c^* \vee \textit{Var}(t) \subseteq \textit{GlobVar}(fg(succ^*(n))) \\ \textit{false} \qquad \text{otherwise} \end{cases}$$

The intuition underlying the definition of the local semantic functional is the same as in the intraprocedural case. Intuitively, an insertion of the $IBCM$-transformation can be delayed to the exit of a node n, if the term t under consideration is not blocked by n (i.e., $\neg Comp(n)$), and if its insertion can be delayed to the entry of n. This holds, if n is an insertion point of the $IBCM$-transformation (i.e., $\textit{Insert}_{IBCM}(n)$), or if the argument of $[\![\, n\,]\!]'_{dl}$ is true (i.e., $b = \textit{true}$).

---

[3] The index dl stands for delayability.

Return Functional. The return functional $\mathcal{R}_{dl} : N_r^* \to (\mathcal{B}^2 \to \mathcal{B})$ of $\mathcal{A}_{dl}$ is defined by

$$\forall n \in N_r^* \ \forall (b_1, b_2) \in \mathcal{B}^2. \ \mathcal{R}_{dl}(n)(b_1, b_2) =_{df} b'$$

where

$$b' =_{df} \begin{cases} b_2 & \text{if } Var(t) \subseteq GlobVar(fg(pred^*(n))) \\ (b_1 \vee Insert_{IBCM}(n_S)) \wedge \neg Comp(n_C) & \text{otherwise} \end{cases}$$

Intuitively, if some of the operands of t are locally declared in the procedure called (i.e., $Var(t) \not\subseteq GlobVar(fg(pred^*(n)))$), then t cannot be used inside this procedure as this concerns a different incarnation of t. Thus, if t is delayable across the procedure call, then it is delayable in one big step and not by moving it stepwise through the called procedure. This, actually, is possible, if t is not passed as an actual parameter (i.e., $\neg Comp(n_C)$), and if the insertion of t can be delayed to the entry of the call node under consideration (i.e., $b_1 \vee Insert_{IBCM}(n_S)$).[4] On the other hand, if all variables of t are global for the called procedure (i.e., $Var(t) \subseteq GlobVar(fg(pred^*(n)))$), t can be delayed across the procedure call, if it can successfully stepwise be delayed to the end of the procedure called (i.e., $b_2 = true$). The correctness of this definition is a consequence of the down-safety and earliestness information encoded in the predicate $Insert_{IBCM}$.

Start Information.

$$Insert_{IBCM}(\mathbf{s}_1) \in \mathcal{B}$$

Intuitively, this choice of the start information reflects that the process of moving computations in the direction of the control flow to "later" program points is initiated at insertion points of the $IBCM$-transformation.

Interpretation. The interpretation of lattice elements in $\mathcal{B}$ is given by the identity on $\mathcal{B}$, i.e., the function $Int_{dl} : \mathcal{B} \to \mathcal{B}$ is given by

$$Int_{dl} =_{df} Id_{\mathcal{B}}$$

11.3.2 Proving Precision

Like for the down-safety and earliestness analysis, we first introduce two lemmas, which simplify the proof of the dl-Precision Theorem 11.3.1. The first lemma can be proved straightforward by means of the definitions of the local semantic functional and the return functional of $\mathcal{A}_{dl}$. The second lemma follows immediately from the definition of interprocedural delayability (cf. Definition 10.5.1).

---

[4] We recall that n_S denotes the procedure call node in S corresponding to n.

Lemma 11.3.1.

1. $\forall n \in N^* \setminus (N_c^* \cup N_r^*) \ \forall stk \in STACK$.
   a) $Comp(n) \Rightarrow top(\llbracket n \rrbracket_{dl}^*(stk)) = false$
   b) $\neg Comp(n) \Rightarrow (top(\llbracket n \rrbracket_{dl}^*(stk)) = true \iff$
   $$Insert_{IBCM}(n) \ \lor \ top(stk) = true)$$

2. $\forall n \in N_c^* \ \forall stk \in STACK. \ top(\llbracket n \rrbracket_{dl}^*(stk)) = true \iff$
   $Var(t) \subseteq GlobVar(fg(succ^*(n))) \land \neg Comp(n) \land$
   $(top(stk) = true \lor Insert_{IBCM}(n))$

3. $\forall n \in N_r^* \ \forall stk \in STACK_{\geq 2}. \ (top(\llbracket n \rrbracket_{dl}^*(stk)) = true \iff$
   $$\left\{ \begin{array}{ll} top(stk) = true & \text{if } Var(t) \subseteq GlobVar(fg(pred^*(n))) \\ (top(pop(stk)) = true \lor & \\ Insert_{IBCM}(n_S)) \land \neg Comp(n_C) & \text{otherwise} \end{array} \right)$$

Lemma 11.3.2. $\forall n \in N^*. \ N\text{-}Delayable^*(n) \iff Insert_{IBCM}(n) \lor$
$(\forall p \in \mathbf{IP}[s^*, n] \ \exists 1 \leq i < \lambda_p. \ Insert_{IBCM}(p_i) \land SameInc_p[i, \lambda_p[\ \land$
$\neg Comp^*_{(p,i)}^{\exists}(p[i, \lambda_p[))$

Descending Chain Condition. Obviously, $\mathcal{B}$ is finite and hence, the corresponding function lattice $[\mathcal{B} \rightarrow \mathcal{B}]$ is finite, too. Thus, we have:

Lemma 11.3.3 (Descending Chain Condition).
The function lattice $[\mathcal{B} \rightarrow \mathcal{B}]$ satisfies the descending chain condition.

Distributivity. We have:

Lemma 11.3.4 ($\llbracket \ \rrbracket'_{dl}, \mathcal{R}_{dl}$-Distributivity).

1. *The local semantic functions $\llbracket n \rrbracket'_{dl}, \ n \in N^*$, are distributive.*
2. *The return functions $\mathcal{R}_{dl}(n), \ n \in N_r^*$, are distributive.*

Proof. The distributivity of the local semantic functions follows immediately from the distributivity of the corresponding intraprocedural local semantic functions (cf. Lemma 4.3.5). Thus, we are only left with proving the distributivity of the return functions. This requires to show:

$$\forall n \in N_r^* \ \forall B \subseteq \mathcal{B}^2. \ \mathcal{R}_{dl}(n)(\bigwedge B) = \bigwedge \{ \mathcal{R}_{dl}(n)(b_1, b_2) \mid (b_1, b_2) \in B \} \tag{11.43}$$

To this end let $n \in N_r^*$ and $B \subseteq \mathcal{B}^2$. Two cases must now be investigated in order to prove (11.43).

Case 1. $Var(t) \subseteq GlobVar(fg(pred^*(n)))$
Here we obtained as desired:

$$\mathcal{R}_{dl}(n)(\bigwedge B)$$
$$= \mathcal{R}_{dl}(n)(\bigwedge \{ (b_1, b_2) \mid (b_1, b_2) \in B \})$$

$$
\begin{aligned}
\text{(Def. of } \textstyle\bigwedge) \quad &= \quad \mathcal{R}_{dl}(n)(\textstyle\bigwedge\{\, b_1 \mid (b_1, b_2) \in B \,\}, \textstyle\bigwedge\{\, b_2 \mid (b_1, b_2) \in B \,\}) \\
\text{(Def. of } \mathcal{R}_{dl}) \quad &= \quad \textstyle\bigwedge\{\, b_2 \mid (b_1, b_2) \in B \,\} \\
\text{(Def. of } \mathcal{R}_{dl}) \quad &= \quad \textstyle\bigwedge\{\, \mathcal{R}_{dl}(n)(b_1, b_2) \mid (b_1, b_2) \in B \,\}
\end{aligned}
$$

Case 2. $Var(t) \not\subseteq GlobVar(fg(pred^*(n)))$

In this case we get the following sequence of equations:

$$
\mathcal{R}_{dl}(n)(\textstyle\bigwedge B)
$$

$$
\begin{aligned}
&= \quad \mathcal{R}_{dl}(n)(\textstyle\bigwedge\{\, (b_1, b_2) \mid (b_1, b_2) \in B \,\}) \\
\text{(Def. of } \textstyle\bigwedge) \quad &= \quad \mathcal{R}_{dl}(n)(\textstyle\bigwedge\{\, b_1 \mid (b_1, b_2) \in B \,\}, \textstyle\bigwedge\{\, b_2 \mid (b_1, b_2) \in B \,\}) \\
\text{(Def. of } \mathcal{R}_{dl}) \quad &= \quad (\textstyle\bigwedge\{\, b_1 \mid (b_1, b_2) \in B \,\} \vee Insert_{IBCM}(n_S)) \wedge \neg Comp\,(n_C) \\
\text{(Def. of } \textstyle\bigwedge) \quad &= \quad \textstyle\bigwedge\{\, (b_1 \vee Insert_{IBCM}(n_S)) \wedge \neg Comp\,(n_C) \mid (b_1, b_2) \in B \,\} \\
\text{(Def. of } \mathcal{R}_{dl}) \quad &= \quad \textstyle\bigwedge\{\, \mathcal{R}_{dl}(n)(b_1, b_2) \mid (b_1, b_2) \in B \,\}
\end{aligned}
$$

which completes the proof of Lemma 11.3.4. $\square$

***dl*-Precision.** The remaining step in showing the precision of $\mathcal{A}_{dl}$ is to prove the coincidence of the interprocedural meet over all paths solution of $\mathcal{A}_{dl}$ with interprocedural delayability in the sense of Definition 10.5.1, which is stated by Theorem 11.3.1. We only prove the first part of this theorem, which is the relevant one for the definition of the *ILCM*-transformation. The second part can actually be proved in the very same fashion. We have:

Theorem 11.3.1 (*dl*-Precision).
For all nodes $n \in N^*$ *we have:*

1. *N-Delayable** (n) *if and only if* $Insert_{IBCM}(n) \vee$
$$Int_{dl}(N\text{-}IMOP_{([\![\ ]\!]^*_{dl},\, Insert_{IBCM}(\mathbf{s}_1))}(n))$$

2. *X-Delayable** (n) *if and only if* $Int_{dl}(X\text{-}IMOP_{([\![\ ]\!]^*_{dl},\, Insert_{IBCM}(\mathbf{s}_1))}(n))$

Proof. As mentioned above, we will only prove the first part of Theorem 11.3.1. For convenience, we abbreviate $Int_{dl} \circ N\text{-}IMOP_{([\![\ ]\!]^*_{dl},\, Insert_{IBCM}(\mathbf{s}_1))}$ and $newstack(Insert_{IBCM}(\mathbf{s}_1))$ by $N\text{-}IMOP$ and stk_0 throughout the proof.

The first implication, "$\Rightarrow$",

$$
\forall\, n \in N^*. \ N\text{-}Delayable^*\,(n) \Rightarrow Insert_{IBCM}(n) \vee N\text{-}IMOP(n)
$$

is according to Lemma 11.3.2 equivalent to

$$
\begin{aligned}
\forall\, n \in N^*.\ (&Insert_{IBCM}(n) \vee \\
&(\forall\, p \in \mathbf{IP}[\mathbf{s}^*, n]\ \exists\, 1 \le i < \lambda_p.\ Insert_{IBCM}(p_i) \wedge SameInc_p[i, \lambda_p[\ \wedge \\
&\neg Comp^{*\,\exists}_{(p,i)}(p[i, \lambda_p[))\ \Rightarrow Insert_{IBCM}(n) \vee N\text{-}IMOP(n))
\end{aligned} \tag{11.44}
$$

Clearly, (11.44) is trivial, if n satisfies the predicate $Insert_{IBCM}$. Thus, in order to complete the proof of (11.44) it is sufficient to show

$$\forall p \in \mathbf{IP}[\mathbf{s}^*, n] \, (\exists 1 \leq i < \lambda_p. \, Insert_{IBCM}(p_i) \wedge SameInc_p[i, \lambda_p[\wedge \atop \neg Comp^{* \, \exists}_{(p,i)}(p[i, \lambda_p[)) \Rightarrow top([\![p[1, \lambda_p[ ]\!]^*_{dl}(stk_0)) = true \quad (11.45)$$

which we simultaneously prove for all nodes $n \in N^*$ by induction on the length k of path $p[1, \lambda_p[$ for all paths p satisfying

$$p \in \mathbf{IP}[\mathbf{s}^*, n] \wedge (\exists 1 \leq i < \lambda_p. \, Insert_{IBCM}(p_i) \wedge SameInc_p[i, \lambda_p[\wedge \atop \neg Comp^{* \, \exists}_{(p,i)}(p[i, \lambda_p[)) \quad (11.46)$$

Obviously, the case $k = 0$ does not occur. Thus, we can start with considering a path $p[1, \lambda_p[$ of length $k = 1$. In this case we obtain $p[1, \lambda_p[= (p_1)$ and $p_1 = \mathbf{s}^*$. By means of (11.46) we obtain

$$Insert_{IBCM}(p_1) \wedge SameInc_p[p_1, p_1[\wedge \neg Comp^*_{(p,1)}(p_1) \quad (11.47)$$

Applying Lemma 10.2.1(1), (11.47) is equivalent to

$$Insert_{IBCM}(p_1) \wedge SameInc_p[p_1, p_1[\wedge \neg Comp(p_1) \quad (11.48)$$

Hence, by means of (11.48), Lemma 11.3.1(1b) yields as desired

$$top([\![p[1, \lambda_p[ ]\!]^*_{dl}(stk_0)) = top([\![p_1]\!]^*_{dl}(stk_0)) = true$$

In order to prove the induction step, let $k > 1$, and assume that (11.45) holds for all paths q with $\lambda_{q[1,\lambda_q[} < k$, i.e.,

(IH) $(\forall q \in \mathbf{IP}[\mathbf{s}^*, n]. \, 1 \leq \lambda_{q[1,\lambda_q[} < k).$
$(\exists 1 \leq i < k. \, Insert_{IBCM}(q_i) \wedge SameInc_q[i, k[\wedge \neg Comp^{* \, \exists}_{(q,i)}(q[i, k[))$
$\Rightarrow top([\![q[1, \lambda_q[ ]\!]^*_{dl}(stk_0)) = true)$

It is sufficient to show that for every path $p \in \mathbf{IP}[\mathbf{s}^*, n]$ with $\lambda_{p[1,\lambda_p[} = k$ satisfying (11.46) holds

$$top([\![p[1, \lambda_p[ ]\!]^*_{dl}(stk_0)) = true \quad (11.49)$$

Without loss of generality we can assume that there is such a path p, which then can be rewritten as $p = p'; (m); (n)$ with $p' = p[1, k[$ and $m = p_k \in pred^*(n)$. Next we must investigate three cases depending on the type of node m.

Case 1. $m \in N^* \backslash (N_c^* \cup N_r^*)$
If $Insert_{IBCM}(m)$ holds, (11.46) implies

$$\neg Comp^*_{(p,k)}(m) = \neg Comp^*_{(p,k)}(p_k)$$

By means of Lemma 10.2.1(1) we therefore have

$$\neg Comp\,(m)$$

Now, Lemma 11.3.1(1b) yields as desired

$$top(\llbracket\, p[1, \lambda_p[\,\rrbracket_{dl}^*(stk_0)) = top(\llbracket\, m\,\rrbracket_{dl}^*(\llbracket\, p'\,\rrbracket_{dl}^*(stk_0))) = true$$

If $Insert_{IBCM}(m)$ does not hold, we obtain by Lemma 10.2.3(1)

$$RhsLev_p^{Var(\Pi)}(k-1) = RhsLev_p^{Var(\Pi)}(k)$$

Thus, we have

$$SameInc_p[k-1, k[\tag{11.50}$$

Additionally, (11.46) guarantees

$$\exists\, 1 \le i \le k-2.\ Insert_{IBCM}(p_i) \wedge SameInc_p[i, k[\wedge$$
$$\neg Comp^*{}_{(p,i)}^{\exists}(p[i, k-2[) \tag{11.51}$$

Combining (11.50) and (11.51), we obtain

$$\exists\, 1 \le i \le k-2.\ Insert_{IBCM}(p_i) \wedge SameInc_p[k-1, k[\wedge$$
$$\neg Comp^*{}_{(p,i)}^{\exists}(p[i, k-2[) \tag{11.52}$$

Hence, the induction hypothesis (IH) can be applied to p' delivering

$$top(\llbracket\, p'\,\rrbracket_{dl}^*(stk_0)) = true \tag{11.53}$$

Now, Lemma 11.3.1(1b) yields

$$top(\llbracket\, p[1, \lambda_p[\,\rrbracket_{dl}^*(stk_0)) = top(\llbracket\, m\,\rrbracket_{dl}^*(\llbracket\, p'\,\rrbracket_{dl}^*(stk_0))) = true$$

which completes the proof of Case 1.

Case 2. $m \in N_c^*$
The case $Var(t) \not\subseteq GlobVar(fg(succ^*(m)))$ cannot occur because of the following implication:

$$\forall\, 1 \le i < \lambda_p.\ Insert_{IBCM}(p_i) \Rightarrow \neg SameInc_p[i, \lambda_p[$$

Thus, we can assume

$$Var(t) \subseteq GlobVar(fg(succ^*(m)))$$

The induction step can now be proved as in Case 1, using Lemma 10.2.3(2) and Lemma 11.3.1(2) instead of Lemma 10.2.3(1) and Lemma 11.3.1(1b), respectively.

Case 3. $m \in N_r^*$
Clearly, we have

$$\neg Comp\,(n) \wedge \neg Insert_{IBCM}(m) \tag{11.54}$$

We must now distinguish, whether t contains local variables of $fg(pred^*(m))$ or not. If all variables of t are global with respect to $fg(pred^*(m))$, i.e., if $Var(t) \subseteq GlobVar(fg(pred^*(m)))$, the induction step follows as in Case 1 using Lemma 10.2.3(3) and Lemma 11.3.1(3) instead of Lemma 10.2.3(1) and Lemma 11.3.1(1b), respectively. Thus, we are left with the case $Var(t) \not\subseteq GlobVar(fg(pred^*(m)))$. Let $p_{k'}$ be the matching return node of $p_k = m$ on p, i.e., $p_{k'} \in N_c^*$, $p_k \in N_r^*$, and $p]k', k[\in \mathbf{CIP}[succ^*(p_{k'}), pred^*(p_k)]$. If $Insert_{IBCM}(p_{k'})$ holds, the induction step follows immediately by means of Lemma 11.3.1(3). Otherwise, i.e., if $Insert_{IBCM}(p_{k'})$ does not hold, (11.46) implies

$$\exists 1 \leq i < k'.\ Insert_{IBCM}(p_i) \wedge SameInc_p[i, k[\wedge \neg Comp^{*\exists}_{(p,i)}(p[i, k'[) \tag{11.55}$$

Moreover, Lemma 10.2.6(2) yields

$$RhsLev_p^{Var(t)}(k') = RhsLev_p^{Var(t)}(\lambda_p) \tag{11.56}$$

This implies

$$SameInc_p[i, k'[$$

and, therefore, (11.55) is equivalent to

$$\exists 1 \leq i < k'.\ Insert_{IBCM}(p_i) \wedge SameInc_p[i, k'[\wedge \neg Comp^{*\exists}_{(p,i)}(p[i, k'[) \tag{11.57}$$

Abbreviating the path $p[1, k']$ by p'', the induction hypothesis (IH) delivers

$$top([\![p'']\!]^*_{dl}(stk_0)) = true \tag{11.58}$$

This implies

$$top(pop([\![p']\!]^*_{dl}(stk_0))) = top([\![p'']\!]^*_{dl}(stk_0)) \tag{11.59}$$

since intervals of call nodes and return nodes on interprocedural paths are either disjoint or one is included in the other (cf. Lemma 7.2.1). Combining (11.58) and (11.59) we get

$$top(pop([\![p']\!]^*_{dl}(stk_0))) = true \tag{11.60}$$

The induction step

$$top([\![p[1, \lambda_p[ ]\!]^*_{dl}(stk_0)) = top([\![m]\!]^*_{dl}([\![p']\!]^*_{dl}(stk_0))) = true$$

now follows from (11.54) and (11.60) by means of Lemma 11.3.1(3).

The second implication, "$\Leftarrow$",

$$\forall n \in N^*.\ Insert_{IBCM}(n) \vee \text{N-IMOP}(n) \Rightarrow \text{N-Delayable}^*(n) \tag{11.61}$$

holds trivially by Lemma 11.3.2, if n satisfies the predicate $Insert_{IBCM}$. In order to complete the proof of the second implication it is therefore sufficient to show

$$\forall p \in \mathbf{IP}[\mathbf{s}^*, n].(top([\![p[1, \lambda_p [ ]\!]_{dl}^*(stk_0)) = true) \Rightarrow$$
$$\exists 1 \le i < \lambda_p. Insert_{IBCM}(p_i) \wedge SameInc_p[i, \lambda_p[\wedge \neg Comp^{*\exists}_{(p,i)}(p[i, \lambda_p[) \quad (11.62)$$

We prove this formula simultaneously for all nodes $n \in N^*$ by induction on the length k of path $p[1, \lambda_p[$ for all paths p satisfying

$$p \in \mathbf{IP}[\mathbf{s}^*, n] \wedge top([\![p[1, \lambda_p[ ]\!]_{dl}^*(stk_0)) = true \quad (11.63)$$

As in the proof of the first implication the case $k = 0$ does not occur, and therefore, we can start with considering a path $p[1, \lambda_p[$ of length $k = 1$. In this case we obtain $p[1, \lambda_p[= (p_1)$ and $p_1 = \mathbf{s}^* \in N^* \backslash (N_c^* \cup N_r^*)$. Hence, Lemma 11.3.1(1) yields

$$\neg Comp(p_1) \wedge Insert_{IBCM}(p_1) = top(stk_0)$$

such that (11.62) holds trivially for $i = 1$.

In order to prove the induction step, let $k > 1$, and assume that (11.62) holds for all paths q with $\lambda_{q[1, \lambda_q[} < k$, i.e.,

(IH) $(\forall q \in \mathbf{IP}[\mathbf{s}^*, n]. \ 1 \le \lambda_{q[1, \lambda_q[} < k).$
$top([\![q[1, \lambda_q[ ]\!]_{dl}^*(stk_0)) = true \Rightarrow$
$(\exists 1 \le i < \lambda_q. Insert_{IBCM}(q_i) \wedge SameInc_q[i, \lambda_q[\wedge \neg Comp^{*\exists}_{(q,i)}(q[i, \lambda_q[)$

It is sufficient to show that for every path $p \in \mathbf{IP}[\mathbf{s}^*, n]$ with $\lambda_{p[1, \lambda_p[} = k$ satisfying (11.63) holds

$$\exists 1 \le i < \lambda_p. \ Insert_{IBCM}(p_i) \wedge SameInc_p[i, \lambda_p[\wedge \neg Comp^{*\exists}_{(p,i)}(p[i, \lambda_p[)$$

Thus, we can assume that there is such a path p, which then can be rewritten as $p = p';(m);(n)$ with $p' = p[1, k[$, $m = p_k \in pred^*(n)$, and $k+1 = \lambda_p$. Similar to the proof of the first implication we must now investigate three cases depending on the type of node m.

Case 1. $m \in N^* \backslash (N_c^* \cup N_r^*)$
In this case we obtain by Lemma 11.3.1(1)

$$\neg Comp(m) \quad (11.64)$$

and by Lemma 10.2.3(1)

$$RhsLev_p^{Var(\Pi)}(k) = RhsLev_p^{Var(\Pi)}(\lambda_p) \quad (11.65)$$

Hence, we have

$$SameInc_p[k, \lambda_p[\quad (11.66)$$

Moreover, Lemma 10.2.1(1) yields

$$\neg Comp(m) \iff \neg Comp^*_{(p,k)}(m) \quad (11.67)$$

If $Insert_{IBCM}(m)$ holds, the induction step follows trivially from (11.64), (11.66), and (11.67) for $i = k$. Otherwise, i.e., if $Insert_{IBCM}(m)$ does not hold, Lemma 11.3.1(1b) yields

$$top(\llbracket p' \rrbracket_{dl}^*(stk_0)) = true \qquad (11.68)$$

Applying the induction hypothesis (IH) to $p';(m)$, we get

$$\exists 1 \leq i_{p'} < k.\ Insert_{IBCM}(p_{i_{p'}}) \wedge SameInc_p[i_{p'}, k[\wedge \\ \neg Comp^*_{(p,i_{p'})}(p[i_{p'}, k[) \qquad (11.69)$$

According to (11.64), (11.66), and (11.67), (11.69) is equivalent to

$$\exists 1 \leq i_{p'} < k.\ Insert_{IBCM}(p_{i_{p'}}) \wedge SameInc_p[i_{p'}, \lambda_p[\wedge \\ \neg Comp^*_{(p,i_{p'})}(p[i_{p'}, \lambda_p[) \qquad (11.70)$$

Thus, the induction step follows for $i = i_{p'}$.

Case 2. $m \in N_c^*$
In this case, Lemma 11.3.1(2) directly yields

$$Var(t) \subseteq GlobVar(fg(succ^*(m))) \ \wedge \ \neg Comp(m)$$

The induction step can now be proved along the lines of Case 1 using Lemma 10.2.3(2) and Lemma 11.3.1(2) instead of Lemma 10.2.3(1) and Lemma 11.3.1(1b), respectively.

Case 3. $m \in N_r^*$
Clearly, in this case we have $\neg Comp(m)$, and can proceed with the following case analysis.

Case 3.1. $Var(t) \subseteq GlobVar(fg(pred^*(m)))$
In this case, Lemma 10.2.3(3) delivers

$$RhsLev_p^{Var(\Pi)}(k) = RhsLev_p^{Var(\Pi)}(\lambda_p)$$

Moreover, Lemma 11.3.1(3) yields

$$top(\llbracket p' \rrbracket_{dl}^*(stk_0)) = true$$

Applying the induction hypothesis (IH) to $p';(m)$, the induction step can be proved as in Case 1.

Case 3.2. $Var(t) \not\subseteq GlobVar(fg(pred^*(m)))$
Let $p_{k'}$ be the matching return node of $p_k = m$ on p, i.e., $p_{k'} \in N_c^*$, $p_k \in N_r^*$, and $p]k', k[\in \mathbf{CIP}[succ^*(p_{k'}), pred^*(p_k)]$. Lemma 11.3.1(3) then delivers

$$\neg Comp(p_{k'}) \qquad (11.71)$$

and

$$Insert_{IBCM}(p_{k'}) \ \vee \ top(\llbracket p'' \rrbracket_{dl}^*(stk_0)) = true$$

where $p''=_{df} p[1, k'[$. Additionally, Lemma 10.2.6(2) and Lemma 10.2.7 yield

$$RhsLev_p^{Var(t)}(k') = RhsLev_p^{Var(t)}(\lambda_p) \tag{11.72}$$

and

$$\neg Comp^{*\exists}_{(p,k')}(p[k', k]) \tag{11.73}$$

respectively. In particular, (11.72) implies

$$SameInc_p[k', \lambda_p[\tag{11.74}$$

Thus, if $Insert_{IBCM}(p_{k'})$ holds, the induction step follows immediately for $i = k'$. Otherwise, i.e., if $Insert_{IBCM}(p_{k'})$ does not hold, we have

$$top(\llbracket p'' \rrbracket^*_{dl}(stk_0)) = true$$

Applying the induction hypothesis (IH) to p'';$(p_{k'})$, we obtain

$$\exists 1 \le i_{p''} < k'. \; Insert_{IBCM}(p_{i_{p''}}) \wedge SameInc_p[i_{p''}, k'[\wedge \\ \neg Comp^{*\exists}_{(p,i_{p''})}(p[i_{p''}, k'[) \tag{11.75}$$

Combining (11.72), (11.74), (11.71), and (11.73), we get that (11.75) is equivalent to

$$\exists 1 \le i_{p''} < k'. \; Insert_{IBCM}(p_{i_{p''}}) \wedge SameInc_p[i_{p''}, \lambda_p[\wedge \\ \neg Comp^{*\exists}_{(p,i_{p''})}(p[i_{p''}, \lambda_p[) \tag{11.76}$$

Hence, the induction step follows for $i = i_{p''}$. This completes the proof of the relevant part of Theorem 11.3.1. □

Applying Lemma 11.3.3, Lemma 11.3.4, and Theorem 11.3.1 we obtain the main result of this section: $\mathcal{A}_{dl}$ is precise for interprocedural delayability. Consequently, the *IMFP*-solution computed by $\mathcal{A}_{dl}$ coincides with the set of all program points being interprocedurally delayable in the sense of Definition 10.5.1.

Theorem 11.3.2 ($\mathcal{A}_{dl}$-Precision).
$\mathcal{A}_{dl}$ *is precise for interprocedural delayability, i.e.,* $\mathcal{A}_{dl}$ *is terminating and dl-precise.*

11.4 IDFA-Algorithm $\mathcal{A}_{un}$: Interprocedural Unusability

In this section we present the specification of the IDFA-algorithm $\mathcal{A}_{un}$ for computing the set of interprocedurally unusable program points.[5] The central result of this section is the $\mathcal{A}_{un}$-Precision Theorem 11.4.2. It yields that the algorithm is precise for this property: it terminates with the set of program points, which are interprocedurally unusable in the sense of Definition 10.5.3.

---

[5] The index un stands for unusability.

We recall that the determination of unusable program points requires a backward analysis of S (cf. Section 8.7 and Section 9.2.1). Therefore, the roles of call nodes and return nodes are interchanged in the definitions of the local semantic functions (cf. Section 11.4.1) and the return functions (cf. Section 11.4.1), and the start information is attached to the end node (cf. Section 11.4.1).

11.4.1 Specification

Data Flow Information. The domain of data flow information of $\mathcal{A}_{un}$ is given by the lattice

$$(\mathcal{C}, \sqcap, \sqsubseteq, \bot, \top) =_{df} (\mathcal{B}, \wedge, \leq, false, true)$$

This is the same lattice as for the delayability analysis, however, the interpretation is different. In the context of the unusability analysis, a data flow information attached to a program point expresses, whether a placement of t is unusable at this point or not. For the same reason as for the delayability analysis, it is not necessary to use a product lattice for storing transparency information explicitly (cf. Section 11.3.1).

Local Semantic Functional. The local semantic functional $[\![\ ]\!]'_{un} : N^* \to (\mathcal{B} \to \mathcal{B})$ of $\mathcal{A}_{un}$ is defined by

$$\forall n \in N^* \ \forall b \in \mathcal{B}. \ [\![n]\!]'_{un}(b) =_{df} b'$$

where

$$b' =_{df} \begin{cases} I\text{-}Latest(n) \vee (\neg Comp(n) \wedge b) \\ \qquad\qquad \text{if } n \in N^* \setminus N^*_r \vee Var(t) \subseteq GlobVar(fg(pred^*(n)))) \\ true \qquad\qquad \text{otherwise} \end{cases}$$

Note that the local semantic functional is the straightforward extension of its intraprocedural counterpart to the interprocedural setting.

Return Functional. The return functional $\mathcal{R}_{un} : N^*_c \to (\mathcal{B}^2 \to \mathcal{B})$ of $\mathcal{A}_{un}$ is defined by

$$\forall n \in N^*_c \ \forall (b_1, b_2) \in \mathcal{B}^2. \ \mathcal{R}_{un}(n)(b_1, b_2) =_{df} b'$$

where

$$b' =_{df} \begin{cases} b_2 \qquad\qquad\qquad\qquad \text{if } Var(t) \subseteq GlobVar(fg(succ^*(n))) \\ I\text{-}Latest(n) \vee (\neg Comp(n) \wedge b_1) \ \text{otherwise} \end{cases}$$

Intuitively, if some operands of t are locally declared in the called procedure (i.e., $Var(t) \not\subseteq GlobVar(fg(succ^*(n))))$, then t cannot be used inside the called procedure as this concerns a different incarnation of t. Consequently,

t is unusable in this case immediately before entering the procedure, if it is unusable immediately after leaving it (i.e., $b_1 = true$) and if it does not occur as a parameter argument (i.e., $\neg Comp(n)$), or if the procedure call node is a potential insertion point of the $ILCM$-transformation (i.e., $I\text{-}Latest(n) = true$). On the other hand, if all variables of t are global for the procedure called (i.e., $Var(t) \subseteq GlobVar(fg(succ^*(n))))$, t is unusable before the procedure call, if this information could be propagated to the entry of the called procedure (i.e., $b_2 = true$).

Start Information. The start information is given by the element

$$true \in \mathcal{B}$$

Note that this information is mapped to the end node of the program because unusability is a backward problem. Intuitively, it expresses that a computation cannot be used after the termination of the program, and therefore a computation placed at the end of the program is unusable.

Interpretation. The interpretation of lattice elements in $\mathcal{B}$ is given by the identity on $\mathcal{B}$, i.e., the function $Int_{un} : \mathcal{B} \to \mathcal{B}$ is defined by

$$Int_{un} =_{df} Id_{\mathcal{B}}$$

11.4.2 Proving Precision

Similar to the other analyses, we first give a technical lemma, which simplifies the proof of the un-Precision Theorem 11.4.1. This lemma can easily be proved by means of the definitions of the local semantic functional and the return functional of $\mathcal{A}_{un}$.

Lemma 11.4.1.

1. $\forall n \in N^* \setminus (N_c^* \cup N_r^*) \ \forall stk \in STACK$.
   a) $I\text{-}Latest(n) \Rightarrow top([\![n]\!]^*_{un}(stk)) = true$
   b) $\neg I\text{-}Latest(n) \Rightarrow (top([\![n]\!]^*_{un}(stk)) = true \iff$
   $$\neg Comp(n) \ \wedge \ top(stk) = true)$$

2. $\forall n \in N_c^* \ \forall stk \in STACK_{\geq 2}$.

   a) $I\text{-}Latest(n) \Rightarrow top([\![n]\!]^*_{un}(stk)) = true$
   b) $\neg I\text{-}Latest(n) \Rightarrow (top([\![n]\!]^*_{un}(stk)) = true \iff \neg Comp(n) \ \wedge$
   $$\left\{ \begin{array}{ll} top(stk) = true & \text{if } Var(t) \subseteq GlobVar(fg(succ^*(n))) \\ top(pop(stk)) = true & \text{otherwise} \end{array} \right)$$

3. $\forall n \in N_r^* \ \forall stk \in STACK. \ top([\![n]\!]^*_{un}(stk)) = true \iff$
   $$\left\{ \begin{array}{ll} top(stk) = true & \text{if } Var(t) \subseteq GlobVar(fg(pred^*(n))) \\ true & \text{otherwise} \end{array} \right.$$

Descending Chain Condition. The finiteness of $\mathcal{B}$ directly implies the finiteness of its corresponding function lattice $[\mathcal{B} \to \mathcal{B}]$. Thus, we have:

Lemma 11.4.2 (Descending Chain Condition).
The function lattice $[\mathcal{B} \to \mathcal{B}]$ *satisfies the descending chain condition.*

Distributivity. Along the lines of Lemma 11.3.4 we can prove:

Lemma 11.4.3 ($[\![\ ]\!]'_{un}, \mathcal{R}_{un}$-Distributivity Lemma).

1. *The local semantic functions* $[\![\, n \,]\!]'_{un}$, $n \in N^*$, *are distributive.*
2. *The return functions* $\mathcal{R}_{un}(n)$, $n \in N^*_c$, *are distributive.*

un-Precision. Finally, we have to prove the coincidence of interprocedural unusability and the interprocedural meet over all paths solution of $\mathcal{A}_{un}$. Like in the previous sections, we only prove that part of the precision theorem, which is needed for the definition of the $ILCM$-transformation. We have:

Theorem 11.4.1 (un-Precision Theorem).
For all nodes $n \in N^*$ *we have:*

1. *N-Unusable$^*(n)$ if and only if $Int_{un}(X\text{-}IMOP_{([\![\ ]\!]^*_{un}, true)}(n))$*
2. *X-Unusable$^*(n)$ if and only if $Int_{un}(N\text{-}IMOP_{([\![\ ]\!]^*_{un}, true)}(n))$*

Proof.
As mentioned above, we will only prove the second part of Theorem 11.4.1. In order to simplify the notation, we abbreviate $Int_{un} \circ N\text{-}IMOP_{([\![\ ]\!]^*_{un}, true)}$ and $newstack(true)$ by $N\text{-}IMOP$ and stk_0 throughout the proof.
The first implication, "$\Rightarrow$",

$$\forall n \in N^*. \ X\text{-}Unusable^*(n) \Rightarrow N\text{-}IMOP(n)$$

is proved by showing the even stronger implication

$$\begin{aligned}
\forall p \in \mathbf{IP}[\mathbf{s}^*, \mathbf{e}^*]. \ p_i = n \Rightarrow \\
(\forall i + 1 < j \le \lambda_p. \ Comp^*_{(p,i+1)}(p_j) \Rightarrow \\
\exists i + 1 \le r \le j. \ I\text{-}Latest(p_r) \wedge SameInc_p[i+1, r[) \quad (11.77) \\
\Rightarrow top([\![\, \widetilde{p]i, \lambda_p} \,]\!]^*_{un}(stk_0)) = true
\end{aligned}$$

which we simultaneously prove for all nodes $n \in N^*$ by induction on the length $k =_{df} \lambda_p - i$ of postfix-path $p]i, \lambda_p]$ for all paths p satisfying

$$\begin{aligned}
p \in \mathbf{IP}[\mathbf{s}^*, \mathbf{e}^*] \wedge p_i = n \wedge \\
(\forall i + 1 \le j \le \lambda_p. \ Comp^*_{(p,i+1)}(p_j) \Rightarrow \quad (11.78) \\
\exists i + 1 \le r \le j. \ I\text{-}Latest(p_r) \wedge SameInc_p[i+1, r[)
\end{aligned}$$

If $k = \lambda_{p]i,\lambda_p]} = 0$, we obtain $p]i, \lambda_p] = \varepsilon$, and therefore

$$top([\![\, \widetilde{p]i, \lambda_p} \,]\!]^*_{un}(stk_0)) = top([\![\, \varepsilon \,]\!]^*_{un}(stk_0)) = top(stk_0) = true$$

holds trivially.

In order to prove the induction step, let $k > 0$, and assume that (11.77) holds for all postfix-paths $q]i, \lambda_q]$ with $\lambda_{q]i,\lambda_q]} < k$, i.e.,

(IH) $(\forall q \in \mathbf{IP}[\mathbf{s^*}, \mathbf{e^*}].\ q_i = n \wedge 0 \leq \lambda_{q]i,\lambda_q]} < k).$
$$(\forall i + 1 \leq j \leq \lambda_q.\ Comp^*{}_{(q,i+1)}(q_j) \Rightarrow$$
$$\exists i + 1 \leq r \leq j.\ I\text{-}Latest\,(q_r) \wedge SameInc_q[i+1, r[\,)$$
$$\Rightarrow top(\llbracket\, \widetilde{q]i, \lambda_q]}\,\rrbracket^*_{un}(stk_0)) = true$$

It is sufficient to show that for every path $p \in \mathbf{IP}[\mathbf{s^*}, \mathbf{e^*}]$ with $p_i = n$ and $\lambda_{p]i,\lambda_p]} = k$ satisfying (11.78) holds

$$top(\llbracket\, \widetilde{p]i, \lambda_p]}\,\rrbracket^*_{un}(stk_0)) = true$$

Thus, we can assume that there is such a postfix-path $p]i, \lambda_p]$, which then can be rewritten as $p]i, \lambda_p] = (p_{i+1}); p'$ with $p' = p[i+2, \lambda_p]$. Next, we have to investigate three cases depending on the type of node p_{i+1}.

Case 1. $p_{i+1} \in N^* \backslash (N^*_c \cup N^*_r)$

If p_{i+1} satisfies the predicate $I\text{-}Latest$, Lemma 11.4.1(1a) yields as desired

$$top(\llbracket\, \widetilde{p]i, \lambda_p]}\,\rrbracket^*_{un}(stk_0)) = top(\llbracket\, p_{i+1}\,\rrbracket^*_{un}(\llbracket\, \tilde{p}'\,\rrbracket^*_{un}(stk_0))) = true$$

Thus, we are left with the case that p_{i+1} does not satisfy the predicate $I\text{-}Latest$. Together with (11.78) this implies

$$\neg Comp\,(p_{i+1}) \tag{11.79}$$

Moreover, Lemma 10.2.3(1) yields

$$RhsLev_p^{Var(t)}(i+1) = RhsLev_p^{Var(t)}(i+2) \tag{11.80}$$

Hence,

$$\forall i + 1 \leq j \leq \lambda_p.\ Comp^*{}_{(p,i+1)}(p_j) \Rightarrow$$
$$\exists i + 1 \leq r \leq j.\ I\text{-}Latest\,(p_r) \wedge SameInc_p[i+1, r[\tag{11.81}$$

is equivalent to

$$\forall i + 2 \leq j \leq \lambda_p.\ Comp^*{}_{(p,i+2)}(p_j) \Rightarrow$$
$$\exists i + 2 \leq r \leq j.\ I\text{-}Latest\,(n_r) \wedge SameInc_p[i+2, r[\tag{11.82}$$

Thus, the induction hypothesis (IH) can be applied to p' yielding

$$top(\llbracket\, \tilde{p}'\,\rrbracket^*_{un}(stk_0)) = true \tag{11.83}$$

Now, by means of (11.79) and (11.83), Lemma 11.4.1(1b) delivers

$$top(\llbracket\, \widetilde{p]i, \lambda_p]}\,\rrbracket^*_{un}(stk_0)) = top(\llbracket\, p_i\,\rrbracket^*_{un}(\llbracket\, \tilde{p}'\,\rrbracket^*_{un}(stk_0))) = true$$

which completes the proof of Case 1.

Case 2. $p_{i+1} \in N_c^*$

If p_i satisfies the predicate *I-Latest*, the induction step

$$top(\llbracket \widetilde{p]i, \lambda_p} \rrbracket_{un}^*(stk_0)) = top(\llbracket p_{i+1} \rrbracket_{un}^*(\llbracket \tilde{p}' \rrbracket_{un}^*(stk_0))) = true$$

is an immediate consequence of Lemma 11.4.1(2a). Thus, we are left with the case that p_{i+1} does not satisfy the predicate *I-Latest*. Similar to Case 1 this implies

$$\neg Comp\,(p_{i+1}) \tag{11.84}$$

We must now distinguish, whether t contains local variables of $fg(succ^*(p_{i+1}))$ or not, and proceed with the following case analysis.

Case 2.1. $Var(t) \subseteq GlobVar(fg(succ^*(p_{i+1})))$

In this case, Lemma 10.2.3(2) yields

$$RhsLev_p^{Var(t)}(i+1) = RhsLev_p^{Var(t)}(i+2) \tag{11.85}$$

As in Case 1, this allows to apply the induction hypothesis to p' yielding

$$top(\llbracket \tilde{p}' \rrbracket_{un}^*(stk_0)) = true \tag{11.86}$$

The induction step

$$top(\llbracket \widetilde{p]i, \lambda_p} \rrbracket_{un}^*(stk_0)) = top(\llbracket p_{i+1} \rrbracket_{un}^*(\llbracket \tilde{p}' \rrbracket_{un}^*(stk_0))) = true$$

follows now directly from (11.84) and (11.86) by means of Lemma 11.4.1(2b).

Case 2.2. $Var(t) \nsubseteq GlobVar(fg(succ^*(p_{i+1})))$

Clearly, the premise of this case implies

$$Var(t) \cap LocVar(fg(succ^*(p_{i+1}))) \neq \emptyset \tag{11.87}$$

Let $p_{i'}$ be the matching return node of p_{i+1} on p, i.e., $p_{i+1} \in N_c^*$, $p_{i'} \in N_r^*$, and $p]i+1, i'[\in \textbf{CIP}[succ^*(p_{i+1}), pred^*(p_{i'})]$. By means of (11.87), Lemma 10.2.7 yields

$$\forall j' \in \{i+2, \ldots, i'\}.\ \neg Comp^*_{(p,i+1)}(p_{j'}) \wedge \neg SameInc_p[i+1, j'[\tag{11.88}$$

Moreover, Lemma 10.2.6(2) delivers

$$RhsLev_p^{Var(t)}(i+1) = RhsLev_p^{Var(t)}(i'+1) \tag{11.89}$$

Hence,

$$\forall i+1 \leq j \leq \lambda_p.\ Comp^*_{(p,i+1)}(p_j) \Rightarrow \\ \exists i+1 \leq r \leq j.\ \textit{I-Latest}(p_r) \wedge SameInc_p[i+1, r[\tag{11.90}$$

is equivalent to

$$\forall\, i'+1 \le j \le \lambda_p.\ Comp^*_{(p,i'+1)}(p_j) \Rightarrow \exists\, i'+1 \le r \le j. \\ \text{I-Latest}(p_r) \wedge SameInc_p[i'+1,r[\tag{11.91}$$

Abbreviating the path $p]i',\lambda_p]$ by p'', the induction hypothesis (IH) delivers

$$top(\llbracket\, \widetilde{p''}\, \rrbracket^*_{un}(stk_0)) = true \tag{11.92}$$

This implies

$$top(pop(\llbracket\, \widetilde{p'}\, \rrbracket^*_{un}(stk_0))) = top(\llbracket\, \widetilde{p''}\, \rrbracket^*_{un}(stk_0)) \tag{11.93}$$

since intervals of call nodes and return nodes on interprocedural paths are either disjoint or one is included in the other (cf. Lemma 7.2.1). From (11.92) and (11.93) we get

$$top(pop(\llbracket\, \widetilde{p'}\, \rrbracket^*_{un}(stk_0))) = true \tag{11.94}$$

The induction step

$$top(\llbracket\, \widetilde{p]i,\lambda_p]}\, \rrbracket^*_{un}(stk_0)) = top(\llbracket\, p_{i+1}\, \rrbracket^*_{un}(\llbracket\, \widetilde{p'}\, \rrbracket^*_{un}(stk_0))) = true$$

is now an immediate consequence of (11.84), (11.94), and Lemma 11.4.1(2b).

Case 3. $p_{i+1} \in N^*_r$
If $Var(t) \not\subseteq GlobVar(fg(pred^*(p_{i+1})))$, the induction step

$$top(\llbracket\, \widetilde{p]i,\lambda_p]}\, \rrbracket^*_{un}(stk_0)) = top(\llbracket\, p_{i+1}\, \rrbracket^*_{un}(\llbracket\, \widetilde{p'}\, \rrbracket^*_{un}(stk_0))) = true$$

holds trivially by means of Lemma 11.4.1(3). Thus, we are left with the case

$$Var(t) \subseteq GlobVar(fg(pred^*(p_{i+1}))) \tag{11.95}$$

In particular, $p_{i+1} \in N^*_r$ implies

$$\neg Comp\,(p_{i+1}) \tag{11.96}$$

Additionally, Lemma 10.2.3(3) yields

$$RhsLev_p^{Var(t)}(i+1) = RhsLev_p^{Var(t)}(i+2) \tag{11.97}$$

Hence,

$$\forall\, i+1 \le j \le \lambda_p.\ Comp^*_{(p,i+1)}(p_j) \Rightarrow \\ \exists\, i+1 \le r \le j.\ \text{I-Latest}(p_r) \wedge SameInc_p[i+1,r[\tag{11.98}$$

is equivalent to

$$\forall\, i+2 \le j \le \lambda_p.\ Comp^*_{(p,i+2)}(p_j) \Rightarrow \\ \exists\, i+2 \le r \le j.\ \text{I-Latest}(p_r) \wedge SameInc_p[i+2,r[\tag{11.99}$$

Thus, the induction hypothesis (IH) can be applied to p', which delivers

$$top(\llbracket \tilde{p}' \rrbracket_{un}^*(stk_0)) = true \tag{11.100}$$

Now, by means of (11.100), Lemma 11.4.1(3) yields as desired

$$top(\llbracket \widetilde{p]i, \lambda_p} \rrbracket_{un}^*(stk_0)) = top(\llbracket p_{i+1} \rrbracket_{un}^*(\llbracket \tilde{p}' \rrbracket_{un}^*(stk_0))) = true$$

which proves the induction step in this case.

The second implication, "$\Leftarrow$",

$$\forall n \in N^*. \ N\text{-}IMOP(n) \Rightarrow X\text{-}Unusable^*(n)$$

is proved by showing the even stronger implication

$$(\forall p \in \mathbf{IP}[\mathbf{s}^*, \mathbf{e}^*]. \ p_i = n). \ (top(\llbracket \widetilde{p]i, \lambda_p} \rrbracket_{un}^*(stk_0)) = true)$$
$$\Rightarrow (\forall i + 1 \leq j \leq \lambda_p. \ Comp^*_{(p,i+1)}(p_j) \Rightarrow \tag{11.101}$$
$$\exists i + 1 \leq r \leq j. \ I\text{-}Latest(p_r) \wedge SameInc_p[i+1, r[)$$

which we simultaneously prove for all nodes $n \in N^*$ by induction on the length $k =_{df} \lambda_p - i$ of postfix-path $p]i, \lambda_p]$ for all paths p satisfying

$$p \in \mathbf{IP}[\mathbf{s}^*, \mathbf{e}^*] \wedge p_i = n \wedge top(\llbracket \widetilde{p]i, \lambda_p} \rrbracket_{un}^*(stk_0)) = true \tag{11.102}$$

The induction base for $k = \lambda_{p]i,\lambda_p]} = 0$ holds trivially.

In order to prove the induction step, let $k > 0$, and assume that (11.101) holds for all postfix-paths $q]i, \lambda_q]$ with $\lambda_{q]i,\lambda_q]} < k$, i.e.,

(IH) $(\forall q \in \mathbf{IP}[\mathbf{s}^*, \mathbf{e}^*]. \ q_i = n \wedge 0 \leq \lambda_{q]i,\lambda_q]} < k).$
$$(top(\llbracket \widetilde{q]i, \lambda_q} \rrbracket_{un}^*(stk_0)) = true) \Rightarrow$$
$$(\forall i + 1 \leq j \leq \lambda_q. \ Comp^*_{(q,i+1)}(q_j) \Rightarrow$$
$$\exists i + 1 \leq r \leq j. \ I\text{-}Latest(q_r) \wedge SameInc_q[i+1, r[)$$

It is sufficient to show that for every path $p \in \mathbf{IP}[\mathbf{s}^*, \mathbf{e}^*]$ with $p_i = n$, and $\lambda_{p]i,\lambda_p]} = k$ satisfying (11.102) holds

$$\forall i + 1 \leq j \leq \lambda_p. \ Comp^*_{(p,i+1)}(p_j) \Rightarrow$$
$$\exists i + 1 \leq r \leq j. \ I\text{-}Latest(p_r) \wedge SameInc_p[i+1, r[\tag{11.103}$$

Thus, we can assume that there is such a postfix-path $p]i, \lambda_p]$. This path can then be rewritten as $p]i, \lambda_p] = (p_{i+1}); p'$ with $p' = p[i+2, \lambda_p]$, and an index j with $i + 1 \leq j \leq \lambda_p$ and $Comp^*_{(p,i+1)}(p_j)$. Similar to the proof of the first implication we must now investigate three cases depending on the type of node p_{i+1}.

Case 1. $p_{i+1} \in N^* \setminus (N_c^* \cup N_r^*)$

If p_{i+1} satisfies the predicate *I-Latest*, the induction step follows trivially for $r = i + 1$. If p_{i+1} does not satisfy the predicate *I-Latest*, Lemma 11.4.1(1b) yields

$$\neg Comp\,(p_{i+1}) \wedge top([\![\,\tilde{p}'\,]\!]_{un}^*(stk_0)) = true \tag{11.104}$$

Applying the induction hypothesis (IH) to p', we obtain

$$\forall\, i + 2 \leq j \leq \lambda_p.\ Comp^*_{(p,i+2)}(p_j) \Rightarrow$$
$$\exists\, i + 2 \leq r \leq j.\ \textit{I-Latest}\,(p_r) \wedge \textit{SameInc}_p[i + 2, r[\tag{11.105}$$

In particular, this implies that

$$r_{p'} =_{df} Min(\{r \mid i + 2 \leq r \leq j \wedge \textit{I-Latest}\,(p_r) \wedge \textit{SameInc}_p[i + 2, r[\})$$

is well-defined. Moreover, Lemma 10.2.3(1) yields

$$RhsLev_p^{Var(\Pi)}(i + 1) = RhsLev_p^{Var(\Pi)}(i + 2) \tag{11.106}$$

Combining (11.104) and (11.106), we obtain that (11.105) is equivalent to

$$\forall\, i + 1 \leq j \leq \lambda_p.\ Comp^*_{(p,i+1)}(p_j) \Rightarrow$$
$$\exists\, i + 1 \leq r \leq j.\ \textit{I-Latest}\,(p_r) \wedge \textit{SameInc}_p[i + 1, r[\tag{11.107}$$

Hence, the induction step follows for $r = r_{p'}$.

Case 2. $p_{i+1} \in N_c^*$

Similar to Case 1, whenever p_{i+1} satisfies the predicate *I-Latest*(p_{i+1}), the induction step follows trivially for $r = i + 1$. Thus, we are left with the case that p_{i+1} does not satisfy the predicate *I-Latest*. By means of Lemma 11.4.1(2b) we directly get

$$\neg Comp\,(p_{i+1}) \tag{11.108}$$

We must now distinguish, whether t contains local variables of $fg(succ^*(p_{i+1}))$ or not, which leads to the investigation of the following two cases.

Case 2.1. $Var(t) \subseteq GlobVar(fg(succ^*(p_{i+1})))$

In this case Lemma 11.4.1(2b) yields

$$top([\![\,\tilde{p}'\,]\!]_{un}^*(stk_0)) = true \tag{11.109}$$

Hence, the induction hypothesis can be applied to p'. Moreover, Lemma 10.2.3(2) implies

$$RhsLev_p^{Var(t)}(i + 1) = RhsLev_p^{Var(t)}(i + 2) \tag{11.110}$$

The induction step follows now as in Case 1.

Case 2.2. $Var(t) \not\subseteq GlobVar(fg(succ^*(p_{i+1})))$

In this case we have

$$Var(t) \cap LocVar(fg(succ^*(p_{i+1}))) \neq \emptyset$$

Let $p_{i'}$ be the matching return node of p_{i+1} on p, i.e., $p_{i+1} \in N_c^*$, $p_{i'} \in N_r^*$, and $p]i+1, i'[\in \textbf{CIP}[succ^*(p_{i+1}), pred^*(p_{i'})]$. As a consequence of

$$top(\widetilde{[\![p]i, \lambda_p]\!]}_{un}^*(stk_0)) = top([\![p_{i+1}]\!]_{un}^*([\![\tilde{p}']\!]_{un}^*(stk_0))) = true$$

we obtain by means of Lemma 11.4.1(2b)

$$top([\![\tilde{p}'']\!]_{un}^*(stk_0)) = true \tag{11.111}$$

where $p''=_{df} p]i', \lambda_p]$. The induction hypothesis (IH), therefore, yields

$$\forall i'+1 \leq j \leq \lambda_p. \; Comp^*_{(p,i'+1)}(p_j) \\ \Rightarrow \exists i'+1 \leq r \leq j. \; \textit{I-Latest}(p_r) \wedge SameInc_p[i'+1, r[\tag{11.112}$$

Similar to Case 1, this implies that

$$r_{p''} =_{df} Min(\{r \mid i'+1 \leq r \leq j \wedge \textit{I-Latest}(p_r) \wedge SameInc_p[i'+1, r[\})$$

is well-defined. Additionally (11.108) and Lemma 10.2.7 yield

$$\neg Comp^{*\exists}_{(p,i+1)}(p[i+1, i'[) \tag{11.113}$$

Moreover, Lemma 10.2.6(2) yields

$$RhsLev_p^{Var(\Pi)}(i+1) = RhsLev_p^{Var(\Pi)}(i'+1) \tag{11.114}$$

Thus, (11.112) is equivalent to

$$\forall i+1 \leq j \leq \lambda_p. \; Comp^*_{(p,i+1)}(p_j) \Rightarrow \\ \exists i'+1 \leq r \leq j. \; \textit{I-Latest}(p_r) \wedge SameInc_p[i+1, r[\tag{11.115}$$

and therefore, the induction step follows for $r = r_{p''}$ in this case.

Case 3. $p_{i+1} \in N_r^*$

Clearly, we have

$$\neg Comp(p_{i+1}) \tag{11.116}$$

If $Var(t) \not\subseteq GlobVar(fg(pred^*(p_{i+1})))$, we have

$$\forall i+1 < j \leq \lambda_p. \; \neg SameInc_p[i+1, j[$$

Together with (11.116) this implies

$$\neg Comp^{*\exists}_{(p,i+1)}(p[i+1, \lambda_p[)$$

Hence, the induction step holds trivially in this case. We are therefore left with the case

$$Var(t) \subseteq GlobVar(fg(pred^*(p_{i+1})))$$

By means of Lemma 11.4.1(3) we get

$$top([\![\tilde{p}']\!]_{un}^*(stk_0)) = true \tag{11.117}$$

Thus, the induction hypothesis can be applied to p'. Moreover, Lemma 10.2.3(3) yields

$$RhsLev_p^{Var(t)}(i+1) = RhsLev_p^{Var(t)}(i+2) \tag{11.118}$$

Hence, the induction step follows as in Case 1. This completes the proof of the second implication, and finishes the proof of the relevant part of Theorem 11.4.1. □

Combining Lemma 11.4.2, Lemma 11.4.3, and Theorem 11.4.1, we get the central result of this section: $\mathcal{A}_{un}$ is precise for interprocedural unusability. This guarantees that the *IMFP*-solution computed by $\mathcal{A}_{un}$ coincides with the set of program points, which are interprocedurally unusable in the sense of Definition 10.5.3.

Theorem 11.4.2 ($\mathcal{A}_{un}$-Precision).
$\mathcal{A}_{un}$ is precise for interprocedural unusability, i.e., $\mathcal{A}_{un}$ is terminating and un-precise.

12. Perspectives

In this chapter we reconsider the anomalies observable for interprocedural code motion from a different point of view giving additional insight into their causes and the differences to the intraprocedural setting. We show that anomalies of this kind are not specific for the interprocedural setting, but have analogues in other programming paradigms and application scenarios. Afterwards, we discuss a variety of pragmatic aspects related to our framework, and, finally, give directions to future work concerning both the framework and the application side.

12.1 Reconsidering Code Motion Anomalies

In Chapter 10 we demonstrated that there are essential differences between the intraprocedural and interprocedural setting regarding code motion. Most importantly, in the interprocedural setting (1) computationally optimal results are in general impossible, and (2) safety is in general not equivalent to the disjunction of up-safety and down-safety. The loss of the decomposability of safety, i.e., the failure of the intraprocedural decomposition theorem for safety (cf. Lemma 3.2.1), turned out to be the source of several placing anomalies showing up when adapting intraprocedural code motion strategies to the interprocedural setting. Extensions of intraprocedurally computationally optimal strategies can dramatically degenerate a program, even if there is a computationally optimal canonic result (cf. Figure 10.18).

Other paradigms and application scenarios. Because of the practical impact of the failure of the decomposition theorem for safety on interprocedural code motion, one should note that this failure is not specific for the interprocedural setting. It has analogues in other programming paradigms and application scenarios causing similar anomalies when extending intraprocedural code motion strategies accordingly. In [KSV3], this has been demonstrated considering code motion in a setting with *explicitly parallel programs* and *shared memory*. For the same program setting, but a different application, the elimination of *partially dead assignments*, this has been demonstrated in [Kn2, Kn3]. In [KRS7], the failure of the decomposition theorem has been proved for the intraprocedural setting considering *semantic* code motion in-

J. Knoop: Optimal Interprocedural Program Optimization, LNCS 1428, pp. 251-270, 1998.
© Springer-Verlag Berlin Heidelberg 1998

stead of *syntactic* one as in this monograph. The point of syntactic code motion is to treat all term patterns independently and to regard each assignment as destructive for the value of every term pattern containing the modified variable. The algorithms for busy and lazy code motion are syntactic code motion algorithms. In contrast, semantic code motion aims at eliminating computations, which are semantically partially redundant, and is thus more powerful than syntactic code motion (cf. [BA, RWZ, St3, SKR1, SKR2]). In this scenario, however, where safety is based on a semantic notion of term equivalence, it cannot equivalently be decomposed into the corresponding notions of up-safety and down-safety. As a consequence, an essential difference between "motion-based" and "placement-based" approaches for the elimination of semantically partially redundant computations shows up: specific partially redundant computations are out of the scope of any motion-based approach, and can only be eliminated by placement-based approaches. Intuitively, a *placement-based* approach is free to place a computation at any safe program point. In contrast, a *motion-based* approach is limited to program points, where the computation can "safely" be moved to, i.e., where in addition all nodes in between the old and the new location are down-safe. As for interprocedural syntactic code motion, also for semantic code placement computationally optimal results are in general impossible. In fact, it is the validity of the decomposition theorem for safety applying to syntactic code motion in the intraprocedural setting, which implies that motion-based and placement-based approaches are of the same power for this scenario.

Interprocedural code motion. We now return to the interprocedural setting, and focus again on interprocedural code motion. As demonstrated in Chapters 10 and 11, the placing anomalies exhibited by interprocedural extensions of intraprocedural placing strategies are not caused by the data flow analyses involved, but by the optimizing transformation itself. In the following, we reconsider these anomalies from a different point of view in order to give additional insight into the differences between the intraprocedural and interprocedural setting. To this end we consider the effect of the as-early-as-possible placing strategy underlying busy code motion for the example of Figure 10.18. Recall that the program of this example is free of any partially redundant computation, and hence, computationally optimal. As illustrated in Figure 10.19, it is dramatically degenerated by an application of the as-early-as-possible placing strategy.

In order to reveal the difference to the intraprocedural setting, we extract the essence of this example and investigate it in a comparable intraprocedural situation established by means of procedure inlining, where we concentrate on the procedures π_3 and π_4 first. The left program fragment of Figure 12.1 shows procedure π_4 after inlining π_3 together with the set of (entry) down-safe and (entry) earliest nodes. The right program fragment shows the corresponding program resulting from busy code motion. As in Figure 10.19 an insertion has been moved into the loop to node **14**, but the computation originally located in the loop could be removed from it by moving it to node **20**. Hence, the programs are in the cernel of the relation "computationally better". In the example of Figure 10.18, the comparable transformation of moving the computation from node **12** to node **20** is prevented by the second call of procedure π_3 located in π_2, which results in the placing anomaly of Figure 10.19. This call, however, is not taken into account in the modelling of Figure 12.1.

Thus, for the sake of a "fair" comparison of the interprocedural and intraprocedural setting, we have to consider the situation after inlining π_3 for both of its calls, where the inlined procedure body is "shared" by the two former calls. The right program fragment of Figure 12.2 then shows the result of busy code motion. Obviously, the defect of the interprocedural situation does not realize. Intuitively, this is because the computation-free execution path from node **6** to node **9** across node **15** is "visible" for program executions reaching node **24**, and prevents moving $a + b$ into the loop to node **23**. This reveals the essential difference to the interprocedural situation of Figure 10.18. Though the corresponding computation-free path is present as well, it is "invisible" at the call site of π_3 in π_4: program executions entering procedure π_3 at the call site at node **22** cannot be completed by program continuations reaching node **9** because the call/return-behaviour of procedure calls would be violated. The validity condition imposed on interprocedural program paths excludes these paths.

Intuitively, this can be considered the *dilemma of customization* of interprocedural DFA for program optimizations, where, like for code motion, the correctness and profitability of a modification at a specific program point (considering code motion, replacing an original computation by its corresponding temporary) relies on a "global" modification of the program text, i.e., on a modification involving several program points (considering code motion, inserting initializations of the temporay). Interprocedural DFA computes information along valid paths only, and thus, provides for every program point including call sites the "most precise" information possible. Customization can thus be considered the central goal of interprocedural DFA. The problems arise on the transformation side, where customization of information concerning call sites gets in conflict with transformations, where the global modifications required for separately justifying the "local" improvements (considering code motion, those temporary initializations, which justify correctness at a particular use site) do not behave "compositionally". Considering code motion, this means inserting or removing computations from procedures, which are called at several call sites. This is the source of potential conflicts. They become effective, if as for instance in the example of Figure 10.19, from the point of view of some call site a computation must be inserted in (removed from) the callee, which, however, is prevented by a different call site because safety and profitability would be affected. In essence, it is this kind of conflict causing the anomalies of interprocedural busy code

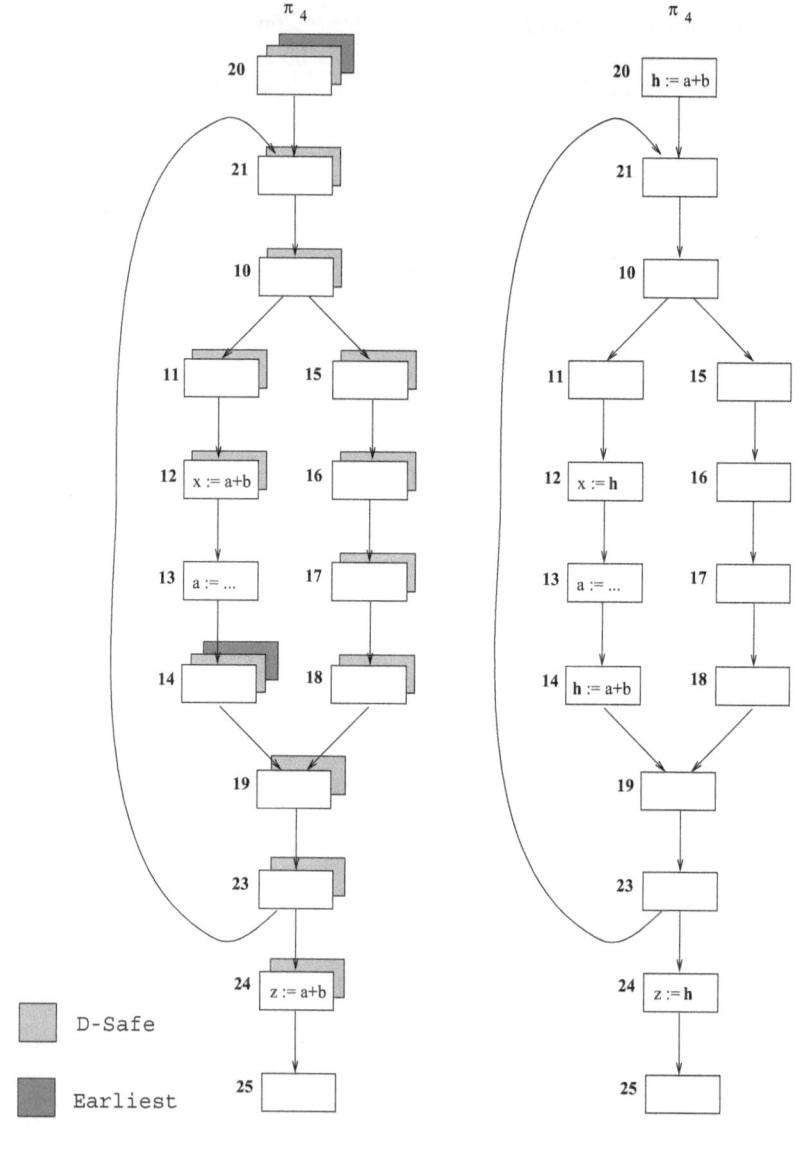

π_4 after inlining of π_3 After the BCM-transformation

Fig. 12.1. Intraproc. situation of the "right" part of Fig. 10.18

motion. Optimizations, which do not require "global" modifications in the sense above, are in fact not affected by this dilemma. A prominent example is *constant propagation* (cf. [Ke1, Ki1, Ki2, RL1, RL2, WZ1, WZ2]). It does not rely on inserting new statements, but on modifying existing ones only.

Hence, its power depends directly on the precision of the DFA information, and thus its customization.

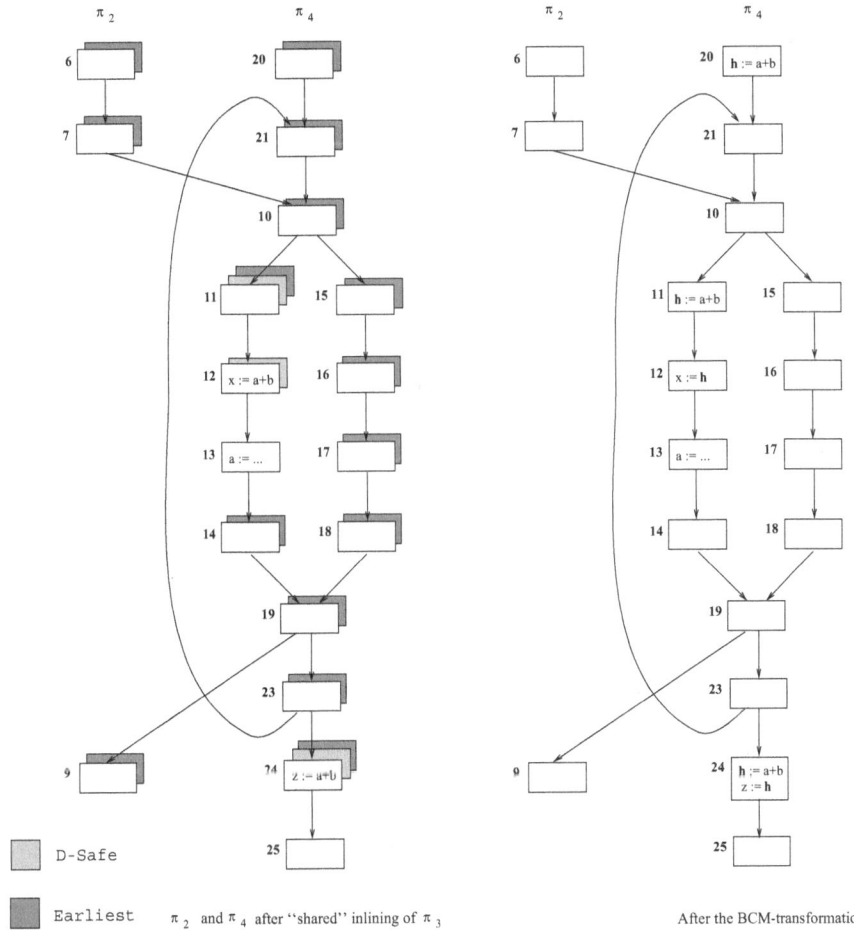

Fig. 12.2. Intraprocedural situation of Figure 10.18

Summary. Considering interprocedural code motion there is no general way of getting rid of these problems as computational optimality is in general impossible. In the following, we therefore sketch three orthogonal approaches centered around *optimality* and *generality* aiming at computational and life-time optimality for specific program classes and applicability to all programs without exhibiting anomalies, respectively.

I. Abstract interpretation of control. Intuitively, the first approach is, in addition to abstractly interpret the semantics of a program, to also abstractly interpret its control flow. An extreme, however, not general approach falling into this group is to consider the interprocedural control flow graph of a program as an intraprocedural flow graph, i.e., computing data flow information according to all paths, not just interprocedurally valid ones as suggested by the example of Figure 12.2. This, however, is limited to data flow properties, which must be satisfied along all program executions reaching a specific program point as e.g. *availability*. Properties, which are justified if they are valid along some program execution as e.g. *partial availability*, are not safely approximated. Thus, problems simultaneously involving existentially and universally quantified properties, cannot safely be approximated, and hence not handled at all.

II. Keeping Optimality. The second approach, which we followed in this monograph, is characterized by retaining optimality for specific program classes at the price of losing generality. Canonicity of the *IBCM*-transformation is the guarantor of the computational and lifetime optimality of the interprocedural versions of busy and lazy code motion, respectively. As demonstrated, generality is lost: in the absence of canonicity, the result can dramatically be degenerated. It is an important matter of future work to characterize further program classes having a computationally and lifetime optimal counterpart together with an algorithm constructing them. Particularly promising is here the class of programs having a computationally optimal canonic counterpart. The *IBCM*- and *ILCM*-transformation provide a good starting-point in order to enhance them accordingly.

III. Keeping Generality. Basically, the third approach is characterized by retaining generality at the price of losing optimality. In essence, this can be achieved by heuristically limiting the motion of computations across procedure boundaries in order to avoid anomalies. The algorithm of Morel and Renvoise of [MR2] is a prominent example following this approach. Another example is the algorithm of [KM2] dealing with the elimination of partially redundant and partially dead assignments in High Performance Fortran programs. Unfortunately, heuristics are often overly restrictive unnecessarily reducing the transformational power of an algorithm. In the following we demonstrate this by illustrating the limitations of the heuristics of the algorithm of [MR2] imposed for avoiding (1) motion anomalies, and (2) unnecessary motions of computations, which, as a side-effect, avoids unnecessarily long lifetimes of temporaries.[1]

(1) Avoiding Motion Anomalies. Intuitively, the constraint introduced by Morel and Renvoise for avoiding motion anomalies prevents hoisting of a computation across a procedure call, if this requires an insertion inside the callee. In the example of Figure 10.18, the algorithm of [MR2] leaves the program thus invariant. However, this constraint is in general overly restrictive as illustrated by the program of Figure 12.3. For this example, the algorithm

---

[1] Morel and Renvoise did not introduce the second part of this heuristics as a means for limiting lifetimes. This is indeed rather a side-effect of avoiding unnecessary motions they were aiming at.

of [MR2] generates the program of Figure 12.4, failing to eliminate the partially redundant computation at node **22** inside the loop. The point here is that because of the motion contraint moving $a + b$ across the call sites of π_3 is prevented because this would require an insertion inside the callee π_3. The constraint is too restrictive in that it does not take into account that in this example all call sites require an insertion inside the callee. For comparison, interprocedural busy code motion generates the computationally optimal canonic result of Figure 12.5.

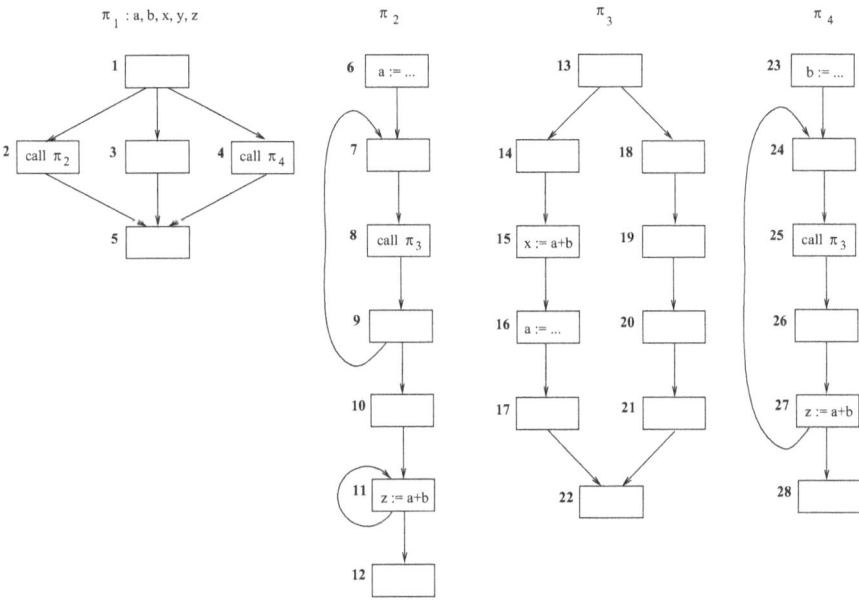

Fig. 12.3. The limitations of the motion-heuristic of Morel and Renvoise

(*2*) *Limiting the Lifetimes of Temporaries.* In order to avoid unnecessary motions of computations, which, as a side-effect avoids unnecessarily long lifetimes of variables, Morel and Renvoise introduced a *profitability* constraint on moving computations into their pioneering intraprocedural code motion algorithm (cf. [MR1]): computations are moved to earlier computation points only if they are *partially redundant*. Intuitively, this means that computations are only moved if at least one program path profits from the move. This avoids some, though not all unnecessary motions of computations, without affecting the computational optimality of the algorithm. As demonstrated by the example of Figure 12.6 this does not carry over to the interprocedural setting. Here, the algorithm of [MR2] generates the sub-optimal result of Figure 12.7 because limiting the motion of computations to partially redundant ones prevents hoisting of the computation at node **8** to node **7**. As a consequence, the insertions in π_2 and π_4 cannot be moved into procedure π_3. The motion

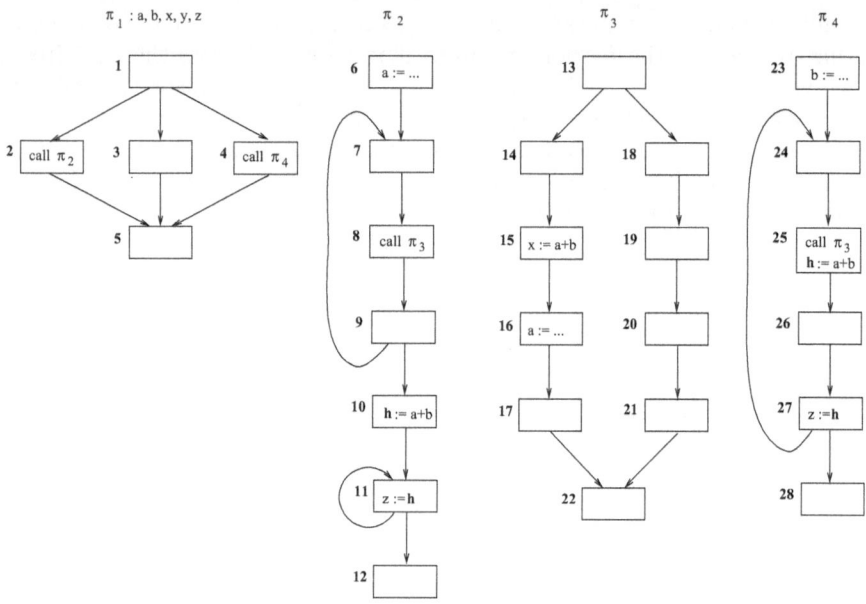

Fig. 12.4. The effect of Morel and Renvoise's algorithm

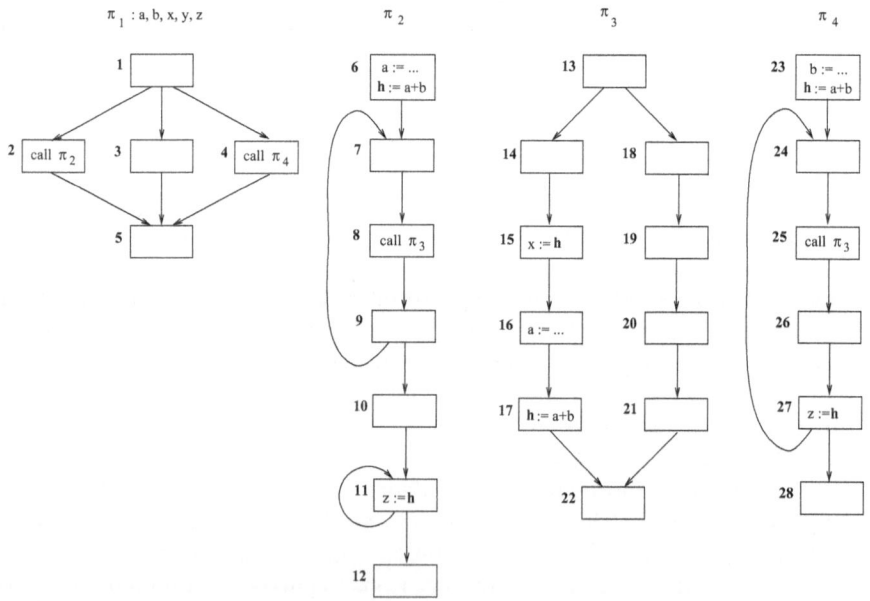

Fig. 12.5. Computationally optimal result of the *IBCM*-transformation

process is blocked. In contrast, interprocedural lazy code motion generates the computationally and lifetime optimal canonic result of Figure 12.8.

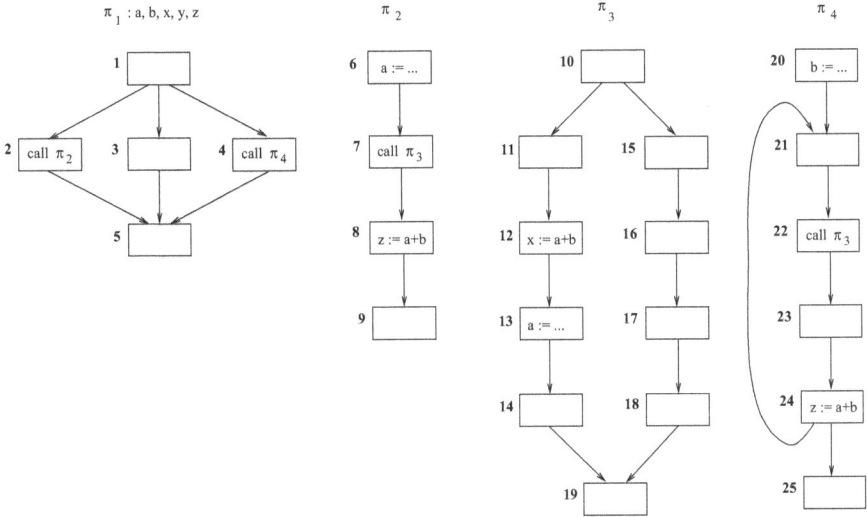

Fig. 12.6. Limitations of the lifetime-heuristic of Morel and Renvoise

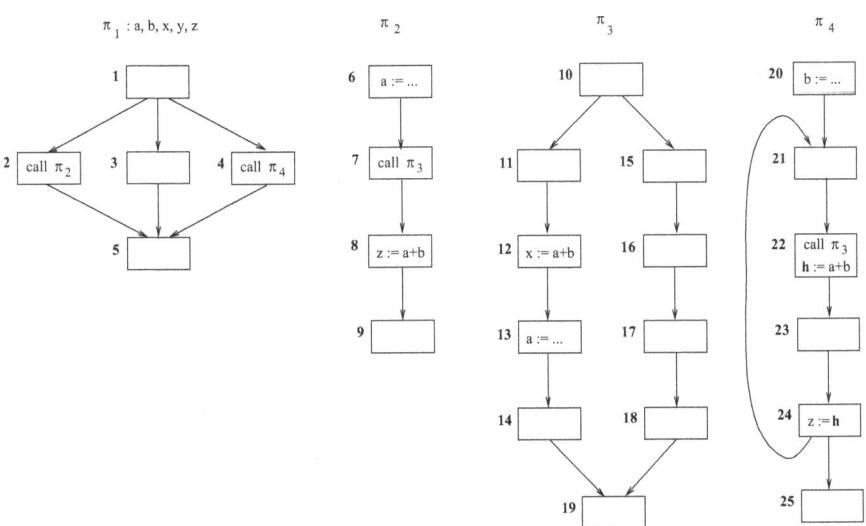

Fig. 12.7. The effect of Morel and Renvoise's algorithm

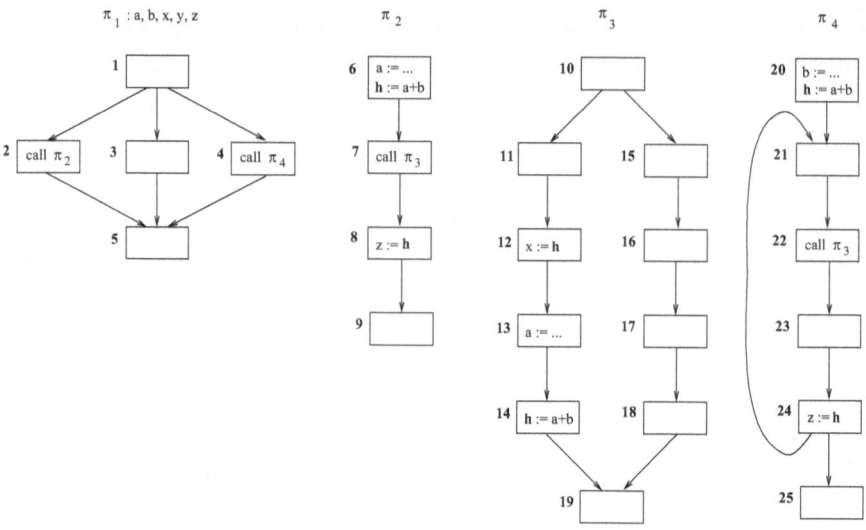

Fig. 12.8. Computationally & lifetime opt. result of the *ILCM*-transformation

12.2 Pragmatics

12.2.1 Static Procedure Nesting and Complexity of IDFA

The framework we presented captures programs with statically nested procedures, which is important concerning its applicability to "real world" programs. It should be noted, however, that programs without statically nested procedures can often more efficiently be analyzed. We illustrate this by means of the down-safety and the earliestness analysis of the *IBCM*-transformation of Chapter 10. In a program containing statically nested procedures the local variables of a procedure are global variables of its static successors. This introduces the phenomenon of variables being "relatively global". It enforces the down-safety and the earliestness analysis besides keeping track on the variables which are modified by an assignment, also to keep track on the static level of their declaration. Considering the down-safety analysis, we therefore used the lattice

$$(\mathcal{C}, \sqcap, \sqsubseteq, \bot, \top) =_{df} (\mathcal{B} \times \mathcal{N}, Min, \leq, (false, 0), (true, \infty))$$

as the domain of relevant DFA-information. Intuitively, the second component of a data flow information stores the static level of the "most globally" declared variable, which has been modified in the current procedure call.

In a program without statically nested procedures, the situation is much simpler. A variable is either "truly" global, if it is an external variable or if it is declared in the main procedure of the program, or it is "truly" local, if it is declared in one of its procedures. Hence, the down-safety and the earliestness analyses must only distinguish between modifications of global and local variables. Regarding the down-safety analysis, this can be achieved by considering the simpler lattice

$$(\mathcal{C}, \sqcap, \sqsubseteq, \bot, \top) =_{df} (\mathcal{B}^2, \wedge, \leq, (false, false), (true, true))$$

as the domain of relevant data flow information. We remark that the choice of this lattice relies on the same intuition as above: the second bit of a DFA information attached to a program point indicates whether a global variable of the term under consideration has been modified. Following [KRS4], the local semantic functional for down-safety simplifies to

$$[\![\ ]\!]'_{ds} : N^* \to (\mathcal{B}^2 \to \mathcal{B}^2) \quad \text{defined by}$$

$$\forall n \in N^* \ \forall (b_1, b_2) \in \mathcal{B}^2. \ [\![n]\!]'_{ds}(b_1, b_2) =_{df} (b'_1, b'_2)$$

with

$$b'_1 =_{df} Comp(n) \vee (Transp(n) \wedge b_1)$$

$$b'_2 =_{df} \begin{cases} b_2 \wedge NoGlobalChanges(n) & \text{if } n \in N^* \setminus N^*_r \\ true & \text{otherwise} \end{cases}$$

where the predicate $NoGlobalChanges : N^* \to \mathcal{B}$ is the analogue of the function $ModLev$ of Section 10.2.1. It is defined by:

$$\forall n \in N^*. \ NoGlobalChanges(n) =_{df} Var_{LhsVar(n)}(t) \subseteq LocVar(\Pi \setminus \{\pi_1\})$$

Similarly, the definition of the return functional $\mathcal{R}_{ds}$ simplifies to

$$\mathcal{R}_{ds} : N^*_c \to (\mathcal{B}^2 \times \mathcal{B}^2 \to \mathcal{B}^2) \quad \text{defined by}$$

$$\forall n \in N^*_c \ \forall ((b_1, b_2), (b_3, b_4)) \in \mathcal{B}^2 \times \mathcal{B}^2. \ \mathcal{R}_{ds}(n)((b_1, b_2), (b_3, b_4)) =_{df} (b_5, b_6)$$

with

$$b_5 =_{df} \begin{cases} b_3 & \text{if } Var(t) \subseteq GlobVar(\Pi) \\ Comp(n) \vee (b_1 \wedge b_4) & \text{otherwise} \end{cases}$$

$$b_6 =_{df} b_2 \wedge b_4$$

The start information, finally, is given by the element

$$(false, true) \in \mathcal{B} \times \mathcal{B}$$

Analogously, also the earliestness analysis can be based on a less complex lattice:

$$(\mathcal{C}, \sqcap, \sqsubseteq, \bot, \top) =_{df} (\mathcal{B}^2, (\vee, \wedge), (\geq, \leq), (true, false), (false, true))$$

The local abstract semantics is then given by the functional

$$[\![\ ]\!]'_{ea} : N^* \to (\mathcal{B}^2 \to \mathcal{B}^2) \quad \text{defined by}$$

$$\forall\, n \in N^*\ \forall\, (b_1, b_2) \in \mathcal{B}^2.\ [\![\, n\,]\!]'_{ea}(b_1, b_2) =_{df} (b'_1, b'_2)$$

with

$$b'_1 =_{df} \neg\, Transp\,(n) \lor (\neg I\text{-}DSafe\,(n) \land b_1)$$

$$b'_2 =_{df} \begin{cases} b_2 \land NoGlobalChanges\,(n) & \text{if } n \in N^* \setminus N^*_c \\ true & \text{otherwise} \end{cases}$$

Correspondingly, the return functional of the earliestness analysis simplifies to

$$\mathcal{R}_{ea} : N^*_r \to (\mathcal{B}^2 \times \mathcal{B}^2 \to \mathcal{B}^2) \quad \text{defined by}$$

$$\forall\, n \in N^*_r\ \forall\,((b_1, b_2),(b_3, b_4)) \in \mathcal{B}^2 \times \mathcal{B}^2.\ \mathcal{R}_{ea}(n)((b_1, b_2),(b_3, b_4)) =_{df} (b_5, b_6)$$

with

$$b_5 =_{df} \begin{cases} b_3 \land \neg I\text{-}DSafe\,(n) & \text{if } Var(t) \subseteq GlobVar(\Pi) \\ \neg b_4 \lor (\neg I\text{-}DSafe\,(n_S) \land b_1) & \text{otherwise} \end{cases}$$

$$b_6 =_{df} b_2 \land b_4$$

The start information is then given by the element

$$(\mathbf{s}_1 \in Range(t), true) \in \mathcal{B} \times \mathcal{B}$$

In the remainder of this section we investigate the impact of static procedure nesting on the computational complexity of the *IBCM*-transformation. More generally, this leads us to the complexity of so-called bit-vector problems, of which the *IBCM*-transformation is a typical representative. Bit-vector problems are characterized by expressing the relevant data flow information in terms of a finite number of predicates. Though the number of the predicates depends on the problem, it is independent of the size of the program being analysed. It thus only adds a constant factor to the complexity estimation. In practice, the number of mutually dependent predicates hardly exceeds two. Thus, the factor is even small. As demonstrated in [KS2], the only blow-up in size for programs without statically nested procedures stems from the fact that bit-vector algorithms usually work on members of linearly growing classes like the set of program variables or the set of program terms. This, however, adds even in the intraprocedural setting a multiplicative factor to the worst-case time complexity because the determination of the properties of the different members proceeds independently, as long as the program being analysed does not satisfy specific structural properties. In a program without statically nested procedures a single member of such a class can be checked in linear time (cf. [KS2]). The proof of this result is as usual based on the assumption that the argument program is "constant branching", i.e., the number of successors of a node in the flow graph system is bounded by a constant. This proof can straightforward be adapted to programs with statically nested procedures, which adds a quadratic factor to the complexity as stated by Theorem 12.2.1. We remark that this theorem relies on the assumption of constant branching. It can be dropped, however, using a refined argument on edges (cf. [KS2]).

Theorem 12.2.1. *The worst-case time complexity of solving a bit-vector problem for a single member of the class of interest is* $O(d^2 * n)$, *where* d *and* n *denote the level of the statically most deeply nested procedure and the number of nodes of a flow graph system, respectively.*

For realistic programs it is reasonable to consider d a constant. Under this assumption, Theorem 12.2.1 yields that interprocedural bit-vector problems can be solved within the same worst-case time complexity as their intraprocedural counterparts. However, a performance comparison in practice must also take the constant factor imposed by the nesting level into account. In essence, the worst-case time complexity is determined by the complexity of computing the semantic functions for procedures. This complexity itself depends mainly on the maximal length of chains in the function lattice representing the domain of the abstract procedure semantics. Denoting by b the number of mutually dependent predicates under consideration, and by n the level of the statically most deeply nested procedure, the maximal chain length in the function lattice can be estimated by

$$2^b * b$$

for programs without statically nested procedures and by

$$d^b * (d * b)$$

for programs with statically nested procedures (cf. [KS2]). Recalling that in practice d can be regarded a constant, this does not affect the worst-case time complexity, but nonetheless it can significantly influence the performance of an implementation. Transforming a program containing statically nested procedures into a program without statically nested procedures before analyzing it can thus often be profitable. Suitable transformations together with general side-conditions of their applicability and effectivity are described in [La2, Ol1]. As a side-effect of these transformations, the resulting programs satisfy the sfmr-property; a fact, which is particularly important in the presence of formal procedure calls.

12.2.2 Aliasing: Call by Name and Call by Reference

As indicated in Chapter 6, the HO-DFA of our framework can also be used for computing (correct (i.e., safe) approximations of) the sets of may-aliases and must-aliases of a name or reference parameter of a procedure (cf. [Ban, Co, CpK2, We]).[2] Alternatively, alias-analyses can also be formulated as IDFA-problems. A straightforward specification utilizes the power set lattice $\mathcal{PS}$ of variable identifiers occurring in a program as the domain of relevant DFA-information. Except for call nodes and return nodes the local semantics of the statements of an interprocedural flow graph is given by the identity on $\mathcal{PS}$. The semantics of call nodes and return nodes is concerned with establishing and releasing the alias relation between the arguments of a call statement and the parameters of the called procedure. Defining the meet operation in $\mathcal{PS}$ as the set union operator and the set intersection operator, respectively, results in IDFA-algorithms for may-aliases and must-aliases. In contrast to the *control flow free*[3] computation of aliases by means of the HO-DFA, the IDFA-algorithms realize a *control flow dependent* computation of aliases (cf. [CpK1]). The practical impact of this conceptual difference concerning precision and complexity remains to be investigated.

In general, IDFA-applications are sensible to alias-information, and must be tailored to use this information properly. Considering the *IBCM*- and *ILCM*-transformation two effects of aliasing must be taken into account. First, a program term is modified if an alias of one of its operands is modified. This requires may-alias information. Second, a program term is computed if it is computed by any of its alias-representations. This requires must-alias information. Actually, the *IBCM*- and *ILCM*-transformation can straightforward be adapted to uniformly capture both effects. For the *IBCM*-transformation this is demonstrated in [KRS4]. It is worth noting, however, that this is a step from a purely syntactically based code motion algorithm towards a semantically based code motion algorithm, since lexically different program terms are considered equivalent, if corresponding operands are aliases of each other.[4] A similar extension to semantically based code motion for communication placement in distributed languages has been proposed by Agrawal, Saltz, and Das by semantically interpreting the assignment of the parameter transfer (cf. [ASD]).

---

[2] We recall that call by name and call by reference coincide as long as there are no complex data structures.

[3] Intuitively, "control flow free" means that a statement can be followed by any other statement of a procedure. In contrast, "control flow dependent" means that the intraprocedural flow of control is respected.

[4] Intuitively, "syntactically" means that only lexically identical program terms are considered equivalent (cf. [BC1, Dh1, Dh2, Dh3, DRZ, DS1, DS2, KRS1, KRS2, MR1, So, St1, St2]). In contrast, "semantically" based code motion algorithms consider also lexically different program terms equivalent, if they are semantically equivalent (cf. [BA, Cl, KRS7, RL1, RL2, RWZ, St3, SKR1, SKR2]).

12.3 Future Work

12.3.1 The Framework Side

The framework has been developed for the family of Algol-like programming languages. Thus, it is settled in the *imperative* programming paradigm, but it is not limited to it. For example, the HO-DFA dealing with formal procedure calls yields a natural interface to other programming paradigms, in particular, to the *functional* and the *object-oriented* one. Its similarity to constraint-based methods for *closure* and *safety* or *type* analysis of functional and object-oriented languages is obvious (cf. [Ag1, Ag2, Ay, Bon, OPS, Pal1, Pal2, PC, PS1, PS2, PS3, PS4]), though the details are different. Current approaches to these problems concentrate mainly on correctness and efficiency, whereas precision in the style of Theorem 6.4.1 is not considered systematically. It is worth investigating to which extent the methods used in proving the correctness and precision of our HO-DFA carry over to the problem of closure and safety analysis of functional and object-oriented languages. This also holds for considering formal procedure calls as higher order branch statements during IDFA. As mentioned earlier, formal procedure calls are thereby automatically treated in a most recent fashion. This directly suggests to apply this technique to LISP and its derivates, to which in contrast to Algol-like programming languages the dynamic scope rules apply. As demonstrated in [SF1, SF2] also extensions to the logical programming paradigm are possible.

Besides this link to other programming paradigms indicated by the HO-DFA, it is also worth-wile to adapt the abstract interpretation based approach centred around a coincidence theorem underlying our framework to both the object-oriented and the parallel programming paradigm, and to develop variants tailored for conceptually quite different object-oriented languages like Smalltalk, C++, and Oberon, and parallel languages like Parallel-C, High Performance Fortran, or to CCS- and CSP-like languages. First results concerning the analysis of explicitly parallel programs with interleaving semantics and shared memory can be found in [KSV1, KSV2]. There it has been shown how to construct for unidirectional bit-vector problems precise analysis algorithms, which can easily be implemented, and are as efficient as their counterparts for sequential programs. This is highly relevant in practice because of the broad scope of applications of bit-vector problems ranging from simple analyses like liveness, availability, very busyness, reaching definitions, and definition-use chains (cf. [He]) to more sophisticated and powerful program optimizations like code motion (cf. [DS2, DRZ, KRS1, KRS2]), partial dead code elimination (cf. [KRS3]), assignment motion (cf. [KRS4]), and strength reduction (cf. [KRS5]). All these techniques require only unidirectional bit-vector analyses, and can now be made available for parallel programs, too. In [Kn2, Kn3] and [KSV3] this has been demonstrated for partial dead code elimination and partial redundancy elimination, respectively. On the object-oriented side we adapted in a first step the abstract interpretation based approach to a Smalltalk- and an Oberon-like language. This extension offers a conceptually new approach for type analysis, which is often more powerful than related previous techniques (cf. [Ag1, Ag2, OPS, PC, PS3, PS4]), and additionally, it opens the object-oriented setting for classical optimizations (cf. [KG, KS4]). Central for both the parallel and the object-oriented extension was to extend the framework of abstract interpretation accordingly, and to prove specific coincidence theorems.

In addition, there are also several worth-wile starting-points for refining and enhancing the framework for the imperative programming paradigm itself. An important and straightforward to realize point is to replace the algorithm for computing the *IMFP*-solution consisting in the version presented here of a preprocess for computing the abstract semantics of procedures and a main process for computing the *IMFP*-solution based on the results of the preprocess by a new computation procedure, which interleaves both steps, and computes the semantics of procedure call nodes by-need only. Though this does not improve the worst-case time complexity of computing the *IMFP*-solution, it can in practice be expected to yield a dramatic performance gain. Similar in spirit it would be to derive a variant of the framework for "demand-driven" data flow analysis in the fashion of [DGS1, DGS2]. The point of this approach is to answer so-called data flow queries. Intuitively, this means answering, whether a given data flow information can be assured at a specific program point. In practice, data flow queries can quite efficiently be answered as only small fractions of the program have to be considered.

In addition to these pragmatically motivated modifications, the following topics are of major importance to further enhance the framework:

1. Extending the framework to functions, i.e., to procedures returning the result of a computation.
2. Enhancing the framework by means of refined alias and higher order data flow analyses.
3. Identifying new practically relevant classes of programs, for which the sfmr-property can efficiently be checked.
4. Developing new criteria guaranteeing the sfmr-property of a program, which can efficiently be verified.
5. Extending the framework to capture programs lacking the sfmr-property.

The first four points can be dealt with in a rather straightforward manner, the last one, however, requires additional care because formal procedure calls can no longer be treated as nondeterministic higher order branch statements without additional precautions. The current treatment of ordinary and formal procedure calls in the framework suggests the following approach. Operationally, to enhance the control flow by a stack component which allows a bookkeeping of the static environment in which a formal procedure call is invoked during the analysis; denotationally, to superpose the computation of the semantics of ordinary and formal procedure calls by a process analogously to the one for computing the semantics of procedure calls (cf. Definition 8.3.2). The practicality of this approach remains to be investigated. In particular, introducing a kind of a control flow stack suggests that it would be limited to programs with a *regular formal call tree* because otherwise the control flow stack can grow arbitrarily. This limitation, however, would have a direct analogue in the field of program verification: a correct and relatively complete Hoare-system for an Algol-like programming language $\mathcal{L}$ exists if and only if every program of $\mathcal{L}$ has a regular formal call tree (cf. [Ol1]).

12.3.2 The Application Side

In this section we sketch a variety of further practically relevant applications, which can be made available for imperative programming languages by means of our stack-based framework. This ranges from bit-vector based optimizations (cf. [He]) over constant propagation (cf. [Ke1, Ki1, Ki2, RL1, RL2, WZ1, WZ2]), strength reduction (cf. [ACK, CcK, CP, Dh4, DD, JD1, JD2, Pa1, Pa2, PK]), and semantically based code motion (cf. [BA, Cl, RWZ]) to the automatic parallelization of sequential programs with procedures (cf. [BC2, Le, LY, Wo, ZC]).

Following the presentation of Section 11, the framework can easily be used for solving the classical bit-vector problems like computing *available (up-safe) expressions*, *very busy (down-safe) expressions*, *live variables*, and *reaching definitions*. In [KRS4] this is demonstrated for a set-up with value and reference parameters. We recall that bit-vector analyses are practically most important because of the broad scope of powerful program optimizations relying on analyses of this type. All these analyses can now be adapted to the interprocedural setting. For example, along the lines of [KRS3] the algorithm for interprocedural lazy code motion could be enhanced to an algorithm for *interprocedural lazy strength reduction*, which would be unique to uniformly combine code motion and strength reduction interprocedurally. Similarly, this holds for the algorithms of partial dead code elimination and assignment motion of [KRS5] and [KRS6], which only require unidirectional bit-vector analyses, too. They can thus be generalized to the interprocedural setting in the same fashion. In [KM2] this has been demonstrated for a similar application, called *distribution assignment placement* (cf. [KM1]), in the context of data parallel languages: avoiding unnecessary distribution assignments in High Performance Fortran programs. In essence, this application combines partial dead code elimination and partially redundant assignment elimination. Usually, the combination of optimizations is the source of intricate interdependencies (cf. [Cl, ClCo, WS2]), which holds for distribution assignment placement as well. The interdependencies and second-order effects of its two component transformations introduce intricate problems into optimality considerations (cf. [GKLRS, KM1, KM2]) making distribution assignment placement from both a theoretical and practical point of view particularly interesting. In [Rü], the impact of interacting code motion transformations on the transformational power and the algorithmic complexity of an application has been investigated in detail for a related (intraprocedural) application scenario. It is an important matter of future work to investigate how the techniques and results developed in [Rü] can be adapted and applied to the application scenario of [KM1] and its interprocedural extension of [KM2]. Likewise this also holds for the stronger notion of lifetime optimality introduced in [Rü], which in contrast to the lifetime notion considered here takes the lifetimes of temporaries simultaneously into account, requiring that the cumulated lifetimes of temporaries are minimized. In [Rü] an algorithm is presented achieving this notion of lifetime optimality for intraprocedural code motion. It is based on busy and lazy code motion, and thus, it is promising to investigate its extensibility to the interprocedural setting.

Going on, intraprocedural reaching definition analysis is another example of a practically relevant application, which can interprocedurally be enhanced in the same fashion allowing the construction of interprocedural *definition-use chains* (cf. [HS]). They are important for an (interprocedural) *dependence analysis* of a program (cf. [FO, FOW, RS]), which is a common prerequisite of the *automatic parallelization* of sequential programs. In addition, definition-use chains are also useful for a simple form of (interprocedural) *constant propagation*.

A different, much more powerful approach to *interprocedural constant propagation* (cf. [CC2, CCpKT, JM, RHS, SRH1, SRH2]) can be based on the decidable class of *finite constants* introduced in [SK1, SK2]. Finite constants are optimal for acyclic programs. The decision procedure for finite constants generalizes and improves in this respect on all previous techniques for (intraprocedural) constant progagation. Basis of the interprocedural extension of this algorithm is the fact that finite constants have a purely *operational* characterization in the sense of the meet over all paths approach, and a purely *denotational* characterization in the sense of the maximal fixed point approach yielding a computation procedure, whose coincidence is a consequence of the coincidence theorem.

Analogously to the interprocedural extension of finite constants, also the semantically based algorithms for code motion and strength reduction of [SKR1, SKR2, KS3, KRS7] can interprocedurally be extended. One should note, however, that in contrast to the bit-vector based interprocedural versions of lazy code motion and lazy strength reduction, which have the same worst-case time complexity as their intraprocedural counterparts, this does not hold for the semantically based algorithms. In practice, the additional computational effort must carefully be balanced with the enlarged transformational power of the algorithms.

In addition to the applications sketched above, which are based on our work, there is a large variety of further applications reported in the literature, both intraprocedurally and interprocedurally. Muchnick provides an up-to-date survey (cf. [Mu]). The stack-based framework can serve as a uniform platform in order to (re-)formulate and to compare algorithms which are designed for related applications. Moreover, because of the large spectrum of language features supported by the stack-based framework this may often allow to enhance these algorithms accordingly, improving thereby their transformational power.

12.3.3 Generators for IDFA and Optimization

In this section we consider a practically important recent trend in optimization: the construction of tools for the automatic generation of data flow analyses and optimizations out of concise specifications. In contrast to the construction of algorithms needed by other compiler phases like the lexical and syntactical analysis or the code generation phase, for which a support by powerful generators is state-of-the-art for years, optimizers are usually still hand-coded. Of course, this is an expensive and error-prone process. Early approaches to improve on this situation concentrated on *peephole* optimizations, which are particularly simple as they do not require global program analyses (cf. [DF, Kes]). They have been complemented by approaches which address the generation of global analyses, but do not support the construction of (complex) program transformations (cf. [AGL, AM, CDG, HMCR, KH, YH]). More recently, systems have been introduced supporting both the construction of global analyses and of optimizations based thereof (cf. [Aß1, Aß2, TH, VF, WS1, WS3]). However, the application range is different. The systems of [Aß1, Aß2, TH, VF] concentrate on "classical" intraprocedural optimizations, whereas the system of [WS1, WS3] is particularly well-suited for local transformations based on data dependency information. This is particularly important for the automatic parallelization of sequential programs.

The stack-based framework we presented here is quite appropriate for serving as a common basis for constructing an interprocedural generator for data flow analyses and optimizations. A prototype, the DFA&OPT-METAFrame tool kit [KKKS, KRS4], has been implemented as a part of the METAFrame-system [SMCB], whose computational cernel is the fixed-point analysis machine of [Kl, SCKKM]. The current prototype, which recently has been complemented by a control-flow analysis generator allowing the automatic generation of flow graphs and flow graph systems from the abstract syntax tree of the underlying program [BKK], supports data flow analysis and optimization of intraprocedural and interprocedural programs along the lines of the framework here, and of parallel programs along the lines of [KSV1, KSV2]. It applies particularly well to optimizations based on bitvector analyses like *code motion, assignment motion, partial dead code elimination, strength reduction*, and (via definition-use chains) also *constant propagation* and *constant folding*. Both interprocedural and parallel DFA-problems can be specified in terms of the local semantic functions giving abstract semantics to statements, the direction of the data flow, and the kind of fixpoint desired corresponding to the cookbook presentation of the framework here. Alternatively, intraprocedural data flow analyses can also be specified in terms of modal logic formulas as proposed in [St1, St2]. First practical experiences show that the generated DFA-algorithms are as efficient as their hand-coded counterparts. A *high level programming language* allows us to combine the results of different analyses for specifying program optimizations. It is the connecting link for combining program analysis and optimization. The generator has successfully been tested on a large sample of program optimizations mentioned above. For interprocedural data flow analysis the current version of the generator supports programs composed of procedures with global variables. An extension to local variables, value, reference, and procedure parameters in order to support the full scope of the framework presented in this monograph is in progress.

Bibliography

[Ag1] Agesen, O. Constraint-based type inference and parametric polymorphism, In *Proceedings of the 1st International Static Analysis Symposium (SAS'94)* (*Namur, Belgium*), Springer-Verlag, Heidelberg, LNCS 864 (1994), 70 - 100.

[Ag2] Agesen, O. The cartesian product algorithm. In *Proceedings of the 9th European Conference on Object-Oriented Programming (ECOOP'95)* (*Aarhus, Denmark*), Springer-Verlag, Heidelberg, LNCS 952 (1995), 2 - 26.

[All1] Allen, F. E. Control flow analysis. In *Proceedings of an ACM SIGPLAN Symposium on Compiler Optimization* (*Urbana-Champaign, Illinois*), ACM SIGPLAN Notices 5, 7 (1970), 1 - 19.

[All2] Allen, F. E. Interprocedural data flow analysis. In *Proceedings of the IFIP Congress '74* (*Stockholm, Sweden* (*August 1974*)). Rosenfield, J. L. (Ed.), Amsterdam: North-Holland, 1974, 398 - 408.

[Ar1] Armbruster, D. Entscheidbarkeit und Bestimmung der Rekursivität von Prozeduren. Ph.D. dissertation, University of Stuttgart, Germany, 1985.

[Ar2] Armbruster, D. A polynomial determination of the most-recent property in Pascal-like programs. *Theoretical Computer Science 56*, 1 (1988), 3 - 15.

[Ar3] Armbruster, D. Polynomial recursion analysis in Pascal-like programs. In *Proceedings of the 1st International Conference on Theoretical Aspects of Computer Software (TACS'91)* (*Sendai, Japan*), Springer-Verlag, Heidelberg, LNCS 526 (1991), 447 - 458.

[Aß1] Aßmann, U. How to uniformly specify program analysis and transformations with graph rewrite systems. In *Proceedings of the 6th International Conference on Compiler Construction (CC'96)* (*Linköping, Sweden*), Springer-Verlag, Heidelberg, LNCS 1060 (1996), 121 - 135.

[Aß2] Aßmann, U. OPTIMIXing. In *Proceedings of the Poster Session of the 7th International Conference on Compiler Construction (CC'98)* (*Lisbon, Portugal*), Departamento de Informática, Universidade de Lisboa, (1998), 28 - 35.

[Ay] Ayers, A. Efficient closure analysis with reachability. In *Proceedings of the 2nd International Workshop on Static Analysis (WSA'92)* (*Bordeaux, France* (*September 1992*)), 126 - 134.

[ACK] Allen, F. E., Cocke, J., and Kennedy, K. Reduction of operator strength. In [MJ], 1981, 79 - 101.

[AGL] Adl-Tabatabai, A.-R., Gross, T., and Lueh, G.-Y. Code reuse in an optimizing compiler. In *Proceedings of the 9th ACM SIGPLAN Annual Conference on Object-Oriented Programming Systems, Languages, and Applications (OOPSLA'96)* (*San Jose, California*), ACM SIGPLAN Notices 31, (1996), 51 - 68.

[AGS] Ayers, A., Gottlieb, R., and Schooler, R. Aggressive inlining. In *Proceedings of the ACM SIGPLAN'97 Conference on Programming Language Design and Implementation (PLDI'97)* (*Las Vegas, Nevada*), ACM SIGPLAN Notices 32, 5 (1997), 134 - 145.

[AM] Alt, M., and Martin, F. Generation of efficient interprocedural analyzers with PAG. In *Proceedings of the 2nd International Static Analysis Symposium (SAS'95) (Glasgow, UK)*, Springer-Verlag, Heidelberg, LNCS 983 (1995), 33 - 50.

[ASD] Agrawal, G., Saltz, J., and Das, R. Interprocedural partial redundancy elimination and its application to distributed memory compilation. In *Proceedings of the ACM SIGPLAN'95 Conference on Programming Language Design and Implementation (PLDI'95) (La Jolla, California), ACM SIGPLAN Notices 30*, 6 (1995), 258 - 269.

[ASU] Aho, A. V., Sethi, R., and Ullman, J. D. Compilers: Principles, techniques and tools. Addison-Wesley, 1985.

[AU] Aho, A. V., and Ullman, J. D. Node listings for reducible flow graphs. In *Proceedings of the 7th International Symposium on Theory of Computing (STOC'75) (Albuquerque, New Mexico)*, 1975, 177 - 185.

[Ba1] Barth, G. Interprozedurale Datenflußsysteme. Habilitationsschrift, University of Kaiserslautern, Germany, 1981.

[Ba2] Barth, G. Interprocedural data flow systems. In *Proceedings of the 6th GI-Conference (Dortmund, Germany)*, Springer-Verlag, Heidelberg, LNCS 145 (1983), 49 - 59.

[Ban] Banning, J. P. An efficient way to find the side effects of procedure calls and the aliases of variables. In *Conference Record of the 6th Annual ACM Symposium on Principles of Programming Languages (POPL'79) (San Antonio, Texas)*, 1979, 724 - 736.

[Bon] Bondorf, A. Automatic autoprojection of higher order recursive equations. *Science of Computer Programming 17*, (1991), 3 - 34.

[Bou] Bourdoncle, F. Interprocedural abstract interpretation of block structured languages with nested procedures, aliasing and recursivity. In *Proceedings of the 2nd International Symposium on Programming Language Implementation and Logic Programming (PLILP'90) (Linköping, Sweden)*, Springer-Verlag, Heidelberg, LNCS 456 (1990), 307 - 323.

[Bth] Barth, J. M. An interprocedural data flow analysis algorithm. In *Conference Record of the 4th Annual ACM Symposium on Principles of Programming Languages (POPL'77) (Los Angeles, California)*, 1977, 119 - 131.

[Bu] Burke, M. An interval-based approach to exhaustive and incremental interprocedural data-flow analysis. *ACM Trans. Program. Lang. Syst. 12*, 3 (1990), 341 - 395.

[BA] Bodík, R., and Anik, S. Path-sensitive value-flow analysis. In *Conference Record of the 25th Annual ACM Symposium on Principles of Programming Languages (POPL'98) (San Diego, California)*, 1998, 237 - 251.

[BC1] Briggs, P., and Cooper, K. D. Effective partial redundancy elimination. In *Proceedings of the ACM SIGPLAN'94 Conference on Programming Language Design and Implementation (PLDI'94) (Orlando, Florida), ACM SIGPLAN Notices 29*, 6 (1994), 159 - 170.

[BC2] Burke, M., and Cytron, R. Interprocedural dependence analysis and parallelization. In *Proceedings of the ACM SIGPLAN'86 Symposium on Compiler Construction (Palo Alto, California), ACM SIGPLAN Notices 21*, 7 (1986), 162 - 175.

[BGS] Bodík, R., Gupta, R., and Soffa, M. L. Interprocedural conditional branch elimination. In *Proceedings of the ACM SIGPLAN'97 Conference on Programming Language Design and Implementation (PLDI'97) (Las Vegas, Nevada), ACM SIGPLAN Notices 32*, 5 (1997), 146 - 158.

[BKK] Braun, V., Knoop, J., and Koschützki, D. Cool: A control-flow generator for system analysis. In *Proceedings of the 7th International Conference on Compiler*

Construction (CC'98) (*Lisbon, Portugal*), Springer-Verlag, Heidelberg, LNCS 1383 (1998), 306 - 309.

[Ch] Chow, F. A portable machine independent optimizer – Design and measurements. Ph.D. dissertation, Dept. of Electrical Engineering, Stanford University, Stanford, California, and Tech. Rep. 83-254, Computer Systems Lab., Stanford University, 1983.

[Cl] Click, C. Global code motion/global value numbering. In *Proceedings of the ACM SIGPLAN'95 Conference on Programming Language Design and Implementation (PLDI'95)* (*La Jolla, California*), *ACM SIGPLAN Notices 30*, 6 (1995), 246 - 257.

[Co] Cooper, K. D. Analyzing aliases of reference formal parameters. In *Conference Record of the 12th Annual ACM Symposium on Principles of Programming Languages (POPL'85)* (*New Orleans, Louisiana*), 1985, 281 - 290.

[CC1] Cousot, P., and Cousot, R. Abstract interpretation: A unified lattice model for static analysis of programs by construction or approximation of fixpoints. In *Conference Record of the 4th Annual ACM Symposium on Principles of Programming Languages (POPL'77)* (*Los Angeles, California*), 1977, 238 - 252.

[CC2] Cousot, P., and Cousot, R. Static determination of dynamic properties of recursive procedures. In *Proceedings of the 2nd IFIP TC-2 Working Conference on Formal Description of Programming Concepts* (*St. Andrews, N. B., Canada (August 1977)*). Neuhold, E. J. (Ed.), New York: North-Holland, 1978, 237 - 277.

[CC3] Cousot, P., and Cousot, R. Systematic design of program analysis frameworks. In *Conference Record of the 6th Annual ACM Symposium on Principles of Programming Languages (POPL'79)* (*San Antonio, Texas*), 1979, 269 - 282.

[CC4] Cousot, P., and Cousot, R. Abstract interpretation frameworks. *Journal of Logic and Computation 2*, 4 (1992), 511 - 547.

[ClCo] Click, C., and Cooper, K. D. Combining analyses, combining optimizations. In *ACM Trans. Program. Lang. Syst. 17*, 2 (1995), 181 - 196.

[CCHK] Callahan, D., Carle, A., Hall, M. W., and Kennedy, K. W. Constructing the procedure call multigraph. *IEEE Trans. Software Eng. SE-16*, 4 (1990), 483 - 487.

[CCpKT] Callahan, D., Cooper, K. D., Kennedy, K. W., and Torczon, L. M. Interprocedural constant propagation. In *Proceedings of the ACM SIGPLAN'86 Symposium on Compiler Construction* (*Palo Alto, California*), *ACM SIGPLAN Notices 21*, 7 (1986), 152 - 161.

[CcK] Cocke, J., and Kennedy, K. An algorithm for reduction of operator strength. *Commun. of the ACM 20*, 11 (1977), 850 - 856.

[CpK1] Cooper, K. D., and Kennedy, K. W. Efficient computation of flow insensitive interprocedural summary information. In *Proceedings of the ACM SIGPLAN'84 Symposium on Compiler Construction* (*Montreal, Canada*), *ACM SIGPLAN Notices 19*, 6 (1984), 247 - 258.

[CpK2] Cooper, K. D., and Kennedy, K. W. Interprocedural side-effect analysis in linear time. In *Proceedings of the ACM SIGPLAN'88 Conference on Programming Language Design and Implementation (PLDI'88)* (*Atlanta, Georgia*), *ACM SIGPLAN Notices 23*, 7 (1988), 57 - 66.

[CpK3] Cooper, K. D., and Kennedy, K. W. Fast interprocedural alias analysis. In *Conference Record of the 16th Annual ACM Symposium on Principles of Programming Languages (POPL'89)* (*Austin, Texas*), 1989, 49 - 59.

[CDG] Chambers, C., Dean, J., and Grove, D. Frameworks for intra- and interprocedural dataflow analysis. Department of Computer Science and Engineering, University of Washington, Technical Report 96-11-02, 1996.

[CKT1] Cooper, K. D., Kennedy, K. W., and Torczon, L. The impact of interprocedure analysis and optimization in the $\mathbf{R}^n$ programming environment. *ACM Trans. Program. Lang. Syst. 8*, 4 (1986), 491 - 523.

[CKT2] Cooper, K. D., Kennedy, K. W., and Torczon, L. Interprocedural optimization: Eliminating unnecessary recompilation. In *Proceedings of the ACM SIGPLAN'86 Symposium on Compiler Construction (Palo Alto, California)*, *ACM SIGPLAN Notices 21*, 7 (1986), 58 - 67.

[CLZ] Cytron, R., Lowry, A., and Zadeck, F. K. Code motion of control structures in high-level languages. In *Conference Record of the 13th Annual ACM Symposium on Principles of Programming Languages (POPL'86) (St. Petersburg Beach, Florida)*, 1986, 70 - 85.

[CP] Cai, J., and Paige, R. Look ma, no hashing, and no arrays neither. In *Conference Record of the 18th Annual ACM Symposium on Principles of Programming Languages (POPL'91) (Orlando, Florida)*, 1991, 143 - 154.

[De] Deutsch, A. Interprocedural may-alias analysis for pointers: Beyond k-limiting. In *Proceedings of the ACM SIGPLAN'94 Conference on Programming Language Design and Implementation (PLDI'94) (Orlando, Florida)*, *ACM SIGPLAN Notices 29*, 6 (1994), 230 - 241.

[Dh1] Dhamdhere, D. M. Characterization of program loops in code optimization. *Comp. Lang. 8*, 2 (1983), 69 - 76.

[Dh2] Dhamdhere, D. M. A fast algorithm for code movement optimization. *ACM SIGPLAN Notices 23*, 10 (1988), 172 - 180.

[Dh3] Dhamdhere, D. M. Practical adaptation of the global optimization algorithm of Morel and Renvoise. *ACM Trans. Program. Lang. Syst. 13*, 2 (1991), 291 - 294.

[Dh4] Dhamdhere, D. M. A new algorithm for composite hoisting and strength reduction optimisation (+ Corrigendum). *Internat. J. Computer Math. 27*, (1989), 1 - 14 (+ 31 - 32).

[DD] Dhaneshwar, V. M., and Dhamdhere, D. M. Strength reduction of large expressions. *J. Program. Lang. 3*, 2 (1995), 95 - 120.

[DF] Davidson, J. W., and Fraser, C. W. Automatic generation of peephole transformations. In *Proceedings of the ACM SIGPLAN'84 Symposium on Compiler Construction (Montreal, Canada)*, *ACM SIGPLAN Notices 19*, 6 (1984), 111 - 115.

[DGS1] Duesterwald, E., Gupta, R., and Soffa, M. L. Demand-driven computation of interprocedural data flow. In *Conference Record of the 22nd Annual ACM Symposium on Principles of Programming Languages (POPL'95) (San Francisco, California)*, 1995, 37 - 48.

[DGS2] Duesterwald, E., Gupta, R., and Soffa, M. L. A practical framework for demand-driven interprocedural data flow analysis. *ACM Trans. Program. Lang. Syst. 19*, 6 (1997), 992 - 1030.

[DK1] Dhamdhere, D. M., and Khedker, U. P. Complexity of bidirectional data flow analysis. In *Conference Record of the 20th Annual ACM Symposium on Principles of Programming Languages (POPL'93) (Charleston, South Carolina)*, 1993, 397 - 409.

[DK2] Dhamdhere, D. M., and Khedker, U. P. A generalized theory of bit-vector analyses. *ACM Trans. Program. Lang. Syst. 16*, 5 (1994), 1472 - 1511.

[DP] Dhamdhere, D. M., and Patil, H. An elimination algorithm for bidirectional data flow problems using edge placement. *ACM Trans. Program. Lang. Syst. 15*, 2 (1993), 312 - 336.

[DRZ] Dhamdhere, D. M., Rosen, B. K., and Zadeck, F. K. How to analyze large programs efficiently and informatively. In *Proceedings of the ACM SIGPLAN'92*

Conference on Programming Language Design and Implementation (*PLDI'92*) (*San Francisco, California*), *ACM SIGPLAN Notices 27*, 7 (1992), 212 - 223.

[DS1] Drechsler, K.-H., and Stadel, M. P. A solution to a problem with Morel and Renvoise's "Global optimization by suppression of partial redundancies". *ACM Trans. Program. Lang. Syst. 10*, 4 (1988), 635 - 640.

[DS2] Drechsler, K.-H., and Stadel, M. P. A variation of Knoop, Rüthing and Steffen's LAZY CODE MOTION. *ACM SIGPLAN Notices 28*, 5 (1993), 29 - 38.

[ERH] Emami, M., Rakesh, G., and Hendren, L. J. Context-sensitive interprocedural points-to analysis in the presence of function pointers. In *Proceedings of the ACM SIGPLAN'94 Conference on Programming Language Design and Implementation (PLDI'94)* (*Orlando, Florida*), *ACM SIGPLAN Notices 29*, 6 (1994), 242 - 256.

[FO] Ferrante, J., and Ottenstein, K. J. A program form based on data dependency in predicate regions. In *Conference Record of the 10th Annual ACM Symposium on Principles of Programming Languages (POPL'83)* (*Austin, Texas*), 1983, 217 - 236.

[FOW] Ferrante, J., Ottenstein, K. J., and Warren, J. D. The program dependence graph and its use in optimization. *ACM Trans. Program. Lang. Syst. 9*, 3 (1987), 319 - 349.

[Gu] Guttag, J. Abstract data types and the development of data structures. *Commun. of the ACM 20*, 6 (1977), 396 - 404.

[GKLRS] Geser, A., Knoop, J., Lüttgen, G., Rüthing, O., and Steffen, B. Non-monotone fixpoint iterations to resolve second order effects. In *Proceedings of the 6th International Conference on Compiler Construction (CC'96)* (*Linköping, Sweden*), Springer-Verlag, Heidelberg, LNCS 1060 (1996), 106 - 120.

[GT] Grove, D., and Torczon, L. Interprocedural constant propagation: A study of jump function implementation. In *Proceedings of the ACM SIGPLAN'93 Conference on Programming Language Design and Implementation (PLDI'93)* (*Albuquerque, New Mexico*), *ACM SIGPLAN Notices 28*, 6 (1993), 90 - 99.

[GW] Graham, S. L., and Wegman, M. A fast and usually linear algorithm for global flow analysis. *Journal of the ACM 23*, 1 (1976), 172 - 202.

[He] Hecht, M. S. Flow analysis of computer programs. Elsevier, North-Holland, 1977.

[HC] Hwu, W. W., and Chang, P. P. Achieving high instruction cache performance with an optimizing compiler. In *Proceedings of the 16th Annual International IEEE and ACM Symposium on Computer Architecture* (*Jerusalem, Israel*), 1989, 242 - 251.

[HK] Hall, M. W., and Kennedy, K. W. Efficient call graph analysis. *ACM Letters on Programming Languages and Systems 1*, 3 (1992), 227 - 242.

[HMCR] Hall, M. W., Mellor-Crummey, J. M., Carle, A., and Rodriguez, R. FIAT: A framework for interprocedural analysis and transformations. In *Proceedings of the 6th Annual Workshop on Parallel Languages and Compilers (PLC'93)*, 1993.

[HRB] Horwitz, S., Reps, T., and Binkley, D. Interprocedural slicing using dependence graphs. In *ACM Trans. Program. Lang. Syst. 12*, 1 (1990), 26 - 60.

[HRS] Horwitz, S., Reps, T., and Sagiv, M. Demand interprocedural dataflow analysis. In *Proceedings of the 3rd ACM SIGSOFT Symposium on the Foundations of Software Engineering (SFSE'95)*, 1995, 104 - 115.

[HS] Harrold, M. J., and Soffa, M. L. Efficient computation of interprocedural definition-use chains. In *ACM Trans. Program. Lang. Syst. 16*, 2 (1994), 175 - 204.

[HU1] Hecht, M. S., and Ullman, J. D. Analysis of a simple algorithm for global flow problems. In *Conference Record of the 1st ACM Symposium on Principles of Programming Languages (POPL'73) (Boston, Massachusetts)*, 1973, 207 - 217.

[HU2] Hecht, M. S., and Ullman, J. D. A simple algorithm for global data flow analysis problems. In *SIAM J. Comput. 4*, 4 (1977), 519 - 532.

[HW] Hoare, C. A. R., and Wirth, N. An axiomatic definition of the programming language Pascal. *Acta Informatica 2*, (1973), 335 - 355.

[ISO] ISO/TC79/SC5N: Specification for computer language Pascal. Third draft proposal, 1981.

[JD1] Joshi, S. M., and Dhamdhere, D. M. A composite hoisting-strength reduction transformation for global program optimization. Part I. *Internat. J. Computer Math. 11*, (1982), 21 - 41.

[JD2] Joshi, S. M., and Dhamdhere, D. M. A composite hoisting-strength reduction transformation for global program optimization. Part II. *Internat. J. Computer Math. 11*, (1982), 111 - 126.

[JM] Jones, N. D., and Muchnick, S. S. A flexible approach to interprocedural data flow analysis and programs with recursive data structures. In *Conference Record of the 9th Annual ACM Symposium on Principles of Programming Languages (POPL'82) (Albuquerque, New Mexico)*, 1982, 66 - 74.

[Ka] Kandzia, P. On the most recent property of ALGOL-like programs. In *Proceedings of the 2nd Colloquium on Automata, Languages, and Programming (ICALP'74) (Saarbrücken, Germany)*, Springer-Verlag, Heidelberg, LNCS 14 (1974), 97 - 111.

[Ke1] Kennedy, K. W. Variable subsumption with constant folding. SETL Newsletter 112, Courant Institute of Mathematical Sciences, New York University, August 1973.

[Ke2] Kennedy, K. W. Node listings applied to data flow analysis. In *Conference Record of the 2nd Annual ACM Symposium on Principles of Programming Languages (POPL'75) (Palo Alto, California)*, 1975, 10 - 21.

[Kes] Kessler, R. R. Peep – An architectural description driven peephole transformer. In *Proceedings of the ACM SIGPLAN'84 Symposium on Compiler Construction (Montreal, Canada)*, *ACM SIGPLAN Notices 19*, 6 (1984), 106 - 110.

[Ki1] Kildall, G. A. Global expression optimization during compilation. Ph.D. dissertation, Technical Report No. 72-06-02, University of Washington, Computer Science Group, Seattle, Washington, 1972.

[Ki2] Kildall, G. A. A unified approach to global program optimization. In *Conference Record of the 1st ACM Symposium on Principles of Programming Languages (POPL'73) (Boston, Massachusetts)*, 1973, 194 - 206.

[Kl] Klein, M. The fixpoint analysis machine. Ph.D. dissertation, Dept. of Computer Science, University of Aachen, Germany, 1996.

[Kn1] Knoop, J. Optimal interprocedural program optimization: A new framework and its application. Ph.D. dissertation, Dept. of Computer Science, University of Kiel, Germany, 1993.

[Kn2] Knoop, J. Partial dead code elimination for parallel programs. In *Proceedings of the 2nd European Conference on Parallel Processing (Euro-Par'96) (Lyon, France)*, Springer-Verlag, Heidelberg, LNCS 1123 (1996), 441 - 450.

[Kn3] Knoop, J. Eliminating partially dead code in explicitly parallel programs. *Theoretical Computer Science 196*, 1-2 (1998), 365 - 393. (Special issue devoted to the 2nd European Conference on Parallel Processing (Euro-Par'96) (Lyon, France) (August 26 - 29, 1996)).

[KG] Knoop, J., and Golubski, W. Abstract interpretation: A uniform framework for type analysis and classical optimization of object-oriented programs. In *Proceedings of the 1st International Symposium on Object-Oriented Technology (WOON'96) (St. Petersburg, Russia)*, 1996, 126 - 142.

[KH] Kwangkeun Yi, and Harrison, W. L. Automatic generation and management of interprocedural program analyses. In *Conference Record of the 20th Annual ACM Symposium on Principles of Programming Languages (POPL'93) (Charleston, South Carolina)*, 1993, 246 - 259.

[KKKS] Klein, M., Knoop, J., Koschützki, D., and Steffen, B. DFA&OPT-METAFrame: A tool kit for program analysis and optimization. In *Proceedings of the 2nd International Workshop on Tools and Algorithms for the Construction and Analysis of Systems (TACAS'96) (Passau, Germany)*, Springer-Verlag, Heidelberg, LNCS 1055 (1996), 422 - 426.

[KM1] Knoop, J., and Mehofer, E. Optimal distribution assignment placement. In *Proceedings of the 3rd European Conference on Parallel Processing (Euro-Par'97) (Passau, Germany)*, Springer-Verlag, Heidelberg, LNCS 1300 (1997), 364 - 373.

[KM2] Knoop, J., and Mehofer, E. Interprocedural distribution assignment placement: More than just enhancing intraprocedural placing techniques. In *Proceedings of the 5th IEEE International Conference on Parallel Architectures and Compilation Techniques (PACT'97) (San Francisco, California)*, IEEE Computer Society, Los Alamitos, (1997), 26 - 37.

[KRS1] Knoop, J., Rüthing, O., and Steffen, B. Lazy code motion. In *Proceedings of the ACM SIGPLAN'92 Conference on Programming Language Design and Implementation (PLDI'92) (San Francisco, California)*, *ACM SIGPLAN Notices 27*, 7 (1992), 224 - 234.

[KRS2] Knoop, J., Rüthing, O., and Steffen, B. Optimal code motion: Theory and practice. *ACM Trans. Program. Lang. Syst. 16*, 4 (1994), 1117 - 1155.

[KRS3] Knoop, J., Rüthing, O., and Steffen, B. Lazy strength reduction. *J. Program. Lang. 1*, 1 (1993), 71 - 91.

[KRS4] Knoop, J., Rüthing, O., and Steffen, B. Towards a tool kit for the automatic generation of interprocedural data flow analyses. *J. Program. Lang. 4*, 4 (1996), 211 - 246.

[KRS5] Knoop, J., Rüthing, O., and Steffen, B. Partial dead code elimination. In *Proceedings of the ACM SIGPLAN'94 Conference on Programming Language Design and Implementation (PLDI'94) (Orlando, Florida)*, *ACM SIGPLAN Notices 29*, 6 (1994), 147 - 158.

[KRS6] Knoop, J., Rüthing, O., and Steffen, B. The power of assignment motion. In *Proceedings of the ACM SIGPLAN'95 Conference on Programming Language Design and Implementation (PLDI'95) (La Jolla, California)*, *ACM SIGPLAN Notices 30*, 6 (1995), 233 - 245.

[KRS7] Knoop, J., Rüthing, O., and Steffen, B. Code motion and code placement: Just synonyms? In *Proceedings of the 7th European Symposium On Programming (ESOP'98) (Lisbon, Portugal)*, Springer-Verlag, Heidelberg, LNCS 1381 (1998), 154 - 169.

[KS1] Knoop, J., and Steffen, B. The interprocedural coincidence theorem. In *Proceedings of the 4th International Conference on Compiler Construction (CC'92) (Paderborn, Germany)*, Springer-Verlag, Heidelberg, LNCS 641 (1992), 125 - 140.

[KS2] Knoop, J., and Steffen, B. Efficient and optimal bit-vector data flow analyses: A uniform interprocedural framework. Institut für Informatik und Praktische Mathematik, Christian-Albrechts-Universität zu Kiel, Germany, Bericht Nr. 9309 (1993), 22 pages.

[KS3] Knoop, J., and Steffen, B. Unifying strength reduction and semantic code motion. Rheinisch-Westfälische Technische Hochschule Aachen, Germany, Aachener Informatik-Bericht Nr. 91-28 (1991), 42 pages.

[KS4]   Knoop, J., and Schreiber, F. Analysing and optimizing strongly typed object-oriented languages: A generic approach and its application to Oberon-2. In *Proceedings of the 2nd International Symposium on Object-Oriented Technology (WOON'97) (St. Petersburg, Russia)*, 1997, 252 - 266.

[KSV1] Knoop, J., Steffen, B., and Vollmer, J. Parallelism for free: Bitvector analyses ⇒ No state explosion! In *Proceedings of the 1st International Workshop on Tools and Algorithms for the Construction and Analysis of Systems (TACAS'95) (Aarhus, Denmark)*, Springer-Verlag, Heidelberg, LNCS 1019 (1995), 264 - 289.

[KSV2] Knoop, J., Steffen, B., and Vollmer, J. Parallelism for free: Efficient and optimal bitvector analyses for parallel programs. *ACM Trans. Program. Lang. Syst. 18*, 3 (1996), 268 - 299.

[KSV3] Knoop, J., Steffen, B., and Vollmer, J. Code motion for parallel programs. In *Proceedings of the Poster Session of the 6th International Symposium on Compiler Construction (CC'96) (Linköping, Sweden)*, Department of Computer and Information Sciences, Linköping University, Technical Report LiTH-IDA-R-96-12 (1996), 81 - 88.

[KU1]   Kam, J. B., and Ullman, J. D. Global data flow analysis and iterative algorithms. *Journal of the ACM 23*, 1 (1976), 158 - 171.

[KU2]   Kam, J. B., and Ullman, J. D. Monotone data flow analysis frameworks. *Acta Informatica 7*, (1977), 309 - 317.

[La1]   Langmaack, H. On correct procedure parameter transmission in higher order programming languages. *Acta Informatica 2*, (1973), 110 - 142.

[La2]   Langmaack, H. On procedures as open subroutines. Part I. *Acta Informatica 2*, (1973), 311 - 333.

[La3]   Langmaack, H. On procedures as open subroutines. Part II. *Acta Informatica 3*, (1974), 227 - 241.

[La4]   Langmaack, H. On a theory of decision problems in programming languages. In *Proceedings of the International Conference on Mathematical Studies of Information Processing (Kyoto, Japan)*, Springer-Verlag, Heidelberg, LNCS 75 (1978), 538 - 558.

[La5]   Langmaack, H. On termination problems for finitely interpreted ALGOL-like programs. *Acta Informatica 18*, (1982), 79 - 108.

[Lak]   Lakhotia, A. Constructing call multigraphs using dependence graphs. In *Conference Record of the 20th Annual ACM Symposium on Principles of Programming Languages (POPL'93) (Charleston, South Carolina)*, 1993, 273 - 284.

[Le]   Lengauer, Ch. Loop parallelization in the polytope model. In *Proceedings of the 4th International Conference on Concurrency Theory (CONCUR'93) (Hildesheim, Germany)*, Springer-Verlag, Heidelberg, LNCS 715 (1993), 398 - 416.

[LH]   Larus, J. R., and Hilfinger, P. N. Detecting conflicts between structure accesses. In *Proceedings of the ACM SIGPLAN'88 Conference on Programming Language Design and Implementation (PLDI'88) (Atlanta, Georgia), ACM SIGPLAN Notices 23*, 7 (1988), 21 - 34.

[LLW]   Langmaack, H., Lippe, W., and Wagner, F. The formal termination problem for programs with finite ALGOL68-modes. *Information Processing Letters 9*, 3 (1979), 155 - 159.

[LR]   Landi, W., and Ryder, B. G. A safe approximate algorithm for interprocedural pointer aliasing. In *Proceedings of the ACM SIGPLAN'92 Conference on Programming Language Design and Implementation ((PLDI'92) (San Francisco, California), ACM SIGPLAN Notices 27*, 7 (1992), 235 - 248.

[LY]   Li, Z., and Yew, P.-C. Interprocedural analysis for program parallelization and restructuring. In *Proceedings of the ACM SIGPLAN'88 Conference* on *Parallel Programming: Experience with Applications, Languages, and Systems (PPEALS'88) (New Haven, Connecticut), ACM SIGPLAN Notices 23*, 9 (1988), 85 - 99.

[Ma] Marriot, K. Frameworks for abstract interpretation. *Acta Informatica 30*, (1993), 103 - 129.

[McG] McGowan, C. L. The "most-recent" error: Its causes and corrections. In *Proceedings of an ACM Conference on Proving Assertions about Programs (Las Cruces, New Mexico), ACM SIGPLAN Notices 7*, 1 (1972), 191 - 202.

[Mo] Morel, E. Data flow analysis and global optimization. In: Lorho, B. (Ed.). Methods and tools for compiler construction. Cambridge University Press, 1984, 289 - 315.

[Mor] Morgan, R. Building an optimizing compiler. Digital Press, 1998.

[Mu] Muchnick, S. S. Advanced compiler design implementation. Morgan Kaufmann Publishers, San Francisco, California, 1997.

[My] Myers, E. W. A precise inter-procedural data flow algorithm. In *Conference Record of the 9th Annual ACM Symposium on Principles of Programming Languages (POPL'81) (Williamsburg, Virginia)*, 1981, 219 - 230.

[MJ] Muchnick, S. S., and Jones, N. D. (Eds.). Program flow analysis: Theory and applications. Prentice Hall, Englewood Cliffs, New Jersey, 1981.

[MR1] Morel, E., and Renvoise, C. Global optimization by suppression of partial redundancies. *Commun. of the ACM 22*, 2 (1979), 96 - 103.

[MR2] Morel, E., and Renvoise, C. Interprocedural elimination of partial redundancies. In [MJ], 1981, 160 - 188.

[Nie1] Nielson, F. A bibliography on abstract interpretations. *ACM SIGPLAN Notices 21*, 1986, 31 - 38.

[Nie2] Nielson, F. A denotational framework for data flow analysis. *Acta Informatica 18*, (1982), 265 - 288.

[Ol1] Olderog, E.-R. Charakterisierung Hoarscher Systeme für ALGOL-ähnliche Programmiersprachen. Ph.D. dissertation, Dept. of Computer Science, University of Kiel, Germany, 1981. (In German).

[Ol2] Olderog, E.-R. Sound and complete Hoare-like calculi based on copy rules. *Acta Informatica 16*, (1981), 161 - 197.

[OPS] Oxhøj, N., Palsberg, J., and Schwartzbach, M. I. Making type inference practical. In *Proceedings of the 6th European Conference on Object-Oriented Programming (ECOOP'92) (Utrecht, The Netherlands)*, Springer-Verlag, Heidelberg, LNCS 615 (1992), 329 - 349.

[Pa1] Paige, R. Formal differentiation - a program synthesis technique. UMI Research Press, 1981.

[Pa2] Paige, R. Transformational programming – applications to algorithms and systems. In *Conference Record of the 10th Annual ACM Symposium on Principles of Programming Languages (POPL'83) (Austin, Texas)*, 1983, 73 - 87.

[Pal1] Palsberg, J. Comparing flow-based binding-time analyses. In *Proceedings of the 6th International Joint Conference on Theory and Practice of Software Development (TAPSOFT'95) (Aarhus, Denmark)*, Springer-Verlag, Heidelberg, LNCS 915 (1995), 561 - 574.

[Pal2] Palsberg, J. Closure analysis in constraint form. *ACM Trans. Program. Lang. Syst. 17*, 1 (1995), 47 - 62.

[PC] Plevyak, J., and Chien, A. A. Precise concrete type inference for object-oriented languages. In *Proceedings of the 9th ACM SIGPLAN Annual Conference on Object-Oriented Programming Systems, Languages, and Applications (OOPSLA'94) (Portland, Oregon), ACM SIGPLAN Notices 29*, 10, (1994), 324 - 340.

[PK] Paige, R., and Koenig, S. Finite differencing of computable expressions. *ACM Trans. Program. Lang. Syst. 4*, 3 (1982), 402 - 454.

[PS1] Palsberg, J., and Schwartzbach, M. I. Polyvariant analysis of the untyped Lambda calculus. Dept. of Computer Science, University of Aarhus, Denmark, DAIMI PB - 386, 1992.

[PS2] Palsberg, J., and Schwartzbach, M. I. Safety analysis versus type inference. *Information and Computation 118*, 1 (1995), 128 - 141.

[PS3] Palsberg, J., and Schwartzbach, M. I. Object-oriented type inference. In *Proceedings of the 6th ACM SIGPLAN Annual Conference on Object-Oriented Programming Systems, Languages, and Applications (OOPSLA'91) (Phoenix, Arizona), ACM SIGPLAN Notices 26*, 11 (1991), 146 - 161.

[PS4] Palsberg, J., and Schwartzbach, M. I. Object-oriented type systems. John Wiley & Sons, 1994.

[Re1] Reps, T. Solving demand versions of interprocedural analysis problems. In *Proceedings of the 5th International Conference on Compiler Construction (CC'94) (Edinburgh, UK)*, Springer-Verlag, Heidelberg, LNCS 786 (1994), 389 - 403.

[Re2] Reps, T. Demand interprocedural program analysis using logic databases. In Ramakrishnan, R. (Ed.): *Applications of logic databases*. Kluwer Academic Publishers, Boston, Massachusetts, 1994.

[Ri] Richardson, S. E. Evaluating interprocedural code optimization techniques. Ph.D. dissertation, Computer Systems Laboratory, Stanford University, Technical Report CSL-TR-91-460, Stanford, California, 1991, 126 pages.

[Ro] Rosen, B. K. Data flow analysis for procedural languages. *Journal of the ACM 26*, 2 (1979), 322 - 344.

[Rü] Rüthing, O. Interacting code motion transformations: Their impact and their complexity. Ph.D. dissertation, Dept. of Computer Science, University of Kiel, Germany, 1997.

[Ry] Ryder, B. G. Constructing the call graph of a program. *IEEE Trans. Software Eng. SE-5*, 3 (1979), 216 - 226.

[RG] Richardson, S. E., and Ganapathi, M. Interprocedural optimization: Experimental results. *Software - Practice and Experience 19*, 2 (1989), 149 - 169.

[RHS] Reps, T., Horwitz, S., and Sagiv, M. Precise interprocedural dataflow analysis via graph reachability. In *Conference Record of the 22nd Annual ACM Symposium on Principles of Programming Languages (POPL'95) (San Francisco, California)*, 1995, 49 - 61.

[RL1] Reif, J. H., and Lewis, R. Symbolic evaluation and the global value graph. In *Conference Record of the 4th Annual ACM Symposium on Principles of Programming Languages (POPL'77) (Los Angeles, California)*, 1977, 104 - 118.

[RL2] Reif, J. H., and Lewis, R. Efficient symbolic analysis of programs. Harvard University, Aiken Computation Laboratory, Technical Report No. 37-82, 1982.

[RS] Ross, J. L., and Sagiv, M. Building a bridge between pointer aliases and program dependencies. In *Proceedings of the 7th European Symposium On Programming (ESOP'98) (Lisbon, Portugal)*, Springer-Verlag, Heidelberg, LNCS 1381 (1998), 221 - 235.

[RWZ] Rosen, B. K., Wegman, M. N., and Zadeck, F. K. Global value numbers and redundant computations. In *Conference Record of the 15th Annual ACM Symposium on Principles of Programming Languages (POPL'88) (San Diego, California)*, 1988, 12 - 27.

[So] Sorkin, A. Some comments on a solution to a problem with Morel and Renvoise's "Global optimization by suppression of partial redundancies". *ACM Trans. Program. Lang. Syst. 11*, 4 (1989), 666 - 668.

[St1] Steffen, B. Data flow analysis as model checking. In *Proceedings of the 1st International Conference on Theoretical Aspects of Computer Software (TACS'91)* (*Sendai, Japan*), Springer-Verlag, Heidelberg, LNCS 526 (1991), 346 - 364.

[St2] Steffen, B. Generating data flow analysis algorithms from modal specifications. *Science of Computer Programming 21*, (1993), 115 - 139.

[St3] Steffen, B. Optimal run time optimization – Proved by a new look at abstract interpretations. In *Proceedings of the 2nd International Joint Conference on Theory and Practice of Software Development (TAPSOFT'87)* (*Pisa, Italy*), Springer-Verlag, Heidelberg, LNCS 249 (1987), 52 - 68.

[SCKKM] Steffen, B., Claßen, A., Klein, M., Knoop, J., and Margaria, T. The fixpoint-analysis machine. In *Proceedings of the 6th International Conference on Concurrency Theory (CONCUR'95)* (*Philadelphia, Pennsylvania*), Springer-Verlag, Heidelberg, LNCS 962 (1995), 72 - 87.

[SF1] Seidl, H. and Fecht, Ch. Interprocedural analysis based on PDAs. Fachbereich IV – Mathematik/Informatik, Universität Trier, Germany, Forschungsbericht Nr. 97-6 (1997), 27 pages.

[SF2] Seidl, H. and Fecht, Ch. Interprocedural analysis based on pushdown automata. *Notes of a Tutorial held in conjunction with the European Joint Conferences of Theory and Practice of Software (ETAPS'98)* (*Lisbon, Portugal*), Departamento de Informática, Universidade de Lisboa, (1998), 30 pages.

[SH] Steenkiste, P. A., and Hennessy, J. L. A simple interprocedural register allocation algorithm and its effectiveness for LISP. *ACM Trans. Program. Lang. Syst. 11*, 1 (1989), 1 - 32.

[SK1] Steffen, B., and Knoop, J. Finite constants: Characterizations of a new decidable set of constants. In *Proceedings of the 14th International Symposium on Mathematical Foundations of Computer Science (MFCS'89)* (*Porąbka-Kozubnik, Poland*), Springer-Verlag, Heidelberg, LNCS 379 (1989), 481 - 491.

[SK2] Steffen, B., and Knoop, J. Finite constants: Characterizations of a new decidable set of constants. Extended version of [SK1]. *Theoretical Computer Science 80*, 2 (1991), 303 - 318.

[SKR1] Steffen, B., Knoop, J., and Rüthing, O. The value flow graph: A program representation for optimal program transformations. In *Proceedings of the 3rd European Symposium on Programming (ESOP'90)* (*Copenhagen, Denmark*), Springer-Verlag, Heidelberg, LNCS 432 (1990), 389 - 405.

[SKR2] Steffen, B., Knoop, J., and Rüthing, O. Efficient code motion and an adaption to strength reduction. In *Proceedings of the 4th International Joint Conference on Theory and Practice of Software Development (TAPSOFT'91)* (*Brighton, United Kingdom*), Springer-Verlag, Heidelberg, LNCS 494 (1991), 394 - 415.

[SMCB] Steffen, B., Margaria, T., Claßen, A., and Braun, V. The METAFrame'95 environment. In *Proceedings of the 8th International Conference on Computer-Aided Verification (CAV'96)* (*New Brunswick, New Jersey*), Springer-Verlag, Heidelberg, LNCS 1102 (1996), 450 - 453.

[SP] Sharir, M., and Pnueli, A. Two approaches to interprocedural data flow analysis. In [MJ], 1981, 189 - 233.

[SRH1] Sagiv, M., Reps, T., and Horwitz, S. Precise interprocedural dataflow analysis with applications to constant propagation. In *Proceedings of the 6th International Joint Conference on Theory and Practice of Software Development (TAPSOFT'95)* (*Aarhus, Denmark*), Springer-Verlag, Heidelberg, LNCS 915 (1995), 651 - 665.

[SRH2] Sagiv, M., Reps, T., and Horwitz, S. Precise interprocedural dataflow analysis with applications to constant propagation. *Theoretical Computer Science 167*, 1-2 (1996), 131 - 170. (Special issue devoted to the 6th International Joint

Conference on Theory and Practice of Software Development (TAPSOFT'95) (Aarhus, Denmark) (May 22 - 26, 1995)).

[SW] Srivastava, A., and Wall, D. W. A practical system for intermodule code optimization at link-time. *J. Program. Lang. 1*, 1 (1993), 1 - 18.

[Ta1] Tarjan, R. E. Applications of path compression on balanced trees. *Journal of the ACM 26*, 4 (1979), 690 - 715.

[Ta2] Tarjan, R. E. A unified approach to path problems. *Journal of the ACM 28*, 3 (1981), 577 - 593.

[Ta3] Tarjan, R. E. Fast algorithms for solving path problems. *Journal of the ACM 28*, 3 (1981), 594 - 614.

[TH] Tijang, S., and Hennessy, J. Sharlit – A tool for building optimizers. In *Proceedings of the ACM SIGPLAN'92 Conference on Programming Language Design and Implementation (PLDI'92) (San Francisco, California), ACM SIGPLAN Notices 27*, 7 (1992), 82 - 93.

[Ull] Ullman, J. D. Fast algorithms for the elimination of common subexpressions. *Acta Informatica 2*, (1973), 191 - 213.

[VF] Venkatesh, G. V., and Fischer, C. N. Spare: A development environment for program analysis algorithms. In *IEEE Trans. Software Eng. SE-18*, 4 (1992), 304 - 318.

[Wal] Walter, K. G. Recursion analysis for compiler optimization. *Commun. of the ACM 19*, 9 (1976), 514 - 516.

[We] Weihl, W. E. Interprocedural data flow analysis in the presence of pointers, procedure variables, and label variables. In *Conference Record of the 7th Annual ACM Symposium on Principles of Programming Languages (POPL'80) (Las Vegas, Nevada)*, 1980, 83 - 94.

[vWMPK] Van Wijngaarden, A., Mailloux, B. J., Peck, J. E. L. and Koster, C. H. A. Report on the algorithmic language ALGOL68. *Num. Math. 14*, (1969), 79 - 218.

[vWMPKSLMF] Van Wijngaarden, A., Mailloux, B. J., Peck, J. E. L., Koster, C. H. A., Sintzoff, M., Lindsey, C. H., Meertens, L. G. L. T, and Fisker, R. G. (Eds.). Revised report on the algorithmic language ALGOL68. *Acta Informatica 5*, (1975), 1 - 236.

[Wi1] Winklmann, K. On the complexity of some problems concerning the use of procedures. Part I. *Acta Informatica 18*, (1982), 299 - 318.

[Wi2] Winklmann, K. On the complexity of some problems concerning the use of procedures. Part II. *Acta Informatica 18*, (1983), 411 - 430.

[Wth] Wirth, N. The programming language PASCAL. *Acta Informatica 1*, (1971), 35 - 63.

[WG] Waite, W. M., and Goos, G. Compiler construction. Springer-Verlag, Germany, 1984.

[WS1] Whitfield, D., and Soffa, M. L. Automatic generation of global optimizers. In *Proceedings of the ACM SIGPLAN'91 Conference on Programming Language Design and Implementation (PLDI'91) (Toronto, Canada), ACM SIGPLAN Notices 26*, 6 (1991), 120 - 129.

[WS2] Whitfield, D., and Soffa, M. L. An approach to ordering optimizing transformations. In *Proceedings of the 2nd ACM SIGPLAN Symposium on Principles and Practice of Parallel Programming (PPOPP) (Seattle, Washington), ACM SIGPLAN Notices 25*, 3 (1990), 137 - 147.

[WS3] Whitfield, D., and Soffa, M. L. An approach for exploring code-improving transformations. *ACM Trans. Program. Lang. Syst. 19*, 6 (1997), 1053 - 1084.

[WZ1] Wegman, M. N., and Zadeck, F. K. Constant propagation with conditional branches. In *Conference Record of the 12th Annual ACM Symposium on Principles of Programming Languages (POPL'85) (New Orleans, Louisiana)*, 1985, 291 - 299.

[WZ2] Wegman, M. N., and Zadeck, F. K. Constant propagation with conditional branches. *ACM Trans. Program. Lang. Syst. 13*, 2 (1991), 181 - 210.

[Wo] Wolfe, M. High performance compilers for parallel computing. Addison-Wesley Publishing Company, Redwood City, California, 1996.

[YH] Yi, K., and Harrison III, W. L. Automatic generation and management of interprocedural program analyses. In *Conference Record of the 20th Annual ACM Symposium on Principles of Programming Languages (POPL'93) (Charleston, South Carolina)*, 1993, 246 - 259.

[ZC] Zima, H., and Chapman, B. Supercompilers for parallel and vector computers. Addison-Wesley Publishing Company, ACM Press, New York, 1991.

Index

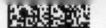